Eyewitness Accounts of the American Revolution

Correspondence and Journals of Samuel Blachley Webb

Edited by Worthington C. Ford

The New York Times & Arno Press

CORRESPONDENCE AND JOURNALS

OF

SAMUEL BLACHLEY WEBB.

VOL. I.

1772- 1777.

Saml B. Webb

CORRESPONDENCE AND JOURNALS

OF

SAMUEL BLACHLEY WEBB.

COLLECTED AND EDITED BY

WORTHINGTON CHAUNCEY FORD.

VOLUME I.

1772-1777.

NEW YORK.
1893.

WICKERSHAM PRESS
LANCASTER, PA

PRINCIPIA NON HOMINES

TO

THE MEMORY OF

MY FATHER

JAMES WATSON WEBB.

CONTENTS OF VOL. I.

(vii)

ILLUSTRATIONS.

PREFACE.

SAMUEL BLACHLEY WEBB was deprived of a notable career by unfortunate conditions, for which he was not responsible. Of sturdy New England ancestry, independent in fortune, and engaged in a profitable West Indian trade, as active in mind as he was in body, his youth gave promise of great things. The Revolution interfered with the natural development of his capacities; and, while setting aside existing circumstances, seemed favorable to give him position and reputation through new opportunities. He was connected with the movement even before the first Congress; for as secretary to Silas Deane, he was the scribe of the Committee of Correspondence in Connecticut. He marched in the Company raised in Wethersfield to succor Boston after the affair at Lexington. In his first experience of war at Bunker's Hill, he distinguished himself by his bravery when others were disgracefully leaving the field of battle. Through the influence of his stepfather, Silas Deane, he was appointed an aid to Major-General Putnam, at that time in high estimation throughout the colonies. His services, ready pen, and connections, soon after led to his entering into the military family of General Washington, naturally the centre of action, and offering such training and friendships as were of great value to a young man.

He left the General only to take a place of higher responsibility, and at the age of twenty-three was ap-

(xxvii)

pointed to command a regiment, where everything promised a rapid advancement and a brilliant career. A short, but exciting service in the Highlands, at a time when the preservation of the posts in that region was of exceeding importance to the American cause, ended in his being taken prisoner by the British. With this misfortune his activity practically terminated. Through no fault of his own, he was held a prisoner on parole for nearly three years, unable to serve his country, and subject to the whims and caprice of the British commanders and of the Continental Congress. Released in 1781, he at once joined his regiment, and remained with it till the army was disbanded, gaining praise for the appearance and discipline of his men, and a deserved promotion to be Brigadier-General.

This, in brief, is the story told from original sources in these volumes. My father has related why the materials used in his memorial volume were so meagre, and his explanation will in a measure serve for me:

From the day he marched from Wethersfield to take part in the battle of Bunker Hill, and for years previous, he (Colonel Webb) never failed, except from illness, to write up his journal of the day. He rarely destroyed a paper, and the accumulated records, embracing the entire period from 1774 to 1784, filled two monstrous chests, not less than five feet long and of proportionate width; and every scrap of paper in this great mass of manuscript correspondence, journals and accounts, was as accurately and carefully filed as are the archives of any court of record, and all these treasures were left to be treated as best suited the whims of children. The letters of Washington, Jay, Hamilton, and other notables, were scattered broad-cast among our school fellows. What was particularly attractive, were the books of blotting paper we prepared for them. And how, think you, was it done? My father, who was exceedingly neat and precise (as well as expensive in his habits), had blank books of uniform size prepared for his journal with covers of soft leather, and between the sheets of writing paper was bound up a sheet of blotting paper. These journals were carefully labelled A, B, C, extending through the entire alphabet ; and then a new series commenced, marked AA, BB, CC, and so on down to PP ; and these invaluable records of our great war of independence, in relation to which he, from his position, knew probably as much as any individual, we children, left to ourselves, deliberately but in true ignorance *destroyed.* We tore out of those journals and destroyed *all the written manuscript contained in them,* and presented the pretty little books of *blotting paper* to our school fellows.*

The comparatively small part which escaped destruction was scattered among different members of the family, and an attempt has been made to bring together what remains. Wishing to give these records a more permanent form, I placed them in the hands of Mr. Ford, and desired him to prepare a volume which should be at once a family memorial and a contribution to the history of the Revolution of lasting and intrinsic interest. The scope of the work widened as it proceeded, and the one volume intended has been extended to three.

The incidents connected with Colonel Webb's military services are naturally the important features of the work, and the manuscript treasures of many public and private collections have been searched for material. The Colonel's military correspondence and journals, even in their fragmentary condition, give the outlines of the history, which have been filled in with letters, orderly books and other records. An attempt is made for the first time to sketch the difficulties that attended the framing of a cartel for the exchange of prisoners

* Reminiscences of General Samuel B. Webb, 32, 33.

between the commanders of the opposing armies. This seems particularly fitting to be given in this connection, as Colonel Webb was present at the first informal exchange or transfer of prisoners by Putnam, before Washington had assumed command of the Continental army; and after his capture he became an active factor in keeping alive the negotiations for a general exchange, and in insisting upon a due recognition of the claims of the prisoners of war to be released from their distressing position. This sketch, given with as much detail as space will permit, will constitute a new and interesting chapter in the history of the Revolution.

In the last volume will be printed a short biography of Colonel Webb, and Mr. Ford will acknowledge the courteous aid afforded by many to the undertaking, which has my grateful recognition. The manuscripts are printed as they were written, as in any other form they would lose much of the writer's personality and local flavor that belong to them. If any error has been committed, it lies on the safer side of too great fulness, lest something of value should be lost by pruning, alteration or omission.

The keen interest taken by my father in preserving in permanent form a part of these records, demands something more than a mere acknowledgment. I have dedicated these volumes to his memory as a tribute of affection, and in remembrance of his sympathetic enthusiasm for the renown of his father, Samuel Blachley Webb.

WM. SEWARD WEBB.

NEW YORK, *January, 1893.*

THE CORRESPONDENCE

OF

SAMUEL BLACHLEY WEBB.

TO MISS SALLY WEBB.

[NEW LONDON, May, 1772.]*

DEAR SISTER :

I have since I last wrote you passed a very disagreeable week at New London. I keep at the Coffee House, tho' repeated invitations to lodge at yᵉ Cott'e. I returned last Tuesday evening. My first inquiry was to know if there was any letters for me from Boston and was much disappointed to find none. Last evening Mr. Joyce from Wethersfield bro't me your letter dated April 22. Where it had been so long I cannot imagine.

After attending church this day I mounted my horse and came to Wethersfield ab't dusk, and am now sitting with my brother. He has sent a servant to Hartford for your letter. When he returns I flatter myself I shall have the pleasure of receiving a large package from you. Till then, I'll turn the subject.

* I am in doubt as to the date of this letter. General J. Watson Webb printed it first in the series of the Webb letters, but assigned no date. It was probably written in May, 1772, as he mentions the receipt of a letter (somewhat delayed) dated April 22d.

Now, my dear Sally, if ever, this is the season to be in the country. It's impossible for you to form a true idea of beautiful Spring. Never has it been known for twenty years back, the spring to be so forward. All nature is in full glory. I want words to tell you what I think. Surely you have not forgot the beautiful meadows at Middletown. I came thro' there this evening just as bright Phœbus was taking his nightly leave of us. I stop'd short my horse and for many minutes sat musing on the goodness of the Almighty. How beautiful all the fields looked! The tender grass shooting upwards for the use of ye beasts, and fruits of various kinds for man's refreshment. There was ye apple, ye peach, ye pear, and ye apricot full of blossoms, giving us warning what in due time they will bring forth; and altho' you are not here to see the present appearance, you undoubtedly will be to reap some of ye fruit from these blossoms. No more till ye servant returns from Hartford.

MONDAY MORN.

I intended last night to have finished my letter, but soon after I wrote the above, Sister Libby who was going to bed in the opposite chamber, ran in to her brother in a surprise and told us there was a fire in the garden. We instantly ran down and found ye smoke house had caught fire. Lucky it was we found it before we went to bed, otherwise, my dear sister, in all probability both houses must have been consumed. Thanks to our God for his protection. I was very much chagrined and disappointed when I found neither you nor Hettie* had said a word to me. I was almost

* Mehitabel Webb.

tempted to commit the above scrawl to the flames, but upon the whole thought it would not be brotherly.

Joe* calls and says he must send the letters immediately to Hartford or the post will be gone, and Hetty will (perhaps) think I have not rec^d a very long letter from her if I do not answer it. My best respects to all the ladies, especially to Miss H——d, as I fancy I am most acquainted with her. I know not how many errors there are in this letter, nor have I time to look over it, but must let it go and doubt not you will correct errors yourself. I am, dear Sally, your friend and very affectionate brother.

TO MISS SALLY WEBB.

WETHERSFIELD, Thursday, Novr 21st, 1772.

DEAR SISTER:

By the date of my letter yo'll see I am once more at our old place of abode—I come now to bid adieu to the few friends I have left here—few indeed, now my dear, dear sisters are absent. Last Tuesday I came up from Middletown to get my cloaths, etc. I got here about sunset. I went into the House, and as usual went to the Chamber where my Sisters used to keep. I opened the Door,—when instead of entering I made a full stop—the Room was dark,—and so altered in appearance since I was last there, that it struck me with a Melancholly I seldom ever felt before,—I hove in my portmanteau, and turned directly about,—it affected me so much that I could not tarry in the House,—I went to the store where I passed the evening (with

* Joseph Webb.

my head reclined on my arm), till 10 o'clock thinking of· my dear sisters,—then went to bed with Jonna in your Chamber. I sought for sleep but it was not to be found; frequently I cri'd, Sweet Sleep come close my Eyes and drive off Melancholly. But in vain,—thus I passed the *long,*—*long* Night,—I arose before Bright Phœbus had made his appearance, from his wat'ry bed, finished my Business and went directly to Middletown, where I passed the evening in dancing,—the Pleasure of the Lady's Company and Madeira made me again

SAM B. WEBB.

I am now in my Brother's Store, 4 o'clock, Sunday Afternoon—good folks all gone to yᵉ old shop,— I am oblig'd to write by candle light,—dare not open the Windows, for fear of offending Conciences,—now what more have I to say to my dear Sisters,—enough if I could see them, But alas fate has decreed it otherwise

> " O Cruel fate, O hard to tell,
>   We're now apart, O Sisters, O farewell "

My vessel falls down the River to-morrow,—and I shall go to New London in about a week—Hope yo'll write me by the return of this post,—for [I will] positively go next Week,—I mean to write to you from New London by the Eastern Post,—Once more Adieu,—that all Blessings of this world may attend my Sisters & that we may again meet in the Spring, is, & shall be the prayer of your most

Affectionate Brother.

FROM JEREMIAH WADSWORTH TO JAMES FLAHERTY.*

NEW LONDON, Dec. 10th, 1772.

DEAR SIR:

This will be handed you by Mr. Samuel Webb, who is to touch at the Mole on his way to Jamaica. This is his first trip to the West Indies. He is a young gentleman of fortune and character, and I shall be particularly obliged to you for your friendly advice, and have no doubt you'll readily give it.

I hope shortly to take you by the hand as I sail in company with the bearer. The schooner Sally, John Barnes, brings you a horse. I hope she will be there as soon as this. I intend to go to St. Mark's if the matter appears well when I arrive at the Mole.

I have a fine cargo of horses in the brig Sam, only waiting for a wind.

If Barnes arrives before me give him your best advice and assistance. Pray inquire thoroughly into the affair of Depresardy's permission. In utmost haste, I am, Dear Sir, your most humble servt

JERE : WADSWORTH.

TO MISS SALLY WEBB.

NEW LONDON, Sunday evening, 13 Decr, 1772.

MY EVER DEAR SISTERS:

Is it possible, can it be, that I am agoing to leave my native shore,—that I am not to see, nor hear from you this winter,—it is & must be so,—Kitty, I have rec'd a Letter from you since I have been here, t'was pleaseing to me,—wou'd now write each of my Sisters a Letter, but time will not admit,—It's now almost a week since I have been here wt. my Horses on board ready to put to Sea,—But the winds have been Contrary,—and the old Seamen have not lik'd the Looks of the wether,—this evening the wind is shifted to North West, & no do'bt we shall put to Sea in the morning, 3 or 4 Days sickness is what I expect when I first go

*From the *Reminiscences of General Samuel B. Webb*, p. 313.

out,—Happy shall I think myself if no other sickness attends me than Sea sickness.—Happy did I say,—that's impossible when absent from my Dear Brothers & Sisters.

I have alter'd my voyage, & shall sail direct for Kingstown in Jamaica,—if either of you should hear of any Vessel that was bound there within three weeks from this (or to Cape Nichola Mole), Beg you will not forget your Brother.—Adieu—my Dear—Dear Sisters, may Heav'ns Blessings attend you prays your

Affec^t. Brother

SAM^L. B. WEBB.

Monday morn 14th Dec^r. —no wind, fine pleasant day—it looks more like May than Dec^r. —I am overwhelmed with a very feeling & tender Melancholly to think of going of—We must part, so our adverse fate Compels & God only knows whether we ever meet again, this is necessarily precarious from the utter uncertainty of Life, all ages are liable to the arrest of Death,—and when the thread of life is spun to its utmost length;—alas how short the space from the Cradle to the grave;—tis a solemn Certainty, that every brest now warm with Hope, or busy with design, will shortly lie cold & inanimate in the Grave; the Eye that reads *this*, will be clos'd in Death, and the Hand that writes it will Crumble into Dust.—O my Sister (consider this as dictated by the ties of nature & inspir'd by the affectionate regard I bear you) let me conjure you to live mindfull of, & with a wise reference to the important future realities of *Death, Judgment & Eternity*. Let us, my Dear Sisters, live in such manner that we may glide serenely, thro' the vale of life, without the Gloom of Terror, or trepidation of Doubt, meet our fate cheerfully & quit the stage like those, who neither wish to live, or fear to Die, that tho' the survivor of us, may mourn the others loss,—yet may have this reflection to console us,—that our separation tho painfull, is but momentary;—while our reunion in the realms of bliss, —will prove Eternal.

Remember what Dr. Parnelle tell us—

> "Absent or Dead, still let a friend be Dear
> A sigh the absent claim ; the Dead a tear."

N. B. I mean to say more or less to you every day till I sail, at present I feel in a pensive melancholly mood—am now agoing to amuse myself by walking.

Dr. Sisters, it is not half an hour since I wrote ye above—My Capt. calls—says fair Wind—and we must make sail immediately—this I write you from on board my Vessel—the schooner *Dolphin*, Capt. Saml. Crowel commander—Adieu my dear sisters—may Heavn Bless and preserve you prays your

Affect Brother
Saml. B. Webb.

FROM THE HOUSE OF BURGESSES OF VIRGINIA.[*]

Virginia, March 19th, 1773.

Sir:

I have received the Commands of the House of Burgesses of this Colony to transmit a Copy of the resolves enter'd into by them on

---

[*] The Virginia House of Burgesses met at Williamsburg on March 4th, 1773, after an unusually long interval had been allowed to elapse since its last meeting in February, 1772. Indeed, it is doubtful if Lord Dunmore, even now looking with hungry gaze at certain promising land ventures in the Western Country, would have summoned it to meet at all, were it not for the discovery that the treasury notes had been extensively forged, and some radical remedy was essen-

the 12th Instant, which they hope will prove of General Utility, if the other Colonies shall think fit to adopt them. They have expressed themselves so fully as to the motives that led to these Resolutions, that I need not say any thing on that Point; and shall only beg you will lay them before your Assembly as early as possible, &

tial to prevent a panic. After doing what was thought necessary in the way of Colonial legislation, the House took up the subject of a Court of Inquiry, constituted by royal commission, to determine and punish those who burnt the armed schooner, the *Gaspee*, in Rhode Island. The dangerous feature of this court was believed to lie in the power given to it to send to England for trial persons committing an offence in the Colonies. A writer in the *Providence Gazette* of Saturday, 26 December, 1772, voiced the general feeling of the people. "A Court of Inquisition, more horrid than that of Spain or Portugal, is established within this Colony, to inquire into the circumstances of destroying the Gaspee schooner; and the persons who are the commissioners of this new-fangled court, are vested with most exorbitant and unconstitutional power. They are directed to summon witnesses, apprehend persons not only impeached, but even suspected; and them, and every of them, to deliver them to Admiral Montague, who is ordered to have a ship in readiness to carry them to England, where they are to be tried." The towns of Massachusetts took the alarm against such "a new and unheard of grievance. . .plainly destructive of the main pillar of the British constitution;" and the agitation spread to the other Colonies.

In Virginia a few of the younger and more active minds of the Burgesses determined to take more positive action than would commend itself to the more conservative members. "Not thinking our old and leading members up to the point of forwardness and zeal which the times required," wrote Jefferson in his autobiography, "Mr. [Patrick] Henry, R[ichard] H[enry] Lee, Francis L[ightfoot] Lee, Mr. [Dabney] Carr and myself agreed to meet in the evening in a private room of the Raleigh [tavern], to consult on the state of things. There may have been a member or two more whom I do not recollect. We were all sensible that the most urgent of all measures was that of coming to an understanding with all the other Colonies to consider the British claim as a common cause to all, and to produce an unity of action: and for this purpose that a committee of correspondence in each Colony would be the best instrument for intercommunication: and that their first measure would probably be to propose a meeting of deputies from every Colony at some central place, who should be charged with the direction of the measures which should be taken by all. We therefore drew up the resolutions . . .[Mr. Carr] moved them, they were agreed to nem. con., and a committee of correspondence appointed, of whom Peyton Randolph, the Speaker, was chairman. The Governor, then Lord Dunmore, dissolved us; but the committee met the next day, prepared a circular letter to the Speakers of the other Colonies, inclosing to each a copy of the resolutions, and left it in charge with their chairman to forward them by expresses."—*Writings of Thomas Jefferson*, Edited by Paul

PEYTON RANDOLPH.

request them to appoint some of their body to communicate from
time to Time with the Corresponding Committee of Virginia.

I am with great respect,

Your most Obedient Servant

PEYTON RANDOLPH.

To the Honorable, the Speaker of the House of Assembly for Connecticut.

[Enclosure.]

RESOLVES OF THE HOUSE OF BURGESSES OF VIRGINIA.

FRIDAY, the 12th of March, 13 Geo. III. 1773.

Upon a Motion made,

The House resolved itself into a Committee of the whole House,
upon the State of the Colony.

Mr. Speaker left the Chair.

Mr. Bland took the Chair of the Committee.

Mr. Speaker resumed the Chair.

Mr. Bland reported from the Committee, that they had directed
him to make the following Report to the House, viz.

Whereas the Minds of his Majesty's faithful subjects in this Colony
have been much disturbed by various Rumours and Reports of Proceedings tending to deprive them of their antient, legal and constitutional Rights :

AND whereas the Affairs of this Colony are frequently connected
with those of Great Britain, as well as of the neighbouring Colonies,
which renders a communication of Sentiments necessary ; in Order,
therefore, to remove the Uneasinesses, and to quiet the Minds of the
People, as well as for the other good Purposes above mentioned :

BE IT RESOLVED, that a standing Committee of Correspond-
ence and Enquiry be appointed, to consist of eleven Persons, to wit,
the Honourable Peyton Randolph, Esquire, Robert Carter Nicholas,
Richard Bland, Richard Henry Lee, Benjamin Harrison, Edmund
Pendleton, Patrick Henry, Dudley Digges, Dabney Carr, Archibald
Cary, and Thomas Jefferson, Esquires, any six of whom to be a
Committee, whose Business it shall be to obtain the most early and

Leicester Ford, i, 7. The committee did hold a session on March 13th, but the
letter to the Colonies was dated March 19th. It is printed, with the resolutions
of the Burgesses, in *Records of the Colony of Rhode Island and Providence Plantations*, vii, 225.

authentic Intelligence of all such Acts and Resolutions of the British Parliament, or Proceedings of Administration, as may relate to or affect the British Colonies in America ; and to keep up and maintain a correspondence and communication with our Sister Colonies, respecting these important Considerations ; and the result of such their Proceedings, from Time to Time, to lay before this House.

RESOLVED, That it be an Instruction to the said Committee, that they do, without Delay, inform themselves particularly of the Principles and Authority, on which was constituted a Court of Enquiry, said to have been lately held in Rhode Island, with Powers to transport Persons, accused of offences committed in America, to Places beyond the seas, to be tried.

The said Resolutions, being severally read a second Time, were, upon the Question severally put, thereupon agreed to by the House, nemine contradicente.

RESOLVED, That the Speaker of this House do transmit to the Speakers of the different Assemblies of the British Colonies, on this Continent, Copies of the said Resolutions, and desire that they will lay them before their respective Assemblies, and request them to appoint some Person or Persons, of their respective Bodies, to communicate, from Time to Time, with the said Committee.*

BY THE HOUSE OF BURGESSES OF THE COLONY OF VIRGINIA.
Extracted from the Journal.
G. WYTHE, C. H. B.

FROM THE COMMITTEE OF CORRESPONDENCE OF VIRGINIA.

WILLIAMSBURG, Virginia, April 6, 1773.
SIR:

The Speaker of the House of Burgesses of this Colony having transmitted to you a Copy of the Resolutions entered into by their

*These resolutions were received by the Speaker of the House of Representatives of Connecticut in May, when that body was in session, and were without delay laid before it. On Friday, May 21st, a decision was reached, approving and adopting the suggestion of Virginia, and appointing a standing committee of correspondence and inquiry. This committee consisted of the following nine persons: Ebenezer Silliman, William Williams, Benjamin Payne, Samuel Holden Parsons, Nathaniel Wales, Silas Deane, Samuel Bishop, Joseph Trumbull and Erastus Wolcott.

House at their last Session, constituting a Committee of Correspondence and Enquiry, permit us to refer you to those Resolutions.
That Committee have appointed us a Select corresponding Commit-
mittee and in pursuance of their Direction we are now to request
the Favor of you to transmit us a full Account of the principles and
Authority on which was Constituted a Court of Enquiry said to have
been lately held in the Colony of Rhode Island with powers to
transport persons accused of Offences committed in America, to
places beyond the Seas, to be tried, together with an Authentic Copy
of their Commission & proceedings.

We have it also in Command to transmit you a Copy of an Act of
our Assembly made at their last Session, to prevent counterfeiting
the Paper Currency of other Colonies.   This Colony having of . late
years sustained the greatest Injury by having their paper Currency
forged, and it having been represented to our General Assembly that
the principal Author of this Mischief is an Inhabitant of North Carolina, they judged it necessary as well to prevent such dangerous
practices in future, as to shew their Regard for the other Colonies to
pass this Act.   Our Governor will transmit Copies of this Law to the
different Governors on the Continent with a Request that they would
be pleased to recommend it to their several Assemblies to enact
Laws of the same Import respecting Virginia, and we are to request
your Countenance and Assistance upon so important an Occasion.
We have the Honor to be very respectfully,

Sir, your most obedt servts

PEYTON RANDOLPH
R. C. NICHOLAS
DUDLEY DIGGES.

FROM THE COMMITTEE OF CORRESPONDENCE OF RHODE ISLAND.

NEWPORT, May 15, 1773.

SIR:

Having received a Letter from the Speaker of the House of Burgesses of Virginia inclosing the Resolutions of that Patriotic and
illustrious Assembly of the 12th March last, and also a Letter from
the Committee of Correspondence and Inquiry by them appointed, I

took the earliest Opportunity of laying them before the House of Deputies of this Colony, who immediately enter'd into the Consideration of them, and persuaded that nothing less than a firm and close Union of the Colonies in the most spirited prudent and consistent Measures can defeat the Designs of those who are aiming to deprive them of their inestimable Rights and Privileges passed, Nemine contradicente, the Resolutions of which I have the Honor to inclose you a Copy.

I beg the Favour of you to lay them before your House of Representatives as soon as possible.

I am with great respect

Your most obedient Servant

METCALF BOWLER.

[Enclosure.]

IN THE HOUSE OF DEPUTIES, May 7th 1773.

Resolved, that a standing Committee of Correspondence and enquiry be appointed to consist of seven persons, to wit : the Honble Stephen Hopkins Esqr , Metcalf Bowler, Moses Brown, John Cole, William Bradford, Henry Ward, and Henry Marchant Esq^{rs}, any four of whom to be a Committee whose Business it shall be to obtain the most early and authentick Intelligence of such Acts and Resolutions of the British Parliament or Proceedings of Administration as may relate to or affect the British Colonies in America, and to keep up and maintain a Correspondence and Communication with our Sister Colonies respecting these important Considerations ; and the Result of such their Proceedings from Time to Time to lay before this House.

Voted p^r Ord^r J LYNDON Cler

IN THE HOUSE OF DEPUTIES, May 7th 1773.

Whereas this House hath appointed a Committee of Correspondence with Committees of other Colonies in North America respecting the Rights and Privileges of the Colonies &c It is therefore resolved by this House that his Honour the Governor be requested to deliver said Committee a Copy of his Commission as one of the Judges of the Court of Enquiry constituted from home, and said to be held in this Colony, and of all such other Papers which were laid before said Court as may be consistant with his Honour as Governor of this Colony.

Voted p.ʳ Ord.ʳ J LYNDON Cler

IN THE HOUSE OF DEPUTIES, May 7ᵗʰ 1773.

Resolved that the Speaker of this House be requested to write to the Speaker of the House of Burgesses in Virginia and to all other Speakers of Assemblies in North America informing them of the Proceedings of this House relating to the Preservation of the Rights of the Colonies.

Voted p.ʳ Ord.ʳ J. Lyndon Cler

The afore written is a true Copy of three Votes of the House of Deputies or Lower House of Assembly of the Colony of Rhode Island.

Teste   JOSIAS LYNDON Cler

RESOLUTION OF THE HOUSE OF REPRESENTATIVES OF NEW HAMPSHIRE.

May 28ᵗʰ 1773. The house Taking into consideration the Letters Rec'd from the Committee of Correspondence appointed by the house of Burgesses of Virginia ; also a Letter from the Speaker of the house of Deputies of the Colony of Rhode Island Directed to the Speaker of this house.

Thereupon Resolved that this house heartily concur in Sentiments with the house of Burgesses & the house of Deputies aforesaid in said Letters Represented.

Resolved That a Standing Committee of Correspondence and Enquiry be appointed to Consist of Seven persons Viz.ᵗ The Hon.ᵇˡᵉ John Wentworth Esq.ʳ, John Sherburne, William Parker, John Giddinge, Jacob Sheafe, Christopher Toppan, & John Pickering Esquires, any four of whom to be a Committee whose Business it shall be to obtain the most early and authentick Intelligence of all such Acts and Resolutions of the British Parliament, or proceedings of administration, as may Relate to or affect the British Colonies in America, and to keep up and maintain a Correspondence and Communication with our Sister Colonies Respecting these important Considerations ; & the Result of such their proceedings from time to time to lay before this house.

Extract from the Journal of the house of Representatives of the Province of New Hampshire.

WILLIAM PARKER Cler of the Assembly.

REPLY OF THE MARYLAND COMMITTEE.

MARYLAND, Decembr 6, 1773.

SIR :

After receipt of your Letter of ye 14th June I took the first opportunity to lay before the House of Delegates of this province, the Resolutions of your House of Representatives. They had rec^d from the Speaker of the House of Burgesses of the Colony of Virginia, the Resolutions of that House, and Letters inclosing Resolutions from the Speakers of other Houses of Representatives. In consequence whereof, they came to the Resolutions I now have the Honor to inclose, and which I have in Command to transmit to you, requesting you will lay them before your House of Representatives at their next meeting. With great respect, I am Sir, y^r mo Obed^t. Servant

MAT. TILGHMAN.*

[Enclosure.]

RESOLUTIONS OF THE HOUSE OF ASSEMBLY OF MARYLAND.

BY THE LOWER HOUSE OF ASSEMBLY,
Friday, October 15th, 1773.

The order of the Day being read, the House took into Consideration the several Letters and other papers communicated to this House by the Honorable Speaker, and addressed to him by the Honorable the Speakers of the several Colonies of Virginia, Massachusetts Bay, Connecticut and Rhode Island ; and resolved unanimously, That this House most cordially accept the Invitation to a mutual Correspondence and Intercourse with our Sister Colonies.

Resolved unanimously, That a Standing Committee of Corre-

---

* Speaker of the Lower House of Assembly of Maryland.

SHIPPED by the Grace of God, in good Order and well conditioned by *Mr Jn. Silas*

Deane Joseph & Sam'll Webb in and upon the good *Wright* called the *Joseph* whereof is Master, under God for this present Voyage, *Marg'tta Brown* and now riding at Anchor in the Harbour of *Newlondon* and by God's Grace bound for *Hispaniola* to say,

Nspt Onions, 32 March flour 2,000 hoop Nutter 2,900 Hoops 136 Hhd
Hhgheads 1400 feet pine leading, 230 March of Mutt — 1141 ℔ Bread
2 Tierces Beans 60 Water Casks 260 Bushels Corn 80 Bush Corn
cont 6 Bar'l Gerial Mini Coy —

being mark'd and number'd as in the Margin, and to be delivered in the like good Order and well conditioned, at the aforesaid Port of *Hispaniola* (the Danger of the Seas only excepted) unto
Jacon. M. Wells — *Nothing being Known — to* or to Assigns,
A or they paying Freight for the said Goods *Being* with Primage and Average accustomed. In Witness whereof the Master or Purser of the said *throx* hath affirmed to *three* Bills of Lading, all of this Tenor and Date; the one of which *Hhgh* Bills being accomplished, the other *two* to stand void. And so God send the good *Wright* to her desired Port in Safety, AMEN. Dated *Newlondon Nov. 24, 1773* —

Barj. Beans

spondence and Enquiry be appointed to consist of Eleven persons, to wit, The Honorable Matthew Tilghman, Esquire, Speaker, John Hall, Thomas Johnson, William Paca, Samuel Chase, Edward Lloyd, Matthias Hammond, Josias Beall, James Lloyd Chamberlaine, Brice Thomas Beale Worthington, and Joseph Sim, Esquires, any six of whom to be a Committee, whose Business it shall be to obtain the most early and authentick Intelligence of all such Acts and Resolutions of the British Parliament or Proceedings of administration as may relate to or affect the British Colonies in America, and to keep up and maintain a Correspondence and Communication with our Sister Colonies respecting those important Considerations, and the Result of such their Proceedings from Time to Time to lay before this House.

Resolved unanimously, That the Speaker of this House transmit to the Speakers of the different Assemblies of the British Colonies on this Continent Copies of the above Resolutions.

Extract from the Journal of the Lower House of Assembly of the Province of Maryland.

P⠗ J͛ᴺ͛ᵒ Duckett,
Cl. Lo. Ho.

FROM SILAS DEANE.

Wethersfield Dec͛ 6th 1773.

Dear Samˡ:

This I trust will be handed you, by Cap͛ Wadsworth,* who will I hope find you in health, & prosperous forwardness of your Business. Neither the Times, nor any Circumstances have materially altered since you left Us. By the appearance of the Season and Weather, the Winter will be open the first part of it, and of necessary Consequence shut the latter part, as was the Case, last year; but this is all uncertain and ought to have no influence on your, or Our Business. Should you be able to dispatch the Brigᵃ in Feb͛ for New York with a Load of Molasses or the greater part of one, and a prospect of Flour Lard & Lumber answering to good acc͛, think it best to exert yourself to effect it, and nothing shall be wanting, on Our power to dispatch her, indeed as She will, & must in such case come

* Jeremiah Wadsworth.

into New York She will not be delayed, in case She can be dispatched at any Rate. But if you find a dull sale, collection, & prospect, it will be by all means best, to close the affairs you already have in hand, and delay the Brig[n] for that purpose, until you can get her a full Cargoe, but not on any other acc[t] , as her Expences are great. Must on your return in the Brig[a] advise you to come into New London preferably to any other port, as the Charge is less, and you may there have advice, how Markets are at New York, Boston, & Philadelphia. But if returning yourself in the Brig[a] and should fall in Westward, you may always off the Capes speak with Pilot Boats from Philadelphia, & by them learn the Markets, but in such case, take into your Calculation, that Port Charges are very high at Philadelphia, and that you run a greater Chance of Strict Treatment respecting duties, than in a Port in which you are acquainted.

Should you send the Brig[a] to N. York in February and wait to return in her yourself the second Tripp, before that, Letters may be lodg'd for you, in Philadelphia, and indeed more certain advice, given & rec[d] on the subject, than at present can be suggested—at all Events, be careful to close all your affairs, before you leave the place, and keep an exact account of all your proceedings, by which should you be ever so unfortunate, you may at least satisfy your Employers whence your misfortunes arose, & if successful a review of your minutes will give you, & them pleasure, after immediate Interest therein ceases to influence. I have known very honest Men, when unfortunate, suffer in their Character, and never retreive their affairs, only because of their being careless, in writing down at the Time, their, various proceedings, and Consequently being unable, to render a fair account, how their misfortunes arose ; Whereas a Man that is able from written Testimony to avouch his proceedings, & shew that no dishonest, or negligent conduct of his—no fraud, or imbezzlement has occasioned his Misfortunes let them be ever so great, he is sure of not suffering in his Character as an honest Man, & of course his affairs are not irretreivable. I do not write thus, on Acc[t] of Suspicion, of your attention to your Business, or integrity therein, but to urge you to keep this alway in mind. It is with pleasure to me, as well as your other Friends, that I see you desirous of, and assiduous in Business, and the Course you have taken, and are pursuing is more likely to advance your Interest than any I know of at present; when once you are (& I doubt not, you soon may be), Master of it.—it is True, the Sea is on many Acc^ts a disagreeable Life, but to Cross it once each Year, as a Factor, and have certain consignments, is nothing, when put in Competition with the vexations, and perplexities of Trade at home, Debts due, & crowding—Debtors breaking, or deceiving, with the thousand disappointments, & consequent Anxieties, which every Dry Good Trader, of any consequence experiences; the fatigues meerly of the Body, are Nothing in comparison of those of the Mind. You must therefore consider the fatigues at Sea as nothing more, than Sauce to give a relish to the enjoyments at home. But in tasting these, never let Appetite run away with Judgment—to pass through life in so austere a manner, as to enjoy none of the Bounties of Providence, is an extreme—to give up Reason, to Sensual Gust, and by attempting to enjoy all, really enjoy none is an extreme—they are equally to be avoided, and a Golden Mean pursued, make yourself so happy, for it is now in Youth absolutely in your power, to be Master of your pleasures, and not let them be the master of you. This will give you the Blessings, of Health, of Peace, & competence which I most sincerely wish you—for your Amusement, & your Friends, I send you the Papers, containing the proceedings respecting the Tea & the Event is still doubtful, but I hope for the best & am wishing you the best of Heaven's Blessings.

Your Affectionate Parent

& Friend

SILAS DEANE.*

TO SALLY AND HETTY WEBB.

MOLE S. NICHOLAS, Jany 22, 1774.

MY DEAR SISTERS:

Your kind favours by Capt. Wadsworth came safe to hand, for which I am truly obliged to you—they gave me a satisfaction which cannot be described. In Receiving one Letter from you in this place, at so great

---

* Endorsed by Col. Webb, " Received at Hispaniola, January, 1774."

a Distance from you gives me more real pleasure than ten would was I in the next town, you must excuse my not answering them by the first Opportunity,—Business prevented or I should have done it with pleasure, —and intended this day to have wrote you a long Letter, came of on Board early in the forenoon for that purpose, and intended to have spent most of the Day in writing my friends,—but was call'd of on Business and have been detained all the afternoon,—I am now writing by Candle light,—and Capt. Chapman Sails in half an hour which Obliges me to be short, and write you both in one—or loose this Opp.ʸ of writeing You— which I do not chose to do,—God only knows when it is probable I may be at home,—but soon I hope—for the place is unhealthy and much I want to see my friends,—Capt. Deane still remaines quite sick—but on the mending hand,—I have had several turns of the fever,—which did not hold but a day or two,—and I trust if prudence etc will give me Health I shall not want for it,—may you my Dear Sisters be blessed with Health and Happiness,—let my lot be what it will, I shall ever wish your prosperity. I want to say many things to you, which must be omitted,—for want of time,—You'll Remember me to all my friends—and ere long I hope to have the pleasure of seeing them,—my compliments to yᵉ Miss Chester & all your fair friends —Adieu my Dear Sisters, & Remember your ever Affect. Brother.

My Love to Jack & Abby.

TO MRS. SARAH SIMPSON.*

WETHERSFIELD, Sunday Evening
8 o'clock [February, 1774].

MY DEAR SISTER:

I sent the servant this afternoon while people were in meeting, in order that he might return seasonably for us to answer our letters—if any—this evening. I have been very Impatiently waiting an hour or two his return,—nor can I Imagine what detains him, and fearing I may not have time after his return, I shall devote a few of the present moments to you, and tho I justly might scold you for not writeing, yet I forbear.

Half past 8 o'clock. The post himself came in while writeing ye above, but sorry I am to say only one letter for Joe, for myself—I am used to being disappointed, I may almost say every Sunday Evening—by haveing no letter from my friends in Boston—but poor Hetty, —she looks as tho: she had lost all her friends,—says 'tis cruell—you cannot Imagin how it Grieves her. I beg of you, my sister, not to neglect her, and Peggy too, she says, "Could she neglect me. No, I am certain the post has lost my letters"—sometime, before I could convince her that there was no letters for her. She would have wrote you and her much Lov'd friend Miss Simpson last week, but her Health prevented,— which I informed our Sister Peggy of by a Billet P^r. Post—agreeable to the desire of Hetty, which I suppose she has received. Much company is with us— and I must leave writeing you—the post lodges here— if time, will say something to Mr. Simpson, & add to this before he goes in the morning.—My best Respects

* Sarah Webb had married John Simpson, of Boston.

to our Good sister your companion,—and to B^r. Jack. Believe me, my Dear Sister, ever y^r. friend & most affec^t. B^r.

SAM. B. WEBB.

Monday Morn. You must excuse me to Mr. Simpson, and tell him the post waits or I would write him. Next post I shall not forget him. Good morning to you.   Adieu. Yrs.   S. B. WEBB.

Brother Jack—Alias Sally's Husband—must excuse there Brother Jose—for not writing this week. Company has prevented my having any opportunity this week. I observe what you say ab^t. Isham. Its a very odd affair, and I'll write particular to Isham—the Law is in full force—& all that I can mistrust is—that he's a Lawyer—Have not rec'd a single line in answer to one of the Letters I [   ] for you.

[JOSEPH WEBB.]

FROM J. WENTWORTH.

PORTSM^o . NEW HAMP^E 7th Feby 1774.

SIR:

Your agreeable favour of the 24th June last Incloseing the Resolves of the Honble House of Representatives of the Colony of Connecticut, I had the honor to Receive and on the first meeting of our Assembly I took the earliest opportunity to lay the Interesting papers before them, [by] whose unanimous direction I have to assure your Honble house that in every Constitutional plan for Secureing the Rights of British America & removing the present Infringements thereon our Sister Colonies may rely we Sincerely join, having no wish for ourselves of an exclusive nature in those matters, ever looking on the whole as embarked in the same Common Bottom, and so Represented it in an Address to Lord Dartmouth at our first meeting after his Lordships appointment for American affairs.

The proposed method of Union in all the Colonies hath ever appeared to us (since the first Recommendation thereof) to be absolutely necessary, for which purpose this house adopted the Resolves of the very Respectable House of Burgesses of the Colony of Virginia and in May last appointed a Committee of Correspondence as you will observe by the Inclosed extract from the Journals. You may therefore Depend on the ready Concurance of this House with the measures tho't necessary to be pursued by the other Colonies in the Glorious Cause of Liberty.

In the Name & by order of the House I have the Honour to be with great Regard,

Sir your most obed^t Humble Servt.

J. WENTWORTH, Speaker.

The Honble Speaker of the House of Representatives of the Colony of Connecticut.

SILAS DEANE TO THE VIRGINIA COMMITTEE.

HARTFORD IN CONNECTICUT
March 10th 1774.

GENTLEMEN:

We wrote you from Newhaven the enclosed, since which yours of the 6th of January last* came to hand, inclosing the form of a Writt of assistance, the resolutions of your Assembly, since, against granting the general one, demanded by the Commissioners of his Majesty's Customs, and your Arguments on the Subject, for which we are much obliged, and consider them at once ingenious and conclusive. —The officers of his Majesties Customs have omitted pursuing their motion, for this Writt, for several Courts past, and we expect the affair will dye in silence with us, but should they revive it, your reasonings will be of service in the cause, and we are confident, they will not obtain the general one in this Colony, nor is there probability of their urging for, or obtaining any, of any kind, as at best such Writts are disagreeable to our Constitution, and of dangerous Tendency, and at this period, when the people in the Colonies are so justly alarmed, our Courts, whatever they might think of such a Writt, as that which has obtained with you, will not be prevailed on to grant

* This letter is printed in the *Calendar of Virginia State Papers*, viii. 6.

any, and indeed as this would not be accepted by the officers of the Customs, the granting it is but Needless.—You have enclosed the act of Our Assembly respecting the Counterfeiting of the Currencies of our Sister Colonies, and take Liberty to hint that were the Laws of the Colonies, respecting their Currencies, and other general Concerns, of one Tenor, as far as particular, local Circumstances will any way admit of it, might have a most happy tendency, towards forming and strengthening that Union of the Colonies, on which their safety, and happiness depends. We consider with pleasure, the step taken by your worthy House of Burgesses in appointing a Committee to keep up a regular Correspondence with your sister Colonies, now followed by almost the whole of them, as a Basis, on which the most lasting, and beneficial Union, may be formed, and supported. No intelligence either public or private has been rec⁴ from Great Britain, or any part of Europe, for almost three months, and we are anxiously expecting the Account how the returned Tea is received, and what Measures the present session of Parliament respecting that, and other American Concerns, will adopt.

We are with great Truth & Esteem, Gentlemen, your most obed! & very Hum̤ Serv̤ᵗˢ *

FROM THE NEW JERSEY COMMITTEE OF CORRESPONDENCE.

BURLINGTON, March 16ᵗʰ, 1774.

SIR:

The Representatives of this Colony having received a Letter from the truly Patriotic House of Burgesses in Virginia, enclosing their Resolutions to obtain the most early Intelligence of all such Acts and Resolutions of the British Parliament, or Proceedings of Administration as may relate to, or affect the British Colonies, and to maintain a mutual Correspondence and Communication concerning these im-

* This letter is in the script of Silas Deane. It is printed in the *Calendar of Virginia State Papers*, viii, 40, but is dated March 8th, 1774, and is signed by William Williams, Samuel Holden Parsons, Silas Deane and Benjamin Payne. It also has a postscript; "Since the above, Intelligence is received from London as late as the 10th of January, with which you are doubtless favored. A quantity of Tea arrived at Boston and met the fate of the former, the particulars of which will be with you before this; enclosed is a paragraph from our last Gazette."

portant Considerations, have come to the inclosed Resolutions, which we have the Honor to send you.

The Utility of the Plan proposed, at a Time when Claims are made on the Colonies to which they cannot give their assent, appeared so evident that they unanimously and chearfully adopted the Design of Uniting in every prudent and Constitutional Measure necessary to defeat every Attempt to deprive them of the inestimable Rights and Priviledges of British Subjects.

The Committee of Correspondence request the Favor of you to direct any Intelligence which your Honourable House may conceive necessary to be communicated to this Colony, to James Kinsey, Esqr , in the City of Burlington, New Jersey.

We are with great Respect, your most obedient Servants,

J. KINSEY   J. WETHERILL

SAM. TUCKER   J$^{NO.}$ HINCHMAN *

HEND^K FISHER

FROM SAMUEL ADAMS TO SILAS DEANE.

BOSTON, May 19, 1774.

SIR:

The Committee of Correspondence for the Town of Boston have before them a Letter signed by yourself, in Behalf of the Honble House of Representatives for the Colony of Connecticut ; and I am desired by our Committee, to return them their hearty Thanks for the Readiness they discover to support this Town, now called forth to stand in the Gap, and suffer the vengeful stroke of the Arm of Tyranny ! God forbid ! they should succumb. I trust in *Him,* we shall never be so servile as to submit to the ignominious Terms of the cruel Edict. Aided by our Sister Colonies, we shall be able to acquit ourselves under so severe a Tryal with Dignity. But that Aid must be speedy ; otherwise we shall not be able to keep up the Spirits of the more irresolute among us, before whom the crafty Adver-

---

* It was on the 8th of February that the assembly appointed from its members a committee of correspondence, comprising: James Kinsey, Stephen Crane, Hendrick Fisher, Samuel Tucker, John Wetherill, Robert Friend Price, John Hinchman, John Mehelm and Edward Taylor.

saries are already holding up the grim Picture of Want and Misery. It is feared by the Committee, that a conference of the Committees of Correspondence, from all the Colonies, cannot be had speedily enough to answer for the present Emergency. If your Hon.ble Committee shall think it proper, to use their influence with the Merchants in the several Seaport Towns in Connecticut, and prevail with those of each Town for themselves, to withhold their Trade with Great Britain and Ireland, and every Part of the West Indies, to commence at a certain time (say the 14th of June next), it will be a great sacrifice indeed, but not greater than Americans have given the World to expect from them, when called to offer it for the Preservation of the publick Liberty. One year's virtuous forbearance, would succeed to our wishes. Your sentiment that "Boston is suffering in the common cause," is just and humane. Your obliging Letter has precluded any Necessity in me, to urge your utmost Exertions, that Connecticut may, at this important Juncture, act her Part in support of that common Cause, though the Attack is made more immediately on the Town of Boston.

Being at present pressed for time, I cannot write so largely as I feel disposed to do. I must, therefore, conclude with assuring you, that I am with very great Regard for the Hon.ble Committee, Sir, your Sincere Friend & Fellow Countryman.

SAMUEL ADAMS.

FROM THE COMMITTEE OF CORRESPONDENCE OF VIRGINIA.

WILLIAMSBURG, VIRGINIA, May 28th, 1774.

GENTLEMEN:

The inclosed Papers will explain to you our present political State here, with Regard to the unhappy Dispute with our Mother-Country. The Propriety of appointing Deputies from the several Colonies of British America, to meet annually in general Congress, appears to be a Measure extremely important and extensively useful, as it tends so effectually to obtain the united Wisdom of the Whole, in every Case of general Concern. We are desired to obtain your Sentiments on this Subject which you will be pleased to furnish us with. Being very desirous of communicating to you the Opinion and Conduct of the late Representatives, on the present Posture of American Affairs as quickly as possible, we beg Leave to refer you to a future Letter, in which we shall more fully express our Sentiments on these Subjects.

We are, with great Respect, Gent.,

Your mo. obed. Servants,

PEYTON RANDOLPH

R. C. NICHOLAS

DUDLEY DIGGES

To the Committee of Correspondence for Connecticut.

SILAS DEANE TO THE COMMITTEES.

WETHERSFIELD IN CONNECTICUT, June 4th, 1774.

GENTLEMEN:

The present alarming measures, systematically adopted and now put in execution, for the absolute destruction of the Liberties of the British Colonies in America, has we doubt not engaged your Attention, so that we need not be particular on the subject, but inform that an Union of Council, by way of Congress from the different Colonies has been proposed, as the most effectual step to give at once Consistency and Weight, to such Measures, as shall be adopted & pursued to counteract the cruel designs of our Enemies.—The lower House of Assembly for this Colony, which closed their sessions this day, were pleased to Approve of the proposal and to recommend to their Committee of Correspondence, to join with those of the Sister Colonies in attending such Congress, should it be Agreeable to them, at such time and place as might be most Convenient, by such number of their Body or others, as they should think best to Appoint.—In Consequence of which we take the earliest Opportunity of laying the proposal before you, and add that should it meet with your Approbation, we Imagine that the last Week in July or first in August, may be as early as it can be held, consistant with giving notice to our Sister Colonies, and Possibly—New York or some Town on your or our side of that Capital, a proper Center of the Colonies represented —If this or something simelar should be agreeable to your sentiments, Shall depend on a line from you in proper season & that you will inform the Committees of the Provinces Southward of you, or such of them as it is probable may be able to attend at the Time—We mention this time and those Colonies, which may be then able to Attend, but could the Congress be so timed that all the Colonies on the Continent might be represented in it, it would to us be a most desirable Circumstance, and which we hope will be affected on some future occasion ; but the present urgency of our Situation seems to call for an earlier Day, than to Permit Intelligence to be sent farther than Virginia. But this we Submit to your Consideration, and shall at all times, as well by Letter, as Personally esteem ourselves happy in a Free & mutual exchange of Sentiments on the great one Important Subject before Us, and in uniteing to Promote the common Cause of American Liberty.

We are with great Respect Your Obedient Servants,

By order, and in behalf of the Committee
of Correspondence for Connecticut
SILAS DEANE

N. B   Simelar to the above has been Wrote to New ⎱
Hampshire, Boston, Newport & New York   ⎰

To James Kinsey, Stephen Crane, Hendrick Fisher, Saml Tucker, Jn Wetherill Esqrs. of ye Committee of Correspondence for New Jersey.

TO THE COMMITTEE OF CORRESPONDENCE, BOSTON.

WETHERSFIELD June 13th, 1774.

GENTLEMEN :

I received last Evening pr Post Your printed Letter of ye 8th Inst* incloseing a Printed Covenant to be signed, which Lettrs was directed to me as of the Committee of Correspondence for Wethersfield.—I must inform You there is no Committee for this Town nor do I know of any for any one Town in this County ; but as you have seen, by my former Letters, there is one general one for the Colony, appointed by the Honorble House of Representatives in May 1773, in whose behalf & by whose order, I have had the pleasure of Corresponding

---

* An address by the citizens of Boston to their countrymen relative to the blockade of their port. It is printed, with the covenant to suspend all commerce with Britain, in Force, *American Archives, Fourth Series,* I, 397.

with You, and the other Committees appointed in the different Colonies—Our Committee being situated remote from each other, at their last Meeting Appointed me their Clerk, and largely Considering the present Melancholly situation of American affairs in General, and of the Town of Boston in particular, directed me to write to you and the other Committees of our Sister Colonies, the Letter You received doubtless by the last post,*—To give you their Sentiments, so far, as they had discuss'd, and determined on the Subject, and in case of any new Event should happen, or fresh Proposal, of general concern, be made to Notice them of it, and call them together. —Our Committee have been from the first Unanimously of the opinion, that a General Congress, was necessary previous to every other measure. The Honorable House of Representatives at their Session in May last, adopted the same Sentiments, and gave us particular Instructions to Promote, and join therein ; Which we have since had the Happiness to find, is also the Unanimous opinion of our Sister Colonies Westward of us †—I shall pursuant to my Instruc-

---

* Printed on page 25.

† The House of Representatives of Connecticut "by a special Act empowered their committee of correspondence and inquiry, to join the committees of their Sister colonies in holding, as early as conveniently might be, a General Congress of the Committees or Delegates by them appointed to take into consideration the present melancholy and alarming situation of America in general, and of our Sister Colony of Massachusetts in particular. Pursuant to this the Committee have wrote to Boston, Portsmouth and New-port on the east; to New York, New [The?] Jersies, Philadelphia and Maryland on the west, proposing the last week in July or the first week in August for the time, leaving the place to be resolved as may best suit the Colonies that may send Representatives to attend, but at the same [time] supposing New York or Philadelphia might be the proper center. "It is, we conceive, of importance that every colony should be represented at such a general conference and much to be desired, but as the present Exigency presses, and it appearing very necessary to us that some general measures should be adopted seasonably, occasioned our taking the liberty of hinting at the time and place, though some other will be equally agreeable to us, if more so to our remote brethren. Your answer in season will much oblige us, by which we shall as far as possible regulate our conduct in this important affair. The wise, spirited and seasonable proceedings of your truly patriotic House of Burgesses, in early proposing a correspondence between and union of the Colonies, has justly merited and universally received the approbation and grateful acknowledgments of British America." *Silas Deane, as Clerk of the Committee,* to the Virginia Committee, 14 June, 1774.

tions summon the Committee to a Meeting and Communicate to
them Your printed Letter &ᶜ Meanwhile give me leave to hint to
you, the Light in which they view'd Associations of this kind, come
into by way of Subscriptions without a General Consent of the Colonies first had, and a consistant uniform plan digested, and Adopted
by the Whole.—"They View the present Attack on Boston, not as
Something Accidental. Not merely to obtain Satisfaction to the
India Company for a wretched Trifle of Tea, or to a Custom House
Officer, for some insult, or Indignity which he Received in Consequence perhaps of his own Insolence—But as part of the general
System, as one Operation of the general plan long since concerted,
for Subjugating the Colonies, and rendering their Lives, and proper-
ties, subservient to the Will & Pleasure, of a British Parliament, or
rather of their Ministry : in opposeing such a Systematical attack, the
greatest Union, and most general Consultation, is, on every Account
absolutely Necessary, to avoid takeing any one step of a Partial, or
Private Nature, or less general, or on less certain, & Determined
principles than the Importance of the cause calls for.—— They consider Subscriptions, however generously designed, as liable to Misrepresentations, and abuse and that, the Confidence which Subscribers at very remote distances from each other, will have in one Another, can never equal that which will be placed in the Resolutions,
and Determinations, of a Congress, in which each Colony will be
Represented by some of the most respectable Characters in it, and
on whom the Individuals have always placed their greatest reliance
& Trust—such a Congress, will carry with it in America the Weight
of a Constitutional Assembly, and have more Influence in all probability at the Court of Great Britain, than any other Association
whatever."——

These being the Sentiments of my Brethren of the Committee, and
confirm'd in them by the unanimous and Patriotic Resolutions of the
Gentlemen in our Sister Colonies, I cannot promote a Subscription
to the Agreement or Covenant You sent Us, untill the other Proposal of a General Conferance, has first taken Place, or until I shall
confer with the rest of the Committee thereon ; indeed by the diction
of it, I apprehend it was at first calculated, rather for the present
exigency untill something more general might be devised, And for
the Province of the Massachusetts in Particular.——

This Town meet on Thursday this Week, in order to take into Consideration, a proposal for Contributeing to the Immediate relief of the Town of Boston, when I shall duly lay before them the Letter You sent, and what other Intelligence I may Receive

I am Gentlemen Your Sympathizing

Fellow Countryman

SILAS DEANE Clk. : of Committee

Correspondence for Connecticut.

SILAS DEANE TO EBENEZER SILLIMAN AND — BISHOP.

WETHERSFIELD, 13 June, 1774.

SIR:

You have seen the Resolutions of our Brethren westward respecting a Congress. Pursuant to the Committee's direction, I have wrote to Boston, New Port, Portsmouth, New York, New Jersey, &c., and per next Post shall receive their answers, which will doubtless be in approbation of the speedy executing the Proposal. Meantime I think it best for us to appoint our members for the Congress in season.

Towns are [holding] Warning Meetings,—Resolutions are forming, subscriptions are circulating in this Colony of such various kinds & complexions that a preparation for a Congress is necessary, if for no other purpose than to prevent that Diversity of sentiment & Confusion into which the People, in Consequence of their present uncertain & apprehensive state of mind, must throw them. I therefore propose a meeting of the Committee, on Wednesday, the 22d instant, at Wethersfield or Middletown, as shall be most Agreeable to you, and the Gentlemen Eastward of the center.*

I am, with great Esteem, Gentlemen, your most obedt very Hum. Servt.

SILAS DEANE.†

* The meeting was held on July 13th, at New London. See introduction.

† This letter is in the writing of Samuel B. Webb.

SILAS DEANE ON RELIEF FOR BOSTON.

[June, 1774?].

MR. WATSON: *

If you can insert the following in your next and think it deserving, do so; otherwise return it P͞r Bearer.

[SILAS DEANE].

" Ruin from Man, is most conceal'd when near
And sends the dreadful Tidings in the blow."—YOUNG.

It is idle,—nay, it is more, for it is the height of madness and desperate Folly, to stand with our arms across, disputing about the rights & privileges of a Country, in the Day of battle, when the Enemy have actually invaded the Land, and are spreading havock, and desolation all around.—What is the present situation of New England?—What the Temper of too great a Number of its Inhabitants, who in words are the foremost in the list of Patriots, & Friends to their Country's Liberty? Our Liberties struck at one blow from their Foundation—our Capital made a Garrison, its harbour shut, its Inhabitants, unequalled in all the rolls of antiquity for patience, perseverance, & the other patriotic virtues, starving by degrees, sinking all their Interest, and loosing every prospect of ease, affluence, & worldly Felicity under the cruel, the iron hand of Tyrannic power— And each Town in fearful & certain expectation of sharing soon their Fate, unless the Acts complained of are repealed, or defeated by a vigorous & decisive Opposition. This is the present situation of New England in particular, & more immediately, of all the Colonies in general, and not much more remote.—The Temper of too great a Number of our Inhabitants is—O tell it not in Gath—O that there were no Necessity of telling it anywhere, but Justice requires that the public know how near to some men's hearts, private property clings, even in this day of immediate distress, & danger.—When in a late Assembly it was motioned that a Sum of Money should be

---

* Ebenezer Watson, the printer of the *Connecticut Courant*. This paper was established in 1764 by Thomas Green, who took Watson into partnership, and removing to New Haven, left him as publisher and editor. The paper continued to be published after Watson's death, by his widow, Hannah Bunce Watson, and a brother, James Watson, was one of the prominent merchants in New York. Samuel B. Webb named a son after him—General James Watson Webb.

voted for the relief of the sufferers in Boston, when urged that it was
what we honestly owed them, as a Debt, not merely a Charity—when
observed, that the hand of charity was seldom very warm, too apt to
grow cold, & that the sums contributed for their relief were no way
adequate to their sufferings—the motion was put by, and the devoted
Town turned over to the Charity of Individuals, or Towns at large,
& that principally by the means of Gentlemen who had not by themselves or Towns given anything.—When proposals were made out,
and the Assembly urged to provide a Quantity of Fire Arms in store,
& furnish the soldiery with Bayonets at the public expense—Interest
stept in, and raised a variety of ingenious Objections which bore
down all before it, and left the Soldiers to provide for themselves,.or
remain in the wretchedly unprovided State in which Too many of
them are unhappily in.—To effect this, it was urged, that it would be
very expensive—That the people would not bear it—That it was
Time enough to take such Measures sometime hence, &c., &c.—
Just as though Lord North would give us warning in season, or that
a paltry sum of private property, a sordid principle, & Love of Interest was to be taken into Consideration at a Day like this—It is rather
in vain now to recriminate—The Enemy have for some time been
in possession of our capital, the strongest by nature of any Town in
his Majesties Dominions, they have been suffered unmolestedly to
fortify, to reconnoiter the country, to lay up their Magazines of Stores,
and settle their planns of future operation—large reinforcements are
ordered, are now probably near our Coasts, while I write they may
be landing, Horse as well as Foot in Boston, and another week may
bring us the news of their being on their March into the Country—
for Horse are not transported from Europe, meerly to parade in the
Streets of Boston, or on its Common, nor are Waggons made meerly
for amusement, nor the extraordinary attention which Genl. Gage
has paid thro : the Winter to perfect his men in the regular modes
of Attacks done meerly for diversion.—As soon as the recruits are
arrived and refreshed, and the proclamation issued, their March will
begin—What the Consequences will be, if motives of sordid Interest,
under the stale device of prudence, prevails to keep us inactive may
easily be foreseen—Is there, my Countrymen, any other Alternative
now left you but to submit, or prepare for resistance even to Blood?
I declare I know of none. Our Petitions dispised, our Liberties

sported away, our private as well as public Interest invaded, and our Lives at the Mercy of a General and his army !—O ye preachers of prudence, of Caution, of parsimony, fly to the General at once and make your Peace.   Bow the knee, and be slaves at once, but no longer infect with your timid conduct those who have the Souls of Freemen, Souls superior to wealth, or *Title, other than* that of Sons of Liberty—If the major part—it is not possible,—but if the major part are of your Sentiments, leave us, who differ from you, at least to Our Fate, permit us to make at least one struggle in favor of our Liberties, disincumbered with your weight eventually operating in the opposite scale.   CASSIUS.

FROM METCALF BOWLER TO EBENEZER SILLIMAN.

NEWPORT, June 20th, 1774.

SIR:

Agreeable to the Directions of the General Assembly I have the Honor to inclose you a Copy of certain Resolutions entered into by them respecting the very alarming Situation of the Colonies.

I have also to inform you that upon this Occasion the Assembly have adjourned to the Fourth Monday in August next.

I am, with very great Regard, Sir,
Your most humble Servant,
METCALF BOWLER.   Speaker.

[Enclosure.]

RESOLUTIONS OF THE ASSEMBLY OF RHODE ISLAND.

At the General Assembly of the Governor and Company of the Eng-
lish Colony of Rhode Island and Providence Plantations in New
England in America; begun and beholden by Adjournment at New-
port, within and for the said Colony, on the Second Monday in
June, in the Year of our Lord One Thousand Seven Hundred and
Seventy-four, and in the Fourteenth Year of the Reign of His Most
Sacred Majesty George the Third by the Grace of God, King of
Great Britain and so forth.

This Assembly taking into the most serious Consideration several Acts of the British Parliament, for the levying Taxes upon His

Majesty's Subjects in America, without their Consent, and particularly an Act lately passed for blocking up the Port of Boston, which Act even upon the Supposition that the People of Boston had justly deserved Punishment, is scarcely to be paralelled in History—for the Severity of the Vengeance executed upon them ; and also considering to what a deplorable State this and all the other Colonies are reduced, when by an Act of Parliament, in which the Subjects in America have not a single Voice, and without being heard, they may be divested of Property and deprived of Liberty, do upon mature Deliberation Resolve

1st. That it is the Opinion of this Assembly that a firm and inviolable Union of all the Colonies, in Counsels and Measures, is absolutely necessary for the Preservation of their Rights and Liberties ; and that, for that Purpose a Convention of Representatives from all the Colonies ought to be holden, in some suitable Place, as soon as may be, in order to consult upon proper Measures to obtain a Repeal of the said Acts, and to establish the Rights and Liberties of the Colonies upon a just and solid Foundation.

2d. That the Honble Stephen Hopkins and the Honble Samuel Ward Esq^rs be and they are hereby appointed by this Assembly to represent the People of this Colony, in a general Congress of Representatives from the other Colonies, at such Time and Place as shall be agreed upon by the Major part of the Committee's appointed or to be appointed by the Colonies in general.

3d. That they consult and advise with the Representatives of the other Colonies, who shall meet in such Congress, upon a loyal and dutiful Petition and Remonstrance to be presented to His Majesty, as the united Voice of His faithful Subjects in America, setting forth the Grievances they labour under, and praying His gracious Interposition for their Relief : And that in Case a major Part of the Representatives of all the Colonies shall agree upon such Petition and Remonstrance they be empowered to sign the same in Behalf of this Colony.

4th. That they also consult and advise upon all such reasonable and lawful Measures as may be expedient for the Colonies, in an united Manner, to pursue, in order to procure a Redress of their Grievances, and to ascertain and establish their Rights and Liberties.

5th. That they also endeavor to procure a regular annual Convenvention of Representatives from all the Colonies to consider of proper Means for the Preservation of the Rights and Liberties of the Colonies.

6th. That the Speaker of the Lower House transmit, as soon as may be, Copies of these Resolutions to the present or late Speakers of the respective Houses of Representatives of all the British Colonies upon the Continent.

A true Copy duly examined,

Witness,   HENRY WARD Secry.

FROM THE COMMITTEE OF CORRESPONDENCE OF MARYLAND.

ANNAPOLIS, 26th June, 1774.

GENTLEMEN:

The inclosed Resolutions which we are directed to communicate, contain the Sense of this Province of a Union and general Plan of Conduct, in Defence of the Liberties of America, in the present dangerous and truly alarming Crisis. We feel ourselves happy in the firm and steady Spirit which animates the people of this Province to pursue those Means which they judge the most Speedy and effectual to prevent the Fall of Boston and the Massachusetts Government, and by such Prevention to save America from Destruction. It is our most fervent Wish and sanguine Hope that your Colony has the same Disposition and Spirit, and that by a general Congress such a Plan may be struck out, as may effectually accomplish the grand Object in View.

We are also directed to propose that the general Congress be held at the City of Philadelphia the twentieth of September next, which we hope will be convenient and agreeable, if not, we shall be ready to attend at any other Time or place that may be generally thought so.

We shall be thankful for a speedy Communication of every Thing you may think of Consequence.

Wé are Gentlemen with the utmost Respect

Your most obedient Servants,

TH. JOHNSON JUNᴿ.

ROBᵀ. GOLDSBOROUGH

Wᴹ. PACA

SAMUEL CHASE

To the Committee of Correspondence for Connecticut—Original sent by way of Philadelphia.

FROM THE COMMITTEE OF CORRESPONDENCE OF BOSTON.

BOSTON, June 28th, 1774.

SIR :

Your favor of the 20th current inclosing the proceedings of the Respectable Town of Weathersfield came duly to Hand. The wisdom, generosity and justice of our worthy fellow Countrymen while they greatly releive our present anxietes, afford us that prospect of a final restoration to the peaceful enjoyment of our invaluable Rights, which bears us up under such calamities as must otherwise stagger the most Resolute. To what lengths administration determines to proceed with us is yet very Uncertain. A collection of all the Troops on the Continent into this Capital, besides those arrived & expected from Europe is undoubtedly intended. The distruction of our Constitution will probably be proclaimed when that force is assembled. In this as in our present trial, our eyes must be [turned] to our Worthy fellow Colonists for that aid they have hitherto so kindly manifested their disposition to afford us.

The Contributions making in Weathersfield for the support of our Poor demand our hearty thanks on this behalf. Yesterday and to Day our Town has been in Meeting by adjournment. Our opponents mustered all their force & moved that the Committee of Correspondance be censured and dismissed. A very fair & free Debate ensued, and the most strict scrutiny into the conduct of the Committee ; which issued in the following vote, viz! :

It was moved and seconded that this Town bear open testimony that they are abundantly satisfied of the upright intentions & much approve the honest Zeal of the Committee of Correspondance & desire that they would persevere with their usual activity & firmness, continuing stedfast in the Way of Well doing.

And the Question being put the same passed in the Affirmative by a Vast Majority.

Signed by order & in behalf of the Committee of Correspondence for Boston.

WILLIAM COOPER, Clerk.

Silas Deane, Esqr .

SILAS DEANE TO CHARLES THOMSON.

WETHERSFIELD, July 4th, 1774.

SIR:

Your favour of the 21st Ult?, inclosing the resolves of the respectable City and County of Philadelphia was duly Received, since which conclude you have seen an account of the Proceedings of the Massachusetts Assembly & of their Dissolution. The Committee of Correspondence for this Colony met on the 13th Inst in order to appoint Deputies, to attend the General Congress of the Colonies at Philadelphia on the first of September Next—pursuant to the advice and Direction of Our House of Representatives at their Session in May last. The Inhabitants of this Colony are unanimous in the common Cause, and have their Attention fixed on the Result of the expected Congress, which they trust will be, the effecting such an Union, of the American Colonies, and the deviseing, and Recommending those Firm, but Just, Constitutional and Spirited Measures in which, all the Inhabitants of these extensive Colonies will unite, & by Union, & Perseverance, effect not only the Salvation of British America, but of Great Britain itself. We have a Report that Govr. Gage has threatned, that he will be Actively present in the Congress. This would be perfectly Incredible, were it not for the equally extraordinary stepps lately taken. His Proclamation of the 29th Ult? forbidding the Inhabitants of his Government, signing or entering, in any Manner, into Associations, against the Importations of British Goods, you will Receive by this Post, on which shall make no other Comment, than this, it Renders the above Report probable or Submitting to the Condition of those Slaves in the Islands, who are not permitted to Convene together in Public, or private, but by the express Liberty of their Masters. Shall lay your Letter before the Commee at their Meeting, and Inform you of their Proceedings as well as every occurance in this Colony deserving public Attention, and shall in return most gladly Receive the like from You, and Your Sentiments thereon, whether in a Public or private Capacity,—meantime I Remain

Sir, Your Most Obedient & very Huml. Servt. *

SILAS DEANE.

* This letter is in the script of Samuel B. Webb.

SILAS DEAN.

Member of the Congress

FROM SILAS DEANE TO THOMAS MUMFORD.*

WETHERSFIELD, 1 August, 1774.

Dᴿ SIR:

I am sorry that Mᵣ Johnson's engagements prevented his attending the Congress, but the more so, that the Consequence of his declining has been a Report to his disadvantage. I know you wish to have justice done to every man's character,—to one of his worth, ability, and who has repeatedly served this Colony, rather to the detriment of his own private Interest, in a more special manner. Now I have only Time to assure you that Dr. Johnson shew no disinclination to the measure proposed of a Congress, but on the other hand highly approved of it, as a most salutary & effectual step.—Nor did he so much as intimate any apprehension, as to his disobliging his Friends in England by attending, but his Reasons were, his previous engagement to attend a Reference of a most important Consequence at Albany, the middle of September next, not as an Attorney, but as a Referee. More than two Hundred Men are interested in the Event, and it had been already adjourned once on his account, and the other Referees belonged to different Governments and of course it could not be put by, but at the greatest inconveniency and expence. This was one Reason. The other was, that he tho't one of the Council could not attend with that propriety as another person, but this latter Reason I judged might have been got over, had it not been for the other—I do for my own part believe the Doctᵣ is as sincere in the Interest of America, as any one person in the Colony, and that he approves of the Congress, and of a Non-importation Agreement, which makes him consider the principal subject on which the Congress will be engaged of a Commercial Nature.—I have [wrote] this not disinterestedly, for I feel myself interested in his behalf I own, and the more so as I know how it feels to have sus-

---

* Thomas Mumford was a prominent merchant in New London, residing in Groton. In June, 1774, he was chosen a member of the Groton Committee of Correspondence, and in 1775 he was one of a company of gentlemen, seven in all, who formed the plan for taking Ticonderoga, giving their individual notes for the money borrowed from the Colony treasury for the venture. In 1775 he was a member of the General Assembly of Connecticut, and in 1778 signed the emissions of colonial bills of credit, and was an agent of the Secret Committee of Congress.—Caulkins, *History of New London*, 506.

picious stories circulated, however groundless, which affect a man's character in degree at least, and that in a most tender manner. And I have wrote to you, knowing your good Opinion of that Gentleman, and your readiness to do him as well as all Mankind Justice within the Circle of your Acquaintance and Connections. I am with Comp^ts to Mrs Mumford & Family, Dr Sir, your most obed^t Hum^l Servt *   SILAS DEANE.

TO JOSEPH WEBB.

PHILADELPHIA, Sat^y 17th Sepr 1774.

DEAR BROTHER:

The Post goes out Immediately—I have got your lett^r to Mr Deane,—he being at ye Congress—which sets till two o'Clock cannot see it. Their Committees Which have been out for 4 or five days past stateing the Rights of y Colonies &c have this morning call'd them together,—and perhaps in a few days we may give you some interesting Intelligence,—Yesterday we Din'd together w^h ye Congress to ye Number of ab^t 400†—Inclosed you have the Toasts Drank—if time I

* From the Ford Collection.

† John Adams noted in his *Diary:* "16, Friday. Dined with Mr. Wallace with a great deal of company at an elegant feast again. 17, Saturday. This was one of the happiest days of my life. In Congress we had generous, noble sentiments, and manly eloquence. This day convinced me that America will support the Massachusetts or perish with her." And to his wife, he wrote on the 18th: "The proceedings of the Congress are all a profound secret as yet, except two votes which were passed yesterday, and ordered to be printed. You will see them from every quarter. These votes were passed in full Congress with perfect unanimity. The esteem, the affection, the admiration for the people of Boston and the Massachusetts, which were expressed yesterday, and the fixed determination that they should be supported, were enough to melt a heart of stone. I saw the tears gush into the eyes of the old, grave, pacific Quakers of Pennsylvania." The action of the Congress on the Suffolk resolutions is given in the *Journals*, September 18, 1774.

The Committee on stating the rights of the Colonies was appointed on September 7th, reported on the 22d, when a copy of its report was made out for each Colony. See *Works of John Adams*, II, 375.

would be particular.—I shall leave this some time next week—when M^r. Deane will write you particular— — He says he shall advise M^r. Simpson to urge his B^{rs} making a public Recantation*—setling matters, and w^h. our Sister to spend the Winter in Weth^d. —M^r. Revere got here Yesterday express from Boston, †—am in the utmost haste

Y^r. Affec^t. B^r.

SAM^l. B. WEBB.

SILAS DEANE TO THE COMMITTEE OF CORRESPONDENCE OF WETHERSFIELD.

PHILADELPHIA, 19 September, 1774.

GENTLEMEN :

I have the pleasure of inclosing to you Two Resolves of the Congress, which were pass'd without one dissenting Voice, though all the Members were present—I wish to have these dispersed through the Colony, into every Town at least ‡—Mr. Webb § can inform you of the general Sentiments of this part of the Continent, particulars will not be published by the Congress, untill they rise, or adjourn, except in those cases where it is judg'd, to be peculiarly necessary. I may take the Liberty however to assure you that the greatest Unanimity has hitherto prevailed among the Members.

I am with regard, Gentlemen, your most Obed^t & most Hum^{le} Servt.

SILAS DEANE.

P. S. Mr. Webb to whom I refer sets out to-morrow, but M^r. Rever going this instant I forward by him.‖

* See introduction.

† "Last Friday Mr. Revere brought us the spirited and patriotic resolves of our county of Suffolk. We laid them before Congress." *Samuel Adams to Charles Chauncey,* 19 September, 1774.

‡ The resolutions on the Suffolk Resolutions.

§ Samuel B. Webb.

‖ From the Ford collection.

TO SILAS DEANE.

WETHERSFIELD, Monday Evening, Octo'r 10, 1774.

DEAR SIR:

By my Brother's letter from you, p^r. Jemmy this evening, I notice you mention my not writing you, since my leaving Philadelphia; but I have frequently heard that a man without any business is the most busy man in the world; this I give as one reason why I have not wrote you since my return. But the principal reason is truly this, that my brother, as I suppose, has given you all such intelligence as would be necessary, amusing, or worth paying postage for. But as it seems you desire I should write, I risk the chance of its being acceptable or amusing, and wish I may find anything to say that may meet with the wished for approbation, —and I take this early opportunity for fear I may not have leisure again between this and next post. My continual uneasiness and anxiety on account of my Sisters, who are now in Boston, has determined me to pay them a visit, and if some unforeseen incident does not prevent, I intend setting off the last of this week; shall take Newport, Providence, &c., in my way, and will, if anything new or interesting [occurs], write you from each place, but more particularly from the present seat of noise and confusion, say Boston; the true situation of it, and fortifications which are now erecting at the only entrance of that large capital. My brother seems more at ease about our Sister, than *you* (by your letter) or *I* do. May all his conjectures be right. That "they [are] as safe there as here," is my most fervent wish,—but much I fear. On the first hostility, such as blood shed by the Troops in Boston, this Colony will most undoubtedly be immediately under arms and march for Boston. The Light Infantry at Middletown, to which I two years belonged, have now a very fine stand of arms which I purchased for them in New York on my return home from Philadelphia. They have given me an invitation to make one of the number, should any emergency call their appearance in the field, which with my whole heart I shall readily accept, if occasion [demands]. But Heaven forbid we may ever arrive to this unhappy Crisis! But all have drawn their arms, and myself among the rest.

On my return, I personally waited on Mr. Davenport at Stamford, and the Selectmen of every other Town which I pass'd through in that county, and have the pleasure to inform you that the Spirit of Liberty which has so long been buried in silence seems now to rear its head. Fairfield has had a meeting and entered into good and spirited resolves, and are now collecting grain for Boston. Greenwich, I am informed, and Stratford are doing the same; the latter I am uncertain of. Mobs, which I fancy you judge ruinous to all good government, will be opposed by every true Son of Liberty in this Colony. Other methods may be adopted more effectual to still our *very few* remaining enemies. A reason, and I think a very good one, is given, that all such riots should be stop'd in their first growth, viz., "A day may come, and in all probability soon will, unless a redress of our grievances can be obtained, that we may be as destitute of all Law and Civil Government as the Massachusetts now is; then, if mobs are allowed to take hold of persons and private property, dissensions will follow, and we soon should be, instead of a United, a broken Body." These are the principles our warmest friends adopt, and, as I before hinted, I think good.

Our Assembly set on Thursday, this week; many plans &c., &c., are formed for our Militia; the best I have seen is by Mr. Hosmer* wth (I suppose) the help of some military genius of that town, and he strongly wish'd you to meet him there, to put forward the thing. Some few remonstrances I hear are to be hove in, but I hope not to be noticed. Permit me, Dear Sir, to ask whether a letter from Col. Dyer, Mr. Sherman and yourself, on this subject to some of your friends, Members of the Assembly, of the Council, &c., (as there is not a possibility of your being present), would not be of Service? I am not the *only one* that thinks it would. But as I am a young, and consequently an inexperienced politician, I shall for the present here drop the subject, and leave it to better judges and more experienced men; tho', young as I am, ever maintain my principles, which I think are justly fixed.

Letters which you mention to have sent by a private hand to New York, for the Thursday's Post, are not yet come to hand; I hope not stopp'd by ——, but I think not improbable, as all parties are on the *look out*. The safest conveyance seems to be by post. Should anything new come to hand I shall mention it. My most respectful compliments await on the gentlemen of the family, Mr[s]. House, Mrs. Trist, and Miss

---

*Titus Hosmer, of Watertown, Connecticut, was a prominent man in his day. He was a member of the Council and Assembly 1773–1778, speaker in 1777, and a member of the Continental Congress in 1778. He died in 1780.

Levy; Mr. Furguson I shall write—"The most Important Man,"—if time before I go.

I am, with most dutiful respects, Dear Sir,
Your very affectionate friend and most humble servt,

SAM'L B. WEBB.

Wednesday, 12th. By Mr. Belding, who goes on to the Assembly this morning, I forward this to New Haven. Joe would write you, but yesterday and the day before were field days,—two companies of Foot and the Troop in the field;—which my Brother was obliged to attend; his respects to you; says he shall write you next post. Mrs. Deane is, she thinks, a little better since her return from Deerfield, and will probably write you soon. I would, as I have promised, write Mr. Furguson, but time will not allow me at present.

Am as above, yours affectionately

S. B. WEBB.

TO MRS. SARAH SIMPSON.

SUNDAY EVENING, 16 October, 1774.

MY DEAR SISTER:

Since I wrote poor Sam has Dislocated his Ancle,—say on Tuesday morning last—otherways before this I should have been *att* or on my Road to Boston, but a very faithfull Attendance has got it so, that I walk tolerably well, and on the morrow, Doct. Porter willing, I set of on my intended Tour. Several very pressing Invitations from Mr. Pease, a little Business &c., has determined me to take New Port and Providence in way. Should I set of to-morrow I go as far as Norwich in Company with M^r. John Chester.*   This Censorious World, my Dear Sister, will—should Miss H. be at Newport—charge my visit that way on her Acc^t. altho: Determined on long before any knowledge of her Intention of going there this fall.   But in all probability she is, or will before my Arrival there, have embarked for Carolina, should that be the case, it will prevent talk.   I should leave my visiting Providence & Newport till my return, but as our Sister Abby will be with me, I think so young as she is, it would not be worth her while to go that way, tho: as Joe is now agoing to enter into a state which will Naturally make him more Confined,† I shall think it *my Duty*, and Surely my Inclination to pay my utmost Attention to my *Two* Remaining Sisters, may they be as well Situated as you are, my D^r. Sister, and B^r. Sam. is Happy; but so long as they remain in a single Life, nothing, that an Affectionate Brother can do shall be wanting to make them Happy.   The very Idea of seeing you and my other friends—so Happy—in Boston as I am taught to think they are, give me an undiscribable Pleasure.   My Love to B^r. Jack & Jonⁿ and Sister P[egg]y.

Adieu my Dearest Sister, believe me your Affec^t. B^r.

SAM^L. B. WEBB.

Dont look for Saml. till he comes, as I must travel slow.

---

* Capt. John Chester was born at Wethersfield, 18 Janua˜y, 1749; married 25 November, 1773, Elizabeth Huntington, a sister of Jedediah and Ebenezer Huntington, who did good service during the Revolution.   Capt. Chester died in 1809, and his widow survived him till 1834.

† On November 22, 1774, Joseph Webb married Abigail Chester, a daughter of John Chester and Sarah (Noyes) Chester.   Abigail was born at Wethersfield, May 27, 1754, and was a sister of Capt. John Chester.

SILAS DEANE TO THOMAS MUMFORD.

28 November, 1774.

DEAR SIR:

Your's I rec^d , and the Two Cheeses; am obliged to you for the Favor of procuring Them. The Petition to his Majesty I gave Govr Trumbull, and have but just now got it back; will endeavor to procure you a Copy of it by To-morrow's post, on the express Condition of its not going out of Your hands.

The Dissolution of Parliament, sudden & unexpected, must cause much Speculation, and as we wish To have things, so we form Our Judgments of what may be the Consequences. But for my own part, confess myself greatly at a Loss to form any determination on the Subject further than this : The motives for the Dissolution, were evidently unfavorable to America, as the plan seems to be, to obtain so Sudden a Reelection, that the People in Great Britain may neither be acquainted with, or alarmed at the Situation of American Affairs.

Capt. Goodrich waits so [   ] not add But am, with Comp^{ts} to Y^r Lady, Sir, y^{rs} ,

S. DEANE.*

TO SILAS DEANE.

NEW YORK, 15thDecem^r, 1774.

GENTLEMEN:

It is with the most painful reluctance that we are Compelled to solicit Your Interposition even in An Affair which most nearly concerns you, as it Certainly Implies a strong Censure on too many of the Inhabitants of this City & Province which we would fain Rescue from the Detestable Reproach of Encouraging a Pensiond Servile Wretch commonly known by the Name of James Rivington who is daily by his Conversation Paper & Pamphlets Insulting Reviling & Counteracting this whole Continent and that in the most rancorous & Malevolent Manner, for Proof of which in part we beg leave to refer You to the Inclosed Piece taken from his Paper of the 1st of this month,† since when he has Published three Different Pamphlets all

---

* From the Ford Collection.

† The article referred to was probably that on " Considerations on the Nature and Extent of the Legislative Authority of the British Parliament," favoring the supremacy of the British legislature over colonial affairs.

Calculated, these & the former as well as the authors knew how, to Defeat the Salutary Intentions of the General Congress partly by Alarming the fears of the Timid & Stirring up the avarice of the Selfish & partly by a rascally attempt in two of the last publications to Ridicule the United Counsells of America all which together with other Corrupt means & Pernicious Influence that Some of you are no Strangers to the report of, have Undoubtedly been the occasion of A most Scandalous Defection in Several parts of this Province.

This being a Brief of the True State of the Case we the Real friends of this Devoted Country have thought it Adviseable for our mutual Safety to offer You & all the other Colonies a Plan which if Carried into Execution cannot fail it is Imagined of making this Enemy & Traitor to Our Common Rights repent of his Impudence & folly, which is to call meetings of Your respective Districts & enter into Resolutions Immediately not to take his paper nor the paper of any Printer on the Continent who Shall dare to Insult this oppressed Country by attempting to Subvert the regulations of the General Congress & also that you will not even have any Dealings with him or those who advertise in his paper or the paper of any other printer whilst he or they continue to print against the proceedings of the Congress and publish the same in all the papers on the Continent this we think if properly conducted will be a lesson to others hereafter & appears the more necessary just now as the Worthy Inhabitants of South Carolina have already by their Representatives Prohibited any more of his papers Coming into that Province when a similar Conduct of the other Colonies would Convince the most Hardy of our American Enemies as well as the ministry of Great Britain that our Unanimity is not to be Violated or attempted with Impunity.

There is also another Reason which we think not an Unimportant one neither & that is that the Enemies of America will Undoubtedly transmit every thing that has been Written against the Congress or their Constituents Informing that it was all done with the Greatest safety to the Printer & with but very little prejudice to his Interest which may occasion a Delay of Conciliatory Measures as well as a further Exertion of Ministerial Influence in Order to Detach us from the Common Cause.

We hope the propriety of the measure will appear in the same Important light to you & all the friends of America as it does to us but do not mean to Dictate by any means, if the present Accounts from Great Britain of the Ministry succeeding in Getting a majority of the old Members returned may be depended on which there is too much reason to believe is the Case we Imagine You will readily Grant that every thing in our Power ought to be done in order to preserve our Union as perfect & Indissoluble as possible.

We are sensible that what we have recommended has partly been advised by the Congress & is Included in the association for which Reason it is thought to be the more Essential as such a measure by Being rather more than the latter Requires will give the Greater Sanction & Stability to their proceedings.

Should this plan be adopted by you we think that you will not fail to render it as Extensive as Your Influence by conveying a Transscript of it where ever there is a prospect of its Utility.

THE FRIENDS OF LIBERTY.

See An Advertisement in his last paper relative to A proposed Raffle for Books than which can any thing be more daring or Insolent.*

TO JOHN AND SARAH SIMPSON.

WETHERSFIELD, Feb? 18th, 1775.

BROTHER JACK:

You do not Deserve a letter—you are Indebted to me almost a quire of paper—and I must insist you Ballance your Acct. . Immediately, without delay. Yours &c., S. B. WEBB.

DEAR SISTER:

I began with an intention to write our Brother, but on second tho't, as I cannot write but to one this week I have alter'd, and shall say a few words to you. I am

---

* In the advertisement Rivington described himself as "a FREE PRINTER, approved such, by both PARTIES," and announced certain political publications in terms that could not but give great offence to the "good people" of the colonies.

not in a humour to write you a long Circumstantial letter. Most of the week I have spent at Middletown —return'd last Evening—and am neither sick or well, but rather in a stupid, senseless mood. M^r. Simpson I suppose e're this reaches you will be on his way here. I cannot but regret his not waiting on you & Miss Peggy up with him. As M^r. Brymer is to accompany him I think it would be very Convenient. I had said every thing in my power on the subject, but 'twas like talking to the Wind, your friends, many of them, think you very Indifferent about them—they are Continually enquireing when you intend paying Us a Visit. 'Tis always the Case when I write at the same table with our Sister Hetty—she twitches away my paper—& has ten thousand Questions of no manner of Consequence to ask me—and so very good natur'd when she gets into one of these Fits that it makes me Laugh—and I cannot but Humour her, let me be ever so much engaged. She Calls me her Old Man, &c.—I Could wish ever to live as Happy as I now do in the Company and Conversation of this our Sister. She is indeed a very good Girl, and seems to put great Dependence & Confidence in me, at the same time 'tis my Duty as well as Inclination to pay a particular, friendly & Brotherly Attention to Her. Jose is married; of Consequence his love and Attention is turn'd to another. Hetty and myself are therefore, at present Insepperable. She goes no where unless Brother Saml. Attends her. While I was this week at Middletown there was a Ball here, M^r. Len^d. C———r* came

---

* Probably Leonard Chester, a brother of Capt. John Chester.

bowing and scrapeing, beging the company of Miss Webb; but no, by no Means, the Old Man, was gone to Middletown, & to be sure, with a toss of the Head, she should not go. I have spun out considerable more than I tho't to when I began, & if it gives you half the satisfaction in peruseing that it has me in writeing, I am fully paid. A number of your friends at Middleton enquired particularly after you, & desired to be Rem'd to you. Adieu, My Comp^{ts} &c. wait on your good Companion & Sister. Believe me, as ever, Your very Affec^t. B^r. & friend

SAM^L. B. WEBB.

To our B^r. Willm I desire to be Remembered.

TO MRS. SARAH SIMPSON.

WETHERSFIELD, Saturday, March 18th, 1775.

MY DEAR SISTER:

Your last letter to me has been fully answered, which now lies by me, and on a second perusal have Concluded not to send it you, but promise you a perusal of it the first time I see you, which I hope may be soon. It alluded particularly to what you said to me in regard to my Conversation with Parson Walter. I wrote it immediately on the Receipt of yours, and no doubt every line shew'd the sentiment of my Heart. Yours to me gave me more uneasiness, and less Satisfaction, than any I ever Receiv'd from you. I shall say no further on the subject, than that I am not the least uneasy for any part of my Conversation with the Parson, —Confident I have said nor done any thing that deserves Censure. God knows I had not in my Heart,

but to treat him with Respect due him.   If plain Honesty is capable of giveing an Offence, I shall, I fear be
often blame'd by this Censorious World.   Be that as
it may,—I will, while I have life, speak the Sentiments
(if I say any thing) & Dictates of an *Honest Heart*, to
Man, Woman, & Child.   Assured of this in my own
Breast—I shall endeavor not to regard the Malicious
designs of too many of my fellow Mortals.   You are
entirely mistaken my Dear Sister in saying "I am the
cause of Hetty's not Visiting you."   The most I ever
said on the subject was when my Advice was ask'd—
"that I could not Advise her to while the present
troubles Remained,"—& I am still of the same Sentiments.   Be assured she is Dear to me, and I ever will
—while I have any Care of her—discharge my Duty
as a friend, & Affectionate Brother.   Her Inclination
shall by me, ever be Consulted; and if she says she has
a Mind to go, I am Ready to attend her immediately.
The last Chat I had with her on the Subject, I told her
I would, she might depend, attend her between this and
the last of May.   By that time my Sister, most probable, we shall know what we have to depend On.—You
must therefore make yourself easy for a few Weeks,
when I hope We may meet you in perfect Health &
Happiness.   Of this be assured you cannot wish it
more than Hetty as well as myself does; this I think
you cannot Doubt.   By late News of my Business
among the French in Hispaniola, I am much afraid I
shall be forc'd some time this summer, to Revisit that
Dismal Clime, Heav'n forbid—but if Business Calls, I
must Obey.   Of this I shall know more in a few
Weeks, but be it as it may, I am Determined on see-

My Affte Bro   May 22, 1775

Long has been my silence, but this indicates
not will assure You, the one reason is that I did
not know where to direct my letters, & another
that I could not say anything but about
Business, wh is now the burden of the song,
I have undoubtedly inform You of my intention
of settling in Quebec, & the plan I go upon wh
I think a more eligible one than to stay here
spending my whole substance. I must earnestly request your assistance as much as
possible in collecting my Debts, as every thing
depends on you too, my Estate is quite at the
Mercy of my Debtors I hope You will influence
them to shew a great deal, without which We
starve, I want £1000 or 1200 as my part of the
stock in my present plan wh I hope you will
be able to help me, to, otherwise I must stay

here cherish as my friends & flock, both of whom & provision are very sonair. I have not received a line from you since the blockade commenced, so don't know what is done with my goods, tho hope you have disposed of the major part for Cash, as I don't have to Creditt any Part of them. You are sensible that Jose has a great deal to do therefore hope you will do as much as possible for me, bear in mind that 1000 now is worth 30 at Any other time, as it may be the means of procuring a subsistance for life ——

Remember that the New London Post, can bring us Letters & don't neglect us, but at the same time remember that all Letters are opend by both partys

I have only to add that We go in about three Weeks & that it being late I must conclude & by assuring I am yr Affectionate Bro & obliedged friend

John Simpson

ing you first. Since the Departure of our Guest and friend M^r. Brymer, I have taken one Excursion with B^r. Jack Simpson, Esqr. ; he is now with Us sometimes Rambling, at others, Reading, Writeing, Whistleing, Singing, Danceing, blowing the Whistle, as the Man told him, &c., &c., &c.

I have not time to add, but shall as often as leisure permits, write You, in Return I hope you will some-times devote a little time to, Dear Sally, Your friend & Most Affectionate Brother

SAM^l. B. WEBB.

P. S. My Respects to your Amiable friend & Sister, to B^r. Willm &c., who I hope is well & in Spirits. Once more Adieu—By the by, I had forgot to tell you, Your Gentleman is as uneasy as a fish out of Water—to get back—tho: we do every thing in our power to make his tarry Agreeable, he says he is as easy here as he possibly can be in any place on Earth, Home excepted.

TO MRS. SARAH SIMPSON.

WETHERSFIELD, Wednesday Evening, 22 March, 1775.

This, my ever Dear Sister, will be Received by our good Brother your M^r. Simpson, who I dare say meets you unexpectedly, and with a satisfaction which I am unable to describe. We are happy on your Account to part with him, on our own quite the Contrary ; if possible my Affection grows more and more for him at every Meeting, & 'tis with regret whenever I am obliged to part. O my Sister had it so have hap-pened, that you and our Sister Peggy could have ac-

companyed him up, you would have given your friends
a satisfaction which nothing but Ocular Demonstration
can give you a true Idea of. You well know every
thing in our power would have been done to make the
Minutes pass Agreeably on, to You I am positive they
would—at the Old place of your Nativity, in Company
with the Man of your Heart, & your Affectionate
Brethren ; to our Sister Miss Simpson—it would have
gone on hand in hand with our good Sister Hetty, who
is very fond of her,—but why do I talk on a matter
which is already past—for no other Reason but with
great expectation you may yet gratify Us with your
presence this Spring. Can you have already forgot
the Beauties of a fine morning in the Country? can
you have lost the sound of the little Warblers? which
every morning surround our Mansion, and seemingly
with various & most pleaseing Notes thank Almighty
Providence for the return of Spring? Can you (in a
word) forget every pleaseing Idea, and many real enjoyments? No You Cannot—Come then (if possible),
my much Lov'd Sister, to your B^{rs} & Sisters; come
with your other self. Come with your Amiable Sister,
friend and Companion ; else perhaps you never again
may see so many of your friends together, in this now
happy family. I do expect Mr Simpson will be obliged
to pay us another Visit between this & May. For that
Reason 'tis I say so much of your comeing—but should
it be otherways, and nothing more than I at present
know of happens, I shall attend my good Sister, and
once more see you at your Happy Seat. 'Tis late, I
am rather Dull ; if anything appears unconnected, look
it o'er with that Sisterly Affection you are wont to do.

Hetty—as she generally does—has been reading what
I have wrote,—she says "Sammy, you have wrote—
very different from what your feelings are to Night,
which I think makes it appear, *Not so Smart* as I have
seen of yours." I Acknowledge I am not in a humour
for writing, my tho'ts are turned another way. I have
something, of no little Consequence that lies on my
mind. I must bid you Adieu,—with a kind Remembrance of our friend & Sister Miss Simpson, & B^r W^m.
Believe me, Dr Sally, your very Affectionate Brother

Saml B. Webb.

FROM SILAS DEANE OR JOSEPH WEBB TO ——.

*Extract of a letter from Weathersfield, in Connecticut, to a gen-
man in New York, dated April 23, 1775.*

The late frequent marchings and counter-marchings into the
country, were calculated to conceal the most cruel and inhuman design ; and imagining they had laid suspicion asleep, they pitched
upon *Tuesday* night for the execution. A hint being got, two expresses were sent to alarm the Congress. One of them had the good
fortune to arrive ; the other *(Mr. Revere)* is missing, supposed to
be waylaid and slain. In the night of *Tuesday* the Company of
Grenadiers and Light-Infantry, from every Regiment, were transported to *Charlestown* in long boats, and at day-break began their
march for *Lexington,* where a number of the inhabitants were assembled peaceably, without arms, to consult their safety. The Commander called them rebels, and bade them disperse. On their refusal,
he fired, killed and wounded nine. They then proceeded towards
Concord, marking their way with cruelties and barbarity, never
equalled by the Savages of *America*. In one house a woman and
seven children were slaughtered (perhaps on their return). At
Concord, they seized two pieces of cannon, and destroyed two others,
with all the flour, &c., in store, but the people secured their magazine of powder, &c.

By this time about four hundred (no accounts make them more than five hundred) of our men assembled, and placed themselves so advantageously, without being perceived, that when the enemy were on the return, they received the full fire of our men. A heavy engagement ensued; the enemy retreating, and our men pressing on them with constant reinforcements. At *Lexington*, they retook their two pieces of cannon, seized the enemy's wagons and baggage, and made about twenty prisoners; continuing to press the Regulars close to *Charlestown*, where they were on the point of giving up (one account says this Brigade was almost all cut off), but a reinforcement, under the command of Lord *Percy*, having been detached that morning from *Boston*, they joined the first detachment in the retreat, and retired with it to *Bunker's* Hill, where they intrenched, and night parted them. Our number increased, and next morning would have surrounded the hill, had it not been for the situation near the water, where, on one side, they were exposed to the fire from a Man-of-War.

We lost thirty men in the action. The lowest account of the enemy's loss is one hundred and fifty. Lord *Percy*, General *Haldimand*, and many other officers, are said to be among the slain. A gentleman of veracity assured me that he numbered, within half a mile from the place where the fight began, one hundred and fifty. The post confirms the same account.

We are all in motion here, and equipt from the Town, yesterday, one hundred young men, who cheerfully offered their service; twenty days provision, and sixty-four rounds per man. They were well armed, and in high spirits. My brother is gone with them, and others of the first property. Our neighboring Towns are all arming and moving. Men of the first character and property shoulder their arms and march off for the field of action. We shall, by night, have several thousands from this Colony on their march.

The eyes of *America* are on NEW YORK; the Ministry have certainly promised by some of your leading men, that your Province would desert us: but you will be able to form a better judgment when you see how this intelligence is relished. Take care of yourselves; we have more than men enough to block up the enemy at Boston, and if we are like to fall by treachery, by Heaven we will not fall unrevenged on the traitors; but if balls or swords will reach them, they shall fall with us. It is no time now to dally, or be merely neutral; he that is not for us is against us, and ought to feel the first of our resentment. You must now declare, most explicitly, one way or the other, that we may know whether we are to go to Boston or New York. If you desert, our men will as cheerfully attack New York as Boston; for we can but perish, and that we are determined upon, or be free. I have nothing to add, but am your friend and countryman, &c.

P. S. Colonel Murray's son one of the Tories, undertook to guide the Regulars in their march to Concord, and on their retreat was taken prisoner; but attempting to escape from our people, they shot him—a death too honourable for such a villain! They have made another of them prisoner, but I do not recollect his name; none of ours were taken.

Will Colonel Grant believe now that New England men dare look Regulars in the face? Eighteen hundred of their best men retreating with loss, before one-third of their number, seems almost incredible, but I think must be called an omen for good. In every struggle Heaven has, as yet, given us strength equal to the day; its hand is not shortened, nor its arm weakened. We are now called upon to show the world "that whom we call fathers did beget us," and that we desire to enjoy the blessings they purchased for us with their lives and fortunes. We fix on our Standards and Drums, the Colony Arms, with the motto, "*qui transtulit sustinet*," round it in letters of gold, which we construe thus: "God, who transplanted us hither, will support us."*

[Silas Deane or Joseph Webb.]

AGREEMENT OF THE WETHERSFIELD COMPANY OF VOLUNTEERS, CAPT. CHESTER, APRIL 23d, 1775.

To all Christian People believing in, and relying on, that God to whom our Enemies have at last forced us to appeal, be it known:

That We, the Subscribers, having taken up arms for the relief of our Brethren, and defence of their, as well as our just rights and

---

* Force, *American Archives, Fourth Series*, II., 362.

privileges, do declare to the world that we from the heart disavow every thought of Rebellion to his Majesty, as supreme head of the British Empire, or opposition to Legal Authority, and shall on every occasion manifest to the world by our conduct this to be our fixed principle. Driven to the last necessity, and obliged to have recourse to arms, in defence of our Lives and Liberties, and from the suddenness of the occasion deprived of that Legal Authority whose dictates we ever with pleasure obey, [we] find it necessary, for preventing disorders, irregularities, and misunderstandings,.in the course of our march and service, solemnly [to] agree to, and with each other, on the following Regulations and Orders, binding ourselves by all that is dear and sacred, carefully and constantly to observe and keep them.

In the first place, we will conduct ourselves decently and inoffensively, as we march, both to our Countrymen and one another, paying that regard to the advice, admonition and reproof of our Officers which their station justly entitles them to expect ; ever considering the dignity of our own character, and that we are not mercenaries whose views extend no farther than pay and plunder, and whose principles are such, that every path that leads to the obtaining these is equally agreeable, though wading through the best blood of their Countrymen ; but men acquainted with, and feeling the most generous fondness for the Liberties and unalienable Rights of mankind, and who are, in the course of Divine Providence, called to the honorable service of hazarding our Lives in their defence.

Secondly,—Drunkeness, Gaming, Prophaneness, and every vice of that nature, shall be avoided by ourselves, and discountenanced by us in others.

Thirdly,—So long as we continue in our present situation of a voluntary Independent Company, we engage to submit on all occasions to such decisions as shall be made and given by the majority of the Officers we have chosen ; and when any difference arises between man and man, it shall be laid before the officers aforesaid, and their decision shall be final. (We mean by Officers, the Captⁿ , Lieutenants, Ensign, Serjeants, Clerk, and Corporals ; the Captⁿ , or in his absence the commanding officer to be the Moderator, and having a turning or casting voice in all debates ; from whom all orders shall from time to time issue.)

Scorning all ignoble motives, and superior to the low and slavish practice of enforcing on men their duty by blows, it is agreed, that when private admonition for any offense, by any of our Body committed, will not reform, public shall be made, and if that should not have the desired effect, after proper pains taken, and the same repeated, such incorrigible person shall be turned out of the Company as totally unworthy of serving in so great and glorious a Cause, and be delivered over to suffer the contempt of his Countrymen.

As to particular orders, it shall from time to time be in the power of the Officers to make and vary them, as occasion may require, as to delivering out provisions, ammunition, rules and orders for marching, etc. The annexed Orders, for the present, we think pertinent, and agreeable to our minds; to which, with the additions or variations that may be made by our said Officers, we bind ourselves by the ties above mentioned to submit.

In witness whereof, We have hereunto set our hands this 23d of April, 1775.

FROM SILAS DEANE.

TUESDAY MORNING, HARTFORD, 25 April, 1775.

DEAR SAMMY:

I received your Favors, and the express waiting have time to say but a word. All are as well here as people can be, so anxious for the Fate of their Country & Friends; to succour and support whom we are constantly employed.—Expresses are gone to New York, and as far as Philadelphia, to secure everything that way. New Haven Light Infantry, Wallingford & Fairfield Forces, passed us this day, well equipped to join the New England Forces. I have wrote my Brother,* & conclude you are with him, and will see his Letter. The Assembly meet to-morrow; & I hope before the next Sunday, you will have proper Commissions, and regulations sent after you by public Authority.—I know not whether I shall attend the Congress or not; if not, I Design to be with you, immediately after the rising of the Assembly.—I fear you will march too fast; be calm, patient, determined; and remember the Dignity of your Character; which

* Barnabas Deane.

is no less than the patriot fighting for his insulted Country and his murdered Friends; which is the highest honor to which human Nature can rise. I have no Time to add save my Compliments to all Friends. I am, wishing you the best protection, yours, &c.

S. Deane.

FROM SILAS DEANE.

Philadelphia, 14th May, 1775.

Dear Saml :

As you will see my letters to Mrs Deane, I shall not enlarge on incidents referred to, and sketch'd out in them—The Military Spirit is higher in this City, even among the Friends, than in Connecticut. Have your Letter of the 7th, and wish your sister was well out of Boston ; let effects go where they will, it is not a Time to dispute about property, when Liberty and Life are attacked. There is a talk of adj[ournin]g to Hartford, but this is out Doors chat, so no dependance can be laid on what the Resolution may finally be. No place offers for your Brother ; indeed Business is but a secondary Object in this City. Young Mr Gadsden is here in bad state of health, will visit Connecticut before he returns.—Our Family is small, & agreeable ; give my compt^s & Love to your Brother and the Family. I am Dear Sam'l, yours

Silas Deane.

JOSEPH BARRELL TO ———.

Salem, 24 May, 1775.

Dear Sir :

I fully Intended by this Conveyance to have seen you in person, as all my baggage was on board Cap. Calahan, & I with my wife * was thus far on our voyage to London ; but on the 17th Ins^t in the evening a fire broke out in the Soldiers' Barracks near my Store,† and as the Govr ‡ had by the most stupid & Extraordinary order se-

---

* Hannah Fitch, whom he married in 1771.

† The fire began in a store used as a barrack on the south side of the town dock, where some soldiers were filling cartridges.

‡ Thomas Gage, who had succeeded Hutchinson.

cured the fire Engines from the Inhabitants, it was a full hour before
they were in use, and then conducted by his Soldiery with such
Stupidity that the flames raged with Incredible fury & Destroyed 30
Stores, which in all probability might have been easily stopt at first,
amongst wch I suffered loss 1000 £ sterling, a sum more than I can
at this time loose without feeling it, prevents my taking passage as I
intended, and I fear I shall never see London, as providence seems
not to favor the attempt,—this being the 2^d time I've been on the
verge of departing & have been prevented. The account I sent you
by M^r. Head of the Running fight of the Red coats I think is at least
as true as any I've since heard, saving that the Number lost on their
side is nearly 300 kill'd & wounded & on ours 40 kill'd & 20
wounded ; since then our people have been forming Regiments &
have now 12,000 Inlisted men at Cambridge & Roxbury, which are
adding to daily, & by the time this reaches you, I think I can promise 30,000, wch is the number we propose from the 4 New England
Governments. Add to this, that when the Alarm is given almost
every man turns out, & I think you may depend they are as Resolute
& Determined as any men on Earth. We are daily expecting the
troops will attempt to go into the Country again, and we do most
ardently wish it, for if they do not, such is the Impatience of our people, 'tis fear'd by the prudent they will attempt the town, wch if they
should carry, it would in all probabillity, be attended with very great
loss on our side. But this I'll stake my life on, let Lord North,
Bute, Mansfield or the Devil ruin the British Nation by hiring foreign troops, still the people of this Country will not give up. We
are ready to die free, but determined not to live slaves. We ardently
wish the people of England, (who we still love as a people, for take
them from their venal Parliaments, & they are just,) would arouse before 'tis too late ; if they approve of the oppression of their rulers
and are determined in the Name of Satan the friend of Tyranny, to
risk their ruin to enslave us, we are determined in the Name of God,
to oppose wth life & fortune & never to give up 'till Death Delivers
us from their Iron Grasp. 'Tis not Boston, 'tis not the prov. of the
Mass^a Bay, 'tis not the four N. E. Provinces only, but 'tis the continent of America joined in the Opposition. New York, that only
prop of the hopes of Wretches, that *Loyal Prov^e* , we find neither
threats, nor the vague promises of superior Advantages can buy from

the General cause. They are foremost in the present time, and even the Prov. of Nova Scotia has lent a feeble Effort by burning the hay procured for *the frightfull Dragoons wch we hourly expect;* and by this have shown they wish well to our Cause, & 'tis not doubted but they will soon break the bonds of Slavish fear & show the world they are Americans, men that wish well to Good Government, but cannot submit to Tyranny. We have many & Daily Reports from every part of this Extended Continent. They seem all determined, and more awake than ever. *Oppression will make a wise man mad;* you will soon be made acquainted with the Spirit of the times. There is not a moment to loose. Between the Colonies & G. Britain every day makes the matter worse, & another Battle, if we are successful, (wch I pray God to grant) may produce Claims higher than ever. I speak for one & I believe speak the Language of a very great Majority of this distressed people. I wish for a reconciliation with Great Britain, but I prefer Death & Beggary to a tame submission to the order of that wretch, that Murderer of the Industrious, & that Destroyer of the poor, whose cruel Expectations, if complied with, would disgrace Human Nature. O my Dear Sir, the Yankees will fight ; they are averse to begin ; but when they once draw the Sword, they throw away the Scabbard, & tho' so loth to shed Blood, yet in revenge of their murder'd friends, 'tis their Delight ; & Depend upon it they will prove that they have a true sense of that freedom wch the God of nature gave & by whose Assistance they will Defend it.

I know not whether you are acquainted with the particulars of the Negotiations between the Govr & the people of Boston. This is the Case after the famous Retreat of the Invincible Red Coats, 1800 of whom fled with speed before 400 Raw Yankees : The Govr stop'd all the passages to the Town, & would on no terms suffer any person to depart. This state of confinement was extremely disagreeable to the Inhabitants, wch they nevertheless indured with fortitude a few days, in wch time it was either hinted, or directly moved by the Govr that if he could be assured of the peaceable disposition of the people he w'd open the communication. On this the Selectmen call'd together a Number of the gent^n of the town to see if any measures could be falling on, to satisfie the Gov. They accordingly prepar'd Votes wch were adopted in a very full town meeting, assure-

Tho:ͦ Gage

ing the Gov. they were & would be peaceable towards him & his
Soldiery, and Reminded him of many of his assurances when he was
fortifying the Town, that he would not thereby incommode or molest
the Inhabitants. This the Gov.ʳ did not consent to, but assured the
Town by the Selectmen, that if the Inhabitants would give up their
Arms to the Selectmen, then they should one & all depart without
Molestation, with their Effects. This he gave not in writing, tho' he
repeated it before his General Officers, & assured the Selectmen it
should be valid as if in writing, and added further, we should remove
by water as well as Land, any where within the Limits of the Cursed
Port Bill, & that he would use his Influence with the Admiral, that
the boats might be employed from all the Ships for that purpose.
This was what he sacredly promised on his part, when the proposal
was made to the Town. Tho' deliverᵍ Arms by an Englishman is
extreamly painfull, yet the distress of our Wives and Children, &, I
may add some of our Men too, workt so powerfully, that after a very
short Debate the Town came to a full Vote, wᶜʰ, being sent to the
Gov.ʳ , he seem'd highly to approve & again promised to fullfill his
part of the Capitulation, and I believe he intended so to do. But
mark the End. His consummate Blockheads, the Mandamus
Gentry, & the Ignoble multitude of Dispicables, Refugees, who had
always continued the same consistant Strain of Lying, & had hereto-
fore assured the Gov.ʳ the Yankees wᵈ not fight, now terrified with
well-grounded fear, Intreated the Gov.ʳ not to suffer the people to depart, that his safety depended on keeping them, and advised him to
do as they had always done, break his most solemn Promise. To
those Scandalous Advisers, the Gen.ˡ lent an ear, & then threw every
possible barr in the way, & it was a week after the Arms were deliver'd before any person was suffer'd to depart ; & then not without
a pass, wᶜʰ with great Difficulty being obtained, they might go, but
not any m'h'd'se or provisions with them. They might indeed carry
their furniture, but subject to the Brutal Search of the most unfeeling
Villain (a Certain Dirty Miserable Dog by the name of Benj. Davis,
a Wretch, to the disgrace of America spawned amongst us), who
breaks open Boxes, Trunks, &c., & searches for Provision & Mhdse,
taking from the poor wanderers a few pounds of Bark, Coffee, Choco-
late, &c., & from the mouths of Babes a morsel of bread. This
cruel, this Savage, Barbarous Delay, prevents people from going, as

none may depart exempt from these Restrictions, and instead of the men of Warr boats being employed & goods moved anywhere within the Limits of the Port Bills, they suffer only 2 Boats to pass, and nothing to be carried only over Charlestown ferry, and those not above 6 hours in a day, when there is always in common times 4 Boats passing 17 hours in the 24 at this Season. 'Tell it not in London, hide it from the Inhabitants of Paris,' Least the English should appear more vile than the Savages, & the poor distress'd Slaves of France should exult in their perfect freedom. Such has been the manner in which this agreement with the Govr has been comply'd with on his part, tho' on the part of the people fullfill'd to a title. Now Sir, this being the Case, I should be glad to know from you whether it co'd not be construed on your side the water that General Gage is accountable for this distruction by fire, if it can be proved that the goods would have been moved out of town but for his shamefull breach of Promise ; & that they would have been saved, had he not taken Charge of the Engines from the Inhabitants & given them to his *Soldiers*.* Add to this that the effects saved from the flames were wantonly Destroy'd by order of his polite officers, & plunderd by the Soldiers & the Swarm of Wretches which follow the Camp. I really should be glad of your Ansr to this part of my Letter, for if times are ever settled, I shall, if I have any Chance try the force of British Law.†

I have given orders to several persons at Baltimore, Halifax, &c., to remit me money to London, and direct to your care. I shall now give different orders ; but if anything should come in that channel, I hope you'l open the Letters & apply to my Credit any bills that may be sent. Pray procure for me a Ticket in the State Lottery, & if any Balle [is] due you, my friend Mr. Head will pay it. Send me the Number of the ticket registered in my Name, & keep the ticket ; & when the £20,000 is drawn in my favor, I'll come myself or give you timely orders what to do with it.

I am with Respect, &c.,

Jo. Barrell.

* He had written *all Conquering and Invincible soldiers*, but struck out the qualifying words.

† The history of this covenant between General Gage and the Selectmen is given in Ellis, *The Evacuation of Boston*, p. 115. A written notice by Gage is reproduced in facsimile in Winsor, *Memorial History of Boston*, iii. 76.

TO JOSEPH WEBB.*

CAMBRIDGE, June 19th, 1775, Monday Morn, 9 o'Clock.

MY DEAR BROTHER:

The Horrors and Devastations of War now begin to appear with us in Earnest. The Generals of the late engagement and present manuvres you will Doubtless hear before this can possibly reach you. However, as you may be in some Doubt I shall endeavour to give you some particulars which I hope will not be disagreeable, tho' it may be repeating. Know then that last Friday afternoon orders were issued for about 1800 of the province men and 200 of Connecticut men to parade themselves at 6 o'clock with one day's provisions, Blankets, etc., and there receive their Order. (Nearly the same orders in Roxbury Camp also.) Near 9 o'Clock they marched (with Intrenching tools in Carts by their side) over Winter's Hill in Charlestown and passed the intrenchments the Regulars began when they retreated from Concord and went to Intrenching on Bunker's hill which is nearer the water & Castle & Shiping. Here they worked most notably and had a very fine fortification which the enemy never knew till morn. They then began a most heavy fire from the Cop's Hill near Dr. Cutler's Church & from all the ships that could play, continued till near night. About one o'Clock P. M. we that were at Cambridge heard that the regulars were Landing from their Floating Batterys, & the alarm was sounded & we ordered to march directly down to the Fort at Charlestown.

* This letter was a joint production of Captain John Chester and Lieutenant Samuel B. Webb.

Before our Company could possibly get there the battle had begun in earnest, and Cannon and Musket Balls were flying about our Ears like hail, and a hotter fire you can have no Idea of. Our men were in fine spirits. Your Bro^r. and I Led them & they kept their Order very finely 2 & 2.*

My Dear Brother, You'll see by this the amazeing hurry we are in,—Capt. Chester is call'd of and begs me to go on with this letter, which I'll endeavor to do, —tho if it appears incorrect and unconnected you must make proper allowance.—After the Alarm, on our March down we met many of our worthy friends wounded sweltering in their Blood,—carried on the Shoulders of their fellow Soldiers—judge you what must be our feelings at this shocking Spectacle,—the orders were, *press on, press on,*—our Bretheren are suffering and will soon be cut of.—We push'd on, and came in to the field of Battle. Thro the Cannonadeing of the Ships, Bombs,—Chain Shot, Ring Shot & Double headed Shot flew as thick as Hail Stones,— but thank Heaven, few of our Men suffered, by them, but when we mounted the Summit, where the Engagement was,—good God how the Balls flew.—I freely Acknowledge I never had such a tremor come over me before.—We descended the Hill into the field of Battle, —and began our fire very Briskly,—the Regulars fell in great plenty, but to do them Justice they keep a front and stood their ground nobly,—twice before this time they gave way,—but not long before we saw numbers mounting the Walls of our Fort,—on which

* Thus far Capt Chester.

Cambridge June 19th 1775
Monday Morn 9 o'Clock

My Dear Brother

The Horrors & Devastations of War now begin to appear
with us in Earnest. The Generals of the late engagement & present manœuvres you will doubtless hear before this can possibly reach
you. however as you may be in some doubt I shall endeavour
to give you some particulars which I hope will not be disagreeable tho', it may be afflicting. Know then that last
Friday afternoon Orders were Issued for about 1800 of the province men & 200 of Connecticut men to parade themselves
at 6 oClock with one days provisions Blankets &c & there
receive their Orders, (nearly the same Orders in Roxbury Camp also)
Near 9 oClock they marched (with Intrenching tools in Carts) by
their way over Winters Hill in Charlestown & passed the intrenchments the Regulars began when they retreated from Concord &
went to Intrenching on Bunkers hill which is nearer the
water & Castle & Shiping, there they work'd most notably & had a
very fine fortification which the enemy never knew till Morn
they then began a most heavy fire from the Shell near Dr Cullers
Church & from all the Ships that could play which continued till
near night. About one oClock P.M. we that were at Cambridge heard
that the regulars were landing from their Floating Batterys, &
the alarm was sounded & we ordered to March directly down to
the Fort at Charlestown. Before our Company could possibly get there
the battle had begun in earnest & Cannon & Musket Balls were
flying about our Ears like hail. & a hotter fire you can have
no idea of. Our men were in fine Spirits your Bro' & I led them
& they kept their Order very finely 2 #2, — My Dear Brother, you'll
see by this the Amazeing hurry we are in. — Capt. Chester is call'd off
and begs me to go on with this letter, which I'll endeavor to do, tho' if
it appears incorrect and unconnected you must make proper Allowance

After the Alarm on our March down we met many of our worthy
friends wounded sweltering in their Blood, — carried on the Shoulders by
their fellow Soldiers, — judge you what must be the feelings at this
shocking Spectacle, — the orders were, press on press on, our Brethren
are suffering and will soon be cut of. — We pushd on and came
into the field of Battle, tho' the Cannonadeing of the Ships, Bombs
Chain shott, King Shot & Double headed Shot flew as thick as
Hail Stones, — but thank Heaven, few of our Men suffered, by
them, but when we mounted the Summit, where the Engagement
was

was good God how the Balls flew, I freely Acknowledge I never had such a tremor came over me before, we descended the Hill into the field of Battle, and began our fire very Briskly, the Regulars feel in great plenty, but to do them Justice they keep a grand front and stood their ground nobly, twice before this time they gave way, but not long before we saw numbers mounting the Walls of our Fort, on which our Men in the Fort were ordered to fire and make a swift Retreat, we covered their Retreat till they come up with Us by a Brisk fire from our smalle Arms, the Dead and wounded lay on every side of me, their groans were piercing indeed, tho long before this time I believe the fear of Death had quited almost every Breast, theymen had possession of our Fort & four field pieces, and lay much the Advantage of the Ground, and to tell you the truth, our Reinforcements belonging to this Province very few of them came into the field but lay sculking the opposite side of the Hill, Our orders then came to make the best Retreat we could, we set off almost gone with fatague, and Ran very fast up the Hill, leaving some of our Dead and Wounded in the field — we Retreated over Charlestown Neck, thro the Pheirest of the Ships fire, here some principle Officers fell by Cannon & Bombs, after we had got out of the ships fire under the Covert of a Hill — near an other Intrenchment of ours, we again Rallied and lined every part of the Road and fields — here we were Determined to Die or Conquer if they ventured over the Neck, — but it grew dark and we saw them pitching Tents, we retired to our Intrenchment & lay on our Arms all Night, keeping vast Numbers of our Troops out on scouting Parties, they keep up a constant fire from the Ships and floating Batteries all Night, but few of them Reach'd Us, — But alas how Dismal was the sight to see the Beautifull & Valeuable town of Charlestown all in Flames — and now behold it a heap of Ruin — with nothing standing but a heap of Chimnays, which by the by remains an everlasting Monument of British Cruelty and Barbanity this Battle tho we lost it, cannot but do Honor to Us, for we fought with less Numbers, are tho they once or twice almost surrounded the Fort we secured their Retreat, but alas in the short fight some Brave Fellows among the Unhappy Number, was our Worthy friend Dr Warren, alas he is no more, he fell in his Countrys Cause, and fought with the Bravery of an Ancient Roman they are in possession of his Body and no doubt will rejoice greatly over it, After they entered our Fort they mangled the wounded in a Most horrid Manner, by runing their Bayonets thro them, and beating their Heads to pieces with the Britch's of their Gun,

in

in this Bloody Engagement, we have lost, Wilson Rowlanson
Roger Fox, Gershom Smith, and Lawrence Sullivan, who we
suppose fell, at least their Bodies into the hands of our Enemies
their souls we hope in the happy Regions of Bliss — Wounded
Daniel Deming, Samuel Delling, Epaphras Stevens, Constant Griswould, — none of them Mortally, are in a fair
way, and likely to Recover — to give you the exact number of
the whole number of our Kill'd and wounded is Impossible,
Opinions are various and no returns yet made to the Council of War
— but the best I can find out is about 120 of our Men Kill'd and
wounded, perhaps there may be double that number, I cannot say
a few days & we shall know exactly, — of the Regulars I doubt not
theirs are many more lost than of ours, the truth of their numbers
tis not probable we shall know, — The Kings troops, to the
number of 2 or 3,000 are now encamped on the same Hill they
were after the Battle of Lexington, — have twenty field pieces
with them, and lie under the Protection of the Ships, our
grand Fortification is on prospect Hill — within a Mile and
a half of theirs, — we have about three thousand Men in it, &
2. 12 Pounders — 2 24 & C. 6 pounders — here we mean to
make a Stand, — should they prove Victorious (which Heaven
forbid) and get possession of this Hill, — we must retire before them
& leave Cambridge to the Destruction of those merciless Dogs
— but Heaven we trust will appear on our side, — and sure I
am many thousands of Us must fall, before we flee from them
— Gage has said that the 19th of June should be made as memorable as the 19th of April is — this is the day and I assure
you we are properly on our Guard,

Monday 1/2 after 6

I have one moments Leisure again to Continue my Scrawl
yesterday we had another Alarm, & I wish it has not been as fully as
as at first. Our men were Marching down in much Better Order
& better Spirit, for Prospect (alias Bunkers) Hill. We heard all
the Light horse with reinforcement enough to Make 2000 in all
were on their March from Bunkers Hill to our intrenchments
But before we had got half way down there were Orders back
again, Gen. Putman Woolcot back from our fort that the Regulars had
made no Movement since last Fight.

Our Retreat on Saturday was Shameful & Scandalous, & owing
to the Cowardice Misconduct & want of Regularity of the Province troops

to do them Justice there was a Number of their Officers & men that were
in the first & a very few others that did honor to themselves by a most
noble manly & spirited Effort in the heat of the engagement, & 'tis
said Many of them the flower of the Province have Sacrificed themselves in the Cause. Some say they have lost more Officers than men
Good Doctr Warren! God rest his Soul! I hope is safe in Heaven! Had many
of their Officers the Spirit & Courage in their whole Constitution that he had
in his little finger, we had never retreated. Many considerable Companies of their men I saw that there was not so much as a Corporal with
them, one in Particular fell in the rear of my Company & marched
with us. We Capts had Mustered & Order'd them to March & tole them he
would overtake them directly, but they never saw him till next Day,
& our number were retreating as we March'd up & within a
quarter of a Mile of the Scene of Action. If a Man was wounded 20
more were glad of an opportunity to carry him away when not more
than three could take hold of him to advantage. One cluster would
be sneaking down on their Bellies behind a Rock & others behind
Hay cocks & apple trees. At last I got pretty near the Action & I
met a considerable Company with their Officer at their Head retreating. I spoke to Lt Webb & told him it would not do to see
so many going back & that we must stop them, by all means
says he. I then enquired of the Officer why he went back. he
made no answer. I told him to proceed if he dare, he still went
on. I ordered my men to make Ready very Loud, & tole him
if he went another step he should have the fire of my whole
Company. My men Declared they would fire if I ordered them.
But the Poor Dogs were forced to come back like Dogs that had
been stealing Sheep. But after the Retreat when we came to rally
& attempt to form again, we found it impossible, for they almost
all said they had no Officers to head them. In short the most of
the Companies of this Province are commanded by a most Despicable
Set of Officers, & the whole Success of the Battle with them depends
on their virtue; for almost all from the Capt General to a Corporal are afraid
to set up proper Martial Authority, & say, as affairs are situated
they think their people will not bear it. But in my humble
Opinion they are very much in the wrong. Publick Business here
goes on very Dull. if any thing of importance heaves up it must go
thro a long dispute in the Congress of near 200 Members & then thro a Committee of Safety & then a Committee of War & a Committee of Supplies & by that
means they are forever doing Nothing

our Men in the Fort were ordered to fire and make a swift Retreat,—we covered their Retreat till they came up with us by a Brisk fire from our small Arms,—the Dead and wounded lay on every side of me,—their Groans were pierceing indeed, tho long before this time I believe the fear of Death had quited almost every Breast,—they now had possession of our Fort & four field pieces,—and by much the Advantage of the Ground,—and to tell you the truth,—our Reinforcements belonging to this Province very few of them came into the field—but lay sculking the opposite side of the Hill.—Our orders then came to make the best Retreat we could,—we set of almost gone with fatague, —and Ran very fast up the Hill, leaving some of our Dead and Wounded in the field—we Retreated over Charlestown Neck, thro the thickest of the Ships fire,— here some principle Officers fell by Cannon & Bombs, —after we had got out of the Ships fire under the Covert of a Hill—near another Intrenchment of ours, we again Rallied and line'd every part of the Road and fields—here we were Determined to Die or Conquer if they ventured over the Neck,—but it grew dark— and we saw them pitching Tents,—we retired to our Intrenchment & lay on our Arms all Night,—keeping vast Numbers of our Troops out on Scouting Parties, —they keep up a constant fire from the Ships and floating Batteries all Night,—but few of them Reach'd us.—But alas how Dismal was the Sight to see the Beautiful & Valuable town of Charlestown all in Flames—and now behold it a heap of Ruins—with nothing Standing but a heap of Chimneys,—which by the by remains an Everlasting Monument of British

Cruelty and Barbarity—this Battle—tho: we lost it,—
cannot but do Honor to Us—for we fought with less
Numbers—and tho they once or twice almost surrounded the Fort, we secured their Retreat,—but alas
in the Fort fell some Brave Fellows—among the unhappy Number, was our worthy friend Dr. Warren,
alas he is no more,—he fell in his Countrys Cause,—
and fought with the Bravery of an Ancient Roman,
they are in possession of his Body and no doubt will
rejoice greatly over it.—After they entered our Fort
they mangled the wounded in a Most horrid Manner,
—by running their Bayonets thro them,—and beating
their Heads to pieces with the Britch's of their Guns.

In this Bloody Engagement, we have lost, Wilson
Rowlanson, Roger Fox, Gershom Smith, and Lawrence
Sullivan,—who we suppose fell (at least their Bodys)
into the hands of our Enemy—their souls we hope in
the happy Regions of Bliss.—Wounded Daniel Deming, Samuel Delling, Epaphras Stevens, & Constant
Griswould,—none of them Mortally,—are in a fair way,
and likely to Recover,—to give you the exact number
of the whole of our kill'd and wounded is Impossible,
—Opinions are various—and no returns yet made to
the Council of Warr—but the best I can find out is
about 120 of our Men kill'd and wounded, perhaps
there may be double that number,—I cannot say,—a
few days & we shall know exactly,—of the Regulars I
doubt not their are many more lost than of ours—the
truth of their numbers 'tis not probable we shall know,
—The kings troop to the number of 2 or 3,000 are
now encamped on the same Hill they were after the
Battle of Lexington,—have twenty field pieces with

them, and lie under the Protection of the ships—our grand Fortification is on prospect Hill—within a mile and a half of theirs—we have about three thousand Men in it, & 2–12 Pounders, 2–9 Do, 2 24 p^r. & 6 6 pounders—here we mean to make a stand,—should they prove victorious (which Heaven forbid) and get possession of this Hill,—we must retire before them & leave Cambridge to the Destruction of those merciless Dogs—but Heaven we trust will appear on our side, —and sure I am many thousands of Us must fall, before we flee from them.—Gage has said that the 19th of June should be made as memorable as the 19th of April is—this is the day, and I assure you we are properly on our Guard.*

MONDAY, 11 o'Clock.

I have one moments Leisure again to Continue my Scrawl. Yesterday we had another Alarm, & I wish it had not been a false one as it prov'd. Our men were Marching Down in much Better Order & better Spirits, for Prospect (alias Spectacle) Hill. We heard all the Light horse with a Reinforcement enough to make 4000 in all, were on their March from Bunkers Hill to our entrenchments. But before we had got half·way Down there we were Order'd back again. Genl. Putnam wrote back from our fort that the Regulars had made no Movement since Last Night.

Our Retreat on Saturday was Shameful & Scandalous, & owing to the Cowardice Misconduct & want of Regularity of the Province troops. Tho to Do them Justice there was a Number of their Officers & men

* Here ended Lieut. Webb.

that were in the fort & a very few others that did honor
to themselves by a most noble manly & spirited Effort
in the heat of the engagement & 'tis said Many of them
the flower of the Province have sacrificed their Lives in
the Cause.   Some say they have lost more Officers
than men.   Good Doct.ᵣ Warren, "God rest his Soul,"
I hope is Safe in Heaven!   Had many of their Officers
the Spirit & Courage in their Whole Constitution that
he had in his little finger, we had never retreated.
Many considerable Companies of their men I saw that
said there was not so much as a Corporal with them,
one in Particular fell in the rear of my Company, &
march'd with us.   The Capt. had mustered & Orderᵈ
them to March & told them he would overtake them
directly, but they never saw him till next Day.   A vast
number were Retreating as we Marchᵈ up & within a
quarter of a mile of the Scene of Action.   If a man was
wounded 20 more were glad of an Opportunity to
Carry him away when not more than three could take
hold of him to advantage.   One cluster would be
sneaking down on their Bellies behind a Rock & others
behind Hay cocks & apple trees.   At last I got pretty
near the Action & I met a considerable Company with
their Officer at their Head retreating.   I spoke to Lt.
Webb & told him it would not do to see so many going Back & that we must stop them, by all means says
he.   I then enquired of the Officer why he went back.
He made no answer.   I told him to proceed if he Dare,
he still went on.   I ordered my men to make Ready
very Loud, & told him if he went another step he
should have the fire of my whole Company.   My men
Declared they would fire if I ordered them.   But the

Poor Dogs were forced to Come back like Dogs that had been stealing sheep. But after the Retreat when we came to rally & attempt to form again, we found it impossible, for they all most all said they had no Officers to head them. In short the most of the Companies of this Province are commanded by a most Despicable set of Officers, & the whole success of the Battle with them depends on their virtue; for almost all from the Capᵗ General to a Corporal are afraid to set up proper Martial authority, & say, as affairs are situated, they think their people will not bear it. But in my humble oppinion they are very much in the wrong. Publick Business here goes on very Dull—if any thing of importance heaves up it must go thro a long dispute in the Congress of near 200 Members & then thro a Committee of Safety & then a Committee of War & a Committee of Supplies & by that means they are forever doing Nothing.*

FROM CHARLES WHITING.

MIDDLETOWN, 20ᵗʰ June, 1775.

MY DEAR SAM:

I most heartily congratulate you Sammy, on your safe return from the Field of Battle. Am highly rejoic'd to hear that you behav'd worthy yourself, and prov'd your courage was genuine. I want much to see you and tell you a thousand things & ask 2,000 questions. Write me, as soon as leisure permits, every thing concerning the engagement, for as yet, amidst the endless variety of accounts, I don't know what to depend on as truth. I much fear that the melancholy tidings of the death of the amiable and worthy Dr. Warren, will prove true. How many and what men have you lost? Yester-

* Col. Chester wrote from the end of Webb's *MS.*

day I rec^d a line from ———— ; he remembers you ; the doct^r is going ; must not add ; my hearty compliments to Capt. Chester, and
squeeze his hand for me.

Adieu ! my Dearest Sam!

C. WHITING.

FROM JOSEPH WEBB TO SILAS DEANE.

*Extract of a Letter from Wethersfield, Connecticut, to a Gentlemen
in Philadelphia, dated June 22, 1775.*

Before this you must know, I conclude, that there has been a
battle, in which fell the honourable, the noble Doctor Warren.   For
fear you may not have the particulars, I will endeavour in part to relate to you how the affair was, according to the best accounts I can
gather by letters from the camp.   Last Friday afternoon orders were
issued for about eighteen hundred of the Provincial Troops, and two
hundred of the Connecticut, to parade themselves at six o'clock,
with one's days provision, equipped with packs, blankets, &c.   Their
orders were given at nine o'clock and they marched with their teams,
trenching tools, &c., on Bunker's Hill, to heave up an intrenchment,
which you are sensible is near the water, ships &c.   They worked
most surprisingly that night, and they were discovered at sunrise by
a sailor from the mast head.   The British Army commenced a heavy
fire from Copp's Hill, near Cutler's Church, in Boston, and from all
the ships which could be brought to play, which continued till near
night.

About one o'clock A. M., the Americans at Cambridge heard that
the Regulars were landing from their floating batteries.   The alarm
was sounded, and they were ordered down to the breastwork at
Charlestown ; and Capt. Chester wr.tes me, that before it was possible for him to get there, the battle had began in earnest, and cannon
and musket balls were plenty about their ears.   Chester and my
brother were both in the engagement.   They re-inforced our men
that had left the breastwork in fine order, though they passed
through the cannonading of the ships, bombs, chain-shot, ring-shot,
&c. ; but then their superiour number of artillery and men, (for they
were three to two,) forced our men to retreat, after a warm engage-

ment of an hour and a half. Thank Heaven, but few of our men fell considering the advantages they had over us, our men being much fatigued with working at the intrenchments, and I believe not in the best preparation to meet an enemy. The British Troops, to their eternal disgrace, shame and barbarity, set Charlestown on fire with torches.

My brother says we were obliged to retreat to Prospect Hill, (alias Winter Hill) where we made a stand, and declared we would all die before we would retreat any farther; but the British Troops did not think fit to come out from under the protection of their shipping. The loss of Americans is supposed to be, of wounded, missing and slain, about one hundred and twenty. A large, genteel, well dressed gentleman, who first mounted our breastwork, was overset by one of our impudent Americans, who took good aim as to prevent his ever mounting another, as he tumbled him into the intrenchment just as he cried, " The day is our own."

We rejoice greatly to hear of the coming of the good, the brave, and great General Washington, and shall receive him with open arms. [JOSEPH WEBB.]

FROM SILAS DEANE.

PHILADELPHIA, June 22ᵈ , 1775.

DEAR SAM:

I wrote you a long Letter a few Days since, to which I intended to have added, but am prevented by the setting off of Genᴸ Washington *—Genᴸ Putnam is made a Major General † of the Continent, he will be allowed Two Aid De Camps. I have wrote to the General in your favor, to be appointed one of them, and advise you to apply in-

* Washington left Philadelphia on the morning of June 23d, accompanied by Major General Charles Lee, Mifflin, and Joseph Reed, and arrived in Cambridge on Sunday, July 2d, about two o'clock in the afternoon.

† On Friday, June 16th, Congress resolved that there should be two Major-Generals appointed for the American army, and eight Brigadiers-General. Provision was made for three aids-de-camp, each to receive thirty-three dollars a month; and a secretary to the General, at a salary of sixty-six dollars a month. On the following day Artemas Ward was elected to be the first Major General, and Charles Lee, the second Major-General.

stantly on the Receipt of this in person ; I think he will not refuse you—I have no Time to add but that I am, D.ʳ Sam

Yours   S. Deane.

FROM JEREMIAH WADSWORTH.

Hartford, [25 June, 1775.]

Dear Sam :

Have only a Minutes time to tell you I rejoice to hear you are well. I read your Letter to J. Webb.* What an unhappy affair. The Massachusetts Bullies turned Tail too. They have the Curses of every good Man.

Your Capt. & you have gained immortal honour ; go on & Prosper. Heaven will Protect you. The Brave have everything to hope. Jo tells me you have no Paper. I have two Reams at your service ; here comes a quire. Tell Charles I remember him, and mean this for him as well as you. Mr. Deane's letter says General Washington will soon be with you. We all rejoice at this, and intend some of us to be with you soon. I hope myself to see you In a week. Adieu.

Wadsworth.

Sunday morning.   Post waits.

FROM SILAS DEANE.

Philadelphia, June 29ᵗʰ, 1775.

Dear Sam.ˡ

I wrote you this Day acknowledging yours of the 7ᵗʰ & 12ᵗʰ instant. Mr. Adams wrote a Letter to you by the same, & enclosed one to his Friend, recommending you to his notice. These I trust you have received.

Gen.ˡ Gates, a long experienced Officer, now joins you, and does me the Favor of giving you this.† I have spoke of you to this

---

* Printed on page 65.

† Gates was chosen by Congress to be Adjutant General of the army, on Saturday, June 17th, 1775, on the special recommendation, it is said, of Washington. He was at the time at his country seat in Berkeley County, Virginia, but set out at once for Cambridge, and arrived in Camp about July 8th. His appointment

Gentleman, and now urge it upon you, to regard whatever instruction you may gain from him & General Lee, in your profession, as coming from persons whose Judgment and experience, renders them Oracles for youth in your Situation.

I am, my Dear Sam, your affectionate parent

S. DEANE.

If you can see, or send to your Sister, tell her my heart bleeds for her every hour. Pray obtain, if possible, her Dismission from that devoted Town & a safe residence in yᵉ Country. I am hurried beyond measure in Congress, and in keeping up my extensive Correspondence ;—but will soon write you at large. By no Means form such Connections, either in the Country or Camp, as will tend in any respect, to draw you from your duty in Camp.   S. D.

TO SILAS DEANE.

CAMP AT CAMBRIDGE, July 11th, 1775.

DEAR SIR :

Your several late letters I have received, and the Book. For your kind remembrance of me to the Commanding officers, I beg leave to return you my most hearty thanks.

General Putnam is a man highly esteemed with us ; he has done me the Honor to appoint me his first Aid-De-Camp.* Since which, I have had the offer of being

was announced in general orders of the 9th, where he is named as "Horatio Gates, Esq., Brigadier-General and Adjutant General of the Army." He had held a Major's commission after the defeat of Braddock.

* As a member of Putnam's family, the young aid doubtless lived at the quarters taken by the General when he first came to Cambridge. This was the "Borland house, popularly known as the Bishop's Palace, directly opposite Gore Hall, on Harvard Street. It had been built about fifteen years before by the Rev. East Apthorpe, of Christ Church, Cambridge, a son of Charles Apthorpe, a Boston Merchant. John Adams says it was 'thought to be a splendid palace, and was supposed to be intended for the residence of the first royal bishop.' Another Boston merchant, John Borland, occupied it up to the outbreak."—Winsor, *Memorial History of Boston*, III, 106.

a Brigade Major from General Gates. They are both
Honorable and agreeable posts. I shall for the present remain with Gen'l Putnam—this post will call me
to be continually with the first company in Camp, by
which I hope to improve.

Our Commander-in-Chief, together with the other
Gentlemen from the Southward, are highly esteemed
by every class—they will be the means of Disciplining
the Army, which was much wanted.*   Your friend Mr.
Miller is a Gentleman my station will call me much
with—he is very obliging to me, and I doubt not will
do me every service in his power.   I should have wrote
you a very particular account of the late Battle fought
in the Valley over Bunker's Hill, but suppose Col.
Saltonstall or my Brother had forwarded you my letter
I wrote them, which contained an exact detail of facts—
I hope you have received them before this.   Mr. Alexander, the Express, leaves town in half an hour, which
will prevent my being as particular as I could wish.
Our Army are now encamped on Prospect Hill, and
have got nearly completed our grand Breastwork reaching from the Hill to Mystic River; on our Right we
have completed several Redoubts and Breastworks not
far distant from each other, so that our lines are now
extended from Mystic over to Charles River.   The

---

*To secure order, discipline and regularity, Washington divided the army into
three great divisions, and each division into two brigades. Brigadiers General
Thomas and Spencer with their brigades were to constitute the right wing or division of the army, to be stationed at Roxbury, under the command of Major-
General Ward. Sullivan's brigade was posted upon Winter Hill, and Greene's
upon Prospect Hill—these two brigades to compose the left wing, to be under the
command of Major-General Lee. Putnam commanded the third division, and to
him was entrusted the defense of the posts north of Roxbury.—*Orderly Book*, 22
July, 1775.

enemy are on Bunker's Hill, and are not idle—they are
fortifying in the strongest manner possible. Their
situation is amazingly strong; ten times their number
could not route them. Directly in the front lies the
narrow neck of Charlestown, on their right four floating batteries in Mystic River—on their left next Boston
two ships and several tenders, floating batteries, &c.,
pointing directly across the Neck—by which it would
be almost impossible to pass. We hourly expect them
to sally out and attempt to carry our Lines. I am
sorry to say we have not men enough; 'tis too true.
Gen'l Washington has desired the Provincial Congress
to send in the Militia to the number of 4 or 5000 till
we can raise more men—this matter we at present
keep a secret for fear our Enemies should take advantage of it, and make their attack in a number of different places, and by that means force our Intrenchments.*
But should they attempt it, 'tis thought by our commander that it will be the most bloody Engagement
our American World ever knew—our men are Resolute and determined. On an alarm (of which we have
had several within a week), our men seem cheerfully
to fly to their Alarm posts. We have several thousands of Pikes, with 12 feet handles, which are placed

---

* On the 9th, Washington called a Council of War, and laid his position before
it. In Massachusetts had been raised less than nine thousand men, and from the
other Colonies had been sent a sufficient number to make his command about
fourteen thousand five hundred men, fit for duty. The Council decided that the
army should be raised to twenty-two thousand men, that the Massachusetts regiments should be recruited, and the Provincial Congress be called upon to supply
a temporary reinforcement. Washington asked for one thousand men to be
stationed at Medford, but some intelligence received from Boston on the 12th
induced him to countermand this request.—*Writings of Washington*, (Ford's
edition,) III, 5, 7.

along our Lines—and most certainly will be very useful if they attempt to scale the walls.   I cannot think
but 500 of them at Bunker's Hill at time of the Battle
would have been a means of saving our work; if we
had we must have gained a complete victory—for after
landing the troops the Boats were all ordered to
'Boston, that there was no retreat left for them.   Fight,
Conquer, or Die, was what their officers was plainly
heard to say very often.   Major Bruce, who served
two years in Portugal with Gen'l Lee, told my brother
Joe at the lines, that it was the hottest Engagement he
ever knew; even, says he, the Battle of Minden did not
equal it.   For my part I confess, when I was descend-
ing into the Valley from off Bunker's Hill side by side
of Capt. Chester at the head of our Company, I had no
more tho't of ever rising the Hill again than I had of
ascending to Heaven as Elijah did, Soul & Body together.   But after we got engaged, to see the Dead
and Wounded around me, I had no other feeling but
that of Revenge; four men were shot dead within five
feet of me, but I thank Heaven I escaped with only the
graze of a musket Ball on my Hat.   I think it my duty
to tell you the bravery of one of our Company.   Edward Brown stood side by side with Gershom Smith in
the Intrenchments.   Smith fell, Brown saw his danger
—discharged his own and Smith's gun; when they
came so close as to push Bayonet over our small
Breastwork—Brown sprang, seized a Regular's gun,
took it from him and killed him on the spot, bro't off
the gun in triumph, and has it now by him.   In this
Engagement we lost four brave men, and four wounded
—the dead are Wilson Rowlandson, wounded, taken

prisoner and since died in Boston Goal—Gershom Smith, Lawrence Sullivan,* Roger Fox, killed on the spot—the four wounded are almost well. I had like to forgot to mention that Col. Parker, wounded in the thigh, was taken prisoner, and carried to Boston, where he lay in a Common Goal and died. Gen'l Lee in particular is much put out; intends writing into Boston very soon in a severe way—and inform them what he thinks of their Barbarity, and further acquaint them that if they continue their savage cruelty that every King's officer on the continent will be closely confined.†
Indeed we all wish and expect they will be secured, es-

---

* Lawrence Sullivan is given as alive in a list of prisoners dated 14 September, 1775. The same list contains a William Rollinson, of Connecticut, as having died after being put in jail—a misprint for Wilson Rowlandson.

† Unless some authority had restrained Lee's "petulant itch for scribbling," it is difficult to conjecture what might not have been written by this erratic character. Before leaving Philadelphia he had entered into a correspondence with Burgoyne, who was then in Boston, urging him to retire from the contest, and showing the folly of contending against the force of one hundred and fifty thous·and men then in arms! Burgoyne was also by no means backward in the use of his pen, and the two arranged a personal conference, which was very properly vetoed by the Massachusetts Provincial Congress. It was not until August 11th that Washington wrote to Gage a very dignified remonstrance upon the treatment of prisoners, a letter that Lee characterized as "a most serious message;" but it did not breathe out threats against all the royal officers then in the Colonies. Gage's answer, written by Burgoyne, stirred Lee to propose a reply, which is printed in the *Lee Papers*, I, 200, and mention is made of an earlier letter sent in to Gage.

Abigail Adams wrote to her husband: "Our prisoners were brought over to the Long Wharf, and there lay all night, without any care of their wounds, or any resting-place but the pavements, until the next day, when they exchanged it for the jail, since which we hear they are civilly treated." *To John Adams,* 5 July, 1775. A list of those thrown into the Boston jail is given in Force, *American Archives, Fourth Series,* III, 712.

" My advice to General Gage has been to treat the prisoners taken in the late action, most of whom are wounded, with all possible kindness, and to dismiss them without terms. 'You have been deluded; return to your homes in peace; it is your duty to God and your Country to undeceive your neighbours.' I have

pecially Elliott of New York,* who is a man of great Importance. My brother Joe has been with us a week, set off for home last evening—he had a cruel Interview within the Regular Guards on Charlestown Neck with Mr. Simpson and my unhappy Sister—but the officers forbid any conversation about leaving town. My heart aches for them, but 'tis in vain—none can be permitted to come from under the clutches of that.Tyrant Gage and his Infernal crew. Mr. Trumbull our Commissary is much beloved by all Ranks of people; 'tis lisped he may be appointed Commissary General of the American Army—none here is so well calculated for that important office—his extensive connexions enables him to procure every necessary with the greatest imaginable dispatch. I fancy he is recommended by our Gen'ls which, with your and his other friends Influence, I doubt not will procure him the Fatiguing Birth. I have received many friendly services from him.† I wish to add many particulars, but the Express waits. Capt. Chester is in a fair way to be appointed Major of

had opportunities to sound the minds of these people. Most of them are men of good understandings, but of much prejudice, and still more credulity; they are yet ignorant of their fate, and some of them expect, when they recover, to be hanged. Such an act of mercy as I have proposed may make an impression, and it may spread. Should it fail, it will at least serve to justify acts of a different nature hereafter; and you are no farther the dupes of it in the meantime than by adding about thirty men now in your power to a stock of as many thousands who are out of it."—*Burgoyne to Rochfort*, June or July, 1775.

* Andrew Elliott, Collector of Customs for the port of New York from 1764 to the Revolution.

† Washington, complaining of the inconvenience in depending upon a number of persons for supplies, pointed out the advantage gained in the Connecticut establishment, the troops of which "are extremely well provided under the direction of Mr. Trumbull." He asked that Trumbull be appointed Commissary General, and Congress did so July 19th.

Brigade. We have burnt the Regular Guard houses on Roxbury*—little skirmishes happen almost every day—the king's troops come off second best. Major Mifflin being very observing on the Marshes with his Glass has been complimented with half a dozen four and six pounders from the Ships and Batteries in Boston, but he is small mark and came off clear. I beg you to write me particular whenever you have leisure.

Be assured I am, Dear Sir,

With Esteem Affectionately Yours,

SAML B. WEBB.†

SILAS DEANE, Esq., Philadelphia.
  Pr. Mr. Alexander's Express.

TO SILAS DEANE.

CAMBRIDGE, June [July] 11th, 1775.

DEAR SIR :

Since the close of my other letter, I find the Express is like to be detained half an hour. I had entirely forgot to mention [to] you the conduct of Gen. Spencer, —which I doubt not you'll hear from several quarters. After intelligence of Putnam's being appointed major-General, (which, by the by, gave universal satisfaction) Spencer appeared much chagrined and disappointed; he began to speak very freely, and finally persuaded

---

* The advanced guards of the British occupied a house of one Brown, standing about a mile from Roxbury meeting house, and near the present location of Franklin Square. On the 8th a party of volunteers from the Rhode Island and Massachusetts forces, under the command of Majors Benjamin Tupper and Crane, drove in the guards, and burnt the house.

† From Frothingham, *The Battle-Field of Bunker Hill*, 31.

the officers to remonstrate to the Assembly of Connecticut; and set off immediately for home, without leave
or licence from Gen. Washington, which displeased
him much.*

I cannot imagine our Assembly will be guilty of so
great imprudence as to take any notice of the matter.
I am sorry to say, your friend Col. [Samuel Holden]
Parsons was forward in this matter. I have since been
to Roxbury, and find the officers, many of them, heartily sick of what they have done; in particular, Major
[Return Jonathan] Meiggs,—who says he had rather
serve under Putnam than Spencer, and says he was
forced to sign what the others did, to keep peace.
You'll find the Generals Washington and Lee are
vastly fonder and think higher of Putnam than any
man in the army: and he truly is the Hero of the day.
They have given him the command of Prospect Hill.
I find the intention of Spencer was to get our Assembly
to remonstrate to the Continental Congress, and beg a
re-appointment; but little did he [think] that this could
not be done without cashiering Putnam,—as he [is in]
possession of his commission; and better for us to lose

* As soon as the appointments of the Continental Congress were known at
Cambridge, Spencer laid plans to have them altered, and on July 5th a remonstrance was drawn up to be signed by the officers of the Connecticut force and laid
before the Assembly. It recited that Spencer had been in command of the Connecticut troops from the first; that he had by his conduct endeared himself to the
men; and that he was degraded in rank by the action of Congress, which made it
impossible for him to remain in the army. This remonstrance was signed by
forty-nine officers, among whom were Samuel H. Parsons, Return J. Meigs, and
Roger Enos. The Assembly wrote to its delegates in Congress expressing its
confidence in Spencer; and to Spencer, urging him not to "precipitate a resolution to resign his command." Spencer and Pomroy in the meantime left camp,
but Spencer returned on the 19th of July, and expressed his willingness to serve
under Putnam.

four S[pencers] than half a Putnam.* I think it my
duty to write thus freely to you, though perhaps not
prudent to have it seen in public.†

Opposite to Putnam is placed Gen. Howe, on
Bunker's Hill. Gen. Burgoyne commands on the
Neck, at Roxbury. He has wrote a long letter to
Gen. Lee, in which he proposes a meeting: whether
this will be complied with or not, cannot say. A certain something runs through the whole of his letter,
which shews they are sick at the stomach. He says:
"If the right of taxation is all we are contending for, he
is empowered to say, Great Britain will give that up."
Why did not they say that six months ago? They
must now remember, that we have an undoubted right
to ask for the expense we have been at in raising an
Army,—and the loss of the beautiful town of Charlestown, which is now a heap of rubbish. We doubt not
Burgoyne means this so as hereafter to say that he
made us generous offers, with a view to compromise
matters. He is as cunning and subtle as the Devil
himself; he writes (if 'twas on the right side of the

---

* " I am sorry to observe that the appointments of the General Officers in the
Province of Massachusetts Bay have by no means corresponded with the Judgment and wishes of either the civil or Military. The great Dissatisfaction expressed on this Subject, and the apparent Danger of throwing the army into the
utmost Disorder, together with the strong Representations of the Provincial Congress, have induced me to retain the Commissions in my hands untill the Pleasure of the Congress shall be farther known, (except General Putnam's, which was
given the Day I came into Camp and before I was apprized of these Uneasinesses.") *Washington to the President of Congress*, 10 July, 1775.

† Deane had a good opinion of Spencer until this incident occurred. " His leaving the forces in the manner I hear he has, shocks it very greatly, and, if true, I
wish him to resign at once and let another take his place." *Deane to Mrs.
Deane*, [July, 1775.]

question,) like a man of abilities; but his wickedness is to be seen in every sentence of his letter.*

We have had one of our sentries desert over to the enemy; and a Frenchmen, who came here in the character of a gentlemen, was detected in stealing; the next day he deserted to the enemy; but he's of no consequence, being a simple, foolish fellow.

We heartily wish for the Riflemen to arrive, and instead of 1,000 we wish it were 3,000. We really want them, and we are in hopes you'll make an addition.

I am in the utmost haste,

Yours most affectl?

SAMUEL B. WEBB.

FROM COMFORT SAGE.

MIDDLETOWN, 14 July, 1775.

DEAR SAMMY:

It gives me the greatest pleasure and satisfaction to hear of your good conduct and Behaviour at all times ; more especially, in the late action at Charlestown, where you played the man in such a manner, that your friends and acquaintances frequently spake of it with pride and pleasure. I pray God Almighty, if you should be called to action, that He would protect and preserve you in Battle & Crown you with success. I should be glad to hear from you at all opportunities.

Little or no news here. Last Monday the King Fisher went up the Sound after a vessel from Sea, and sent her Barge with 16 men

* Printed in *Lee Papers*, I, 188. Burgoyne wrote that if the contest was being waged for a relief from taxes, " the quarrel is at an end; there is not a man of sense and information in America, who does not know it is in the power of the Colonies to put an end to the exercise of taxation immediately and forever. I boldly assert it, because sense and information will also suggest to every man, that it can never be the interest of Great Britain, after her late experience, to make another trial."

on shore at Branford. A number of people collected and cut her off, & took the Barge with the people. The Bearer, Capt. Warner from Newport, has taken shelter with his family, together with three other families from there, in that place. He is a Gentleman of fortune & character; and I should esteem it a particular favour if you'll notice him accordingly. He is accompanied by my son Eben'r, who has been ill about six weeks. He made a pretty good voyage. On their return I expect to set out for the Camp.

I am with esteem, your real friend & obt Servt

COMFORT SAGE.

My best respects to all friends and acquaintances.

FROM SILAS DEANE.

PHILADELPHIA, July 16, 1775.

DEAR SAML

The Bearer Mr. *Chas Craig* is a Lieut. in a Compy of Riflemen, & he being a Stranger in the Army, I recommend to your notice, and introduce to the Gentlemen of your *Corps;* which I am sure you will take the greater pleasure in doing, as he comes to share with you the common dangers of your glorious exertions in our Common Cause; and indeed the Cause of Mankind in general.—I have received no letter in Answer to any of mine, tho' I have wrote by every Opportunity since the departure of Genl Washington, as well as previous thereto. This makes me conclude your letters must have miscarried; for I never can believe, for your, as well as my sake, that you are unmindful of me. Let your next relieve me from the least doubt on this head.

I have nothing new worth sending so far. I sent you a Book; hope you received it. Write me particularly by the next post, which will encourage me to continue more at large a Course of Letters consequent on what I entered upon in my first, and afterwardes hinted at by Gen'l Gates. I am wishing you success equal to the justice & extent of the Cause, My Dear Samuel, yours affectionately,

S. DEANE.

MAJOR GENERAL CHARLES LEE TO SILAS DEANE.

CAMBRIDGE, July ye 20th, 1775.

DR. SIR:

I rec'd your two notes respecting your relation Mr. Webb, who is already plac'd about General Putnam as Aid de Camp, but any service I can render him he may command, both from your desire and his own merit, for he seems a sensible, alert, active young man. You will much oblige me in your correspondence when you have leisure, tho' I cannot make any returns to the long letters I wou'd wish from you, as I have scarcely an hour's time in a week upon my hands. Our lines are fourteen miles in extent, and I am scamperer General. I am seldom less than twelve hours on horseback—the want of Engineers has occasion'd a fatigue to me scarcely credible. I cannot conceive what the Devil put it into some of your N. England Gentlemen's heads that you were sufficiently furnish'd with able men of this denomination. I do not believe there is one capable of constructing an oven—however with these disadvantages three or four days more hard labour will make us so secure that I flatter myself not a single post can be forc'd without a loss of men too great for the enemy to spare. We shall then have time to bring your Troops into some arrangement and introduce some method amongst 'em. Yours, Connecticut, are already tolerable, the Rhode Islanders still better ; but amongst the Massachusetts hitherto has reign'd an absolute anarchy. As to the materials (I mean the private men), they are admirable— young, stout, healthy, zealous, good humor'd and sober. Had we but uniforms, compleat arms, more Gentlemen for officers, I really believe a very little time and pains wou'd render 'em the most invincible Army that have appear'd since the first period of the Roman Republic in the world. The more we consider the affair of Bunker's Hill, the more wonderfull it appears—fiveteen hundred, the most disorderly Peasantry, without a single officer to command 'em, in the most disadvantageous situation imaginable, resist and repulse three thousand very good regular Troops, under the command of the very best officer in the British service. They are indeed at length forc'd, but not before they had done most dreadful execution. You will receive the list from General Washington, as likewise the return of the kill'd and wounded on our side.—For God's sake, be at

Cambridge July ye 20th 1775

Dr Sr

I rec'd your two notes respecting your relation Mr Webb, who
is already plac'd about General Putnam as aid de Camp, but my
service is due under him. He may command both from your desire
and his own merits, for he seems a sensible clever little
young Man — You will much oblige me in your correspondence
when you have leisure, tho' I cannot make you any return
to the long letters I wou'd wish from you, as I have scarcely an
hours time in a week upon my hands — our lines are fourteen
miles in extent, and I am scampering forward — I am seldom
less than twelve hours on horse back — the want of engineers
has occasion'd a fatigue to me scarcely credible. I can
scarcely conceive what the Devil put it into your & your
Gentlemen's heads that you were sufficiently provid'd
with able men of this denomination — I do not believe there
is one capable of constructing an oven — however with these
disadvantages three or four days more hard labour will
make us so secure that I flatter myself not a single piece
can be forc'd without a loss of men too great for the enemy
to spare — We shall then have time to bring your troops
into some arrangement and introduce some method & regularity
Yours are already tolerable, the Rhode Islanders still
      Connecticut
better: but amongst the Massachusetts folks who has rupid
an absolute anarchy as to the Materials (I mean the private
Men) they are admirable — young stout healthy active

good humour'd and sober — had we but uniforms compleat we are
now Gentlemen for Officers & I really believe a very little
time and pains wou'd render for the most invincible Army
that have appear'd since the first period of the Roman
Republic in the world. — the more we consider the affair of
Bunker's Hill the more wonderfull it appears — fourteen
hundred the most disorderly Peasantry with a single Officer
to command em in the most disadvantageous situation imagi-
-nable resist and repulse three thousand very good regular
Troops under the command of the very best Officers in the
British Service. — They were evidently at length forc'd but not
before they had done most dreadfull execution — You will
receive the list from General Washington as likewise the
return of the kill'd and wounded on our side — for God's
sake be at the expence of hunting shirts for these
poor People. it will be money well laid out — it will be
oeconomy in the end — I am sorry to find that the Congress
have again descended to petition that callous tyrant
of St J — it can possibly do no good — it may do harm
. . . .
amongst you — You must work upon his fears by his
baggage and his pride — actions — they you will bear this be
adieu My Dr Sir Yours
R Lee

the expence of hunting shirts for these poor People. It will be money well laid out—it will be œconomy in the end. I am sorry to find that the Congress have again descended to petition that Callous Tyrant of St. J[ames]. It can possibly do no good—it may do harm*
* * * * amongst you. You must work upon his fears, by high language and decisive action. I beg you will burn this letter. Adieu, my Dr Sir, yours

C. Lee.†

MR. LEE'S PLAN.

A Battalion consisting of one Colonel, one Lt Colonel, Two Majors, four Captains, four Captain Lieutenants, sixteen Lieutenants, eight Ensigns, Thirty two Sergt's, Thirty two Corporals, six hundred and fivety eight Private, sixteen Drummers or Musick Men, 24 Colour Guards, one Adjutant, one Sergt : Major, one Musick or Drum Major. There must likewise be annex'd a Company of light Infantry, of a Capt. Lt., three L'ts, four Serj'ts, four Corporals, two horn or Conch Sounders, and seventy six Privates. The whole will consist of seven hundred and 48 rank and file. This Battalion is to be form'd into four Companies. Each is to have a Standard and an equal number of officers. There is likewise to be one Regimentary or Great Colour, by which the four Standards of the four Companies are to regulate their advances, their retreats, their Conversions and all their Movements. The four Standards must be of different Colours—for instance, the first or right hand may be red ; the 2d or left hand white ; the 3d or right hand center blue ; the 4th or left hand center green. The colour of the Regiment may give the name to the Regiment : if it is orange, the Reg't may be call'd orange. This Colour must be much larger and shou'd be much more showy than the Standards. If the Regt is the Orange all the men of the Battalion must have an orange colour'd cape to their jacket, and an orange Cockade ; but an epaulette on one shoulder of the Colour of the standard of his respective Company. This will distinguish the Reg't and particular Company he belongs to. In the Colour and the standards must be embroider'd the word liberty.

* One line illegible.

† Compare with Lee's Letter of the same date to Dr. Benjamin Rush, printed in *Lee Papers*, I, 196.

The Colonel should be distinguish'd by some mark in his Cap or hat—as a feather or tuft dy'd of the Colour of his Reg't. The other field officers the same but with some difference in their size—the Capt's a tuft of the Colour of their particular Standard, the Capt. L'ts the same, but smaller than the Capt's. The Subalterns must have likewise some badge to specify their rank. The Sergt's and Corporals must have likewise some.

This Battalion on the Parade, form'd two deep—

F	2 Capt.	F	F	F	3 Capt.	F	1 Capt.
1 Capt.							
Capt. Lt.		Capt. Lt.		C. Lt.		C. Lt	
			Lt. Col.				

2 of ye Lt must be rang'd in the intervals of the Front; two [   ] in the rear; ensigns posted in the rear behind the Standards. The Corporals to be divided in equal files on the two flanks of the respective Companies. Serj'ts, half to be in the interval of the front, and half in the rear at proper distances. The Drums or Musick men to be half behind their respective Colours in the rear; the other half of the whole behind the Reg'ts Colour. A major to be on each Flank. The Adjutant with the Colonel, the Serj't Major with the Lt. Colonel—the Majors to be allow'd two each of the most alert and intelligent light infantry to be orderly on their Persons. Twenty four men or twelve file of men of the most esteem'd valour are always to compose the grand Colour'd Guard, which is to be posted in their Center. Some extraordinary pay or exemptions ought to be allow'd to these Colour Guards—and they must be sworn never to abandon it, as may each Company with respect to its proper standard bearers, of which there are to be four to each Company.

The light infantry Company may either be subdivided on the wings of the Battalion, or scatter'd along the Front as the General or Colonel directs. In short, they can have no fix'd station. The chief things to learn are to load and fire without confusion, to march in front or retreat without crowding or opening their files too much; to wheel and change their front. This will be done well, of course, if those who carry the standards are practiced to know the necessary distances; for which reason all the Standard bearers, as well as colour guards, are to be soldiers of capacity and judgment. There must be four to each Company, who must have the same distinctions and exemptions with the Colour Guards. The ensigns being in the rear will be able to assist 'em much.*

CAPT. JOHN CHESTER TO ————†

CAMP AT CAMBRIDGE, July 22d, 1775.

REV. AND MUCH RESPECTED SIR:

Your favor of the 4th instant I received the day before the Fast, and should have answered it by the bearer, Mr. Miles, had I not been that day on fatigue duty. The day after Fast Mr. Miles set off for home, from Roxbury. I want words to express my gratitude for your religious advice, your many useful and important hints, your arguments and reasons for our animation and support in the glorious struggle for freedom, and your tender expressions of friendship for my family, as well as your anxious concern for my own personal safety.

I shall endeavor, as far as my time and business will permit, to give you, sir, the particulars of the battle of Charlestown. Though, as to the greater part of account published, I may not be able to mend it.

In the latter part of the day before the battle, an adjutant informed me that orders were issued from headquarters that 1800 province men, and 200 Connecticut men, parade themselves [* * * *] clock, with provisions for twenty four hours, blankets [* * *] there wait for further orders. About nine o'[clock t]hey were ordered to march to Bunker Hill, a n[umbe]r of wagons accompanying them with intrenching tools, &c. Just about twelve o'clock at night they began intrenching, and went on with great vigor till daybreak, and were then discovered by the regulars, who were heard to swear most terribly about the Yankees; and they began a heavy fire before sunrise from the ships and Cops Hill, which was kept up with little or no cessation till afternoon. But finding our people paid

---

* An undated paper, but probably prepared while at Cambridge, and sent to Silas Deane. It is endorsed by Deane "Gen'l Leigh's plan."

† Supposed to have been written to Rev. Joseph Fish, of Stonington. The letter is printed in Frothingham, *History of the Siege of Boston*, 389.

little regard to their cannon, and knowing the great importance of
the post, they landed (I believe it was about two o'clock), and
formed in three or four solid columns, and advanced towards the
fort. Those on their right soon changed their position into a line for
battle, and marched on very regularly, rank and file. They were
very near Mystic River, and, by their movements, had determined
to outflank our men, and surround them and the fort. But our officers in command, soon perceiving their intention, ordered a large
party of men (chiefly Connecticut) to leave the fort, and march down
and oppose the enemy's right wing. This they did ; and had time
to form somewhat regularly behind a fence half of stone and two rayles
of wood. Here nature had formed something of a breastwork, or else
there had been a ditch many years agone. They grounded arms. and
went to a neighboring parallel fence, and brought rayles and made a
slight fortification against musquet ball. Here they received the
enemy to very tolerable advantage. Our officers ordered their men
not to fire till the word was given. Lieut. Dana tells me he was the
first man that fired, and that he did it singly, and with a view to
draw the enemy's fire, and he obtained his end fully, without any
damage to our party. Our men then returned the fire, well-directed, and to very good effect, and so disconcerted the enemy
that they partly brok[e and re]treated. Many of our men were
for pursuing, [but by] the prudence of the officers they were
prevented lea[ving s]o advantageous a post. The enemy again
rallied and ad[vanc]ed, and in the same manner were repulsed
a second, and some say, a third time. But at last they stood
their ground, and the action was warm, till the enemy carried the
fort which was on their left wing, and soon there was a retreat of the
whole of the provincials. I am told that a gentleman on Chelsea side
saw the whole engagement, and that he said it lasted thirty-five minutes with the musquetry, and that our first firings swept down the
enemy most amazingly. The men that went to intrenching over
night were in the warmest of the battle, and, by all accounts, they
fought most manfully. They had got hardened to the noise of cannon ; but those that came up as recruits were evidently most terribly
frightened, many of them, and did not march up with that true cour-
rage that their cause ought to have inspired them with. And to this
cause, I conceive, was owing our retreat. Five hundred men more,

that might easily have been there, if they were in any tolerable order and spirits, might have sent the enemy from whence they came, or to their long homes.

I wish it was in my power to give you a satisfactory reason " why our intrenchments were not supported with fresh recruits from Cambridge, and why that important pass over Charlestown neck was not guarded against annoyance from Mystic River, as well as the other side from the fire of the ships and floating batteries, and our retreat secured," &c., &c. Possibly the whole attempt was rather premature, and not thoroughly well planned. If we might again attempt it, we should, undoubtedly, have contrived and executed much better. Perhaps it may be better, however, to prepare ourselves well for some future attempt, than to lament the important success of the last, which we cannot now possibly mend.

As to my own concern in it, with that of my company, would inform, that one subaltern, one sergeant, and thirty privates, were draughted out over night to intrench. They tarried, and fought till the retreat. Just after dinner, on Saturday, 17th ult., I was walking out from my lodgings, quite calm and composed, and all at once the drums beat to arms, and bells rang, and a great noise in Cambridge. Capt. Putnam came by on full gallop. What is the matter? says I. Have you not heard? No. Why, the regulars are landing at Charlestown, says he ; and father [Gen. Putnam] says you must all meet, and march immediately to Bunker Hill to oppose the enemy. I waited not, but ran, and got my arms and ammunition, and hasted to my company (who were in the church for barracks,) and found them nearly ready to march. We soon marched, with our frocks and trousers on over our other clothes, (for our company is in uniform wholly blue, turned up with red,) for we were loath to expose ourselves by our dress, and down we marched. I imagined we arrived at the hill near the close of the battle. When we arrived there was not a company with us in any kind of order, although, when we first set out, perhaps three regiments were by our side, and near us ; but here they were scattered, some behind rocks and hay-cocks, and thirty men, perhaps, behind an apple-tree, and frequently twenty men round a wounded man, retreating, when not more than three or four could touch him to advantage. Others were retreating, seemingly without any excuse, and some said they had left the fort with leave of the officers, because they had been all night and day on fatigue, without sleep, victuals or drink ; and some said they had no officers to head them, which, indeed, seemed to be the case. At last I met with a considerable company, who were going off rank and file. I called to the officer that led them, and asked why he retreated? He made me no answer. I halted my men, and told him if he went on it should be at his peril. He still seemed regardless of me. I then ordered my men to make ready. They immediately cocked, and declared if I ordered them they would fire. Upon that they stopped short, tried to excuse themselves ; but I could not tarry to hear him, but ordered him forward, and he complied.

We were then very soon in the heat of action. Before we reached the summit of Bunker Hill, and while we were going over the Neck, we were in imminent danger from the cannon-shot, which buzzed around us like hail. The musquetry began before we passed the Neck ; and when we were on the top of the hill, and during our descent to the foot of it on the south, the small as well as cannon-shot were incessantly whistling by us. We joined our army on the right of the center, just by a poor stone fence, two or three feet high, and very thin, so that the bullets came through. Here we lost our regularity, as every company had done before us, and fought as they did, every man loading and firing as fast as he could. As near as I could guess, we fought standing about six minutes, my officers and men think   *   *   *

FROM CAPTAIN JOHN CHESTER.

ROXBURY CAMP, 11 August, 1775.

DEAR SAMMY :

I perceive by General Orders, that the General proposes honouring those gentlemen who behaved well in the action on Bunker Hill.*

* " As there are several vacancies in the different Regiments, if there are any particular gentlemen who signalized themselves in the action on Bunker's Hill, by their spirited behaviour and good conduct, and of which sufficient proof is adduced to to the General, he will, in filling up the commissions, use his endeavors to have them appointed (if not already commissioned) to some office, or promoted if they are; as it will give him infinite pleasure at all times to reward merit, wherever it is to be found." *General Orders*, 9 August, 1775.

For my part, I am determined not to tarry longer than the time I first thought of, and am not anxious for promotion ; and if I was, I imagine there is no vacancy nor like to be for me. But two things have determined me to write to you & request your advice on this subject. And first—By the way I am no preacher & never intend to be one—I say then firstly : Will not a censuring world say, in case we make no representation of our behaviour on Bunker Hill after so fair an opportunity given us by the General, that we fear to have our conduct looked into, & that we cannot make good our pretensions, & the story we have told of our conduct?

Again : Would it not be doing injustice to our subalterns & under officers not to represent their behavior and good conduct? For whatever you or I might think of the matter, *they all* are desirous of it, & hope for promotion or notice in some way or other, in consequence of what the General has published. I have conversed with them and know their opinions in the matter.

Now if you think best, after what I have said, to say anything to yᵉ General about the matter, I should be much obliged to you to do it. I am free to ask it of you as you are on the list, & as you are perfectly acquainted with the whole matter, & can do it to as good advantage as any man.

A certain big bellied General, will make the most of his great doing, I very well know. I wish his conduct could be fully known.

The Blins have had 10 lashes each, this morning, for desertion.

With regard to rank, &c.,—had I best try to make any advantage of my commission at home as Major, or justice, or having been sundry times a member of assembly, &c. &c. Write me & tell me how you do, & how you go on at Cambridge, & if you have a convenient opp[ortunit]y, come and bring it yourself. Thereby you'll greatly gratify your friend & most obliged humble servᵗ

JOHN CHESTER.*

* From the *Reminiscences of General Samuel B. Webb*, p. 28. Captain Chester was discharged from the army on the termination of his service, 17 December 1775. He re-entered in the following year.

WASHINGTON TO LUND WASHINGTON.

CAMP AT CAMBRIDGE, Aug.t 20.th, 1775.

DEAR LUND:

Your Letter by Capt.n Prince came to my hands last night—I was glad to learn by it that all are well.—The acc.t given of the behaviour of the Scotchmen at Port Tobacco & Piscataway surprised & vexed me.—Why did they Imbark in the cause?—What do they say for themselves?—What does other say of them?—Are they admitted into Company?—Or kicked out of it?—What does their Countrymen urge in the Justification of them?—They are fertile in invention, and will offer excuses where excuses can be made.—I cannot say but I am curious to learn the reasons why men who had subscribed, & bound themselves to each other, & their Country, to stand forth in defence of it, should lay down their arms the first moment they were called upon.

Although I never hear of the Mill under the direction of Simpson,* without a degree of warmth & vexation at his extreame stupidity, yet, if you can spare money from other Purposes, I could wish to have it sent to him, that it may, if possible, be set agoing before the Works get ruined & spoilt, & my whole money perhaps totally lost.—If I am really to loose Barrand's debt to me, it will be a pretty severe stroke upon the back of Adams, & the expence I am led into by that confounded fellow Simpson, & necessarily so in seating my Lands under the management of Cleveland.†

Spinning should go forward with all possible des-

* Gilbert Simpson.

† James Cleveland. See *Writings of Washington* (Ford), II, 459.

patch, as we shall have nothing else to depend upon if these disputes continue another year—I can hardly think that Lord Dunmore can act so low, & unmannerly a part, as to think of siezing Mrs Washington by way of revenge upon me; howev^r as I suppose she is, before this time gone over to Mr Calvert^s, & will soon after retu^g, go down to New Kent,* she will be out of his reach for 2 or 3 months to come, in which time matters may, & probably will, take such a turn as to render her removal either absolutely necessary, or quite useless—I am nevertheless exceedingly thankful to the Gentlemen of Alexandria for their friendly attention to this point & desire you will if there is any sort of reason to suspect a thing of this kind provide a kitchen for her in Alexandria, or some other place of safety elsewhere for her and my Papers.†

The People of this government‡ have obtained a Character which they by no means deserved—their officers generally speaking are the most indifferent kind

---

* The place of Burwell Bassett.

† Lund Washington had written : " Many people have made a stir about Mrs. Washington's continuing at Mount Vernon, but I cannot think there is any danger. The thought I believe originated in Alexandria; from thence it got to Loudoun, and I am told the people of Loudoun talk of sending a guard to conduct her to Berkeley, with some of their principal men to persuade her to leave this place and accept their offer. Mr. John Augustine Washington wrote, pressing her to leave Mount Vernon. She does not believe herself in danger. Lord Dunmore will hardly himself venture up this river; nor do I believe he will send on that errand. Surely her old acquaintance, the attorney [John Randolph], who with his family is on board his ship, would prevent his doing any act of that kind. You may depend I will be watchful, and upon the least alarm persuade her to remove." Samuel Washington, a brother of the General, lived at Berkeley. There is an interesting paragraph on this subject in one of the fictitious letters issued in 1776. *Spurious Letters attributed to Washington*, 70.

‡ Massachusetts.

of People I ever saw.—I have already broke one Col?
and five Captains for Cowardice, or for drawing more
Pay & Provisions than they had Men in their Companies—there is two more Col^{os} now under arrest, &
to be tried for the same offences—in short they are by no
means such Troops, in any respect, as you are led to
believe of them from the acc^{ts} which are published, but
I need not make myself enemies among them, by this
declaration, although it is consistent with truth.—I dare
say the men would fight very well (if properly officered)
although they are exceeding dirty and nasty people.—
Had they been properly conducted at Bunkers Hill
(on the 17th of June) or those that were there properly
supported, the Regulars would have met with a shameful defeat, and a much more considerable loss than
they did, which is now known to be exactly 1057
killed & wounded—it was for their behaviour on that
occasion that the above Officers were broke, for I never
spared one that was accused of Cowardice but brot. 'em
to immediate Tryal.*

* See letter to Richard Henry Lee, 29 August, 1775, in my edition of the *Writ-ings of Washington*, III. 96.

The "black list" included the following: Captain John Callender, cashiered for cowardice, and dismissed from the anny. Captain Oliver Parker, cashiered for defrauding his men of their advance pay, and for drawing provisions for more men than he had in the company and selling the excess. Captain Christopher Gardner, of Rhode Island, cashiered for deserting his post. Captain Kilton, sentenced to receive a severe reprimand from the commanding officer, at the head of the regiment, for neglect of duty. Captain Ballard, convicted of profane swearing and beating his men. Captain Jesse Saunders, found guilty of drawing more provisions than he had men in his company to consume. Captain Eleazer Lindsay, discharged as a person improper to sustain a commission. Col. Samuel Gerrish, cashiered for behavior unworthy an officer. This ends the record on August 19th. The two Colonels under arrest were probably Col. John Mansfield and Colonel Ebenezer Bridge. Col. Bridge was acquitted, but Col. Mansfield was cashiered.

Our Lines of Defence are now compleated, as near so at least as can be—we now wish them to come out, as soon as they please, but they (that is the Enemy) discover no Inclination to quit their own Works of Defence; & as it is almost impossible for us to get to them, we do nothing but watch each other's motions all day at the distance of about a mile, every now and then picking off a stragler when we can catch them without their Intrenchments, in return, they often attempt to cannonade our Lines to no other purpose than the waste of a considerable [quantity] of Powder to themselves which we should be very glad to get.

What does Doctʳ. Craik say to the behaviour of his Countrymen, & Townspeople?—Remember me kindly to him, & tell him that I should be very glad to see him here if there was anything worth his acceptance; but the Massachusetts People suffer nothing to go by them that they can lay hands upon.*

I wish the money could be had from Hill, & the Bills of Exchange (except Colᵒ. Fairfax's,† which ought to be

---

* Washington, more than once, complained that under the organization of the army by Congress every commission was monopolized by the four New England governments, and he induced that body to so alter the rules of appointments as to give greater scope for choice. The result produced some dissatisfaction.

"Some advantages arose to our Colony by the Congress adopting the army raised in New England the last spring; but among other circumstances attending it, this was one, namely that it being now a Continental army, the gentlemen of all the Colonies had a right to and put in for a share in behalf of their friends in filling up the various offices. By this means, it was thought, that military knowledge and experience as well as the military spirit, would spread through the Colonies; and besides, that they would all consider themselves the more interested in the success of our army, and in providing for its support. But then there was less room for persons belonging to the Colonies which had first raised the army, and who were well worthy of notice. Many of our friends were discontented, who did not advert to this as the true cause why they were not promoted." *Samuel Adams to Joseph Palmer*, April, 1776.

† Col. George William Fairfax, who was then in England.

sent to him immediately) turned into cash; you might
then, I should think, be able to furnish Simpson with
about £300: But you are to recollect that I have got
Cleveland with him to pay also.—I would not have you
buy a single bushel of wheat till you can see with some
kind of certainty what Market the flour is to go to—
& if you cannot find sufficient Imployment in repairing
the Mill works, & other things of this kind for M^r
Roberts and Thomas Alford, they must be closely Im-
ployed in making Cask, or working at the Carpenters
or other business otherwise they must be discharged,
for it is not reasonable, as all Mill business will probably be at an end for a while, that I am to pay them
£100 a year to be Idle.—I should think Roberts himself must see, & be sensible of the reasonableness of
this request, as I believe few Millers will find Imploym^t
if our Ports are shut up, & the wheat kept in the straw,
or otherwise for greater Security.

I will write to Mr Milnor to forward you a good
Country Boulting Cloth for Simpson, which endeavour
to have contrived to him by the first safe conveyance—
I wish you would quicken Lanphire & Sears about the
Dining Room Chimney Piece (to be executed as mentioned in one of my last Letters) as I could wish to
have that end of the House compleatly finished before
I return.—I wish you had done the end of the New
Kitchen next the Garden as also the old Kitchen with
rusticated Boards; however, as it is not, I would have
the Corners done so in the manner of our new Church
(those two especially which Fronts the Quarter)—
What have you done with the well?—Is that walled up?
Have you any acc^{ts} of the Painter?—How does he behave at Fredericksburg?—

I much approve of your sowing wheat in clean ground, although you should be late in doing it, & if for no other purpose than a tryal.—It is a growing I find, as well as a new practice, that of overseers keeping Horses, & for what purpose, unless it be to make fat Horses at my expence, I know not, as it is no saving of my own Horses. I do not like the custom, & wish you would break it—but do as you will, as I cannot pretend to interfere at this distance.

Remember me kindly to all the Neighbors who enquire after

Y^r. affect^e. friend & Servt.

G^o. WASHINGTON.*

FROM REV. ABIEL LEONARD.

WOODSTOCK, Augst 22^d, 1775.

MY DEAR FRIEND:

After two days I arrived to my family. My horse was sick and I was obliged at length to leave him on the road and hire another. Upon my arrival I found a very tasty wig that the Post from Hartford had left for me hearing of my return—which I have worn once or twice, that when I return to Cambridge I may not be an absolute Stranger to myself. It fits me admirably well and my own people are pleased with it, and say it becomes me the best of any I ever wore. To you, Sir, I am indebted for this and hope I shall have the pleasure the beginning of next week of personally acknowledging the Receipt of this Token of your friendship.

Tho' I have the pleasure of an agreeable wife and pleasant children around me, yet I am at Cambridge sleeping and waking, impatient to know every manœvre. Will you gratify your friend by writing a few minutes of what has passed in his absence in doors and out and sending it by the present Post?

Mr. Baylor Aid de Camp to General Washington had an horse in

---

* From the collection of Dr. Thomas Addis Emmet.

my keeping which I have sent down according to his desire—will you
be so kind to see that he has it?

Give my duty to General Putnam, my most respectful Compliments to M.ʳ Commissary General [Joseph Trumbull] & regards to
all friends as tho' personally named.

I hope you have your health by this time confirmed and that you
rise superior to every &c. &c. &c. &c.

I sincerely wish you every Divine Blessing and that a kind providence would order every circumstance in your Life agreeable and
pleasant to you.

from Your Obliged friend and

Very humb.ˡ Ser.ᵛᵗ

ABIEL LEONARD.*

FROM SILAS DEANE.

WETHERSFIELD, 1.ˢᵗ Sept., 1775.

DEAR SAMMY:

We returned Saturday Morning Mrs. Deane very ill with the
Asthma, but on her return recruited.   I set out To-morrow, or Next
Day for my old Station at Philadelphia ; The News from New York
you will hear before this arrives.   My Brother *Simeon* was present,
and is now returned, he left matters, in a very unsettled situation.
On Sunday last Letters passing between Capt.ⁿ Vandeput, & the Town.
All the Guns mounted on Carriages were removed to the Number of
Twenty-one, chiefly Forty-two pounders, & secured on this side the
City, the rest of the Cannon, lye on the Ground, on the Battery, full
in the reach of the Asia, and I apprehend, cannot be moved without
great, perhaps too great a Loss of Men.   Governor Tryon returned,
and harangued the City to little purpose ; the Sum is that he gives
up the Government, & promises not to intermeddle, but wishes them
to behave in the most *peaceable* manner, & puts himself absolutely
into the hands of the Citizens.—

We hear that *Plow'd hill*† is occupied by the Provincials and that

* He was chaplain in General Putnam's regiment.   See the entry in the *Journal* for 29 July, 1777, *post.*

† Now Mount Benedict.   It was occupied on the night of Saturday, 26 August,
1775.

some few Shot have been exchanged, I wish for all the particulars as early as possible. Where are your floating Batteries that I hear nothing from them—I have a nice Hatt, in The True military stile, also a Coat Superfine *Damascene Brown* with buff Facings, I got them first, for myself, with little Altering they will suit You—You shall have them at first Cost, or Gratis, if Boston is in our possession before the 1st of January. I am absolutely too poor in Consequence of our public affairs to give away any thing of much value, or I confess you should have the offer of them before any man in the World. I do not expect to make anything, on the Contrary I expect to sink ; but wish to sink, with a little Consistency, & in degree with my Neighbors, faster, I am willing—but not all at once unless the occasion require it, & then Life & all shall go without a Sigh—You will mention your resolution on this to Me in Your Next. Where is Col. Arnold, I write to him but am not certain where it will find him, tell me what You know of his Situation—let me urge on you, patience & assiduity, in your present Station untill you can honorably be advanced, remember, that suffering, and industry are two capital ingredients in a Soldiers Character—you suffer Nothing at present,— when called to traverse barren, or uncultivated Desarts in constant danger, & frequent Attack, to Suffer Hunger, Thirst, Cold & Wounds untended then you will know What a Soldiers life is, or the roughest side of it, for this prepare yourself, now in season if you mean to be a Soldier, & in doing it do not exert yourself on sudden Occasions violently, but by a moderate, uniform course bring yourself to the habit of bearing all these or more if called—We have some droll stories, about a late Long Island Campaign, & am sorry to find, they all agree, in this : That the Stock from *Plumb*, & *Gardiner's* Islands might have been saved, had there not have been some misapprehensions at least some where—keep your pen going at every leisure, not to write Letters only, but to minute down the material occurrencies, of the Army, they may be of Service hereafter—you may now with little pains, be master of all the principles of forming, training, regulating, & encamping a great Army, not the least thing ought to escape your Notice, the most trifling at present, may rise into importance hereafter,—my Complim[ts] to Gen'l Putnam & Family, Mr. Leonard in Particular if returned—& to Mr. Whitney if present.

I am wishing you every Blessing

Dear Sammy Yours S. DEANE.

Forward or deliver the inclosed to Col. Arnold as soon as may be.

SUNDAY, Sept. 3, 1775.

Since writing the above rec'd a Line from Col. Dyer by which I am detained untill Tuesday next, when I set forward—yours of the 31ˢᵗ I receiv'd and in return, do not think after what passed between the General, & me, at parting, but that it would be unseasonable & a Trespass on the goodness of his disposition to Trouble him with a Letter on that subject at this Time, circumstanced as the Army is, & the apparent probability of a great, & general action coming on, for which every precaution in preparing is Necessary, and must take up his whole Time and Tho'ts, the want of which, must most materially alter your present situation one way or the other, at a proper Time you know I cannot be unmindful of you, nor inattentive to your welfare,—in addition, to what I have before advised let me urge you to get a clever bound Book of the size of J. Webb's or my Letter Book, in which carefully enter down at night, the Transactions and Orders of the Day, with your own Observations—This will be of vast help to you hereafter—experience does as much as reading and Study, in forming a Soldier, one of your Generals has both, in a most eminent degree—Another has hardly anything of the latter, yet with a large share of the former is excellent in his way—you can never be the Scholar in the learning of Antiquity which one of them is, but you may by attention have the same advantages from experience, which joined with a knowledge of the Books printed in our own Language on the Art of Warr may make you one Day equally eminent, & useful—to do this effectually you must not Trust barely to Memory, but treasure up the incidents, & the circumstances leading to them, as in a magazine, for your future Instruction which Joined with your Memory, will make every thing plain, & fresh before your Eyes at any future period—Tell General Putnam I hope to wait on him in Boston as soon as the Congress adjourns—Adieu—There is no news here of any kind—once more write me where Arnold is & what you imagine, he is about to be sent upon.—Compˢ to Col. Reade &c &c &c to all the Circle.*

* From the collection of Dr. John S. H. Fogg, of Boston.

INSTRUCTIONS FOR CAPTAIN WEBB.

Sept: 3, 1775.

1. You are to proceed immediately to a Town about 17 miles hence & receive from Capt. Wharton of Philad. 3 Prisoners, Major French, Ensign Rotton, & M: McDermott with whom you are to proceed to Hartford & there deliver them to the Committee * with the Letter you will have herewith.

2. You are keep an Account of all Expences you may be at in this Service & render it on your return to General Washington.

3. You will advise with M: Wharton as to the best & cheapest Mode of travelling, and either use the Carriage & Horses in which the Prisoners have come, or procure others as you find most convenient.

JOS. REED,
Secrty to Gen. Washington.

FROM MORGAN LEWIS.

NEW YORK, 4th September, 1775.

DEAR SIR:

After a journey of eight Days, we last Wednesday arrived in safety here. The Badness of Col. Gadsden's Horses prevented us from traveling with any great Expedition, and must have rendered our Jaunt very disagreeable, had not a variety of pleasing anecdotes and

---

* On Saturday, August 12th, the Committee of Safety for Philadelphia received information of the arrival at Gloucester of a vessel from Cork, the Hope, Captain Curwin, with some officers of the British army, and some clothing for the ministerial troops at Boston. An order was given to apprehend the officers and seize the clothing. The prisoners were Major Christopher French, Major of his Majesty's Twenty Second Regiment of Foot; John Rotton, Ensign in the Forty Seventh, and Terence McDermott, a cadet or volunteer. They were placed under parole and sent to Washington in charge of Captains Richard Willing and John Wharton; but as their presence in camp would be attended with many inconveniences, they were ordered to Hartford. "Captain Webb has orders to accompany you to Hartford., and is particularly enjoined to show you every mark of civility and respect. It is not doubted but that you and the other gentlemen will make his duty easy." *Joseph Reed to Major French*, 3 September, 1775. A somewhat curious correspondence passed between Washington and French. *Writings of Washington*, III, 148.

pretty Girls we met with in every part of the country proved a sufficient Compensation. We reached Wethersfield on Saturday Noon, where we staid till Sunday Morning, and notwithstanding we were treated very politely and experienced many civilities from your Brother and Mr. Deane, you will excuse me if I tell you I could have wished we had made our stay there much shorter. I need hardly inform you that on Saturday evening at Mr. Deane's, Politicks was the General Topick. New York was, according to custom, lugged in Head & shoulders by Col. Gadsden. I was determined to remain neuter, but being at last provoked by the frequent epithets of *rascally, infamous,* &c., repeatedly applied indiscriminately to the Inhabitants of this Province, I held myself bound in honor to defend the Characters of some Individuals, and accordingly engaged in a very unequal conflict with Messrs. Saltonstal, Deane & Gadsden. The Disputes ran very high, till finally Mr. Deane, I believe was induced (and as I think without Reason) to stigmatize me for a Tory. —I could wish that Charity was a Distinguishing characteristic of a Whig. However, thank God, many of them are blest with it, who I hope will never banish so Christian a Principle from their Breasts till they conceive it dangerous to the Liberties of their Country.

You doubtless have by this time heard that the Asia Ship of War, Ct Vandeput, has fired eight and twenty cannon, besides grape and cannister shot, into our City in consequence of our People's moving some cannon from off the Battery by virtue of an order from the P[rovincial] Congress. *Our* People returned the salute with their musquetry, by which means one of their People was killed and (as we supposed) several others were wounded. Three of *our* People were wounded, none killed. But how will you be surprised when I inform you that our pusillanimous Congress, notwithstanding these daring Insults, have been driven by their fears to a compromise, and have promised to supply the ship as usual with provisions. But we have more virtue out of Doors, than in the Cabinet. The People, roused by a just sense of their Injuries, have burnt two long boats that were seen coming from the Man of War, and yesterday had the pleasure of taking a large sloop with twelve Tories on board, who were supplying one of the Transports with provisions for Boston. The scene was really diverting, and our taking her with so much ease rather Providential.—A very heavy gale came on Saturday evening which lasted till Sunday morning ten o'clock, about which time the sloop parted her cables, and the wind blowing hard up the River, after several fruitless attempts to reach the Asia, she bore away before it. Our People immediately pursued her in small boats. The Asia's tender with about 70 marines besides seamen pursued her. But Vandeput, seeing us mounting some twelve pounders upon two sloops and manning them very strong, guessed at our Intentions and prudently hove out a signal for the Tender's return, which to our great mortification she instantly obeyed. After a ten miles chase they came up with the Boat, and altho' every man on board was doubly armed, took her without exchanging a single shot. When they got her to the shore, it being very wet and cold, their compassion induced them to set her on fire, by way of warming the Passengers Fingers.

We yesterday received an account here that our People had been fortifying plowed Hill, that the Regulars had the next day attacked the Lines upon said Hill, were three times repulsed with great slaughter, & that an Aid-de-Camp of G. Lee's was killed. Pray tell me the Truth of it.

Agreeable to promise, I shall expect from you, my dear sir, an impartial account of every Public Transaction at Cambridge, for by the time that any Intelligence reaches this it becomes so adulterated with Lies and Embellishments that a man must be endued with a spirit of Divination to make Head or Tail of it.

To avoid therefore Impositions of this kind, and to hear from one I much esteem, induces me to request of you a Relation of every public Affair that turns up. My best respects to the worthy old Gentleman you have the Honor of being Aid du Con to, and to every Gentleman in general of my acquaintance at Cambridge, but particularly to Messrs. Melcher, Griffin & Randolph. Accept, sir, of the good wishes of one who shall ever esteem it an Honor to subscribe himself, with the utmost sincerity, your real Friend & h'ble Serv:

MORGAN LEWIS.

FROM CAPTAIN CHESTER.

ROXBURY, SATURDAY MORNING, 6 o'Clock,

[September, 1775].

DEAR SAMMY:

You'll be surprised to hear our Regiment have Caballed & I believe every Officer on the Ground signed a petition & remonstrance*

---

* In general orders of 20 September, 1775, announcement was made that the commissions were ready to be delivered to the officers serving in the army of the United Colonies,—continental commissions to take the place of colonial. Some disputed claims of rank arose, and among the difficulties encountered was this protest against the issue of a commission to Ebenezer Huntington. The matter was brought before Washington, who declined to interfere, for the reasons set forth in the following letter:

TO BRIGADIER GENERAL JOSEPH SPENCER.

SIR: HEADQUARTERS, 26 September, 1775.

I have perused and considered a petition, or rather a remonstrance, directed to you and signed by several captains and subalterns, on the appointment of Mr. Huntington to the lieutenancy of Captain Chester's company.

The decent representation of officers, or even of common soldiers, through the channels of their colonel, or other superior officers, I shall always encourage and attend to; but I must declare my disapprobation of this mode of associating and combining, as subversive of all subordination, discipline and order.

Should the proper officers refuse or neglect to receive their complaints, an immediate application to their general officers would be proper. Much as I disapprove the mode of opposition to this gentleman, I disapprove the opposition itself still more. To yield to it would be in effect to surrender the command of the army to those whose duty it is, and whose honor it ought to be, to obey. Commission should be ever the reward of merit, not of age, and I am determined never to put it out of the proper power to reward a deserving, active officer, whatsoever may be his standing in the army, or the pretensions of those, who have no other merit than that of having been born or enlisted before him.

In an army so young as ours, the claims arising from real service are very few, and the accidental circumstance of obtaining a commission a month or two sooner can with no reasonable person claim any superior regard, or make such a scrutiny of any consequence. This army is supported by the whole continent, the establishment is entirely new. All provincial customs, therefore, which are different in different provinces, must be laid out of the question. The power which has established, and which pays this army, has alone the right to judge who shall command in it, from the general to the ensign. To put it into any other hands would be a high breach of my trust, and would give birth to such factions and cabals as must soon end in the dissolution of the army, and the ruin of our country.

As no objections are made to Mr. Huntington's character, nor any other reason directed to Gen! Spencer agt Huntington's having a Commission in the Regiment. Huntington will be with you himself & can tell you Particulars better than I can write them. Capt Pettibone * brot it to me yesterday morn to sign. I refused & gave my reasons. I told Goodrich & Butler † I was surprised to see they had signed after what they had said to me. I have conversed with several of our Sergts & Privates & find they are in favor of Huntington rather than to take it up along as it may Chance. But it's very probable the officers may succeed so far as to rout H—n—. In that Case I would gladly disapoint their Malice of its full Glut, & therefore would desire you if you think proper & could be willing to hold your Commission as Lieut that so I may not have any awkard, Long shank, Black, Ignorant Old Grey headed fellow to fill up the place. You & Ebby Huntington ‡ must lay your heads together & plague them a little.

assigned than his not rising by graduation, I can make no alteration in his appointment. At the same time I declare, that I shall upon all occasions pay a proper respect to long service, and as far as lies in my power give it all the preference, which is consistent with the welfare of the army and the duties of my station. I make no doubt, therefore, when these and all other officers (who, in such cases, are both parties and judges) divest themselves of prejudice and partialism, they will cheerfully acquiesce in such appointments as are made, and manifest their sincere attachment to their country, and the great cause in which we are engaged, by a ready and hearty obedience to all orders and rules judged necessary for the general interest. I am, Sir, &c.

Go WASHINGTON.

* Abel Pettibone, of the 7th company, in Spencer's regiment. He enlisted from Simsbury, 1 May, and was discharged from service 10 December, 1775.

† Lieutenant Stephen Goodrich and Ensign Charles Butler, of Capt. Chester's company.

‡ Ebenezer Huntington, born 26 December, 1754, was a student in Yale College when the battle of Lexington was fought; at once enlisted in a company of volunteers, and marched to Boston. He was on September 8th appointed first lieutenant in a company of Connecticut troops commanded by Captain John Chester, and in June, 1776, was promoted to a captain's commission, in the regiment of Col. Samuel Wyllys, and near the end of the campaign did the duties of brigade major under General Parsons. Soon after, he joined Major General Heath at the Highlands, as deputy adjutant general and deputy paymaster. On the formation of the "additional" regiment, commanded by Col. Webb, Huntington received the commission of major, and when the Colonel (Webb) of the regiment was made a prisoner by the British, and the Lieutenant Colonel (Wm. S. Livingston) had retired in October, 1778, the command of the regiment devolved

Is it not remarkable that Capt Wells * should advise Ebby to try for the place & offer to write him Recommendatory Letters to ye Govr for that purpose, & tell him he should be Glad to salute him as a Bro.^r Capt & yet sign ag.^t Him?—Willis † too?—The Devil take the Old Boy.

I hope to see you over here Monday next by 8 o'Clock in ye Morning. If that is impossible & you can be at Leisure that Day, send me by Ebby, & I must try to come & see you. If I must come, mind, I must have a whole day with you.

Write me all the Pretty stories about Wethersfield your Leisure will allow by Ebby. Had he best to tarry on the Whole.

From Your Most Sincere Friend & very

Humble Servt

JOHN CHESTER.

You never told me a word how Polly Huntington does.

FROM SILAS DEANE.

PHILADELPHIA, 16 September, 1775.

DEAR SAM:

You owe me a Letter, & a particular one,—but this is not to continue the advice I had begun to give you in a systematical manner, or to complain of you not paying me. I have no time for the former, and impute to the same Cause your deficiency in replying; but just to recommend to your notice a worthy Gentleman of this City, Mr. Clymer, the Bearer, whom I doubt not you will shew such civilities as the nature of your situation will admit of. I expect a long & minute Letter, but take care that it come by a safe hand.

I am, Dear Saml , yours most Tenderly

S. DEANE.

My compliments to Genl Putnam & Friends. I mean writing to Gen. Washington soon.

upon Major Huntington. He joined the main army, was at Yorktown as a Lieutenant Colonel in Scammell's Light Infantry, and at the end of the war retired, serving in many military and civil offices. He died in Norwich, 17 June, 1834.

* Captain Levi Wells of Colchester.

† Captain Samuel Wyllys of Hartford.

SILAS DEANE TO THOMAS MUMFORD.

PHILADELPHIA, Oct? 15th, 1775.

DEAR SIR:

Yours of the 3ᵈ I received this Moment, and am obliged to you for the useful hints contained in it, as well as for your kind remembrance to Me. Sure I am, you will not think me Neglectful of you, when you consider my Situation ; in a word, distress'd as I am, at the prospects before Me & the cross, and untoward Accidents daily happening, I should well nigh go distracted were it not, that a continual Attention to Business every hour of the Day & Night, save those of Sleep, drive away reflection. Our People at Westmoreland have conducted in a most shocking manner, so as to alarm this province & City to its very Center.—A few Days before the adjournment, of the Congress, in August, information was given that the Settlers under the Connecticut, & those under Pennsylvania had bickerings, & that there was danger of a Civil intestine dissention in that Quarter. After some Consultation on the Subject publicly in the Congress, & in private between the Delegates of the two Colonies, in which some warmth was shown by individuals on both sides, we came to this Resolution : that We would write to the Settlers, under the different Claims, to remain peaceably on the lands they had taken up, during the present Contest. For my own part, I th't that Our Letter, would have such an effect, that I pledg'd myself, to the Congress, that the peace of the Colonies, would receive no interruption, from that Quarter ; for give me leave, in confidence to Tell you, That the indiscreet zeal of Col. Dyer did the Cause no service, and had, as I could plainly perceive, much hurt himself among the people of influence, interested in those Lands. The Col? meant well, but disputing on the Connecticut claim in all Companies, by means of artful & designing men, served to increase, & inflame the Apprehensions of the people. Mr. Sherman & myself pursued quite a different plan ; for my own part, I avoided the dispute wholly, and when forced upon it, express'd my warmest wishes for a friendly settlement. By this means I stood well with the more dispassionate of the other party, when we left Philadelphia, & I fondly hoped that my influence with the settlers (to whom I had wrote in the most peremptory stile to keep quiet,) was such, that I should have no Trouble from that Quarter. Judd & Slumans expedition you have heard of ;

it is differently related. I will therefore pass no positive judgment on every particular, but on the whole, it was the most pernicious step they could have taken. This whole province is alarmed. Judd & Sluman were a few Days since bro't under a strong guard to this City, and their Friends denied all access to them at the first—& the people in this City thrown into such a Flame, that Nothing but Col. Dyer's character as a Member of Congress, protected him for a few Days at first from personal insult. The most opulent inhabitants of this City, have lately become interested, under the Proprietaries in those Lands; they assembled, & fell to raising Money to employ an Armed Force to drive off all Our People without exception. Artful Enemies to the general Cause of America blew up the Flame, in hopes of breaking the general Union. I need not be more particular, to give you an Idea of the distress which this Affair threw me into, in a word I publicly, & sincerely condemned their Conduct. The Chief Justice ordered y.m to procure Bail for their appearance, with Sureties, Freeholders of the province. This could not be procured, & they were committed. The Congress ordered the Delegates of the Two Colonies to confer, & labor, a Settlement. They did, but hitherto in vain, tho I think the Storm subsides, and that a Temporary Settlement may be bro't about, if rightly managed; which, believe Me, is a most delicate, as well as arduous task. Sluman & Judd will probably think hard of my censuring them so severely as I have; but I have done it in Sincerity Nor has anything they have said to Me, altered my Opinion. Tho' did I think otherways, I should be in no way of serving them, by attempting to justify them, while the Confidence which the Delegates of this Colony, & other cool persons here have in Me will enable Me I trust to help on the healing of this unhappy breach between the Two Colonies. Thus, my Friend, You see the critical Situation into which this mad frolic of these Men has thrown Us, and indeed the very Union of the Colonies.

I have wrote many Letters into Connecticut, but have received few Answers.—As to Commerce, it is my Opinion that it will be opened soon with all Foreign States, but no decision has yet been had. The Congress early appointed a Committee on the Subject of which I was one; We made a Report, which is now under Consideration. You shall early be informed of whatever it may be.—You

ask Me, when I shall return, which Question I am in no way of answering, but will give you my particular Situation.—The Congress
have appointed a Board of Claims, of which I am one, & cannot of
course be able to return untill the Acc'ts of the Expences of this
Campaign at least is Settled.—On this Business, We set every Morning.—The Congress have also appointed a Secret Committee, for
Supplying the Continent with certain Necessary Articles; of this I
am one, and wish I could see you, or some other of my Connecticut
Mercantile Friends, here, as it would be in my power, to help them,
& in theirs to serve their Country, this all I can give, on this head,
& if you will come down, the Sooner, the better.—A Naval Force, is
a Favorite object of mine, & I have a prospect now, of carrying that
point, having succeeded in getting Our Connecticut, & the Rhode
Island Vessels into Continental pay; which motion I was seconded
in beyond any expectations, and was further directed by Congress to
lay before them an Estimate of the Cruisers on this Coast. This
I shall lay before them this Day, and am of your Opinion, that N.
London harbor is well situated for the rendevous of an American
Navy; &, my Friend, is it not worth while, for N. London to labor,
to obtain the advantages of such a Collection of Navigation spending
their Money there? I think it prudent & adviseable, therefore, for
you or some other to come instantly down here, by which you may
undoubtedly procure an advantageous employment for your Navigation.—As to the Assembly choosing New Delegates, the Congress
will not interfere, either in the Mode, or Time, agreeable to any
Colony. I think, however, it would be best for the Assembly to
make a New Election, or at least to re-elect their Delegates annually. As to myself, I know not how I stand in their estimation,
but make this rule, to serve them cheerfully, To the best of my Abilities, when called upon, and with equal Cheerfullness to give place,
to better Men. By what I have said above you will see I have no
idle Time. My Comp'ts to all Friends in Assembly, particularly to
Mr. Hosmer. I wish he was here, & if you make a new choice he
must be one. I have wrote to him a long Letter, and several short
ones without any Answer.—How does his Lead Works go on? I am,
Sir, Your most Obedt & very Huml Servt.

SILAS DEANE.

P. S. Where is the Maccaroni, & how have you succeeded in procuring a most Necessary Article?* Will it not be prudent to àrm one half the Militia with pikes of handles of about Ten feet in length, the heads Three square, with sharp strips of Iron running down about One feet on the handle from the head, to prevent the enemy laying hold with their hands in the Action. Will a Battery on Winthrop's Neck, another on Mamecock, & a few Guns on the heights on the [eastern] Shore, secure that Harbor? How far up the Norwich River is their Sufficient Depth of Water for a Twenty Gun Ship?†

TO SILAS DEANE.

CAMP IN CAMBRIDGE, Oct. 16th 1775.

DEAR SIR:

By Mr. Bird,‡ a Gentleman Volunteer returning Home, I have a moments leisure to inform you I wrote you three weeks ago a long letter to which I have received no answer. I could wish you might find leisure to write me more frequent than you do,—in my last I mentioned the building the flat Bottom Boats which are now almost compleated and the men are daily exercising in them, such as learning to Row—paddle— land & clime a precipice & form immediately for Action, —they behave much beyond expectation,—this exercise will be of great service if ever we land on the shore of our Enemies, which it seems they much fear as they have hall'd up another Frigate in the Bay back of Mount Whoredom.—Doctr Franklin and the other Gentlemen arrived here last Evening, I have not yet

* Powder.

† From the Ford Collection.

‡ Probably Otway Byrd, who came to camp on October 2nd, with a letter from Robert Carter Nicholas. *Writings of Washington*, III, 170. It is not likely that he did return home, as he was appointed an aid to Major General Charles Lee, on the 25th.

TTLE AT CHARLESTOWN June 17th 1775.

A CORRECT VIEW of THE LATE BA

seen them.* The Representation of the Battle of Charlestown lately struck of in Phil<u>a</u>. is what ought never to go abroad—there is not a single Representation but is *very* erronious. Our little Fortification was on the right more than half way between Charlestown Ferry and Mistic River, he has placed it on the left, the whole is much out of the way. I am in great haste or should be more particular—I am

Affectionately Yours
SAM<u>L</u>. B. WEBB.

JOSEPH BARRELL TO JOSEPH GREEN.†

WESTOWN, 3 NOVEMBER, 1775.

HON<u>D</u> SIR:

I have heard with great pleasure of the very agreeable & pleasant Passage & safe arrival of you & my Aunt. I wish I had been favor'd with a line from you, & hope for the pleasure by some opp<u>y</u> or other.

Every day convinces me of the propriety of your departure for

---

* This was a committee from the Continental Congress, composed of Benjamin Franklin, Thomas Lynch, and Benjamin Harrison. The New England colonies sent representatives also: Governor Nicholas Cooke from Rhode Island; James Bowdoin, Joseph Otis, William Sever and Walter Spooner from Massachusetts, and Matthew Thompson from New Hampshire. The conference assembled on October 18th, and continued its sittings daily till the 22d. Its proceedings are printed in Force, *American Archives, Fourth Series*, III, 1156.

† Joseph Green was an uncle of Joseph Barrell, a resident of Boston, where he was born and spent the greater part of his life as a merchant. He was born in 1706, graduated at Harvard College in 1726, and was one of the leading wits of the day. Little of his writings remain, but a few verses and epigrams may be found in the prints of the day. He lived on School Street, near the " Cromwell's Head," and is said to have had the largest private library in New England. Winsor, *Memorial History of Boston*. A Loyalist, he left Boston in 1775, and, going to London, resided there till his death in 1780. His portrait after a crayon drawing by Copley is printed in Winsor, III, 132. His wife, Elizabeth—died in London, October, 1800, aged 87.

London ; for I'm sure you must have been compleatly miserable in that scene of distress *the Garrison Boston*. From people come out within a few days, we are assured the misery of the Inhabitants increases daily—without provisions and without fuel at this inclement season. Yesterday's paper contains a Proclamation from M.ʳ How, which obliges the Inhabitants to take arms, or perish, as the same Paper has other proclamations forbiding on pain of Death the Departure of any Inhabitant without special leave from himself obtained. You know I promised to write nothing but what might be depended on. I think I have never once done it, & I venture to say the Acc.ᵗ published in London of the Battle of the 17th of June on Bunker hill, said to be from Gen. Gage, is absolutely & essentially false ; but as truth seems of no Acco't in London, I shall instance in one particular only the men that fought defending the Breast work did not exceed 700, not ⅓ of the num.ʳ that Acco't says the Gen. employ'd, but if any Judgment can be formed of 70 boats going, I believe 'twould be full as near truth had the Acco't said "something above 4000," instead of "something above 2000." However that may be, 'tis certain at that time the Army bore no kind of Comparison to its present state, and every Officer suspected, has been try'd & some broke for their Cowardice, w.ᶜʰ has an amaizing Effect on y.ᵉ rest, and I believe they'l find a second Breast work better defended. For since Genl. Washington's Appointment everything [is] carried on with regularity, and the men supplyed with every necessary both for Cloathing & Provisions. Beef, fat and good, the Contractors purchaise for 1.d & 1¼ ster.ᵍ p.ʳ pound, & such is the plenty, that large flocks of Cattle are daily return'd into the Country for want of Purchaisers. This I am an eye witness of, for I am situated on the great Road, where some days 300 teams pass loaded for the Army, many of w.ᶜʰ come quite from Connecticut, & Phill.ᵃ . I am not versed in the Language of the Brute Creation, but I fancy I hear Innumerable Curses from those Beasts of Burthen heaped upon the Tyrant North & his Assistants, who depend upon it, however their chimerical heads have formed the strange Notion of subjugating these Colonies, they never will accomplish it. If these are their measures, their Conquest will be defeat, and their Union an Eternal separation. They might (had they been earlier in their cursed Cruelty) have destroyed all the Seaports, but since the Brutal Burning of great parts of Fal-

mouth, Casco Bay, by that Pompous Puppy, Mowett, the other Ports
are fortifying with Battery beyond Battery, & in many they have
sunk Piers, that 'tis probable may entrap some of those Licensed
Pirates, should they attempt further to push their savage purpose.
But should they absolutely destroy our Seaports, will that end the
matter? Far the contrary. The Landholders, the people in the
Country, then swear an eternal Enmity, & if that hated consequence
of these oppressions has not already taken place, then it surely will.
I mean an entire Separation from Britain, that place from whence
our troubles lately come. If the last Addresses to the king & people
of Britain has no effect, that place, once the Residence of our
Friends, will be so detested, that the very name will be treason to
the Ears of America, & it may then be too late for that Sleepy People to regain our friendship, even by the Distruction of those Advisers of the present Plan.

You have undoubtedly heard that a ship from Bristol with flour
for the Regulars & several others, have fallen into our hands. Possibly news of this kind may very soon be multiplyd in your ears, for
the Americans, always wise in the afternoon, have now adopted such
scheems as bid fair for it. I confess for my own part my first wish
is that this matter may terminate better than the present prospect
promises—even in a happy reconciliation; but my next is, that
America may never be conquer'd, but that every Weapon found
against her peace, the Wretch that found & the fool that attempts
to prosecute it may meet their distruction therein.

The article of Saltpeter being of Consequence, our Gen. Court has
passed an Act engageing to give 4 / L[awful] m[one]y p.r pound for
every pound made before the 1st of June next, & also 3 / L. money
as a bounty on every pound so made. This Act passt both houses 3
days since, but luckily for the Continent (for all these Matters are a
Continental Charge), before the Act came abroad, a simple Countryman brought into the House ½ bushel of Saltpetre, allowd by
Judges to be as good as ever was made & better than we import, &
informd the Court the process was Simplicity itself, and that more
might be produced by June than there was money in the Prov. to
pay for; that he himself makes 14 lbs p.r week, only as a Specimen.
His method is to take the earth from under old houses, Barns, &c.,
& put it lightly into a hogshead or Barrel, & then fill it with water, w.ch

immediately forms a lie. This lie he then puts into an ashes leach that has all the goodness extracted before, this being only as a strainer. After it is run thro' w^{ch}, he boils the Lie so clarified to a certain Consistance, & then puts it to cool, when the saltpetre forms, & is immediately fit for use ; & from every Bushel of earth he produces ¾ lb. saltpetre. On this information, wch is far easier than any yet found out, the Act above was suppressed for Amendment, & the Court proposes to give this person some Bounty, & the scheme is immediately to be made publick, when every Potash work will be converted into Saltpetre Works, & when peace takes place this will be an Article of export no doubt of very considerable value. The truth of this you may depend on. I had it from a very intelligent Member of the Court who saw it tryd & approved. "Necessity is the Mother of Invention."

Dr. Church is under guard for giving Intelligence to the enemy, one of his Letters in Characters being intercepted & Decypherd ; he has not yet had his tryal.

The present Army engaging only till last of December next, a new one is now forming, or rather New Inlistments are prepairing for the old Soldiers. They are now to be dresst in Uniform, a very large q'ty of coarse goods being purchaised by the Continental Congress at Philadelphia, & sent to Head Quarters. The present Engagement is for one year longer, & if matters are not settled this winter, we expect in the Spring 60,000 men in arms in different Parts, & when you consider the very easy method we have of Raiseing Money, namely the Charm of converting a p^s of paper not worth a farthing into a 30 dollar bill,—the largest I've seen of the Continental Currency,—& when you are assured (wch you may be) that it gains Credit with all, & is preferred by many to Gold & Silver, you will not dispute that such an Army may be easily raised upon a Continent of upward 3 Millions of Inhabitants, almost to a man enthusiastick in the cause of Liberty. I pray God to prevent this by some happy measures this Winter on your side the Water. From this Continent 'tis supposed you have the final proposals ; reject them, & the sword alone decides this unnatural Contest. From the Expedition to Canada we have no Accot the last week. The last Acco'ts were very favorable, & 'tis hoped before this day we have it in possession.

Joseph Barrell,

From a drawing by John Singleton Copley

Pray give my Love to Bro. Colburn & his wife, in which my wife joins. Also our Duty to my aunt ; tell her I long to see her, & have repented my not going with you only once—which is ever since ; for I've been oblig'd to [ ] on a Life of Idleness since your Departure, without a Shadow of Business. I expect to murder the Winter in the same Manner ; but in the spring, if it is possible, I will do something. My Trunk of Linnen in Cap. Calahan I've heard nothing of. I hope you'll be kind eno' to keep it until it may with safety be sent to this Country. If ever that happy time arrives, I hope for the pleasure of seeing you again.

[Jo : Barrell.]*

FROM NATHANIEL SHALER.

Middletown, Nov. 4th, 1775.

Dear Sam :

A long time it is since I have set Pen to paper to write, to any of my friends ; therefore you'l not think yourself neglected by the Omission.

And now, what shall I write you but a sorrowfull account of my misfortunes which, I may truly say, have kept pace with the calamities of my Country. Not long since I was bereft of the Partner of my wishes, since which, the little Representative which she left behind, and which seem'd some consolation to me under that irrepairable loss, is snatch'd from me, and I am left as it were, alone, to bemoan my hard fate. You see, my dear Sam, that I am oblig'd in the early period of my life to drink large draughts of the bitter Cup. This may at least serve as a lesson to teach us, not to depend Too much on anything in this Life, since it is but Temporary and everything in it is attended with such uncertainty. What prospects I had for what the world calls happiness, you well know. How are they cut off and vanish'd in a moment from my View. What further misfortunes may fall to my lott, time will produce ; but whatever they are, or whenever they may come, I hope to have fortitude sufficient to bear up under them as a man, and if I do it as a good one, happy for me.

* The draft is endorsed: "To Jos. Green, Esq., Sent by Capt. Jacob Rogers, Passenger in the Packet."

This theme, my dear Sam, although a melancholy one, pleases me to dwell on, and knowing your good nature, and having a claim to your friendship, I take the greater liberties in laying open to your view the sorrows of my heart; when you and myself used to occupy my little South Chamber, we knew no troubles, all then was smooth, easy and joyous; how is the scene chang'd? Not only with me, but even with yourself. When we take a Retrospective view of former times and compare them with the present, what an odds;—where are all our dreams of happiness flown; time has slid away, and we have not as yet catch'd the Phantom which was pursued; she still eludes our eager Grasp; and plainly tells us, she is not possess'd by mortals in this life.—Fix, my dear Sam, your views beyond it, and let's no longer trifle in pursuing pleasures, which, when possess'd, lose their delights in the moment of enjoyment.—Write me by the first opportunity—Heaven be your protection—Adieu, My dear Sam, yours sincerely,   NATH⁺ SHALER.

FROM WILLIAM COIT.

PLYMOUTH, Nov. 7, 1775.

SIR:

Since I parted with you, I have made a blackguard snatch at two of their provision vessels,* and have them safe at Plymouth, and if you were where you could see me and did not laugh, all your risible faculties must perish. To see me strutting about on the quarter-deck of my schooner!—for she has a quarter-deck—ah, and more than that too—4 four pounders, brought into this country by the company of the Lords Say and Seal, to *Saybrook* when they first came. A pair of cohorns that Noah had in the Ark; one of which lacks a

---

* "This morning Capt. Coit, after a cruise of thirty-six hours, brought into this port the schooner Industry, Charles Coffin, master, and the sloop Polly, Sibeline White, master, both from Nova Scotia, bound to Boston, with provisions for the garrison there." *William Watson to Washington*, 6 November, 1775.

"I had just finished my letter when a blundering Lieutenant of the blundering Captain Coit, who had just blundered upon two vessels from Nova Scotia, came in with the account of it, and before I could rescue my letter, without knowing what he did, picked up a candle and sprinkled it with grease; but these are kind of blunders which one can readily excuse. The vessels contain hay, live-stock, poultry, &c., and are now safely moored in Plymouth harbor." *Washington to Joseph Reed*, 8 November, 1775. Moylan looked upon Coit as a "mere blubber."

touch-hole, having hardened steel drove therein, that she might not be of service to Sir Edmund Andros—Six swivels, the first that ever were landed at Plymouth, and never fired since.

Now, that is my *plague;* but I can tell you somewhat of my comfort. My schooner is used to the business, for she was launched in the spring of 1761, and has served two regular apprenticeships to sailing, and sails quick, being *used to it.* Her accommodations are fine ; five of us in the cabin, and when there, are obliged to stow spoon fashion. Besides, she has a chimney in it, and the smoke serves for bedding, victuals, drink and choking. She has one mast too, which is her foremast ; she has a mainmast, but it was put in so long ago, that it has rotted off in the hounds. She has a deck, too. When it was first made, it was new ; and because it was ashamed of being old, the first time we made use of a clawed handspike, it broke a hole through ; notwithstanding the wench knew it was directly over the magazine. Upon the whole, if there comes peace, I would recommend her and her apparatus, to be sent to the Royal Society ; and I dare eat a red-hot gridiron if ever they have had, or will have, until the day of judgment, any curiosity half equal to her. I haven't time to give you her character in full, but, in short, she is the devil. But while I can keep the sea, and light only on unarmed vessels, she will do very well. But if obliged to fire both guns of a side at a time, it would split her open from gunwale to her keelson.*

* The description of the vessel (it was named the *Harrison*) showed it to be bad enough, yet the crews of the privateers were even more unreliable. They were, as a rule, draughted from the army to serve on these ships, and the agent could speak of them only as a " set of the most unprincipled, abandoned fellows." Washington lost patience with them. " Our rascally privateer men go on at the old rate, mutinying if they cannot do as they please." In November he wrote to the President of Congress : " The plague, trouble, and vexation I have had with the crews of all the armed vessels, are inexpressible : I do believe there is not on earth a more disorderly set. Every time they come into port, we hear of nothing but mutinous complaints." Somewhat later, when the profits of privateering became greater, a great desire to engage in it was shown. So far was this carried, that the colonies considered measures to forbid privateering, as so many men went into it, that it was deemed prejudicial to the recruiting service. Plunder was the main support of these vessels, and little regard was paid to nationality or purpose of the captured vessels, so long as they offered some prize money. The blockade of the coast by the British ships in the end made such buccaneering ventures unprofitable.

Pray make my compliments to all friends. Tell friend White, Plymouth is better than all the Rhode and Newport to boot. My mast will be finished to-morrow, I hope, and then away goes your most humble servant,*   WILLIAM COIT.

FROM SILAS DEANE.

PHILADELPHIA, Nov. 22d , 1775.

DEAR SAM:

I have not wrote you for some time past, merely thro' the multiplicity of Business in which I have for some time since, been engaged. I have seen Col. Reed who is much your Friend, and if the Office you referr to should be established, I have no doubt of procuring you the Birth. I hear that Mr. Chester intends retiring, but I do not advise you to accept his place ; for if you can be appointed, Gen'l Gates's Deputy, & assistant Secretary, it will place you at head Quarters under the General's Eye, in the best Company for improving in knowledge & good breeding, and be in a genteel Station, as well as a good one, for any future advancement. You are now entered on the Military Course, & are fortunate in your first office, & Connections—everything hereafter depends on yourself, and as I must advise you, to pursue that Track, for Life, I must urge you, to improve every leisure moment in reading the best Treatises on Warr, & histories of Sieges, &c. Also that you slip no Opportunity, of being present at and acquainting yourself with every Military Operation of any Consequence, and that you now keep a Journal not for entering down Trifles, as they may Daily occur, but of every Operation of Consequence, with your own Observations on it at the Time and afterward of ye Event. Also now enter all the regulations for an Army, such as their Rations, Cloathing, Arms, &c., &c., which you may find of vast service in future to you, in your military Departments—how

---

* Capt. Ephraim Bowen, Jr., was sent to Plymouth by Washington, to superintend the equipment of a vessel intended to intercept the enemy's supplies. Bowen kept a journal, from which we learn that on November 1st he arrived at Plymouth, and found Coit's vessel aground. On the next day, the ship was got off, but being detained by bad weather, succeeded in getting aground on the third or fourth. It sailed on the 5th, and the next day returned with the two prizes. On the 13th Coit sailed for Cape Cod, where a vessel was reported to be at anchor.

long the present unnatural War may last, is dreadfully uncertain, but should it close within a year, or Two, you may so well lay the first Rudiments of Military knowledge, as to introduce you with *éclat* into any other Service, for Wars will continue in one part of the World, or another, untill the Millennium arrive, & that is not, nor will soon I imagine.

As to Mr. Simpson I am sorry for his Situation, and wish his Character stood fairer in the Country than it does, many People in the Country asserting that he was unnecessarily Subservient to Gen! Gage, & that party, and therefore I fear he will suffer in his Interest, as Confiscations are you see begun in Rhode Island.* I shall probably see you as soon as I am dismissed from this Place, which by the Influence of some of my Friends will take place in January. I am in haste, Dear Sir,

Yours Affectionately
Silas Deane.

Mrs. Deane has paid me a Visit, & I returned as far as N. York in her Company, being sent there on Business of the Congress which happened in my Way. Your Brother was with Me, & I returned but yesterday. You must send Me an Acc! of the Number, & force, of the Armed Vessels, now Cruising to the Eastward. I want it for public purposes.

---

* Of John Simpson, the husband of Webb's sister, I can learn but little. His brother, Jonathan, graduated at Harvard in 1772, was an addresser of Gov. Hutchinson in 1774, and was appointed one of the "mandamus counsellors" by the King in the same year. Popular indignation and threats led to his resigning the commission, but he and his brother remained loyal. Sabine (*Loyalists of the American Revolution*, II., 303,) says that John was at Providence, Rhode Island, just before the controversy with Great Britain came to blows; and "finding one morning that his doors and window-shutters had been tarred and feathered, he hastened back to Boston." The two brothers left Boston at the evacuation, and went to Halifax, N. S. John must soon have gone to New York, where he died in 1777 or 1778. Jonathan was proscribed and banished by the Massachusetts act of 1778, became a Commissary of Provisions in the British army, and returning to Boston after the peace, he died there in 1834, aged eighty-four years.

FROM JOSEPH REED.*

PHILADELPHIA, Nov. 26, 1775.

DEAR SIR:

I have defer'd writing to you hitherto in Expectation of having some thing agreeable to say upon the Subject of our last Conversation, which I have faithfully kept in mind. As soon as I came home I went to Mr. Dean[e] & he thought it a matter of some Difficulty and Delicacy for him to appear in ; on which I en[deavored] to put it in another Train, but the Congress are so engaged upon other matters & averse to making any new Appointments that I despair of doing any Thing in it. I had several Matters in Charge from the General which yet lay unsettled owing to the Multiplicity & Importance of their Business. They are fitting out some Vessels here for the Sea, but their other Business is a profound Secret to us, tho' it it well known every Week in New York.†—Toryism has been showing itself both here & there in a very dangerous Way, viz., refusing to receive Continental Currency in Payment.—The Congress have taken up the matter, & we expect every Day a thundering Curse upon these Recusants.‡

We had a small Importation of Powder here a few Days ago, & 50 fine Musquets.—The Captain tells us a Vessel arrived from Europe with a pretty handsome Cargo of Ammunition, the Chief of which was taken by some New England Vessels who were waiting for it. If this is true it will not be long before you will have some good News to send us upon this Subject.

Since the late Skirmish at Lechmore's Point § we are led to expect a General Attack. I wish, with all my Soul, it may be made before the Troops are discharged from Service ; but I cannot believe the

* At this time the Secretary and aid to Washington, and the member of his military family in whom he placed most confidence.

† James Brattle, formerly a servant of Governor Tryon, was now living with ames Duane, a member of the New York delegation in the Continental Congress. He copied the minutes and papers that Duane had, and sent them regularly to ryon; and in the case of this fleet he was enabled to minutely describe it, the umber of guns, weight of metal, number of men and the names of officers. eing detected, he fled, and was sent to England by Tryon.

‡ *Journals of Congress*, January 11, 1776.

§ *Writings of Washington*, III, 216, 217.

Enemy such Fools as to attack a strong Army, when by waiting a while they will have the chance of a weak one.*

In a few Days after this reaches you the Face of your Camp will be changed—Mrs. Washington, her daughter,† and Mrs. Gates set out to-morrow from hence. No bad supply I think in a cold Country where Wood is scarce. They are very agreeable Ladies, & I heartily wish they had better Roads & a pleasanter season for this Journey than I imagine they will have. As the General will now stand in Need of a very gallant Aid-de-Camp, I believe I must make an Interest for you with the Ladies here ; if they scruple my judgment, I can refer them to Mrs. Temple & her fair Daughter for further particulars.‡

* As the terms of service for the greater part of the army would expire by the end of the year, it became necessary to frame a new arrangement. In doing this great difficulties were encountered. " Many of the officers sent in their names to serve, in expectation of promotion; others stood aloof to see what advantage they could make for themselves; whilst a number, who had declined, have again sent in their names to serve. So great has the confusion, arising from these and many other perplexing circumstances, been, that I found it absolutely impossible to fix this very interesting business exactly on the plan resolved on in the conference [note on page 111, *ante*], though I have kept up to the spirit of it, as near as the nature and necessity of the case would admit of. The difficulty with the soldiers is as great, indeed more so, if possible, than with the officers. They will not enlist, until they know their colonel, lieutenant-colonel, major, captain, &c.; so that it was necessary to fix the officers the first thing; which is, at last, in some manner done; and I have given out enlisting orders. You, sir, can much easier judge, than I can express, the anxiety of mind I must labor under on this occasion, especially at this time, when we may expect the enemy will begin to act on the arrival of their reinforcement, part of which is already come, and the remainder daily dropping in." *Washington to the President of Congress,* 11 November, 1775. In spite of these difficulties, and of the fact that the British were fully aware of the weakness of the American army, the issue was favorable. " Search the vast volumes of history through, and I much question whether a case similar to ours is to be found; to wit, to maintain a post for six months together, without [powder], and at the end of them to have one army disbanded and another to raise within the same distance of a reinforced enemy." *Washington to Joseph Reed,* 4 January, 1776.

† Nelly [Calvert] Custis, the wife of John Parke Custis.

"CAMBRIDGE, December 14, 1775.—Last Monday night [December 11th] came to town from Virginia, the lady of his Excellency General Washington, and the lady of the Hon. Adjutant-General Gates, accompanied by John Custis, Esq., and lady, and George Lewis, Esq."

‡ Mrs. Robert Temple. See note to letter from *Robert Temple to General Washington,* 21 April, 1777, *post.*

I was much disappointed in not meeting your Brother here—some how we passed each other on the Road. He has an Acct, the stationery Part of which properly belongs to the General, & will be paid when sent in. There were also 2 p's of Nankeen. Mr Pierce, who writes for the Adjutt Genl took one piece & will pay for it on being made acquainted with the price, which I will also do for the other, when I have the like Knowledge. I must beg your kind Attention to it.

The Riffle Men carry off all the Honour of repulsing [the] Enemy from Lechmore's Point, & that too at the [expense of the] other Troops. I hoped we should have had no more of the Scenes of Bunker Hill revived. I don't hear a Word of our good old General* that Day, tho' this was in his Department. He did not use to leave it to others to urge on the Troops, which makes me suspect our Southern Gentlemen are too partial to their own Corps.—If you have Leisure you will oblige me much in letting me hear from you as often as you conveniently can. The Post comes twice a week. I shall most chearfully return you all the news passing here, & if my Writing at any Time to the General will favour & promote your Wishes, you will give me great Pleasure in letting me know it as I am, with real Regard, Dr Webb, your affect; Hbble Servt.

Jos: Reed.

Please to forward the enclosed into Boston.

FROM EBENEZER HUNTINGTON TO ANDREW HUNTINGTON.†

Camp at Roxbury, December 1st, 1775.

Dear Brother:

I wrote you pr Mr. Kinsman last Week in great haste since which, have receivd none of your favours—I mentioned the death of Sister‡ but not so particularly as I should have been glad to do, suppose you must have Recd the particulars by this time.—Doubtless you have

---

* Putnam.

† A merchant in Norwich.

‡ Faith (Trumbull), the wife of Jedediah Huntington, who died at Dedham, Mass., when on her way to camp to join her husband. She was a daughter of Governor Jonathan Trumbull.

heard before this reaches you the good news that our People at Capan in a privateer have taken a Store Ship with 2500 fire Arms with Accoutrements 31 tons Musquet balls a 13–10–& 8 Inch Mortars with a number of other Articles very suitable for us at this time*—Last Saturday night a 20 Gun Ship in the mouth of this harbour was consumed by fire—Occasioned by Lightning—Yesterday I was on main guard, when a flag of truce went in by Permission of Gen. Washington desiring a Conference, with some particular gentlemen whom Col. Miflin, Deac. Storer & others wanted to see. They came out with five Officers at 12 o'Clock, I went on the lines with Col. Miflin : the Officers were very Complaisant. You must note that one of the Officers we met was Sir Colbourne a Cole of the 49th Mentiond the Disagreeableness of their Situation Coopd up in one (so small a) town—I told him we were all very sorry that matters were so situated but was determined to persist & that it would be very agreeable to us to have a free passage into Boston, he told me with great Complaisance that If I had a desire to go into the town he would pledge his honour that I should come out in an hour's time If I had a mind so to do—much of this passed between us—but nothing was said only in an Audible Voice so as to be heard by all present—The Connecticut men have this day taken the liberty to leave the Camp without Leave (I mean some of them). Majr Trumbull & Capt Chester are sent after them to bring them back they have not yet returned tho' 8 o'Clock—A party went from Cambridge in the same manner among whom was a Sergeant whom the Genl has determined to send to Connecticut in Irons with a Label on his back telling his Crime—to be dealt with as the Authority of the Colony shall think proper—The men universally seem desirous of mutiny because the men had not a bounty—the Genl is about ordering in Minute men to supply the places of those persons who shall so Poltroon like desert the lines.†

---

* This was the brig *Nancy*, Captain Robert Hunter, captured by the schooner *Lee*, under the command of Captain Manley. The prize was taken to Cape Ann, and contained among other stores, 2000 muskets, 100,000 flints, 30,000 round shot, more than 30 tons of musket shot, eleven mortar beds, and a brass mortar weighing nearly 3000 pounds, to which Putnam gave the name *Congress*. The full invoice is printed in Force, *American Archives, Fourth Series*, III, 1721.

† Washington wrote to Governor Trumbull on the " late extraordinary and re-

Give my respects to Mamma, love to Sisters & Brothers while I subscribe myself your loving tho' Afflicted Brother——

EBENEZER HUNTINGTON.

P. S. I could lengthen the letter by minute trifling matter rather tedious than Otherwise but as it is well for length will defer it.

I begun the letter to father but as I had not time to write more than one Concluded to you.*

FROM JEREMIAH WADSWORTH.

HARTFORD, DEC. 31st, 1775.

DEAR SAM:

I was abroad when yours of the 21st inst, came to hand per post.

Have been to New Haven with the two French gentlemen who came from Cambridge.† Joseph Webb went with me through Middletown, where we procured Joseph Johnson to attend them, and discharged their former interpreter, who was unfit for their service.

I have been much indisposed with a violent cold, which has

---

prehensible conduct of some of the Connecticut troops." Many went off, and though the utmost vigilance and industry were used to apprehend them, several got away with their arms and ammunition. "The behavior of our soldiers has made me sick; but little better could be expected from men trained up with notions of their right of saying how, and when, and under whom, they will serve; and who have, for certain dirty political purposes, been tampered with by their officers, among whom no less than a *general* has been busy." *Silas Deane to his wife*, 15 December, 1775. When, on the 16th, the term of service expired, the Connecticut men, who were determined to return home, were paraded with bag and baggage, and in passing through the lines of other regiments were "lavishly hissed, groaned at and pelted." General Greene wrote that the people on the road expressed so much abhorrence at their quitting the army, that it was with difficulty they obtained provisions, while such was their unfavorable reception at home that many returned to the camp. Governor Trumbull could only express his "grief, surprise and indignation," and say that "the conduct of our troops is not a rule whereby to judge of the temper and spirit of the colony." See also *General Orders*, 3 December, 1775. In the course of December some of the troops of New Hampshire, Rhode Island and Massachusetts were afflicted with the same desire to "retire unto a chimney-corner."

* From the Ford collection.

† Penet and Pliarne, who had come to America from Nantes by way of Cape François to contract with the colonies for a supply of arms and warlike stores.

brought me to spitting blood, and I am yet unwell, but hope to weather out this the severest attack I ever experienced from a cold.

Our General Assembly have passed an act to punish persons unfriendly to the liberties of America, which I have enclosed to Mr. Trumbull. Our delegates must come home notwithstanding all the endeavours of their friends; but Mr. Deane, being Chairman of the Naval Committee, will be detained there.*

The widow will be uppermost with you yet. You tell her Mars is the ruling *God*, but I believe Venus comes in for her share. Oh you sly dog! Do you think to blind me with your "*Old Buts*,† *your balls, shells, &c.*" No, no, Sam; I have not been in the oven for nothing. However, make yourself easy, the widow is safe and sound. If any idle dog attacks her in your absence I'll send you word, or drive him off. I wish fortune may for once play fair, and you may meet what you hope for, but be prepared for a disappointment. It may happen. This long silence about the matter forebodes no good.

You write me for two volumes of Entick's History, I never saw but one here, and that your mother sent for. One volume of Knox's Journal is here, and shall be sent by the first opportunity.

Your advice about Middlebrook politicians is not good. Do you think from my knowledge of that noble animal, the horse, I can do anything with such devils? No, no! You have injured the whole species of horses—ask pardon of them, from the General's best horse down to the poor old cart horse in Cambridge. I don't wonder your horse puts your head in the ditch. Why! do you think the beasts will carry you when you disgrace them by such comparisons?

L. C——r ‡ has set up a pin and stocking manufactory, and puts in a memorial to the late assembly for the loan of £1,000 without interest for two years; [he] has not succeeded. He has two girls

---

* On December 11th a Committee composed of a number from each colony was appointed in Congress to devise ways and means for furnishing these colonies with a naval armament. The members were: Josiah Bartlett, Samuel Adams, Stephen Hopkins, Silas Deane, Francis Lewis, Stephen Crane, Robert Morris, George Read, William Paca, Richard Henry Lee, Joseph Hewes and Christopher Gadsden.

† Probably a misprint for " Put "—a reference to Putnam.

‡ Probably Leonard Chester.

in ye pin business, but I believe they will make legs to all the stockings.

The rain will spoil our sport, and I fear yours.

I am coming to Cambridge as soon as my health will allow me. In the interim make my compliments agreeable to all friends, and believe me, dear Sam, your friend and humble servant

JERE WADSWORTH.*

FROM JOSEPH REED.

PHILADELPHIA, Jany 16, 1776.

DRAR SIR:

I have waited some Time with Impatience for a private oppy to thank you for your Favour of the 6th last month. I esteem you too much to be unmindful of your Interest and wishes, & have made both the subject of friendly Conversations with your good Friend Mr. Deane. After beating the Bush upon the Subject we had first in View, we found it must originate with the General or there would be no Prospect of success. As I know he is very particular in the creating new offices, it settled my mind on the Subject at once—as you would I think have a better Chance of being one of his aids than getting him to create or advise any new office. If there is no such Alteration of Affairs at Cambridge as to make a Change in your Sentiments, I shall with great Pleasure use my Interest for the latter Purpose. We correspond almost every week & his Letters are in the most friendly Style.

The Peculiarity of my Situation detains me & will do so till some remarkable change in publick affairs cut asunder the Cords which tie me down here. In that Case, I shall be happy in renewing the Rights of Fellowship with my good friends at Cambridge.—I perfectly long to see the old General†—we toast him every Day, which I assure you is doing a great Deal for a Connecticut Man, as the late Disputes at Susquehanna have created an Antipathy between the two Provinces that was proceeding to dangerous Lengths if the Congress had not interposed.

Our worthy Friend Deane is going to leave us, much regretted by

* From the *Reminiscences of General Samuel B. Webb*, p. 311.
† Major General Putnam.

every Man in and out of Congress who has the Pleasure of his Acquaintance—The latter have given him a most ample Testimonial of his Conduct & Character. The cursed narrow Politicks of Connecticut would never cease working till they ousted him & I am much mistaken if some Folks at Roxbury are not at the Bottom of it.*

Tell your worthy old General that we give him credit for a Part of Manly's Success, as he brought him to us. Is it not very strange that he should monopolize all the Honour of the Sea. What is become of Coit? I expected he would have disputed the Lauril with Manly.—We are fitting out a Fleet from this city of no inconsiderable Force & expect soon to send you an Account of some brilliant Stroke. Manly excepted, we have not shone in that Way as yet.—Apropos—We have a very diverting Account here of a secret Expedition plann'd by a certain General of Winter Hill who wanted to carry off the Honours of the Campaign from the Major General,—but by some unlucky mistake Water was taken for smooth Ice & the whole Detachment came out lopping their Ears & shaking themselves like so many Water Spaniels.—That our Troops scorned to take an Enemy by Surprize & fired a Warning Gun as they marched up, which had the desired Effect of alarming the Enemy : in short, they give a very ludicrous Account of the whole Night's Work, & at no small Expence to the Hero of the Night.†

That Army must be destroyed if possible this Winter, in my opinion the Salvation of America depends upon it—if there is no other way they must be burnt out. I am not Master enough of the subject to judge of the effect of Carcases & shells for this purpose : But if it can be done I hope to God no Time will be lost.—It is universally

---

* Deane had been dropped from the Connecticut delegation in Congress, and was appointed agent to France.

† "[December] 28th.—A strong detachment from Winter Hill marched, in the night, to surprise the British outposts in Charlestown. They passed on the south side of Cobble-Hill, and were to cross the cove on the ice. When they came to the channel, it was found to be open. A soldier slipping down on the ice, his piece accidentally went off, which caused an alarm, and the detachment returned."—Heath's *Memoir*.

"In Lee's absence, a friend of ours on the Hill thought to have plucked some laurels on Bunker's Hill, but it ended in fume, as I believe everything in that quarter will do, if he is absent—oh! how he fretted on his return, for giving an alarm : it interfered with a favorite plan, which must now be postponed." *Stephen Moylan to Joseph Reed*, 2 January, 1776.

expected that some Stroke will be struck this Winter & I hope there will be no Disappointment.—We are getting Powder in small Quantities; but we imported 57 Tons of Salt Petre in our Vessels the other Day.

L.ᵈ Dunmore has burnt Norfolk, one of the most considerable trading Towns to the Southward, & killed several women & children in the course of the Cannonade.—It has made a very great Impression here, they have nothing more to do than burn a Town in each Provience & we shall bring Matters to a short Issue.

I shall always be happy in hearing from you when you have Leisure, but especially when any [Thing] material happens.—I shall make it a Test of your [Friendship], and am willing you should make it so of mine. Make my affectionate Compliments to your General & tell him there is not a Man on Earth who esteems him more. Compliments to Dr. Leonard.

Health, Honour & Happiness attend you, and believe me with sincere Regard, with much Esteem, Dr. Webb.

Your affect., hbble Serv.ᵗ

J. REED.

JOURNAL.

CAMP IN CAMBRIDGE, March 1ˢᵗ, 1776.

The continual hurry and Bustle of Camp Life, since my commencing a Soldier, has prevented my keeping a regular Journal as formerly. The ever-to-be-remember'd 19ᵗʰ of April, 1775, the day on which the Ministerial Butchers under Gen.ˡ Gage march'd out to Lexington and Concord, and there in a most Barbarous manner, spilt the Blood of our Countrymen, is too fresh in every ones memory to need being particularly mentioned,—I then accepted of a first Lieutenancy in the Connecticut Troops under Capt. John Chester, in which Birth I continued until July, when I had the Honor of being appointed first Aid-de-Camp to the

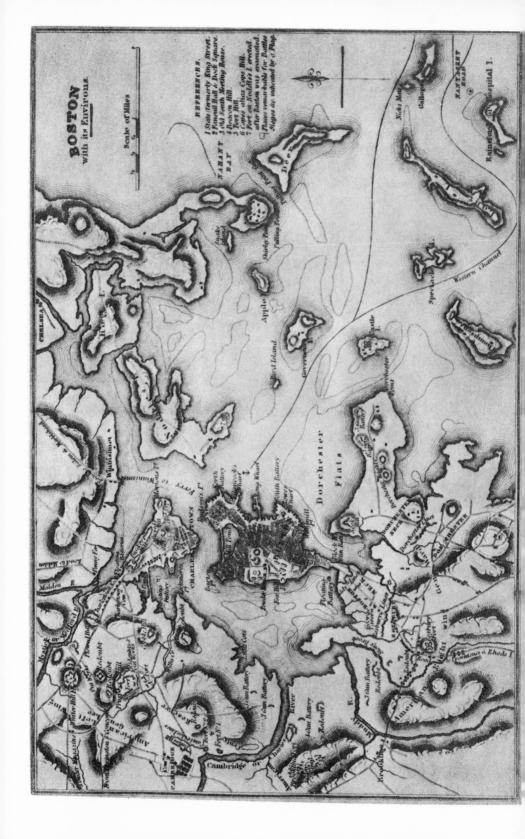

BOSTON
with its Environs.

Scale of Miles

REFERENCES.
1 State (formerly King) street.
2 Faneuil Hall & Dock Square.
3 Old South Meeting House.
4 Beacon Hill.
5 Fort Hill.
6 Copps or thus Copp Hill.
7 Fort on Noddle's I. erected after Boston was evacuated.
▢ Places remarkable for Battles
Sieges &c. indicated by ✶ Flags

Hon'ble Major Gen[l]. Israel Putnam, in which Station I
now continue.

Our affairs growing now to a Critical Situation, I
can no longer neglect minuteing the daily occurances
and Manœvers of our Army, & that of our Enemy,
which has been besieged and close Blockaded by land
ever since the 19th of April last,—by an Army which
they have called a set of Paltroons and Cowards,—in
which they must have altered their Sentiments, or they
would have ventured an Attempt to raise the Seige,—
the greatest preparations are now makeing to approach our Enemies with an endeavour to Rout them
from their Garrison—for while the Sea is open to them
they will get Supply'd with Provision,—and they are in
hourly expectation of large Reinforcements from England, their Garrison at present amount to about 6000
Effective Men, Boston being a Peninsula they are for-
tifyed in the strongest Manner possible, even the
strong Fortifications of Gibralter is said not to equall
them, they have cut a Canal thro' the Neck, by which
Boston is now an Island, on the South & west sides
they are strongly fortified by a chain of Forts both on
the Ridge of Hills running the whole length of the
Town, and below all round the Waters Edge,—on the
North & East sides lie a number of Ships of War—
which sufficiently prevent our attempting to penetrate
in that way—having no Naval force equal to that lying
in the Harbour,—opposite the North East of the Town
lies Noddle Island, which at low water you can get on
to from the Main at Chelsea,—this point runs off in
Bluff—and looks over the shiping—not more than 400
yds Distance—Nor exceeding 600 to ye thick settled

part of the Town,—directly East of the old Fortification Gates on the south part of the Town lies Dorchester Point, which commands the South part of the Town, and is at least 600 yards within their outer lines on the Neck next Roxbury. A strong Battery erected on this Point, would enable us to cut of the communication between the Town and their outworks on the Neck, at the same time annoy the ships and Town,—Neither of these two Posts are taken possession, owing on the side of the Enemy to want of a proper number of Men to Garrison them, and on ours Powder & Artillery to maintain them, but having lately been supplied with some of Both these Necessary Articles, we are now making preparations to take possession of both,—by erecting great number of Facines, Gabions,—pressing Hay &c. &c.*

* On February 16th, Washington called a council of war, believing that the ice formed from Dorchester Point to Boston Neck and from Roxbury to the common, offered a fair opportunity to make an assault upon Boston, before the expected reinforcements from England should arrive. The British force was thought to be only four thousand, while the Americans had nearly nine thousand in camp (8,797), and fifteen hundred on command, who might be ordered to join their respective regiments on short notice. In addition to this army, there was a militia, who should number, when completed, seven thousand men. The council were opposed to making an attack, on the ground that the army was too deficient in arms and powder. It was, however, decided to make preparations to take possession of Dorchester Heights, and also of Noddle's Island.

" I proposed it [an assault] in council; but behold, though we had been waiting all the year for this favorable event, the enterprise was thought too dangerous. Perhaps it was; perhaps the irksomeness of my situation led me to undertake more than could be warranted by prudence. I did not think so, and I am sure yet that the enterprise, if it had been undertaken with resolution, must have succeeded; without it, any would fail; but it is now at an end, and I am preparing to take part on Dorchester, to try if the enemy will be so kind as to come out to us. Ten regiments of militia, you must know, had come to strengthen my hands for offensive measures; but what I have here said respecting the determinations in council, and the possessing of Dorchester Point, is spoken under the rose." *Washington to Joseph Reed*, 26 February, 1776.

Our Commander-in-chief is determined to loose no time in putting into Execution this plan,—for should the Enemy be enabled by reinforcements to maintain these Posts—they would enlarge their limits greatly by which means have it in their power Frequently to make excursions into the Country adjoining, & lay waste with fire and Sword our Villages, Farms, Houses &c. The enemy seem equally Sensible of the Importance of these two Posts, and 'tis said their Commander has Swore if we brake Ground on either he will Sally on us—if he was sure of looseing two thirds of his Army. This is what we wish for,—trusting (thro: the assistance of Heav'n) This would be a means of rescuing from their hands our Capital, and many of our friends, who are now confined there contrary to the Solemn Compact made between Genl. Gage & them, —Should they not sally on us,—we have a prospect of makeing them to take to their ships & flee, in this case we fear the loss of the Town, by their seting fire to it, —but this is trifeling in Comparison to the loss of our Invaluable Privileges,—Which may God preserve us in the enjoyment off. The Enemy are erecting two Batteries on Mount Whoredom, against ours on Lechmores point, and the one on Cobble-Hill known by the name of Putnam's Impregnable Battery,—The Continental Congress have ordered Major Genl Lee to repair immediately into Canada and take Command of the Army before Quebec now under command of Brigadier Genl Arnold*—Genl Schuyler to take command of the

* This resolve was taken on February 17th; but by a subsequent resolve Congress formed the middle and southern departments, and on March 1st. directed Lee to assume command of the southern.

Troops in New York on the Departure of Genl Lee. Our worthy commander in Chief (in orders a day or two past) has in the most pathetic terms told the Soldiery that on our present conduct depends the Salvation of America, that in all probability e'er long we shall be call'd to the field of Battle—that he is confident his troops will behave as deserves the cause we are contending for, but that in all Army'ş their are those who would flee before a much smaller number, & that should any such be found Sculking or retreating before the Enemy without orders—they must expect Instant Death by way of example to others.*

Saturday, March 2. 'Tis intended this night to convince the Enemy we have it in our power to disturb their camp, by Shells, and to keep them under Arms, for which purpose One 13 & one 10-Inch Mortar are carried down to Lechmore's point, & 1 13-Inch to Lamb's Dam on the Roxbury side. 12 at Night—At half past 1 o'Clock we fire'd one 13 Inch Shell and several 18 pound Shot into the Town, which has alarm'd the Enemy & they fail not to Salute us Warmly from Barton's point (opposite Lechmore's) with 2 Mortars and a three Gun Battery. I am unhappily confined to

---

* "As the season is now fast approaching when every man must expect to be drawn into the field of action, it is highly necessary that he should prepare his mind, as well as everything necessary for it. It is a noble Cause we are engaged in, it is the cause of virtue and mankind; every temporal advantage and comfort to us, and our posterity depends upon the vigor of our exertions; in short, Freedom or Slavery must be the result of our couduct: there can therefore be no greater Inducement to men to behave well: But it may not be amiss for the Troops to know, that if any man in action shall presume to skulk, hide himself, or retreat from the enemy, without the orders of his commanding officer, he will be *instantly shot* down, as a example of Cowardice; Cowards having too frequently disconcerted the best formed Troops by their dastardly behavior." *General Orders*, 27 February, 1776.

my Room, but from my window have a most pleasing
and yet dismal View of the firey Ministers of Death
flying thro the Air, poor Inhabitants our friends we
pity most sincerely, but particularly the Women &
Children.

Sunday, March 3, 1776. We continued fireing on
the Town once an hour from Lechmore's Point &
Roxbury with Shells and Cannon but had the Misfortune to Split both our Mortars on Lechmore's Point
about Day dawning, which fortunately hurt none of our
Men. The Enemy returned our fire warmly all night,
but have ceased this morning, our whole Army was
under Arms an hour before Revalle beating this morning in some expectation that the Enemy would sally
out but they have Disappointed us. We likewise had
the Misfortune of splitting a 13 Inch Mortar last night
at Roxbury. This Afternoon the General has ordered
down a fine 13 Inch Brass Mortar, the one taken by
Capt Manly in the Ordinance Store Brigg known by
the Name of "The Congress"—she is to be placed in
Putnam's Impregnable Battery on Cobble Hill, The
Enemy have kept up a feint Bombardment on our advance works all day which we return'd by throwing
some 24-pound Ball into Town.

Monday, March 4th, 1776. We began at 9 o'clock
last night to Bombard and Cannonade on the Town
just fast enough to keep the Enemy alarmed, they did
not fail of warmly returning the Salute—tho thro. the
whole of the night they neither kill'd or wounded a
single Man. About 12 at night we had the Misfortune
to split the Brass Mortar in her Chamber—what cause
to attribute our Mortar splitting to, I Know not; some

conjecture tis want of knowledge in the Bombarders, some one thing & some another, but tis hinted— Treachery, if the latter I hope it may come to light.* About ten oClock, Intelligence came that the Enemy were embarking in Boats opposite Lechmore's point— the whole Army was immediately under Arms, and waited at their alarm Posts—2 Hours. We found some of the Enemy had Embarked, but seeing our readiness to receive them they did not choose to meet us.

Tuesday, March 5th, 1776. Last night at 7 oClock we began a heavy Cannonade on the Town of Boston, from our Forts on Cobble-Hill, Lechmore's Point, & Lamb's Dam on Roxbury side, this way to draw the Enemy's attention, while 3,000 of Troops under the Command of Brigadier Genl. Thomas went on to the Hill on Dorchester call'd—with a vast number of Gabions Facines, &c., and went briskly to work,—in the meantime we keep up a regular cannonade from the about mentioned Posts,—and a few Shells. The Enemy in turn did not fail of returning our Salutes, it lasted till day light, during which time we had one Lieut. & one private Kill'd and two privates slightly wounded. What loss the Enemy met w^t. we had not yet been able to learn. Our Shell rak'd the houses terribly and the Crys of poor Women and Children frequently reach'd our Ears,—we would that they were out of the Devoted Capital, but 'tis not in our power. About Sun rise the Enemy discovered us on Dorchester which to appearance put them in very great Confusion,

---

* Heath notes that the mortars were " not properly bedded, as the ground was hard frozen." *Memoirs*, 39.

our whole Army was immediately under Arms, it was expected at high water the Enemy would endeavor to dislodge us, which would be about 12 oClock maj^r. gen^l. Putnam w^t. the Brigadiers Sullivan & Green[e] were paraded on the Common in Front of the Colledges at the head of 4,000 Men, ready in case the Enemy sallied on Dorchester, to embark in 60 Boats prepared for that purpose in Charles River—and land at the foot of Mount Whoredom on the West part of Boston and immediately take possession of the Heights, by which means we were in hopes of totally routing the Enemy from their Garrison,—we were much Disappointed in their not coming out, which entirely put an end to this plan. Brigadier Genl. Heath was to have been second in Command in the Room of Genl. Sullivan. 'Tis said he declined,—and as it is now told, reflects much on his Honor. In all probability I shall have occasion to mention this subject again; till then I leave mentioning particulars.*

* General Heath, in his *Memoirs*, throws some light upon this matter. When the council of war had determined upon the occupation of Dorchester Heights, it was supposed the British would sally to dislodge the Americans. To make a diversion, it was proposed to send a large detachment from Cambridge, in boats, down the river, to land in Boston, near the bottom of the Common. To this Heath " made a most pointed opposition; alleging, that it would most assuredly produce only defeat and disgrace to the American army; that the British General must be supposed to be a master of his profession, that as such, he would first provide for the defense of the town, in every part, which was the great deposit of all his stores; that when this was done, if his troops would afford a redundancy, sufficient for a sally, he might attempt it; but it was to be remembered that, at any rate, the town would be defended; that it was impossible for troops, armed and disciplined as the Americans then were, to be pushed down in boats, at least one mile and a half, open to the fire of all the British batteries on the west side of the town, and to their whole park of artillery, which might be drawn to the bottom of the Common long before the Americans could reach it, and be flanked also by the works on the Neck; that under such a tremendous fire, the troops

Wednesday, March 6ᵗʰ, 1776.   Camp in Cambridge.
Majʳ. Genˡ. Putnam with the Brigadiers Sullivan &
Green[e] and 4,000 Men are ordered to hold themselves in readiness to embark in the Flatt Bottom
Boats for Boston on the shortest Notice, this will not
take place but in case the Enemy Salle out upon us
on the other side.   The heavy Gale from S. E. last
night blew two of the transports on shore in the harbour of Boston, the Wind is too high this day for them
to come out in Boats.*

could not effect a landing; and he would never give his vote for it.   It was however carried, that the attempt should be made." Under the date March 5th he
wrote: "The British, it was expected, would attempt to dislodge the Americans
from Dorchester Heights.   Signals had been prepared at Roxbury meeting-house
to mark the moment.   The detachment at Cambridge (designed to push into
Boston in the boats) was paraded, not far from No. 2, where it remained a good
part of the day.   But kind Heaven, which more than once saved the Americans
when they would have destroyed themselves, did not allow the signals to be made.
About 3500 of the British troops, it was said, had been sent down to the Castle,
with the intent to have made an attack on the Americans; but, about midnight,
the wind blew almost a hurricane from the south; many windows were forced in,
sheds and fences blown down, and some vessels drove on shore; and no attempt
was made on the works.   *Some* were ready to blame our General [Heath], for the
sentiments which he expressed against the going into Boston, as was proposed,
in the Boats, and attributed it to the want of firmness: But the opinion of every
military man, since that time, whether *American, French,* or *British,* who have
taken a view of the land and water which was to have been the scene of action,
with the concomitant circumstances, (as far as we have heard) hath been coinci-
dent; and those who may in future review them, will for themselves determine,
whether the *independence of spirit and sentiments* of our General, expressed on
the occasion, merited *applause* or *censure*: For himself, he has been frequently
heard to say that he *gloried in them.*"

    * "On Tuesday evening, a considerable number of their troops embarked on
board of their transports, and fell down to the Castle, where part of them landed
before dark.   One or two of the vessels got aground, and were fired at by our
people with a field-piece, but without any damage.   What was the design of this
embarkation and landing, I have not been able to learn.   It would seem as if
they meant an attack; for it is most probable, that, if they make one on our
works at Dorchester at this time, they will first go to the Castle, and come from
thence.   If such was their design, a violent storm that night, and which lasted

Thursday, March 7th. Intelligence this morning, that a transport Ship bound from Boston to the Southward is on Shore near Cape Ann,—the Capt and Crew are on their way to head Quarters. She is ballast with Cannon shott and Shells, had some Money on board.* Our Works go on Briskly at Dorchester, the Enemy seem moveing their Cannon, whether to put them on Board Ship or not cannot say.

Camp in Cambridge, Fryday, 8th, 1776. By Capt Erving, of Salem,† who last night stole out of Boston, we have the following Interesting Intelligence, viz. that our shott & shells did great Damage the several night we fir'd on the Town,—that Genl Howe had draughted 3,000 of his best troops on Tuesday which

till eight o'clock the next day, rendered the execution of it impracticable. It carried one or two of their vessels ashore, which they have since got off. In case the ministerial troops had made an attempt to dislodge our men from Dorchester Hills, and the number detached upon the occasion had been so great as to have afforded a probability of a successful attack's being made upon Boston; on a signal given from Roxbury for that purpose, agreeably to a settled and concerted plan, four thousand chosen men, who were held in readiness, were to have embarked at the mouth of Cambridge River, in two divisions, the first under the command of Brigadier-General Sullivan, the second under Brigadier-General Greene; the whole to have been commanded by Major-General Putnam. The first division was to land at the powder-house, and gain possession of Beacon Hill and Mount Horam; the second at Barton's Point, or a little south of it, and, after securing that post, to join the other division, and force the enemy's gates and works at the Neck, for letting in the Roxbury troops. Three floating batteries were to have preceded, and gone in front of the other boats, and kept up a heavy fire on that part of the town where our men were to land." *Washington to the President of Congress,* 7 March, 1776.

* This was a vessel sent express to New York. It got on shore and bilged at Cape Cod, and the despatches on board were destroyed. About four thousand cannon-shot, six carriage-guns, a swivel or two, three barrels of powder and some coal, formed her cargo.

† Washington says Irvine. The information the Captain gave is printed in my *Writings of Washington,* III, 454.

were to have attack'd the Hill on Dorchester at 5 oClock Wednesday morning, but the heavy Storm prevented. Lord Piercy was to have Commanded,— and Genl. Howe was now getting on Board all the Heavy Cannon, Ordnance Stores, Ammunition, &c., to embark as soon as possible either for New York or Halifax fearing we should make it too warm for him to stay in Boston. On this Intelligence Genl. Washington is determined to carry on our approaches with double vigour, but not to molest them provided their Departure is speedy and they do not attempt to fire the Town. Capt. Manly in the —— Privateer yesterday took and carried into Plymouth * a transport Ship from London for Boston loaded w^t. Coal, Porter, Cheese, &c.—&c.

Saturday, 9th *March*, 1776. Three Inhabitants and one Soldier last night deserted to us from Boston— they confirmed the accounts Rec'd yesterday and say Genl. Howe is makeing all possible Dispatch to get every thing on Board the Transports ready to Sail,— Genl. Washington immediately dispatch'd Expresses to the Southward with this Intelligence, that they may be ready to receive them. It will be a happy Circumstance for us, for them to leave the Town, provided they do not set fire to it, we think they cannot get so firm foot hold on any other part of the Continent.

Sunday, 10th. The Enemy fir'd on our people at 7 oClock last Evening from Boston to Dorchester, they being seated round a large fire—they kill'd 4—we immediately began a heavy Cannonade on them from all our Batteries, which they could answer only on that

---

* Washington says the vessel was carried into Portsmouth.

side next Dorchester, which is sufficient to Convince us their Cannon are remov'd on Board Ships. We continued fireing till ab^t. 3 in ye morn^g .*

* The journal ends abruptly at this point, the next entry being written at New Haven, July 4, 1777. The British evacuated Boston in the forenoon of Sunday, March 17th, and a few hours after their departure the Americans were in possession. Sullivan was ordered to occupy Charlestown, and Putnam, Boston. It was the intention of Washington to send Putnam to New York; but the enemy's lingering in the harbor determined him to send on only five regiments, and keep the rest of the army for an emergency, or until the plans of the British were more fully developed. Brigadier-General Heath was sent on with these advance columns, and it was not until the 29th, that the instructions for governing Putnam's march were prepared. " Six more battalions under General Sullivan march this morning [29th] by the same route, and will, I hope, arrive there in eight or ten days at the farthest. The rest of the army will immediately follow in divisions, leaving only a convenient space between each division, to prevent confusion and want of accommodation upon their march. You will no doubt make the best dispatch in getting to New York. Upon your arrival there, you will assume the command, and immediately proceed in continuing to execute the plan proposed by Major-General Lee, for fortifying that city and securing the passes of the East and North Rivers. If, upon consultation with the brigadier-generals and engineers, any alteration in that plan is thought necessary, you are at liberty to make it; cautiously avoiding to break in too much upon his main-design, unless where it may be apparently necessary so to do, and that by the general voice and opinion of the gentlemen above mentioned.

" You will meet the quartermaster-general, Colonel Mifflin, and the commissary-general at New York. As they are both men of excellent talents in their different departments, you will do well to give them all the authority and assistance they require; and should a council of war be necessary, it is my direction they shall assist at it. Your long service and experience will, better than any particular directions at this distance, point out to you the work most proper to be first raised; and your perseverance, activity, and zeal will lead you, without my recommending it, to exert every nerve to disappoint the enemy's designs." *Washington's instructions to Major-General Putnam*, 29 March, 1776.

Putnam arrived in New York on the evening of April 3d. On the 5th he issued the following general order : " The soldiers are strictly enjoined to retire to their Barracks and Quarters at tattoo beating, and remain there until the reveille is beat.

" Necessity obliges the General to desire the inhabitants of the city to observe the same rule, as no person will be permitted to pass any sentry after this night, without the countersign. The inhabitants, where business requires it, may know the countersign, by applying to any of the Brigade Majors."

See the Memoir of Webb, *ante*.

PLAN OF OPERATIONS.

[6 OR 7 APRIL, 1776.]

Plan for General Putnam's consideration, to employ the armed vessels under his comnand, and which will prevent the King's Ships being supplied with fresh Provisions by the enemies of America; likewise being very useful to protect the vessels bound here with Ammunition, and distress those bound here with Stores from Great Britain and West India Islands, which are now on their way for this Port.

First. Colonel Tupper, commanding the sloop Hector, with a number of whale-boats, to protect the western shore, from Amboy down to Sandy-Hook.

Second. The armed schooner Mifflin, with four whale-boats, to attend Barren Island and Hog-Island Inlet, near Rockaway.

Third. The armed sloop General Schuyler, with two whale-boats, to attend the Inlet at Fire-Island, where vessels of ten feet of water may go in, and which is near about the middle of the south side of Long-Island.

Fourth. The armed schooner General Putnam to proceed down to Shrewsbury Inlet, Shark River, and Cranberry Inlet, even down to Egg-Harbor, on the Western Shore; near one hundred and forty miles range from Sandy-Hook; which will protect the western coast, and having several inlets to run the vessel in, in case they are overmatched; and which will be very useful to the vessels now expected there with ammunition.

General Putnam, in concurrence with the Committee and Colonel Tupper, approves of the within plan.

S. B. WEBB, *A. D. C.*

RECOMMENDATION.

WETHERSFIELD, CONNECTICUT, April 15th, 1776.

If the Bearer of this Mr. Dean should be taken by any of His Majesty's Cruisers I think it incumbent on me to recommend him to any of the Officers of the said Cruisers, for the Civilities received by Gentlemen of this Place since I have been a Prisoner, particularly his Brother Mr. Barnabas Dean, and flatter myself should he fall into the hands of any of my Brother Officers that they will treat him with as much Politeness as the Gentlemen Prisoners here has received from his Friends.

WM. HUNTER.

*Late Commander of His Majesty's Brigg Gaspée taken Prisoner at St. Johns.**

MAJOR GENERAL PUTNAM TO GENERAL WASHINGTON.

NEW YORK, Tuesday, May 21, 1776.
Past 12 at night.

DEAR GENERAL:

Captain William Goforth arrived here about an hour since with the enclosed letters, express from Canada, which I mean to forward on to Amboy very early in the morning, and beg your Excellency's particular answer in regard to what you would have forwarded from this place. Captain Goforth commanded the schooner in the river St. Lawrence ; he says that not more than one hundred men are taken prisoners, and these all sick ; the frigate gave him chase ; he crowded all sail possible, but found it in vain ; he then quitted with his crew, save a son of Colonel McDougall's, and one more, who were so obstinate they would not leave the vessel, and were taken prisoners. · He further says that he did not see a single man land from the ships that came up, nor does he believe the enemy sallied

---

* From the cabinet of the Connecticut Historical Society.

out on our troops; of this he is confident, that not a gun was fired but between the frigate and himself. The troops from the Island of Orleans, Point-Levi, and all out-guards had got safe off, and joined General Thomas.

Misfortune on misfortune. A vessel from France arrived yesterday on the back of Long Island, and came to anchor, loaded with twelve tons of powder, five hundred small arms, and dry goods. The English captain, with a boat's crew, came on shore for assistance to land his goods; soon after, the French Captain, who was on board, saw a small sloop to leeward beating up to him; it is supposed he thought them friends; he immediately weighed anchor and bore down for them, when, unluckily, it proved to be one of the Asia's tenders, who took and carried her into the Hook. I have seen the Captain; he was owned by Mr. Brown, of Providence; she was seen coming into the Hook this morning, in company with the tender, so that there can be no doubt of the truth of it.

The Committee this evening applied to let the armed Periaugur cruise off the back of the Island, to protect a number of vessels which are hourly expected in with arms and ammunition. She is a very swift sailer and draws but little water, and probably may be of great service to us in this way; this request I shall comply with, unless otherwise ordered by your Excellency.

I have the honour to be your Excellency's most obedient and very humble servant.

ISRAEL PUTNAM.*

REPORT OF THE COMMITTEE.

22 May, 1776.

To THE HONOURABLE THE GOVERNOUR AND THE COUNCIL OF THE COLONY OF CONNECTICUT, CONVENED AT HARTFORD.

May it please your Honours:

Pursuant to your Honours' orders and directions given us, two of the Committee, taking with them a constable, went immediately to Governour Skene's lodgings, found the door of his room locked, and said Skene was not at home; and leaving said Committee to guard the room, the others proceeded after Governour Skene;

---

* This letter was written by Major Webb.

found him returning home from this side of the river, and brought him before the Committee. He was asked if he had carried on any correspondence with those who were enemies to America. He answered, that the engagements he had laid himself under by his parole, he had sacredly kept ; that he had no papers but what con cerned his private affairs, which had passed the inspection of the Congress ; that he had the keys in his pocket, and was willing to show us his papers, we might depend on it we should not find them ; and if we accused him, he was an Englishman, and we must prove it.

He was asked if he knew beforehand anything of his negro being about to be chosen Governour by the negroes, and whether he had directly or indirectly any hand in bringing it to pass. He answered, that he did not know anything of it except some words that passed between William Williamson and his negro a day or two before, which he took to be jocose ; and that he had no hand in bringing it to pass, directly or indirectly. He was asked if he did not give his negro money to make a treat, &c., for the negroes. He answered, that he gave his negro a half-joe to keep election with ; and that he was not at Mr. Knox's on Friday evening, after the election when they had their treat, and that he knew nothing about it ; that on Friday, he heard that the negroes had chosen his negro their Governour ; he feared it would excite jealousies, and avoided speaking to him for fear of suspicion ; and declared upon his honour that he had no papers about him.

Then the negro was examined, who told us that one Harper, a negro fellow, first mentioned to him about his being Governour ; that he did say, that if the negroes would choose him Governour, he would give a treat of twenty dollars ; and that it had cost him five and-twenty dollars. He declared that none of the regular officers or soldiers ever said anything to him about it ; that there was no plot nor scheme ; that what he said and did was of his own head merely, as a piece of diversion, and that he meant no harm to the country ; that he had never seen an election ; understood they chose a Governour every year, so he thought he would set up for it. He was asked where he got the twenty-five dollars. He said he had them of his own earnings, got by going in a vessel upon the lakes, where he had certain perquisites which brought him in a great many dollars, which he was allowed to keep. He said he had a paper which Governour Cuff gave him, appointing him Governour, which was at home in his coat pocket, and was willing to show it.

One of the Committee kept Governour Skene's room all night. Next morning, Colonel Wadsworth and Captain Wadsworth went over with him, unlocked his door, and found his trunk of papers gone; of which said Skene seemed to be ignorant. Upon which they searched the other rooms, and the garret, and did not find it. Presently Williams searched a hole in the garret, behind the chimney, and there found the trunk; brought and gave it to Governour Skene, who made strange of it, and said that he supposed that his negro, upon the alarm they had the other day, thinking that his papers were about to be searched, had hid the trunk. The Committee searched the papers, which Governour Skene very frankly offered, and no letters were found, except one found among his clothes from Hugh Wallace, of New York, dated August 2, 1775; also found one lying on the table from said Wallace, dated December 21, 1775, superscribed to Mr. Joseph Webb, Weathersfield, which we herewith lay before your Honours, with the paper appointing his negro Governour, which was written by Nearn, a Regular sergeant, that keeps at William Lord's.

We examined Skene's negro further: how many trunks his master had that he kept papers in. He said one. Asked him of what color it was, and which he described rightly. We asked him how he came to hide it. He constantly denied he ever did. We asked him how his master came by the paper Cuff gave him. He declared he left it in his pocket, and knew not how he came by it.

We examined Nearn, the sergeant, who declared that he wrote it at Cuff's desire; had no design, but thought of it as a piece of fun. We examined Cuff, who gave the same account with Nearn. We asked Cuff, who advised him to resign his Governourship to Skene's negro. He said a good many people—some of our own and some of the Regulars; but remembered none in particular by name.

We had sundry of our own negroes under examination. It appeared that there was no election of Skene's negro but by Cuff's appointment aforesaid; and that they spoke against it, and declared they would not have a Tory for a Governor. It appears that the negroes had an entertainment and a dance at Mr. Knox's, on Friday night, after the election, and that the reckoning was about fifty shillings, of which our negroes were not allowed to pay any part. Major French told us that the day before the election, he dined with Governour Skene, when it was mentioned that Jack was to be chosen Governour. Governour Skene told him he would give him a half-joe, and Major French he would give him two dollars; and Mr. Dermott told us that he gave him two dollars to make a treat with; and that when the reckoning was called for, they, (viz: Major French and Mr. Dermott) interposed, and would not suffer our negroes to pay anything; told Jack to pay it, and accordingly the reckoning was paid, and our negroes excused from paying anything.

All which is humbly submitted to your Honours, by your Honours' most obedient, humble servants, the Committee.

Per order:

JESSE ROOT, Chairman.

NEW YORK, December 21, 1775.

DEAR SIR:

I received the favour of yours of the 18th. I am extremely obliged to you for your attention to G. S. Your humanity and good disposition must fix you high in the esteem of all good men. Yours W. S. I have not seen lately his friend; he sailed for Boston a few days ago, and was in good health.

Be so good as to make my compliments to G. S., and any gentleman of my acquaintance that comes within your knowledge. We have no news here. The October packet has not yet arrived. I find that is the last regular packet we are to expect.

I am, dear, sir, your most obedient servant,

HUGH WALLACE.

To J. WEBB, WEATHERSFIELD, Connecticut.

FROM JOSEPH WEBB TO SILAS DEANE

DEAR SIR: [1776.]

I cou'd write you a Vol. of Accurances, but Mrs Deane says she has given you in full.

The Affair has almost blown over. Govr Skeen says He will wait with patience until you come home. Thinks He is used excessive ill. He now resides at the House that was Timothy Seymour. Pray let me know your private sentiments, then the public sentiments of Him. If I cou'd contrive to get the Mony to [Pelatiah]

Webster* I woud pay it rather than hear any more abot it, tho it is realy a great Damage to me, and in short not right that I shou'd pay it. But as I said before I have some Mony by me and woud pay Him. But Where or how shall I pay it in Philadelphia can He Order it paid in Newyork? Sammy writes me they are now examingᵍ Several Deserters from the Ministerial Camp.

I have Recᵈ the Gun Locks you sent me & have done Very Clever with 'em. Pray do not fail of sending me five or Six dozen more. What Can I get One Hundred pᵗ of Corse Soldier linnin Hose at? What will they ask for Corse Yarn? Our people are afraid You adjournd to N. Haven. They do not think N. Haven as been Hearty eno : to deserve it. They are likewise afraid they may Three or four Hundred come in the Harbor and surprize You. Six Transport sail'd a report says from Boston No one knows where.

Four Men of War lay at New London last Saturday soundᵍ Norwich River. Stewart & Moffatt was aboard. It causes much speculation. Are they coming to Vissit Connectiᵗ ? Mᵗ Mumford thinks hard you do not write Him. Do not forget my Gun Locks it Helps poor Joseph this Evil Time. Capᵗ Chester Urg'd me to write You for such a Screen as you got before, only one Size better with a scieve for flaxseed, Corn, Wheat, Oats. He'll take it a particular favor. I enclose you a Copy of a Letter from Simeon. All yr family are well. Mᵗˢ Webb, Hetty & family, Return their most sincer Respects Duty &c.

I am most Aff ᶫʸ

Your friend & H Sert

JOS. WEBB.†

MAJOR GENERAL PUTNAM TO GENERAL WASHINGTON.

HEAD-QUARTERS, New York, May 24, 1776.

SIR:

I received yours of the 22d from Amboy, and waited immediately on the Provincial Congress ; they gave me the enclosed invoice of articles they had forwarded on for Albany. Most of the articles

* A prominent merchant in Philadelphia, and one of the best informed writers on Continental money. His volume of *Essays* (1791), is still of great value.

† From the cabinet of the Connecticut Historical Society.

General Schuyler wrote for I have already shipped, and will this day proceed up the river. Colonel Knox has sent two conductors to King's Bridge, to pick out twelve cannon suitable for the vessels, and have them ready by the time the vessel gets up.

Last evening came to hand by Mr. Cobbit, the enclosed letter and invoice from General Ward, which I thought proper to keep by me till this morning, as Mr. Cobbit had an exact copy of it with him; many of the articles Colonel Knox says he wants very much for the artillery.

The Commissary has shipped from this place seventeen hundred barrels of pork for Albany since the 15th of April. Three large vessels are hourly expected in from Connecticut, loaded with pork, part of which he says shall be forwarded on for Albany immediately on its arrival.

We have no lead to spare in this place. Colonel Knox informs me there is a great plenty at Boston. I have sent express to General Ward for two tons to be sent immediately on; likewise Colonel Putnam's demand, which I now enclose.

The express is just setting off for Albany; by him I shall advise General Schuyler of what I have sent forward to him. We are completing our works as fast as possible. Shall endeavor to comply with all your orders.

I am, with respect and esteem, your Excellency's most obedient, most humble servant.*

ISRAEL PUTNAM.

P. S. I have just received advice that Captain McKay and his servant both deserted from Hartford last Sunday evening; it is suspected he is gone for Canada.†

* This letter was written by Major Webb.

† "Captain Samuel McKay, a prisoner taken at St. Johns, and sent to Hartford by General Schuyler, being under a parole, a copy of which was transmitted to Congress, by him renewed, and given on the 10th day of May instant, did, in the night after the 18th instant, make his escape in violation of his parole, and took with him Daniel McFarland, a soldier belonging to the artillery, who was his waiter, and being pursued, were retaken at Lanesborough, and brought back to Hartford, with one John Graves, of Pittsfield, who assisted them in making their escape, and were all three committed to prison on the 22d instant. Said McKay has a horse, which the Committee have in custody."—*Hartford Committee to the President of Congress*, 27 May, 1776.

JOURNAL.*

June 21ˢᵗ, 1776. Agreeable to this day's orders Colᵒ Cary and myself, removed to Head Quarters as Aid de Camps to His Excellency General Washington.

Some days past, the General received Information that a most horrid plot was on foot by the vile Torys of this place and the Adjacent Towns and Villages. Haveing taken the necessary precautions, at two o'Clock in the morning a number of Officers & Guards went to different places & took up many of their principles; among whom, was David Matthews, Esqʳ. Mayor of the City; and to our great astonishmⁿᵗ we found five or more of the General's life Guard to be accomplices in this wicked plan; which was, at a proper time, to Assassinate the person of his Excellʸ & the other Genˡ Officers, blow up the Magazine,

---

* In 1846 an editorial note was printed in the Philadelphia Gazette, stating that a gentleman had come in possession of an orderly book with other memoranda, kept by Samuel B. Webb in 1776. General James Watson Webb at once wrote to William B. Reed, in whose hands the volume was, and claimed it as being the son of the writer. This request called out the following letter:

PHILADELPHIA, Sept. 24, 1846.

MY DEAR WEBB:

I intended to see you before you left town and say what I now must write. Your father's journal, which of its kind is a perfect historical gem, ought to belong to you, and you ought take good care of it.

By the express of to-morrow, you will receive it. As I have some doubt of my right to part with it, I wish you to consider it in your hands subject to restoration, and say so in a note to me. There is no probability of any demand being made.

Among my papers I find an incidental notice of your father in a skirmish on December 4, 1777, near Chestnut Hill. In haste, truly yours

WILLIAM B. REED.

Mr. Reed has confused Colonel Charles Webb with Lieutenant Colonel Samuel B. Webb, in the reference to the affair at Chestnut Hill. The journal was loaned by General James Watson Webb to George Bancroft and Washington Irving, each of whom made use of it in their historical works.

G. Washington

FROM THE PAINTING BY COL TRUMBULL

Eng^d by J.B. Hall & Sons New York

spike the Cannon, &c. It was to be put in Execution as soon as the Enemies fleet appeared, if no proper time offered before—but thank God, they are discovered, and many of them in close Custody; where, I hope, they will receive the punishment due such Infamous wretches.*

June 22^d. By express from Canada we have the Disagreeable Intelligence, that on the morning of the 8th Inst., General Thompson, at the head of 1500 men, attack'd the Enemy at Trois Riveres, supposeing their number to be about 500. But, unluckily for us, the Evening before the enemy received reinforcements to the number of about 4,000 Men, wth General Burgoyne at their head; by which means General Thompson was defeated and obliged to retreat. On his retreat he, with five officers, fell into the hands of the Canadian Militia, and were carried Prisoners to General Burgoyne's Camp. This unfortunate affair, we fear, will oblige our little army to leave Canada. When the express came away, General Sullivan, with the remaining part of our Army, ab^t. 2,500 men, was fortifying themselves at the Sorrell. We wish to hear of their safety. Officers taken prisoners in this affair, viz. General Thompson, Col^o. †

June 23^d. The Detachment under Col^o. Jacobs are to go on fatigue near King's Bridge. Att one o'Clock, this evening, a detachment of about 250, under the Majors ―――― and Livingston, march'd to rout a

---

* The history of this " conspiracy " is told in *Minutes of a Conspiracy against the Liberties of America*, Philadelphia, 1865. Also in *New York City during the Revolution*, p. 66.

† The paragraph ends abruptly.

number of Tories in the Swamps on Long Island, and to pick up such men as are known to be notoriously Inimical to the Liberties of America. Success attend them.

June 24.th The Guard, at the City Hall,. has in charge those Traitors to their Country, who were concerned in the late horrible Plot.

June 28th This Morning we hear our Cruizers of [f] the back of Long or Nassau Island, have retaken four prizes—which the Greyhound Man of War had a few days before taken—The sailors inform that General Howe was on board the Greyhound and had arrived at Sandy-Hook; that 130 sail of transports, &c., were to sail from there for this place the 9.th Inst. If this be true, we may hourly look for their arrival.* Agreeable to yesterday's Orders, Thomas Hicky was hang'd in presence of most of the Army—besides great numbers of others — spectators — he seemed much more penitent than he was at first. †

Saturday, 29.th' *June.* This morning at 9 o'Clock, we discovered our Signals hoisted on Staten Island, signifying the appearance of a fleet. At 2 oClock P. M. an

---

* These prizes were taken by the armed sloop *Schuyler*, and one other cruiser. Howe arrived on the 25th.

† Thomas Hickey, a member of the General's guard, was implicated in the " conspiracy," and on trial was convicted of having enlisted into the British service and engaged others. He was sentenced to be hung. "The unhappy fate of Thomas Hickey, executed this day for Mutiny, Sedition and Treachery, the General hopes will be a warning to every soldier in the army to avoid those crimes and all others, so disgraceful to the character of a soldier, and pernicious to his country, whose pay he receives and bread he eats. And in order to avoid those crimes, the most certain method is to keep out of temptation of them, and particularly to avoid lewd women, who, by the dying confession of the poor criminal, first led him to practices which ended in an untimely and ignominious death."—*Orderly Book*, 28 June, 1776.

express arrived, informing a fleet of more than one
Hundred Square rig'd vessels, had arrived and anchored in the Hook—This is the fleet which we forced
to evacuate Boston ; & went to Halifax last March—
where they have been waiting for reinforcements, and
have now arrived here with a view of puting their
Cursed plans into Execution. But Heaven *we hope
and trust* will frustrate their cruel designs—a warm
and Bloody Campaign is the least we may expect;
may God grant us victory and success over them, is
our most fervent prayer. Expresses are this day gone
to Connecticut, the Jerseys, &c., to hurry on the
Militia.

July 1ˢᵗ—By express from Long Island, we are informed that the whole fleet weighed Anchor and came
from Sandy Hook, over under the Long Island shore,
and anchored abᵗ half a mile from the shore—which
leads us to think they mean a descent upon the Island
this Night. A reinforcement of 500 men were sent
over at 9 oClock this Evening to reinforce the troops
on Long Island under General Green—We have also
received Intelligence that our Cruisers on the back of
Long Island, have taken and carried in one of the ene-
mie's fleet laden with Intrenching Tools.

N. Yᵏ. July 2ᵈ — Att 9 oClock this morning the
whole Army was under Arms at their several Alarm
Posts, occasioned by five large Men of War coursing
up thro: the narrows—We supposed them coursing on
to attack our Forts—never did I see Men more chear-
full; they seem to wish the enemies approach—they
came up to the watering place, about five miles above
the narrows, and came too—their tenders took three

or four of our small Craft plying between this and the Jersey Shore—Att 6 oClock P. M. about 50 of the fleet followed and anchored with the others—Orders that the whole Army lie on their Arms—and be at their Alarm Posts before the Dawning of the Day. A Warm Campaign, in all probability, will soon ensue, relying on the Justice of our Cause, and puting our Confidence in the Supreme being, at the same time exerting our every Nerve, we trust the design of our enemies will be frustrated.

July 2ᵈ. [3ᵈ]. This day Arrived in Camp, Brigadier General Mercer, from Virginia, being appointed and ordered here by the Honᵇˡ Continental Congress* —likewise General Herd wᵗʰ the Militia from New Jersey†—by order of his Excellency Genˡ. Washington.

Thursday, July 4ᵗʰ—Last night—or rather at day light this morning—we attack'd a sloop of the enemies mounting eight Carriage Guns—She lay up a small river, which divides Staten Island from the main —call'd the *Kills.* We placed two 9 pounders on Bergen Point—and soon forced the crew to quit her— by the shrieks, some of them must have been kill'd or wounded—the sloop quite disabled.

N. Yᵏ. July 7ᵗʰ By several Deserters from the fleet and Army on Staten Island, we learn that the number of the enemy is abᵗ. 10,000 ; that they hourly look for Lord Howe from England wᵗʰ a fleet, on board of which is 15 or 20,000 men ; that they propose only to

---

* Hugh Mercer. He was sent to command the operations in New Jersey.

† Nathaniel Heard. He had just been sent to Staten Island to drive off the stock.

act on the defensive 'till the arrival of this fleet, when they mean to open a warm and Bloody Campaign, and expect to carry all before them—but trust they will be disappointed.

N. York, July 9th, 1776. Agreeable to this day's orders, the Declaration of Independence was read at the Head of each Brigade ; and was received by three Huzzas from the Troops—every one seeming highly pleased that we were separated from a King who was endeavouring to enslave his once loyal subjects.* God Grant us success in this our new character.

July 10th, 1776—Last night the Statue of George the third was tumbled down and beheaded—the troops having long had an inclination so to do, tho't this time of publishing a Declaration of Independence, to be a favorable opportunity—for which they received the Check in this day's orders.†

* " The Honr: the Continental Congress, impressed by the dictates of duty, policy and necessity, having been pleased to dissolve the Connection which subsisted between this country and Great Britain, and to declare the United Colonies of North America free and independent STATES : The several brigades are to be drawn up this evening on their respective parades, at six o'clock, when the declaration of Congress, showing the grounds and reasons of this measure, is to be read with an audible voice.

" The General hopes this important event will serve as a fresh incentive to every officer and soldier, to act with Fidelity and Courage, as knowing that now the peace and safety of this country depends (under God) solely on the success of our Arms : and that he is now in the service of a State, possessed of sufficient power to reward his merit, and advance him to the highest Honors of a free Country."—*Orderly Book*, 9 July, 1776.

† " Though the General doubts not the persons who pulled down and mutilated the Statue in the Broadway last night were actuated by zeal in the public cause, yet it has so much the appearance of a riot and want of order in the army, that he disapproves the manner and directs that in future these things shall be avoided by the soldiery, and left to be executed by the proper authority."—*Orderly Book*, 10 July, 1776.

New York, July 12th, 1776.—At 12 oClock, this day, we discovered two of the Enemies ships, with three tenders, standing up for the Town—with the tide at flood and a very strong Breeze of wind in their favour —As soon as abreast of Red-Hook, our Battery from that, opened upon them, and all our Batteries for three Miles on end, till they got entirely past. They keep a Warm fire the whole of the time on us—tho with no effect—a number of our shots hulled them. In this fray, we lost six Men by our Guns carelessly. When abreast of Mount Washington, 12 miles above the the Town, Genl. Mifflin gave them a Warm Reception—but did them no great damage. Their view, probably, is to cut of our Communication wth Albany and the Northern Army—I hope we may frustrate their designs.* The same day arrived Admiral, Lord Howe, in the Eagle Man of War, and join'd the Fleet at Staten Island.

The ships that went up ye River this day, are ye Phoenix of forty guns, commanded by —— Parker, † the Rose, of twenty guns, by —— Wallace. ‡

---

* The purpose of this move was to distress the American army by obstructing supplies coming down the river, and " other good consequences dependent on that measure:" and also, in all probability, to encourage the loyal inhabitants of that country to come out openly for the King. After passing the fire of the American batteries, the vessels anchored off Tarrytown; remained there until the 16th, when they proceeded up the river, and anchored off Haverstraw, taking soundings to within gun-shot of Fort Montgomery, occasionally firing a shot as they passed a house on the western shore, and plundering and burning. They did not fall down the river again to Tarrytown till the second or third of August. In view of the ill success of this expedition, Dawson believes it was intended to tamper with the inhabitants on the river, and bring them to the support of the royal army by means other than force.

† Captain Hyde Parker.

‡ Captain James Wallace.

N. York, July 14th, 1776.—A Flag of Truce from the fleet appeared, on which Col[o.] Reed and myself, went down to meet it, about half way between Governors and Staten Islands. Lieutenant Brown, of the Eagle, offered a Letter from Lord Howe, directed George Washington, Esq[r]., which on acc[t.] of its direction, we refused to Receive, and parted with the usual Compliments.*

It is to be noticed, that the frequent repetitions in General orders, is occasioned by new Regiments & Companies daily arriving in Camp—and quite unacquainted with Garrison or Camp Duty—time alone can remedy this inconvenience.

15th *July*, 1776.—The Court of Enquiry ordered y[e] 14th to set on Colonel Rodolphus Ritzema, report, that after the strictest enquiry and maturest deliberation, they are of opinion, that Colonel Ritzema is clear of the 8 crimes alleged ag[st] him, save the last, respecting L[d] Stirling—Lord Stirling thinks proper to pardon that—he is, therefore, acquitted with honour.†

16th *July*, 1776.—A Flag this day, to send to General Howe some spirited Resolves of Congress respecting the Cruelty and Barbarity of the King's Troops and Savages to the Northward, and acquainting him, Retaliation shall immediately take place, unless a final stop is put to such inhuman and Barbarous Conduct.

---

* See Memoir of Col. Webb in these volumes.

† On July 14th a court of inquiry was ordered to examine into the conduct of Colonel Ritzema, charged with " practices contrary to the rules and discipline of the army." Ritzema at once wrote to Washington, tendering his resignation. Washington expressed surprise that at so critical a juncture, and when in such a predicament, an officer of that rank should wish to resign. The trial took place, with the result noted in the orders.

The same day forwarded a Copy of s.^d Resolves to the Northern Army, to be sent General Burgoyne in Cannada.*

N. Y.^k, 17th *July*, 1776.   A flagg from the Enemy, with an answer from General Howe, ab.^t the Resolves sent yesterday directed George Washington, Esq. &c., &c., &c.—which was refused.

July 19th—A flag appeared this morning, when Col.^o Reed & myself went down.   Aid de Camp to General Howe met us—and said, as there appeared an insurmountable obstacle between the two Generals, by way of Corresponding, General Howe desired his Adjutant General might be admitted to an Interview with his Excellency General Washington—On which Col.^o Reed, in the name of General Washington, consented; and pledg'd his honor for his being safe returned.—The Aid de Camp said the Adj.^t Genl would meet us to-morrow forenoon.

July 20th—At 12 oClock we met the Flagg, took Lieut.^t Col.^o Paterson, of — regiment into our Barge and escorted him safely to Town to Col.^o Knox's Quarters; where his Excellency General Washington attended with his Suit and Life Guards, Received and had an Interview of about an hour with him.   We then escorted him back in safety to his own Barge— In going & comeing, we pass'd in front of the Grand Battery—but did not blind fold him:—Sociable and Chatty all the way.

The same Evening arrived an Express from Charles Town, South Carolina, with the agreeable News of Genl Lee's having defeated the Enemies Fleet, after a

---

* *Journals of Congress*, 10 July, 1776.

warm engagement of 12 hours. Dureing the Cannon-ade on the fort, Gen¹. Clinton and L⁴ Cornwallis made several attempts to Land with the Army ; but were beaten off by Col⁰ Moultrie, with 300 men—'tis to be hoped every attempt of our Cruel Invaders may meet with the same fate.

This day ten large Ships arrived with Scotch Troops on Board, to reinforce the Troops at Staten Island— by the best Accounts we can get from Deserters— they contain about 10,000 men.

N. Y^k , *July* 23.—By intelligence this day, it appears the Two pirates up the North River, have made sev-eral Attempts to land, and as often repulsed—having left at different times, fifteen Dead behind them—who were kill'd by our people—after getting to the shore.

N. Y^k. July 25th, 1776.—This day five ships arrived, supposed to come from England. Whether Store Ships or Men of War, could not say.

N. Y^k. July 26th, 1776.—Arrived eight Ships and joined the Enemies fleet.

July 28th.—Arrived to the Enemy Three Ships & one Sloop.

N. York, July 29th, 1776—This day and last Even-ing, about twenty large Ships have arrived—these with the others which have come in for several days past, have troops on Board and are supposed to be. part of Lord Howe's fleet, with the Foreigners.*

---

* " Voted, that an order be drawn on the committee of lead mine at Middle-town in favor Mr. Jos. Webb, of Wethersfield, for one thousand weight of lead, to replace the same quantity sent by the selectmen of Wethersfield by request and delivered Cap. Wadsworth, for the army at Cambridge. *Order given, de-livered to Mr. Hosmer.*" *Connecticut Council of Safety,* 16 July, 1776.

TO MAJOR-GENERAL WARD.

HEAD QUARTERS, NEW YORK, July 18, 1776.

SIR :

His Excellency General Washington, having occasion to ride out early this morning, has dictated and ordered me to acknowledge and answer your two letters of the 11th instant, which came safe to hand by yesterday's post. He is not a little displeased at the Agent's * taking the liberty of removing, or rather disposing of the cargoes of the prizes without your knowledge, and begs you immediately to forbid anything of the kind again. He is surprised that, out of upwards of four hundred prisoners, only seventy-three arms have been sent on, as he supposed every man must have had his arms with him. He begs your attention in collecting, from the agents and others, all the arms that have been taken, and forward them immediately to this place, where they are much wanted. Enclosed is a list of articles he has taken from the invoices, and would have you send on as soon as may be.

By express, yesterday, we learn of the arrival of the Northern army at Crown Point, where those infected with the small-pox will be immediately sent to a distant Hospital, so that the troops from your State bound that way need not be under any apprehension of danger from that disorder. The enemy on Staten-Island remain as when I last wrote.

I have the honor &c.

SAMUEL B. WEBB, *A. D. C.*

* J. Bradford.

[Enclosure.]

List of articles, taken in the Transports, which his Excellency General Washington requests General Ward to forward from Boston to New York as soon as possible.

From Ship *George:* All the fusees, small-arms, and bayonets, shoulder-straps, gun-straps, leather bullet-pouches, hair knapsacks, canvass knapsacks, belts, flints, markees, and soldiers' tents, common tent poles, tin canteens, camp-kettles, blankets, watch-coats, soldiers' clothing, stockings, black plumes.

From Ship *Anne:* All the checked and striped Hollands, check shirts, writing paper, thread stockings, check trowsers, men's shoes, ticking trowsers, men's hats.

From Ship *Lord Howe:* All the small-arms, bayonets, and cartouch-boxes, part of canteens and kettles, soldiers' blankets, cutlasses, canvass knapsacks, markees.

From brig *Annabella:* All the small-arms, shoes, soldiers' tents, sheet lead, pack-saddles, cartouch-boxes, leather bullet-pouches, shoulder-straps, gun-straps, cutlasses. bayonets, and belts.

By order of his Excellency General Washington.

SAMUEL B. WEBB, *A. D. C.*

TO GOVERNOR TRUMBULL.*

HEAD-QUARTERS, NEW YORK, July 18th, 1776.

SIR :

The General has rode out this morning and directed me to acquaint your Honor, that on the first arrival of the Light Horse under command of Col? Seymour† he acquainted them that they could not be of use as Horsemen, on which they concluded to tarry and do duty as foot till the arrival of the new Levies. The latter part of the time they grew uneasy and refused their duty as Soldiers, tho' their services were much

* From the *Trumbull Papers* in the Massachusetts Historical Society.

† Thomas Seymour.

wanted; pleading in excuse, that there was an express Law of the Colony which exempts them from doing duty seperate from their horse. It was only requested they should mount guard, which they refused, on which the General was obliged to discharge them yesterday, altho but a small proportion of the new Levies had arrived.*

I have the honor to be with due Respect your Honor's Most obedient humble Servant

SAMUEL B. WEBB, *A. D. C.*

TO MRS. SARAH SIMPSON. †

HEAD-QUARTERS IN NEW YORK, July 28th, 1776.

MY DR. SISTER:

With Impatience I have waited for an opportunity to write You. The wish'd for day is come. Col⁹ Paterson, Adjutant General to the Army under Command of General Howe, very politely offered to forward a letter to You, and as a Flagg is to be sent in a

---

* Governor Trumbull, fearing that the Connecticut militia might not reach camp in time, ordered three regiments of light horse to go forward. Washington, on the arrival of the first division, not having the means to support them, "thanked the gentlemen for their zeal, and the attachment they have manifested upon this occasion, and informed them that I cannot consent to their keeping their horses, at the same time wishing them to stay themselves." *Washington to the President of Congress,* 10 July, 1776. A large number of the force, "men of reputation and property," sent their horses to be pastured near King's bridge, and remained for a few days, but were soon discharged, peremptorily refusing all kind of fatigue duty, or even to mount guard. As granting such exemption would set a bad example to the other troops, Washington deemed it best to send them home, "though their assistance is much needed, and might be of essential service in case of an attack."

† Although Colonel Webb supposed his sister to be at Halifax, she had returned in the fleet, and was off New York.

day or two to Staten Island, I have taken the first leisure hour to assure you of my unalterable Affection. My anxiety on your and Peggy's account has been very great. I have much to say but the delicate Situation we are in, will prevent my giveing you a long Circumstantial letter. It shall be my endeavour to confine myself to Ideas and Sentiments that will not make it inconsistant with Col? Paterson's Duty to forward it. On the first intelligence of General Howe's Determination to leave Boston I wrote you, and handed it in over the Lines. Had it have reach'd You, I am confident M^r. Simpson never would have left Boston. On Saturday the 17th of March, we perceived the embarkation of the Troops, and immediately entered the Town in Boats from the Mouth of Cambridge River. I soon obtained leave and flew on the wings of Impatience to the well known Mansion of my Sister and friends; here would be a place for me to describe the various emotions of my Heart, &c. Let your Imagination paint to You what I would, but cannot say. Our Brother Joe who had come down on purpose to see and meet You, entered the House with Me. The fair Inhabitants had fled; the House look'd more like a covering for the Dead than a habitation for the liveing. I waited on your friend Doct. Bulfinch, who gave me a particular account of M^r. Simpson's unsettled state of mind for several days before his departure. I can hardly forgive his Conduct in doubting my Affection or imagineing I should suffer him to be any ways ill treated or insulted by our Army or the Country people.—He knew I was in the family of a Gentleman who held a principal Command, and whose Sentiments of Generosity and humanity have never been disputed by his greatest Enemies. By repeated Indulgencies granted Me, he must have imagined he would have protected any of my friends from ill-treatment; indeed there was not the most distant reason for any one who had acted in so Neutral a Line as M.ʳ Simpson to have quitted his Mansion. That he differed in Sentiment with us in the present most unhappy dispute I was sensible, but had carefully avoided takeing an Active part; in that Situation he might have continued. No one would have desired of him to have taken Arms. He might have retired in the Country, liv'd in a Circle of friends without ever haveing occasion to enter upon a Political Subject. That he did not, I am truly sorry. He, 'tis true, can endure hardships and ruff it thro: This troubled Scene: but for yourself and Peggy I fell excessively unhappy. Your Sister mourns your Absence, and most ardently wishes for the day that may make you happy in Meeting. As soon as I found there was no probability of your return from Nantucket Road, I carefully pack'd the Spinnet, Desk, & book case, and other Articles you left in the House and sent them immediately to Wethersfield. In Peggy's Desk I found a number of papers and little matters, which I carefully forwarded to the care of her friend Miss H. att Wethersfield.

TO COLONEL HENRY KNOX.*

HEAD-QUARTERS, N. Y., July 29th, 1776.

SIR :

The General directs me to acquaint you M^r. Belton the Bearer is Recommended by a member of Congress as an ingenious man and proposes making some

See Mr.
Adams' letter
No. 5.
{ experiments on the Enemies Ships—would have you lend him every Assistance in your power—he wants 2 or 3 old Cannon which you may furnish him with—'tis of Consequence every thing of this kind should remain Secret.

I am Sir Your

Most Hum Servt.

SAMUEL B. WEBB, *A. D. C.*†

* From the *Knox Papers* in the cabinet of the New England Genealogical and Historical Society, by whose courtesy I am allowed to use it.

† It was Franklin who wrote the letter introducing Joseph Belton to the attention of Washington. Belton had "petitioned the Congress for encouragement to distroy the enemy's ships of war by some contrivances of his invention. They came to no resolution on his petition, and, as they appear to have no great opinion of such proposals, it is not easy in the multiplicity of business before them, to get them to bestow any part of their attention on his request. He is now desirous of trying his hand on the ships that are gone up the North River; and as he proposes to work entirely at his own expense, and only desires your countenance and permission, I could not refuse his desire of a line of introduction to you, the trouble of which I beg you to excuse. As he appears to be a very ingenious man, I hope his project may be attended with success."—*Franklin to Washington*, 22 July, 1776.

Nothing further is known of Belton. On June 21st, the Pennsylvania Council of Safety appointed John Hazelwood to be Captain and superintendent of the fire rafts, fire vessels, and guard boats under its jurisdiction. Just one month later William Duer, of the New York delegation in Congress, wrote to the Secret Committee: "The Committee of Safety, of Philadelphia, have sent three Persons to New York, in Order to assist us in making Fire Ships—one of whom a Mr. Hazelwood, with whom I have conversed, is particularly Clever. The Fire Ships charged in his Manner must, I am confident, prove Destructive to any vesse they fix upon. I have spoken concerning our wish to destroy the Phœnix and Rose, now in this River, and he is ready to undertake it, not doubting but he

FROM. JOSEPH REED.*

HEAD-QUARTERS, 10 September, 1776.

MY Dᴿ WEBB:

The Hurry of Business & an irksome Complaint (the Piles) have prevented my writing to you before. How do you do? Do you get better? Do you want any Thing from here, that I can procure you? Answer me these Questions as soon as you can. You know I take a sincere Interest in your Welfare & should be happy to promote it. Letters are come to Day from Mᴿ Deane ; he was safe at Bourdeaux the 1ˢᵗ July much caressed by the People there, especially of Rank. We do not know his Success in Politicks, as his letters are to Members of Congress, & the Genᶫ does not chuse to open them.

You gave Mᴿ Tilghman and me some Expectations you would lend him your Mare—he is so obliging as to stay here & do Duty, but has no Horse, nor can we provide him. If you can spare her conveniently, it would be very convenient to us—We are at present very bare in point of assistance. The fiery Sons of Carolina, who

will meet with generous Encouragement. I applied to General Washington to get Leave for him to come up the River; but his Presence will still be wanted in Town, for the Ships there Loading, till this Day Week, when he will wait on your Committee if you send him Notice by Express. He Lodges at Mrs. Graham's in Broad Street. I flatter myself, however, that either one or the other of you will set off for Town immediately on the receipt of this Letter, in which case you can engage him in our Service, and send him up immediately with the necessary material." Belton may have been one of the two companions of Hazelwood, yet to neither belongs the credit of using fire ships against the *Phœnix* and *Rose.* For while Hazelwood remained at Poughkeepsie until the latter part of August, and constructed some fire ships, it was Anderson who designed the two fire-vessels that were sent against the British frigates. Anderson may have been the third of these sent on from Philadelphia, for he was specially recommended to Washington by the President of Congress. "The fire-ships are going on under Mr. Anderson's direction, but rather slowly." *Washington to the President of Congress,* 27 July, 1776. On the eighth of August two such vessels (sloops) were sent up the river, but the attempt to use them was not made till the night of the 16th, and was unsuccessful, save that it frightened the enemy, who returned to New York. See Dawson, *History of Westchester County,* 214.

* After the battle of Long Island, Washington retreated to New York, and at the date of this letter Col. Webb was at or near Kingsbridge, presumably carrying out some of the General's orders.

GENERAL REED,

Member of the Congress.

were so apprehensive there would be an Action before they came, have taken Wing.

Gen. Sullivan has returned. The Congress have appointed D.̇ Franklin, M.̇ Adams & M.̇ Rutledge to meet L.̇ Howe in a friendly Conference at Amboy or Staten Island, as his Lordship chooses. I fear it will come to nothing.* Our Militia are all gone except a very few. One Regiment returns 24. I hope this will open the Eyes of every Man upon(?) such miserable & futile Dependencies.†

God bless you & give you better Health.

Yours Aff'y,   J. REED.

* General Sullivan had been made prisoner on Long Island, and Howe, in his character of peace commissioner, thought him a fit person to convey his advances to Congress. He proceeded to Philadelphia, and on September 2d, delivered a verbal message from Howe to Congress, which was put into writing on the next day. The British commander, while asserting his inability to treat with Congress as a body, expressed the wish to have a conference with some of the members, as private gentlemen. In his eagerness, Sullivan appears to have said too much of Howe's intentions, for he represented him as willing to set the tax act of Parliament aside, and to accede to the view that Parliament had no right to tax America, or meddle with her internal policy. The suggestion of a conference met with some opposition in Congress, but it was finally accepted, and a committee of three appointed to meet Howe, and hear such propositions as he might submit. Franklin, Edward Rutledge and John Adams proceeded to Staten Island, and nothing was accomplished. See *Journals of Congress*, 17 September, 1776; *Works of John Adams*, III, 75–80, IX, 446; *Writings of Washington*, IV, 401.

† "The dependence, which the Congress have placed upon the militia, has already greatly injured, and I fear will totally ruin our cause. Being subject to no controul themselves, they introduce disorder among the troops, whom you have attempted to discipline, while the change in their living brings on sickness; this makes them impatient to get home, which spreads universally, and introduces abominable desertions. In short, it is not in the power of words to describe the task I have to act. Fifty thousand pounds should not induce me again to undergo what I have done. Our numbers, by sickness, desertion, &c., are greatly reduced." *Washington to John Augustine Washington*, 22 September, 1776.

FROM GOVERNOR TRUMBULL TO JAMES BABBEDGE.

LEBANON, Septr 27th, 1776.

SIR:

As Governor Brown is now to be exchanged for Lord Sterling,* and the State of your Health and other Circumstances may leave you in a more unhappy Situation than you have hitherto been, I have determined, agreeable to your request and proposal, to permit you to return to your Family, either with Governor Brown, or Capt Walker, as you may elect, upon your giving your parole in writing, not to bear Arms against the States of America during the present War, and not to say or do any thing to the prejudice of the Interest of said States, or any of them, and also to return to such place as may be appointed, when required by the Continental Congress, the General & Commander in Chief of Our Army or by the General Assembly or Governor & Commander in Chief of this State.

If you accept of these Terms Mr Hosmer is authorised to take your Parole & permit your Departure.

I am Sir

You Obed^t

Hum^e Ser^t

JONATHAN TRUMBULL.

JAMES BABBEDGE, ESQR.

MIDDLETOWN, Septr 28th, 1776.

I hereby Certify that the within named James Babbedge Esqr hath given his Parole of the Purport, as within Directed. I do therefore Permit his Departure accordingly.

TITUS HOSMER.

* Washington had written to Lord Howe proposing to exchange Lord Stirling for General Donald McDonald, who had been captured by Colonel Caswell, the day after the action of Moore's Creek Bridge, in North Carolina [27th of February]. The British commander declined to exchange McDonald for a Brigadier, on the ground that his real rank was that of Major. As McDonald held a commission as Brigadier-General from Governor Martin, of North Carolina, Congress refused to exchange him at a lower rank. Howe then proposed to receive Governor Montfort Brown for Sterling, and this exchange was effected.

TO MAJOR-GENERAL HEATH.

HEAD-QRS. 10 oClock Tuesday Eveng

[1 October, 1776]

The General has this moment Received Information from yᵉ Committee of West Chester County that several Companies are formed & forming to Join Genˡ. Howe, and that it is more than probable they intend to pass this Night or in a day or two. I am therefore to acquaint You His Excellʸ expects your Guards keep the strictest Watch from Harlem River as far up as they are posted.

I am Sir Yʳˢ &c.

SAMˡ B. WEBB

*A. D. C.**

TO HIS BROTHER.†

HEAD QUARTERS ON HARLEM HEIGHTS,

3 October, 1776.

MY DEAR BROTHER :

I am not a little disappointed in not hearing from you by the post. I expected a circumstantial letter.

We have been up ever since two this morning, occasioned by our sentries firing on a reconnoitering party of the enemy. They then ran in and informed that the enemy were approaching. Our army were immediately turned out. A party of Rangers went out, fell in wᵗʰ them and exchanged a few shots, without damage, when the enemy retired to their main body. I want my blue cloth immediately made into a coat. I have neither buttons, facings, linings or any

* From the *Heath Papers* in the Massachusetts Historical Society.

† Probably Joseph.

other trimmings. These I beg you to forward me, or
if you think Mr. Stanley can make it in the newest
taste, agreeable to Gen'l Washington's new form, it
will be more agreeable to me, and I will send you the
cloth by next post. I am likewise in want of a buff
waistcoat and breeches. Mr. Stanley has my measure.
I wish you to furnish the cloth and have them made.
The waistcoat is to be made with skirts and full
trimmed, as the General's dress has no belts to the
waistcoat.

Should anything new turn up, you may expect the
particulars from me. The gentlemen of the family desire their compliments. Remember me affectionately
to my good sister, J. Webb, to Hetty, Jack and Abby,
and believe me, with unalterable affection y^r. friend
and B^r.

SAM^L. B. WEBB.

A general court-martial has been sitting for three
days past, trying one of the captains for not landing
on Montresor's Island ye night young Henly fell. If
our people are in a hanging mood, I think he stands a
chance to swing*.

* Learning from two deserters of a small British force on Montresor's Island,
Heath planned a descent, giving the command to Lieutenant-Colonel Michael
Jackson of the Massachusetts line. Two hundred and forty men were detailed
in three boats, in the first of which were Jackson, Major Hatfield and Major
Henly, the last of whom was one of Heath's aids, and had insisted upon accompanying the expedition. The party in the first boat made a landing, but on
meeting with opposition, saw themselves deserted by the other two boats.
Henly was killed, and Jackson wounded. A court martial was appointed September 29th to try "Captain Weisner and Captain Scott for cowardice and mis-
behavior in the attack made upon Montresor's Island, on the morning of the 23d
instant." Capt. John Wisner was of Col. Nicoll's regiment of the New York
levies, and was sentenced to be cashiered by the verdict of the court. This verdict was unsatisfactory to General Washington. "To convict an officer of the

TO MAJOR-GENERAL HEATH.

HEAD-QUARTERS ON HARLEM HEIGHTS, 6 October, 1776.

SIR :

I am directed by his Excellency to inform you that in the night, about twelve o'clock, our men distinctly heard the enemy throwing tools into boats from Montresor's and Blackwell's Islands, and that boats were moving up the Sound most of the night. About daylight twenty boat loads of men rowed up, and landed on one of the islands called the Two-Brothers.

The General thinks the above Manœuvre should not, in the least draw your attention from Morrisania, though a good look-out should be kept on all their movements; and at the same time bids me add that no time should be lost in taking possession of the hill you yesterday mentioned to him, below the gut.

I am, Sir, your most humble servant,

SAM^L. B. WEBB,

A. D. C.

FROM MRS. PHILLIPS.

PHILLIPSBOROUGH, Monday [October, 1776].

Mrs. Phillips Compliments, & thanks Coll? Webb for his polite note of yesterday, & the very Acceptable pacquet from Middletown. Mrs. Phillips acknowledges herself much obliged to Coll? Webb for his attention in forwarding his letters, & is much indebted to his goodness for the early receipt of them—Miss Phillips begs her com-

crime of cowardice, and in a case where the enterprise failed on that account, where several brave men fell because they were unsupported, and to impose a less punishment than death, he [Washington] is very apprehensive will discourage both officers and men, and render it, hereafter, difficult, if not impossible, to make an exemplary punishment, and especially in the case of a common soldier, who will suppose distinctions are made by officers in the case of an officer."

pliments to Coll? Webb with many thanks for her letter from Miss
Van Horne and his punctuality in enclosing the one she sent to Mrs.
Van Horne : she shall on Wednesday again take the liberty of troubling Coll? Webb.—Mrs. Phillips has by Mrs. Pintard sent another
letter to Coll? Webb's care—she begs her comp?s to General Washington.*

TO MAJOR-GENERAL BENJAMIN LINCOLN.

HEAD Q?RS ON HARLEM HEIGHTS, Oct. 11, 1776.

SIR :

I am directed by his Excellency to inclose you some
minutes delivered him by the Commissary; he conceives the Stores and Provisions to be in very great
Danger, and would have every method taken for their
Security. He desires you will as soon as may be
have the Regiments mentioned Posted in such manner
as may be of the greatest Security to that part of the
Coast where Stores are hourly collecting—I am

Sir, Your most Hum^ble^ Servt.

SAM^L^ B. WEBB,

A. D. C.†

FROM NATHANIEL SHALER.

MIDDLETOWN, Octo? 21st, 1776.

DEAR WEBB :

I Received your favour of 17th by Peat, and agreeable to your
desire delivered the Letter inclos'd to Col? Philips together with
your Compliments, and offers of your friendly service in takeing care
that his Letters to Mrs. Philips, (in case they came to your hand)
should be forwarded to her, for which care he will be much oblig'd

* A letter from Washington to Mrs. Phillips, dated 22 October, 1776, is printed
in my *Writings of Washington*, IV. 501.

† From the collection of Dr. John S. H. Fogg, of Boston.

to you. It gives me the greatest pleasure to find that you have recovered your health after a long and dangirous fit of sickness, that thretned to deprive me of one of those friends which are dearest to me in Life.

How chang'd the Scene my Dear Sam from those Times of Peace and Tranquility, when Law and justice gave security to the upright; and depriv'd the Villain of the power of injureing the Innocent. When the Honest man was a friend to his Country and Virtue respected for Virtues sake—when I look around me and see the altiration (caus'd by these unhappy Times) I am almost persuaded my life has been nothing more than a Dream—when I see the Man who I have ever known for his Honesty, Probity, and just dealing, his Friendly Benevolent Intentions to all Mankind, torn from his Family, his friends his Interest and every thing that can make life worth preserving, to Live in Disgrace and Exile, (and all this perhaps by the fals insinuations of Envy and Malice, without a Crime alledg'd or a Tryal had) I am almost ready to think that something is not right, and that however the Policy of States may reconcile these things, old Native Honesty must look on with Indignation at the Insult offered her, and Pity the Sufferer, and Almighty Justice will in its own good Time give to Merit what is Merits due, and follow with punishment the man who under pretence of zeal for his Country, makes the Virtuous Miserable only to answer the base designs of his unfeeling Heart. This gives me some consolation under the many Vicissitudes in Life, and helps me to support my Spirits under every misfortune my Enemies have been able to Heap on me or my friends: and I, still am in hopes of seeing the day (however gloomy the present aspect) when Peace, Harmony, and good neighbourhood, will get the better of Confusion, Discord, and their attendants, that we may again embrace as friends, and injoy ourselves in Tranquility. My Compliments to your friend Col? Cary and believe me to be with sincerity

Your friend &c.,

NAT. SHALER.

P. S. Col? Philips desired his Comp^t and to acquaint you that he sent Letters last week to Mrs Philips under cover to you which have not been received by her. The inclos'd you forward to her.

TO JOSEPH TRUMBULL.

HEAD QUARTERS IN NEWARK, 24ᵗʰ Novʳ , 1776.

DEAR TRUMBULL :

Your letter, together with the packet for his Excellency, came safe to hand last Evenᵍ, tho it would have been much more agreeable to Us all to have seen your and Jerre's* venerable presence. I have been in hopes his Excellency would lay his commands on you to have you with Us. Your Department has been damnably neglected in this Quarter You ask me a true Account of our Situation ; 'tis next to Impossible to give it to you ; I can only say that no lads ever shew greater activity in retreating than we have since we left You. Our Soldiers are the best fellows in the World at this Business. Fatal necessity has obliged Us to give up to the Enemy much of a fine country, well Wooded, Watered & Stock'd ; not only that, but our Cannon, Mortars, Ordinance Stores &c are mostly gone. Our whole Body did not amount to Two Thousand at the time the Enemy landed in the Jerseys, of consequence we had it not in our power to make a stand, 'till we arrived at this place, where we have collected our Force, & are not only ready, but willing, to Meet the Lads in blue & Red as soon as they think proper. 'Tis a sacred truth they never yet have ventured to Attack Us but with great Advantages ; they pursue no faster than their heavy Artillery can be brought up. With this they Scour every piece of Wood, Stone Walls, &c, before they approach. If they come on soon we shall I trust give a good accᵗ to our

* Jeremiah Wadsworth.

Country. This must be before ye 1st of December, as most of the troops on this side are then their own Masters. I have not time to be so particular as I could wish. Make my Compliments to our friends, be kind enough to tell Jerre I am uneasy to know where my trunks are. I wish he would inform Me.

I am in haste Your friend
& Obed^t. Servt,
SAM^L. B. WEBB

Mifflin gone for Philadelphia
Reed to Brunswick, Burlington &c
I shall be particularly obliged if you will write a line to Jos: Webb & acquaint where we are; I have not a moments time or I should now enclose a line for him.*

FROM COLONEL JOHN TRUMBULL.

Colonel Trumbull's compliments to Colonel S. B. Webb, and asks how he is. Pray forward Barnard in delivering his letters to General Washington, and get his warrant signed, and despatch him back again as soon as may be. What are you about on your side? We can hear nothing from you that we can rely on. Write a line if you can.

North Castle, 26th Nov^r , 1776.

FROM HENRY BABCOCK.

STONINGTON, 27th Nov. 1776.
DEAR SIR:

Tho' late, I most sincerely congratulate you upon your being appointed A. D. C. to his Excellency Genl. Washington, to whom, as well as yourself, I most sincerely wish success, and a whole Harvest of Laurels; please to give my most respectful Compliments to him.

If your Leisure will permit, do be so good as to squeeze out half

* From the cabinet of the Connecticut Historical Society.

an Hour to let me know your present Situation, and that of the Enemy's, and how my good old Friend Gen! Putnam does; who be so good as to salute from me.

You have had a very bustling campaign; and all I wish [is] that Gen! Washington had better Troops to command, and a few better officers, tho' he has some very good Officers. The Congress at last are hit upon the right Plan of having Soldiers by raising them during the War.

As Trade & Merchandize makes Merchants, so does War make Generals. As you are now in his Exc[ellenc]y's Family, in due time you may reasonably expect Preferment, which none of your friends wishes more sincerely than him who has the Pleasure to be with great esteem, D! Sir, your most obedient & most humble Serv!

HENRY BABCOCK.

Compliments to M! Harrison, and tell him he owes me a letter—tho' I know his time as well as yours, is much taken up in the Public Service.

TO JOSEPH TRUMBULL.

HEAD QUARTERS PENNSYLVANIA IN BUCKS COUNTY }
ON DELAWARE, Dec! 16th, 1776. }

DEAR COL?

Yours of 13th Instant from Morristown came to hand last Evening, a little before we had the news of the unfortunate Captivity of General Lee. I wish it may not despirit the people; this is what I most fear. His services as an Officer were great, but this in some measure can be made up. The General is much surprised Gen! Lee should venture to lodge from Camp in a Country where he must have known we had many Enemies. Indeed we shall find hard work to convince many Officers and Soldiers that he is not a Trayter. I do not speak of this as tho' any at Head Quarters have the most distant tho't of his Integrity, but it's difficult to convince the common people. I am extreamly sorry you have disappointed Us; you might have come as well as sent another person; 'tis nothing, only your laziness. I hope Miss D . . r will put fresh vigour into You. You ask me our Situation; it has been the Devil, but is to appearance better. About 2,000 of us have been obliged to run damn'd hard before abᵗ 10,000 of the Enemy. Never was finer lads at a retreat than we are. 'Tis said the Enemy are bound for N. York Via South Amboy; it wants Confirmation. I wish it may be true. No fun for us that I can see; however, I cannot but think we shall drub the Dogs. Those gone for New England will meet their Deserts. I hope, sure I am, the Lads of that Country will not behave in the dam'd cowardly, rascally manner the people of this Country have. Never mind, all will come right one of these days. Time will not permit my being so particular as I could wish. I wish you a pleasant journey and a happy sight of the Dear Girl. Poor Cary has got into the Limboo's, and will in all probability be Married in ten days to a Miss Low. God Bless You. Adieu.

Yours, &c.,   SAM. B. WEBB.*

FROM RICHARD CARY.†

PHILᴬ 22ᵈ Decʳ 1776.

DEAR BOYS:

I hardly know whom to address particularly & therefore you may take it all together. If I am not by this time as much forgot as if

* From the Cabinet of the Connecticut Historical Society.

† Richard Cary was descended from James Cary, draper, from Bristol, England, who came to America and settled in Massachusetts prior to 1647. According to

I had never existed, saving as far as respects promising the Breeches, Stockings, Boots, &c. it may possibly be worth while to tell you that I am a very happy fellow, & have been *really* so since the night before last. I am very agreeably accommodated by Mrs Yard with two Rooms and have everything provided in an elegant neat manner so that I have not the smallest trouble in my new state as a Housekeeper—absolutely I dont envy the happiest man on Earth. Tell the old [——] he was more than half right in his remarks & lessons—but I beg his pardon for the impolite appellation. —Mr Harrison,* I have taken all possible pains to get your Breeches & Stockings, but as yet have no prospects of success, however, I will persevere till I obtain them if to be had in the City. Mr Webb, you have no chance at present for your Boots, but dont despair—dear Sam—dont loose sight of your matrimonial intentions —take my advice—Capt Gibbs † your letter went forward before I arrived here—hope it got safe to hand—please to send mine by Cris. God bless you all my dear Boys health & happiness ever attend you my most dutiful Respects to our worthy General.

R. C.

I expect a letter from some of you.

I have detained the Boy more than an hour in expectation of two tooth brushes which I had the promise of last evening, but am now told the person has not one left.

WASHINGTON TO THE ASSEMBLY OF MASSACHUSETTS.

[1776.]

GENTLEMEN:

This will be delivered you by Mr. Gilman who conducted 7 Penobscot Indians into this Camp & expects to meet a larger num-

the King's Chapel Records this Richard Cary married Anna Phillips, 12 July, 1771, he then being of the 14th Regiment. His second wife was Anna Low, daughter of Cornelius P. Low, of New York. Wyman, *Genealogies and Estates of Charlestown*, I., 180. He was a distant cousin of the Virginia Carys, and his father, of the same name, was a prominent merchant of Boston. In the General Orders published on August 15th, 1775, it was announced that "Richard Carey, Esq.," is appointed Brigade Major, to the Brigade commanded by the eldest Colonel. He became an aid to Washington and his appointment was announced on the same day with that of Col. Webb.

* Robert Hanson Harrison.

† Caleb Gibbs.

ber on his Return. As he desired my Instructions with Respect to the latter, I have given them founded on the advancement of the Season, & the little Probability of deriving any essential Benefit from them at this Time, when both Armies are most probably retireing into Winter Quarters. My Directions to him are not to have them advanced farther at present, but to return with them and take such further Orders from You with Respect to their future Destination as you from your knowledge of their Circumstances & Situation shall think best. Whatever Expence has or may accrue on their Account will certainly be brought into the Continental Account, & I make no doubt but such gratuities will be also allowed as you may think proper & necessary. Should there be any other Disposition of them arising from Circumstances not now known I must beg leave to observe to you that this Army is so unprovided with all kinds of Woollens, that I have not the most distant prospect of supplying them with those Necessaries here, & it is so much to to be feared that any Disappointment would make the most unfavorable Impressions on their Minds. Should they therefore proceed to this Camp, I flatter myself they will be furnished with the Articles necessary for the Season before they proceed hither.

If they are to be put into service the next Season in Consequence of any Engagements already entered into, or which may be done, I would suggest the propriety of keeping them collected together in some proper place, rather than suffering them to disperse into their several Towns from which it may be difficult to gather them, when wanted.

I am &c.*   G<u>o</u> W———N.

FROM JOSEPH WEBB.

WETHERSFIELD, January 4<u>th</u>, 1777.

MY DEAR BROTHER:

Yours of the 27<u>th</u> ulto, was handed me on Thursday Morning.   I

* The body of the letter is in the *MS.* of Webb.   I am unable to fix the date of this letter save by an indorsement.   There is no draft in the *Washington Papers*, in the Department of State, and it is possible the letter was not sent to the Assembly.

opened it at Breakfast, and never was more pleased in my life. It was agreeable and unexpected news. Joy overcame us so much that scarcely one of us could finish our breakfast. Col. Knox's Lady was in comp⁷. She has been at our house these several days on her way to Boston. Heavens be praised for this lucky, happy and Important turn in our favour. Nothing in life could happen at a more critical juncture*—in every place and almost every face, you may see almost a surprising alteration—tho' no one was willing to own any doubts or fears before.

I must own New England has fewer Tories than I think Jersey or Pennsylvania has—yet we have some. Good God ! has his Excellency met with any misfortune? My Blood chills at the very Reflection. Heaven reward and preserve him. I believe Jack will accept under Sheldon.† He seems pleased with it, and I think Jack will make a very genteel, good officer. I think this bids fair to be a very genteel corps. Accept my sincere thanks for your attention in writing me ; I acknowledge myself under the greatest Obligation for 'em. Your Chest & Baggage are at Jere Wadsworth's—the needful shall be done. The Bearer is waiting, cannot add, except that I am affectionately yours

Jos. WEBB.

I shall write you by next Post—but I have not been so good in writing, on acc⁺ of the uncertainty of the times which you must excuse. Its a remarkable Healthy time, and our connections are well.

FROM MAJOR CALEB GIBBS.

HEAD QUARTERS, NEWTOWN, 7 January, 1777.

DEAR WEBB :

I received your agreeable favor of the 5th Instant, and was exceedingly glad to hear our Dear General and all the rest of the fam-

* The affair at Trenton.

† Elisha Sheldon was appointed by Congress on December 12th, 1776, to command a regiment of cavalry on the continental establishment, with the rank and pay of a colonel of foot. John Webb, a younger brother of Samuel, was appointed a lieutenant in this regiment of "light dragoons" on 10 January, 1777, and was promoted to a captaincy 1 January, 1778. He is said to have served for a brief period in 1780 as an aid to General Greene, and in 1781 became an aid to General Robert Howe.

ily was alive and well, and I heartily congratulate you all on the happiness of your good success. It is utterly impossible for you to conceive the anxiety we were in till we heard that you were all well and in the land of the living, for various were the accounts we received, and the most dreadful. We heard that our dear General was wounded, & Col? Fitzgerald* was either killed or taken prisoner; yet everything we heard, seemed to be no wise certain and raised our expectations. I received the letter for Col? & Mrs. Cary, and am very happy to hear the marriage is so agreeable to Mr. Low. I shall forward them the first opportunity. Give me all the news and particulars you possibly can, for we are in great sufferance to hear. If you should providentially fall in near Paramus, remember me to you know whom. Tell her just as you would if it were your own case, and be serious with her. You know more than any one else does, the particulars between us, & if you should be so happy I shall depend on your friendship & sincerity. Make mention of my letter and tell her to write.

> Tell her I love her; If she asks how well,
> Tell her I love her more than tongue can tell.

I hope, if matters turn to expectation, to see her not long hence. My greatest love and respect to our dear General, giving him meet joy for his happy success. Regards to all the Lads. I have sent a keg of the old wine and two loaves of sugar, and should have sent some spirits, but could not get anything to put it in. If you want anything let me know it. Tell Harrison I don't think his horse grows much better. Adieu, & believe me to be yours sincerely.

C. GIBBS.

P. S. If you should see a certain Miss B. at Millstone, I make my best regards. I have sent some letters which were left here for you and several others.†

Lieutenant Colonel John Fitzgerald, an aid to Washington.

† From the *Reminiscences of General Samuel B. Webb*, p. 187.

RELEASE OF PRISONERS.

[From the *Connecticut Courant*, 31 January, 1777.]

HEAD QUARTERS IN MORRISTOWN,

10 January, 1776 [1777].

I have it in command from his Excellency General Washington, to request you will publish the following list of gentlemen, officers and volunteers, who are released from their paroles, which they gave General Carleton, by an exchange of others of the same rank and number belonging to the British army.

I am, &c.   SAM: B. WEBB,

A. D. C.

Majors [Return Jonathan] Meigs [of Connecticut].
    [Timothy] Bigelow [of Massachuserts].
Captains [John] Lamb [of New York].
    [John] Topham [of Rhode Island].
    [Simon] Thayer [of Rhode Island].
    [Daniel] Morgan [of Virginia].
         Goodrich [of Massachusetts].
    [Oliver] Hanchet [of Connecticut].
Lieutenants [Stephen] McDougall [of New York].
    [S   ] Cranston [of Massachusetts].
    [S   ] Clark [of Massachusetts].
    [James] Webb [of Rhode Island].
    [Christian] Febiger [of Pennsylvania].
    [William] Heth [of Virginia].
    [Abijah] Savage [of Connecticut].
    [S   ] Brown [of Massachusetts].
    [Francis] Nichols [of Pennsylvania].
    [Bryan] Bruin [of Virginia].
    [Archibald] Steel [of Pennsylvania].
Ensign   ] Tisdal.
Volunteers [Eleazer] Oswald [of Connecticut].
    [Charles] Porterfield [of Virginia].
    [Mathew] Duncan [of Pennsylvania].

[John] McGuire [of Virginia].
[Samuel?] Lockwood [
[John J.] Henry [of Pennsylvania].*

TO COLONEL SAMUEL B. WEBB.

[Instructions.]

Whereas the honorable Continental Congress, by a resolve of the 27th ultimo, have appointed sixteen battalions more to be raised, in addition to eighty-eight voted in September last, and have authorized me to nominate and commission the officers for the same, know you, that I, reposing the utmost confidence in your abilities and attachment to the United States of America, by virtue of the power aforesaid, do constitute and appoint you a colonel of one of the said battalions, giving and granting you authority, by and with the advice of your other field-officers, to appoint all officers under the rank of field-officers necessary for the same, nevertheless reserving to myself the right of ratifying or rejecting such appointments; and, as many good officers may have been overlooked in the new appointments by the committees of the several States assigned for the discharge of that business, it is my wish, that you give a preference to such of them, as you know to be deserving of notice.

I do hereby require and injoin you, forthwith to take measures for recruiting such battalion, in the most expeditious manner, to serve for the term of three years, or during the continuance of the war with Great Britain, and upon such pay, bounties, and allowances, as have been resolved on by Congress for the eighty-eight battalions aforesaid.

Given at Head-Quarters at Morristown, this 11th day of January, 1777. G? Washington.

* They were taken prisoners under the walls of Quebec, after the death of Montgomery. For more than six months they were confined in the Seminary, Quebec, and early in August were released on parole. It was not till September 23d that the vessel bearing them reached the harbor of New York. Lamb received notice of his exchange in January, 1777, and it is probable the others were released from their paroles at the same time.

FROM GENERAL WASHINGTON.

MORRISTOWN, Jan. 12th, 1777.

SIR:

Instructions—Recruiting orders—and a Warrt for —— Dollars to Recruit with, are Now Inclosed to you—Copies of the Recruiting orders are to be given to the officers so soon as they are nominated, & I should think if only part of the bounty was given to the men at the time of Inlisting them, and the residue when they joined the Regiment, it might be a means of preventing Desertion.

You are to fix upon some Central place for the Rendezvous of your Recruits where you are to attend in order to receive—form—cloath —discipline and provide necessaries for your Regiment—the Recruits with proper officers are to be assembled at that place as fast as they are Inlisted—and you are, once a week to advise me of the state of your Regiment, and how you proceed in the Recruiting of it.

The short time allowed us for the most vigorous preparations will I am persuaded render arguments unnecessary to stimulate you to the speedy completion of your Regiment & preparing it for the Field— in this business I heartily wish you success and am Sir

Yr most obedt Servt

Go WASHINGTON.*

FROM CAPTAIN JOHN CHESTER.

WETHERSFIELD, 17 January, 1777.

MY DEAR FRIEND:

We all congratulate you on the Place of honor you have lately shared in the victories over our common enemy, and pray for a continuation of successes, till they may be obliged to quit the Land, or Kneel to Great George the American.   You cannot conceive the joy and raptures the people were universally in, as we passed the road. 'Tis good to be the messenger of glad tidings.   We were the first that brought the news to Peekskill, of ye Trenton affair.   Gen'l Heath thought it a matter well worth forwarding by Express to Boston, which he did.   We have such vague, uncertain accounts of these

* These instructions were given to the colonel of each of the "Additional Regiments."

matters in general, that I cannot but think that it would richly pay the expenses of forwarding accounts of this kind by Express. They make an amazing alteration in the faces of men and things.

Our assembly are determined, at all events, to fill up their 8 Battalions, if possible. They have granted a bounty of £10 Sterling in addition to the encouragement given by Congress; which, if money will induce men to engage, one would think was sufficient. The good news we have lately heard is worth £100,000 to Connecticut alone in raising.

Report says that the Gen'l has desired you to ride into Connecticut to stimulate your Brethren in the good old cause; and that you declined leaving him at this critical season. How is it?

I wish you to transmit us the earliest accounts of any actions that may happen; we shall, in all cases, be able to improve them to good advantage. So many lies circulate that we are loath to believe the truth unless it comes well authenticated, from under hand and seal from headquarters.

Thos. Wooster has lately been with me, on his road to Boston, and begs me to write you about a Grenadier Regiment he heard you talk of; and which, he thinks, will be raised and hopes not to be forgot.*

I am told that the assembly (which, by the way, have now been sitting more than 4 weeks at Middletown) have at last formed the Militia into Brigades and appointed their General officers. Great doings in Connecticut. Col. Jabez Huntington is appointed Major General; Col. Dyer Saltonstall, Erastus Wolcott, Oliver Wolcott, Gen'l Wadsworth and Col. Sullivan† are appointed Brigadiers. Old Gen'l Wooster takes command of them all as Major General. I wish and hope, that it may answer some good purposes; tho' I much despair of the militia's doing any great things, after my last summer's experiences. Your humble servant has the honor to be appointed Lieutenant-Colonel under Col. Belding, Col. Talcott having

---

* On February 23, 1777, Wooster was commissioned a captain, in Colonel Webb's regiment.

† There are some evident misprints in this sentence. In December, 1776, Jabez Huntington, of Norwich, was appointed "second Major-General over the whole militia of the State." Erastus Wolcott, Gurdon Saltonstall, Eliphalet Dyer, Oliver Wolcott, James Wadsworth, and Gold Selleck Silliman were commissioned Brigadiers-General.

resigned.*   But sooner will he go in the Ranks than submit to be commanded by those who he has threatened to Court Martial, and call'd them all the lifeless, stupid, dull souls, that could be thought of.

The inhuman treatment our prisoners met with while in New York is beyond all description.   Humanity cannot but drop a tear at sight of the poor, miserable, starved objects.   They are mere skeletons, unable to creep or speak in many instances.   One vessel lost 27 in her passage from York to Milford, and 7 died the night they were put ashore ; and they are dying all along the road.   Most who have got home in the neighboring towns, are taken with the small pox, which undoubtedly was given them by design—all this does not seem to discourage the few surviving ones.   They pray that God would only give them health and strength again, and they are determined to have sweet revenge, and all swear they will never be taken again.   Is this a proof of the much boasted humanity of Britons?   Is this a generous return for the kind and hospitable treatment their prisoners have rec'd at our hands?   Do they think by these mean, low arts to dishearten our countrymen?   Depend on it, they have universally a contrary effect ; for men who determined never to fight are bent on it now.   Write me the news of the day.

Mrs. Chester and family join me in compliments to you.

Your sincere friend and humble serv‡

JOHN CHESTER.†

TO GENERAL WASHINGTON.

STRATFORD IN CONNECTICUT, Jany 22^d, 1777.

I am sorry to inform your Excell^{cy} that this State in their late Sessions have pass'd an Act giving £10

---

* Elizur Talcott was colonel of the Sixth Regiment of the State militia, a regiment raised principally from Wethersfield and Glastonbury. In October, 1776, he resigned, and was succeeded by the Lieutenant-Colonel of the regiment, Thomas Belden.   Chester declined to serve, and his place was filled by Howell Woodbridge.

† From the *Reminiscences of General Samuel B. Webb*, p. 30.

(equal to 33⅓ᵈ Dollars)* to each Soldier over & above what Congress have given, that shall enlist during the War or for three Years,—this they say—they have done in order that their Eight Battalions might be full and ready to take the field very early.—I wish no bad Consequences might follow from this step, but I conceive it tends to depreciate the Paper Curr.ᶜʸ and debauch the Soldiery.—At any rate it prevents the raising any Men on the footing which I am sent out on. I propose waiting on the Governor as soon as possible. Perhaps they may advance me the Additional Sum they are to give to those of the Eight Battalions, if so I can go on with my Recruiting business, otherways I must lie Idle till I can receive your further Instructions. I beg your directions on this head by Mr. Oswald,† who waits on you by ord.ʳ of General Knox on the same Subject.

---

* A committee of delegates from the New England states had met at Providence, and among other measures had recommended that a bounty of thirty-three dollars and one-third of a dollar be added by the State to the Continental bounty of twenty dollars. The legislatures treated this recommendation variously. Massachusetts doubled it, making the additional bounty sixty-six dollars. New Hampshire followed the example of Massachusetts, while Connecticut and Rhode Island adopted the sum named at Providence. Governor Trumbull wrote a defence of the policy, pleading the greatly increased cost of living since the War began, and the impossibility of supporting a family on the regular soldier's pay. Yet these additional bounties added greatly to the difficulties and vexations of the Commander-in-Chief. Connecticut extended the bounty so as to apply to the "additional" regiments. "It gives me pleasure to hear that your State has come to the resolution of granting the Colonial bounty to Colonel Webb's additional regiment; and if the other States will do the same, it will in a great measure obviate the objection which I made to their granting a higher bounty than was allowed by the resolves of Congress." *Washington to Governor Trumbull,* 3 March, 1777.

† Eleazer Oswald, an Englishman by birth, had joined the Governor's Foot Guards on the Lexington alarm, served as a volunteer in the Quebec expedition, was taken prisoner and exchanged. He became Lieutenant-Colonel in Lamb's

I have the Honor to be your Excellencies Most
Obd'. Serv'.

SAM^L. B. WEBB.

————————

TO GENERAL WASHINGTON.

WETHERSFIELD IN CONNECTICUT, January 25, 1777.

I wrote your Excellency the 22^d. Instant from Fairfield, in which I mentioned the additional Bounty of
33⅓^d. Dollars given by this State to the Soldiers for
the Eight Battalions they are to raise. I arrived here
last Even^g and find 'tis not in the Governor's power
to grant me the same, but by consent of the Assembly,
which unluckily was adjourned two days before my
arrival. I wish your Excellency to write Governor
Trumbull on the Subject; otherways 'twill be impossible for me to fill my Regiment. Men will not enlist
for 20 Dollars with Me when others will give them 53.
Many of my officers are ready to go Immediately on
the recruiting Service, & with equal encouragement
others have Rec^d I doubt not I should be able to take
the field very early.*

I have the Honor to be
Your Excellencies Most obed'. Hum^l. Serv'.

SAM^L. B. WEBB.

regiment of artillery, and in 1778 retired from service, and joined William God-
dard in publishing the *Maryland Gazette*. This journal gave great offence to
many by printing some queries by Major-General Charles Lee, directed against
Washington, and led to Oswald's challenging Colonel Samuel Smith, who declined
to fight. His subsequent career as a journalist lay in Philadelphia and New York,
and he later returned to Europe. See *Pennsylvania Magazine of History and
Biography*, IV., 252.

* "The General positively forbids all recruiting officers whatever, giving a
greater bounty for men, or making them any other promises, than what is partic

FROM COLONEL FITZGERALD.

MORRIS TOWN Jan. 27, 1777.

DEAR SIR :

Your favor of 22' Inst. came to hand this day. His Excellency is much surpriz'd that the People of Connecticut should adopt a plan, which in his opinion cannot possibly be of the least assistance to that State in the recruiting Service, and must of course be injurious to every other. He cannot at present advise you what to do, as it is neither in his power or Inclination to give the additional Bounty —I'm sorry to inform you under your present circumstances that unless you are pretty soon fit to take the Field, your Battalion will be young in the Line, as the Troops here and to the Southward are raising very fast—Inclos'd you have two Letters one of which has been here some time. The other came this day Inclos'd to the General, and if I am not deceiv'd in the Ticket in which it was sent, I think it will make *you* some amends for the Discouraging news above, tho perhaps it may not to the *Public.*—I have not drawn any Money for the Accot you left in my hands, when I do shall furnish you with the Balla.

I am Dear Webb, with Compliments to Colo. Livingston

Sincerely Yours

JOHN FITZGERALD,

A. D. C.*

FROM GOVERNOR TRUMBULL.

LEBANON, 31 January, 1777.

DR. SIR :

Received yours on the 29th inst, and am most cheerfully ready to give évery assistance in my power towards facilitating the raising a regiment which you are appointed to command, but it is not in my power or of the Council of Safety to give you orders for receiving the ten pounds additional bounty granted by the State to the eight battalions to be raised here ; and that, indeed, was done in conformity to the other States in New England. You will be sensible, no

ularly mentioned in the Resolve of Congress for that service."—*Orderly Book,* 1 February, 1777.

* From the collection of Dr. John S. H. Fogg, of Boston.

doubt, that if this bounty were given to the regiment you are about to raise, their encouragements would be superior to the eight batallion men who enlisted only for three years, as I understand yours will have the encouragement of 100 acres of land, which the others will not, unless such as enlist during the War.   The land may make more impression on some than the ten pounds.   Hope you will succeed in your attempt, and I am, sir,

Your humble serv^t

JON^A TRUMBULL.*

FROM GENERAL WASHINGTON.

HEAD QUARTERS, MORRISTOWN

Feby 8th, 1777.

DEAR SIR:

I last night received your letter of the 1st Inst, and am sorry to find that you meet with so many difficulties in raising your Regiment.

I cannot request Governor Trumbull to advance the Extra bounty. That would be approving a measure which I have always condemned as impolitick and injurious to the General interest, and would be promoting a proceeding, so far from being authorized by the voice of the States in Congress, that it has been reprobated.   I am glad you have set His Honor the Governor right in respect to the encouragement to the additional Battalions—there is no difference.   Troops who engage for three years, or during the War, receive the same.   I wish as many to be enlisted for the latter Term as possible.   I am persuaded no exertions on your part will be wanting, to make up your Regiment : perhaps industry and perseverance will get the better of the Obstacle you mention, tho I am not very sanguine in my expectation that they will.

I am Dr Sir,†

Y^r Most Obed^t Servt.,

G^o WASHINGTON.

* From the *Reminiscences of General Samuel B. Webb*, p. 300.

† The body of the letter is in the *MS.* of Robert Hanson Harrison.

JOSEPH WEBB TO JOSEPH TRUMBULL.

SATURDAY EVENING, 1st March, 1777.

MY DEAR SIR:

I snatch a moment from the Crowd & throng of Officers, &c., &c. I am almost tir'd, Yet the ones I meet with are fine fellows, Jovial and Clean, but I have been quite ill and Confined to the House, but after Bleading and Cleansing out I am better, but still am confined to my Room—to ask you how you do? and may I say your Wife, at least I may say, your Good Lady. Sally Chester and Hetty Webb are Spirts, for they Chatt at such amazing Rate that I hardly know what I write. But to Business—let Mr Dyer purchase all the potash that is Merchantable and Good for us. I suppose you have taken Care of the Necessary for my Brig. I am, Dear Sir, with Comp^t to yourself and Lady,

Your most Aff Friend,

JOS. WEBB.

Mrs Webb says I should have told you to have Bro^t Mrs Trumbull with you. Jack Chester and Mr Webb had serious tho^{ts} of finding out in due season when you was to be married, and have come upon you Coup de Main. But our friend Jack is desired by a Number of the Militia to go after their Wages. Between you and me, Friend Jack is Sorry He's not in the Service; He's a worthy fellow. Cant we yet work A trump that may yet give him a Good Game.

Yours Sincerely,

J. WEBB.*

BRIGADIER-GENERAL PARSONS† TO GENERAL WASHINGTON.

LYME, 6th March, 1777.

SIR:

Since my last of ye 23^d ul^o, I receiv^d your Excellency's Letters of ye 8th, 10th & 18th of Feb^y,‡ before I rec^d those Letters I had establish^d Hospitals in several Parts of this State for innoculating the Re-

---

* From the cabinet of the Connecticut Historical Society.

† General Parsons had been sent into Connecticut to superintend the recruiting service.

‡ Two of these letters—those of the 8th and 10th—are printed in my *Writings of Washington*, V., 225, 227.

cruits ; most of those who had not the Small Pox before are now in the Hospitals : Some will come out in about ten days.

I shall pay a particular attention to your Excellency's Orders to send on the Levies to the Army as they are arm^d & cloth^d , I hope to be able to furnish four or five Hundred in about Three Weeks ; I find its exceeding difficult to arm the Soldiers : I have sent to the eastern States for our Proportion of the Prize Arms, if any are remaining there, with what Success I have not yet heard.

Innoculating the troops renders it Impossible for me to make a Descent on Long Island with Continental Soldiers, I have heard nothing from Colonel Livingston,* but have sent an Express to Fish Kill to Know what Number of Troops he will imploy in that Service, & have applied to the Governor & Council of Safety to furnish some more. They incourage me to Supply Three Hundred Sometime next Week ; this number with Col. Livingston's I hope will be Sufficient to effect the End your Excellency proposes, unless the Enemy's Force there should be considerably increas^d before that Time.

I have not receiv^d the account of Arms from McCheever which he was order^d to transmit ; when it comes to hand I shall endeavor to bring the Colonels to account for those rec^d in their Regiments.

I have not yet been able to produce Returns of the Numbers of Men inlisted with any considerable Exactness, but expect soon to make Returns with Some Degree of Certainty I have sent to Rhode Island to inform myself of the number of Levies in that State, but have no Returns. The Several Regiments in this State by the best Information I have been able to produce will not greatly vary from the following Numbers :†

C. Webb's	80	Chandler's	80
Huntington's	250	Durkee's	140
Wyllys's	250	Swift's	80
Bradly's	220	S. Webb's	80
Douglass's	200		1380

* Colonel Henry Livingston.

† These were Colonels Charles Webb, Second Regiment; Jedidiah Huntington, First Regiment; Samuel Wyllys, Third Regiment; Philip Burr Bradley, Fifth Regiment; William Douglas, Sixth Regiment; John Chandler, Eighth Regiment; John Durkee, Fourth Regiment; Heman Swift, Seventh Regiment, and Samuel B. Webb, "Additional Regiment."

Four of the Regiments by a Variety of Accidents have but lately began to recruit; Col. Sam! Webb has had the Bounty of this State extended to his Reg! but lately; I think he will soon fill that Regiment.

I am of Opinion I have not estimated the Number too largely in any Regiment: but hope soon to have certain Returns.

Nothing on my Part shall be wanting to promote recruiting and forwarding the Troops or any other Service which shall be Assign⁴ me.

I am with the greatest Respect

Your Excellency's most obed! hb! Serv!

SAM! H. PARSONS.

CIRCULAR LETTER TO THE RECRUITING COLONELS.

HEADQUARTERS MORRISTOWN, 12 March 1777

SIR:

Your are hereby required immediately to send me an exact return of the state of your regiment; and to march all the recruits you have, after they get over the small pox, to join the Army; leaving a sufficient number of proper officers to carry on the recruiting service, who are to follow as fast as they are ready. No pleas for delay, drawn from the dispersion of the officers and men, can be admitted. Every commanding officer should know where his inferior officers, and these where their recruits are; and should be able to collect them in the most expeditious manner.

You are to remain behind to complete your regiment, sending forward your Major, and as circumstances shall permit, your Lieutenant Colonel, also,

I am, &c̥   G⁰ WASHINGTON.

FROM LIEUTENANT-COLONEL ALEXANDER HAMILTON.

HEAD QUARTERS, MORRIS TOWN, March 13, 1777.

D͟R SIR:

If General Knox has not passed through on his way here, and gotten out of your reach, you will be pleased carefully and expeditiously to convey the enclosed letter to him; as it is intended to hurry him on to Camp.   If he is out of reach, destroy the letter, for it will be of no consequence to return it.

The family are all well, and hope soon to see you here, at the head of your bloody myrmidons.

I am Dr Sir

Your most hum Servant

A. HAMILTON, *A. D. C.*

P. S.   If the General has not yet come from the Eastward, send the letter to him by express.*

TO MRS. SARAH SIMPSON.

WETHERSFIELD IN CONNECTICUT,

16 March 1777.

MY DEAR SISTER :

Your friendly and very affectionate Letter dated New York, February 11th, I duly receiv.^d —which with sincerity I can say gave me more real satisfaction than any letter I ever read.   It gave us to know you were enjoying Heav'n's greatest gift—*Health.*   Long may it continue, my ever Dear Sister, is the fervent prayer of a fond B.^r —Inclosed you will find a letter wrote for you last summer while in New York, it would have been forwarded, but for particular Reasons which you may hereafter know.   Joe & myself have this after-noon given up Church to do the last friendly office, to our much loved Brother and Sister, that is to give them our Candid and Impartial advice, 'tis impartial because I am not Interested (only in general terms for your welfare)—'tis candid for it comes from a Heart that despises dissimulation, and feels *too* sensibly for its partakers.   Without further prelude, my Dear Sally,

---

* Endorsed by Col. Webb " Express to Genl Knox Cost £11. 16 . 9."

let me tell you, for your present & future Happiness in this world (futurity in another belongs to God alone) to come if possible to the tender Embraces of your *Numerous Friends* and Acquaintance, persuade y.ʳ good *Husband*, sister *Peggy* and *B.ʳ W.ᵐ* that here they may find Domestic ease and Happiness. I would most cheerfully add y.ʳ B.ʳ Jonathan, but that I know his conduct has been very exceptionable—and he might be liable to Insults. But for B.ʳ Jack & family I will be answerable, even with life. He never has been censured but for one thing—which was his leaving Boston, in preference to trusting himself & interest to his friends here.—But for this I have given sufficient Reasons to those who have been the enquirers.—If he comes, he at once collects all his Debts, sets down in Ease, and a genteel sufficiency for a country life, 'till this cruel and unnatural War is at an End. If other-ways, and he still prefers the noise and Bustle of an ARMY, and the gay Scenes of a Town without order, he must abide the Consequences. I will even go so far as to suppose BRITAIN will conquer in the End (which by Heav'n I think is supposing an Impossibility). Where then is the Money due him in this *State?* No better to him than if sunk in the Sea. Suppose, on the contrary, he comes out and *they conquer.* Surely his conduct has been so unexceptionable on the part of the Crown, that his own property will be safe. If he comes out, no one can doubt but he may collect his Interest, and dispose of it agreeable to his mind. But should you conclude still to *follow the British army*, let us make another—much the most probable supposition— that America will rise Triumphant and Rout the cruel

Invaders of its once happy Shores from the Continent, then where are you? Gone to enjoy Britain's Fall, and consequently her troubles. For God's sake, my Dear *B*ͬ. , *Sister and friend*, believe me truly sincere, if there is truth in a human being, and I declare I have no Interest in view but yours. That it will add to my Happiness to see you here I honestly and freely confess. Hettie, Joe, in a word, all your friends, feel extreamly unhappy. The expectation and present prospect we have of soon seeing [*MS. torn.*]

*   *   *   *   *   *

what he says to you on the subject. You may rely on him as a friend of the family's, and one who would not advise contrary to what he tho't their Interest.

I have much to say—the Sum and Substance I have given you. 'Tis impossible for me to give you my Sentiments now so fully as I hope to soon. Again, my Dear Sister, let me tell you to come. Send to me when, what day you will be out, & I will meet you at the lines prepared to convey Mr. S[impson], Miss P[eggy], and Mᵣ W[illia]m S[impson] to this happy Mansion. Should you conclude on this, inform the Bearer, Capt. W——s; if it cannot be done while he is in Town, and you should afterwards conclude, you must find some safe and certain conveyance to give us notice. Hetty now sits leaning on my shoulder, and begs me to write as full as possible. However, enough is said. Remember me affectionately to your good Mr. S., Miss P[egg]y, and Wᵐ. If Mr. Brymer*

---

* Probably Alexander Brymer, a merchant of Boston, and mentioned on page 48 *ante*. Alexander Brymer was an addresser of Gage in 1775, and leaving Boston with the loyalists at the evacuation, was proscribed and banished in 1778.

is in existence, tell him God bless him—his old friend
S. B. W. has not forgot him.   I wish you lasting peace
and Happiness.   Adieu—adieu.

Yours very affectionately,

S. B. WEBB.

FROM ROBERT HANSON HARRISON.

HEAD QUARTERS, MORRISTOWN, 21 March, 1777.

DEAR WEBB:

I was this minute favoured with yours of the 16th. Inst. I am
happy to hear you are recruiting with so much success. Do, my
good lad, push matters as much as possible—believe me, when I tell
you, the situation of our affairs calls loudly for great exertions. Could
we but get an army directly in the field, we might hope for, nay be
certain of the most happy events.

In respect to the arms you mention, which were in the hand of
Col? Lee, application was made for them some time ago by the Council of Massachusetts State for some of their 15 Regiments, and an
order given for their delivery. Your officers have been much spoken
of, and I have no doubt that they will do honour to themselves &
their Country. They are gentlemen, which is the best security for
their well doing.

I am extremely obliged by your kindly excusing my not writing.
You have, my good friend, *hit* upon the true cause. We have more
and more business daily. We have not time to. I have mentioned
you with great respect to our worthy Gen! , & to all your friends.
They all thank you for your remembrance & have their regards for
you.

I have nothing material to inform you of, & if I had, time would
not permit. I rejoice to hear of the capture you mention, but is it
to be depended on? You know the necessity of posts & authenticated Water Town intelligence.

One of the same name was a member of his Majesty's Council of Nova Scotia in
1782, and this councillor died in England in 1822, aged seventy-five. Sabine,
Loyalists of the American Revolution, I., 273.

My Compliments to your Brother, Mr. J. Webb, to Major Huntington, and not forgetting Chester, wishing you all happy.

I am your affec. H'le Serv!

ROB! H. HARRISON.*

WASHINGTON TO BRIGADIER-GENERAL WEEDON.

MORRISTOWN, 27 March, 1777.

DEAR SIR:

Your Letter of the 10th Ins! from Philadelphia came duly to hand. In answer to that part of it which respects Cap^{ns} Thornton & Washington, I have to observe, that upon look^g over the list of Virginia officers, and finding that neither of these Gentlemen in the common course of promotion (notwithstanding the number of vacancey's which had lately happened in those reg^{ts}) would, by several [degrees?] come in as Field officers; I thought however great their merit might be, the advancing them at once to the rank of Lieu! Colonels wou'd (considering the connection between us,) be looked upon as the effect of partiality; I have therefore made Captain Washington Major of Moylan's light Dragoons—and Cap! Thornton, Major of a regiment to be raised by Col? Thruston in Virginia, with the chance of being Lieu! Colonel of it, if Angus McDonald refuses that offer.—This appointment must, I should think, be more agreeable to Thornton than to be thrown into an Eastern Regiment, provided it could be raised, of which there is little prospect, as the Massachusetts have added a large additional Bounty to that allow'd by Congress, which puts a total stop, Henly writes me, to his enlisting a single man.—Thornton is authorized to facilitate the recruiting of

---

* From the *Reminiscences of General Samuel B. Webb*, p. 195. The writer was born in Maryland in 1745, and studying law, practised in Alexandria, where he became acquainted with Washington. When Joseph Reed ceased to act as the General's private secretary, Harrison was appointed his successor (6 November, 1775), with the rank enjoyed by an aid—that of Lieutenant-Colonel. He was appointed by Congress in 1777 a member of the Board of War, but declined the office. He was often employed by Washington in military negotiations, and proved his good sense and trustiness. He remained in the army till 1781, when he accepted the office of chief justice of the general court of Maryland. Washington in 1789 nominated him as one of the United States Supreme Court, but received a declination. Harrison died 2 April, 1790.

Thruston's Regiment, & will, I hope, exert himself to the utmost in getting it compleated, especially as Thruston's wound will render it impossible for him to take an active part for some time to come, & McDonald's acceptance of the Lieut Colonelcy much doubted here.

I have not yet seen any of the recovered soldiers of the third regiment, spoken of as ordered to this place by you ; It is next to impossible, I find, to get either officers or men out of comfortable Quarters, Issue what orders you will for this purpose—nothing I am convinced, but the breaking of Two or Three officers in every regiment will effect a radical *cure* of their negligence, inattention, and in fact downright disobedience, which is now so prevalent among the officers of this army,—and this remedy shall most assuredly be administered.

You Conclude your letter, my good Sir, with an assurance that you shall see me early in the Summer. Surely you meant this by way of joke or trial only—can you possibly conceive that my consent would be obtainable for such an absence as this? Could I stand justified do you think, in the opinion of the Public, to Suffer the officers of the States to be absent so long at the most important and active part perhaps, of the Campaign? No Sir, it is neither to be done, nor expected ; no man wishes more to gratify officers than I do—nor can any man feel more for their Private inconveniences, because no Person Suffers more by an absence from home than myself —but when I forgo all the advantages of Private Interest, and have more cause to regret my confinement, and may suffer more by it from a peculiarity of circumstances than any other man in the Service from a sense of Duty to the Public, it cannot be presumed that that sense which totally restrains my own wishes can give unbounded indulgencies to others—I must therefore inform you, that I cannot consent to your being longer from the Army than the 10th of May— that will allow you as many months as I should be sincerely thankful for weeks, to go Home and return in.

Your old Lieut. Colonel Marshall is not yet returned to Camp. I must therefore desire, that in my name, you will Order him and every other officer of the Virginia Troops, not actually engaged in recruiting by proper authority, nor on Furlough, nor on business, having written leave, and written instructions from General Stephen or myself, to join their respective regiments immediately if they went from the Army—If they are from any of the Corps coming on, to execute the Orders they are charged with & come on without delay— My comp^ts to all Friends.

I am, &c

G? WASHINGTON.*

FROM HENRY LIVINGSTON.

BOSTON, March 28, 1777.

Good Friday.

DR COLONEL:

The happy sight of you ere this did my expectation paint to me; but, alas! in vain, and I suppose now I shall not see you till I come to Wethersfield, which will be soon, as I find you will not come here —For shame! not pay a visit to the great town of Boston, and see the amiable Miss Temple—Her father dined with me yesterday, and to-morrow I will do myself the honor of sipping tea with her. Your commission to kiss her I dare not yet attempt—as yet—but as the old Proverb says a faint heart never wins a fair lady, I believe I will seal my lips to hers ere long—she far exceeds my description— *Venus de Medicis* is a fool to Miss Temple, now what do you think? Believe me I have not forgot your *wife* ir all this description, it is happiness we seek.

I have to beg the favor of Major Blagden to take your buttons for you, 12 doz. in coat, and 10 doz. in westcoat. I hope they will suit your regimentals, they are the best I could get, tho' your Major did not like them. They would have been sent before did I not expect to have seen you ere this.

Any favors that you or your friends want down here that is in my power to execute, I shall be happy of your command.

Adieu. My best wishes attend your true Friend and your wife. Believe me, D'r Colonel, your true

Friend and Humble Servant

HENRY LIVINGSTON.

To Colonel Webb,
    Hospitality Hall, Wethersfield.†

* An unpublished letter, inserted to show the difficulties attending the recruiting service.

† From the *Reminiscences of General Samuel B. Webb*, p. 241.

TO GENERAL WASHINGTON.

WETHERSFIELD IN CONNECTICUT, 1 April, 1777.

SIR :

Want of proper intelligence from my recruiting officers has been my principle reason for not giving your
Excellency a proper return before this and I am yet
unable to do it with that accuracy I wish.   The whole
of my returns amount to One Hundred and Thirty-four,
a number of the officers out—a considerable distance
from this have yet made me no returns, that I cannot
but hope my number is more considerable than I yet
have heard of.

A few days since I received a letter from General
Parsons, inclosing a circular one from y^r. Excellency to
the several Colonels in this State dated 12th Instant,* in
consequence of which I have sent orders to all my
recruiting officers to send into this Place all those they
may have enlisted which have had the Small Pox.
This number can be but few, for in general setting
aside Old Countrymen (which I had rather not have in
my Regiment), not more than one in ten have had that
disorder, and agreeable to my orders those enlisted
have been, and now are, going into the most convenient
Hospitals.   I shall as soon as possible form a Company and forward on to Head Quarters.   General
Parsons calls on me, the same as on those who began
recruiting more than two months before me.   'Tis unreasonable to suppose I can be so forward as they are,
but hope not to be much behind them in taking the field,

* Printed on page 191 *ante.*

I have and will continue to exert myself as much as possible, and doubt not your Excellency will make every reasonable allowance for the many difficulties I have struggl'd thro since my arrival in this State.

I wrote Lieut. Col. Livingston some time since requesting him to call for a further supply of money—it was for the purchase of Arms, which I tho't there was a prospect of; but am disappointed, having been able to get none,—I have now sent Ensign Verstilee to your Excellency to obtain an order for 500 stand of those lately arrived at an Eastern Port, which if granted I will immediately go or send and have them here seasonably for my men. This is the only prospect I see of arming my Reg^t. To take the field at the head of a Reg^t. undisciplined, and almost totally Ignorant of the common Exercise, would not only be disagreeable, but running a Risk of Reputation I should wish to avoid. I mentioned 500 above, supposing y^r. Excell^{cy} would not be willing to order me a full complement for a Reg^t. —If other ways & any should remain on marching my last division I will see them safely conveyed to Head Quarters.

With my most Respectful Compliment to your Lady, and Gentlemen of the family,

I have the Honor to be Your Excell^{cy} s

Most Obed^t. and Very

Hum^{ble} Ser^t

SAM^L. B. WEBB.

BRIGADIER-GENERAL PARSONS TO GENERAL WASHINGTON.

N. HAVEN, 4th April, 1777.

SIR:

Some of The Troops of this State began their march to join the Army yesterday ; they probably will arrive at the North River about next Tuesday or Wednesday. The number I am not able to inform your Excellency as they march from distant Parts of the State, & are to rendezvous at Danbury, where I expect Lt. Col. Butler will take the Command of the Party ; I shall be able by next Post to give the numbers which have march'd, & also the Number of Recruits in the State ; I have never been able to procure any Return from Col. [Charles] Webb or Col. Chandler nor has Col. Swift made one with that certainty that I can rely upon, but I believe I shall have his Return soon ; I shall send on the Troops as fast as I can possibly but a Subaltern's Command from a Reg^t & believe you may expect the men to arrive in small Detachments every week or perhaps more than once a week ; I feel myself exceedingly distres'd that the Troops are so backward & the recruiting service so slowly prosecuted. I am conscious I have omitted no Pains to arm, cloth & forward the marching the Levies & nothing on My Part shall be wanting : the Reg^{ts} from which I have Returns are at present as is subjoin'd exclusive of Officers. I don't know when, or whether ever I shall procure Returns from the other Regiments unless Y^r Excellency should give such Orders as would render it my Duty to take measures with those officers which will be disagreeable.

I am Y^r Excellency's h^l Servt

SAM^l H. PARSONS.

Huntingdon	250	Douglass	276
Wyllys.	193		———
Bradly	320		1402
Durkee	163	Swift suppos'd	150
S. Webb	130		———
Meig's 3 Com^{ps}	70		1552
		Webb	
		Chandler	

BRIGADIER-GENERAL PARSONS TO GENERAL WASHINGTON.

NEW HAVEN, 6th April, 1777.

SIR:

I have rec^d your Letters of ye 6th, 12th, 20th and 29th of March : The first Detachment of the Troops from this State will March from Danbury on Tuesday Morning, under the Command of Lt Col^o Butler of Wyllys's Reg^t Nothing has been or shall be wanting on My Part to forward to Camp every Person who is able to March ; from My Soul, I ardently wish & desire your Excellency May receive every necessary Aid from this and every other State ; I think your Excellency's Censure on the Conduct of some recruiting officers but too well founded.

I have spent My whole Time in riding from place to place in the State to animate the Officers to their Duty & endeavor to put every Thing in forwardness to March.

The Genl who commands this detachment is a worthy brave officer, and I hope will meet your approbation. A more Particular answer to your Letters I will Send by next Post.

I am y^r Excellency's Obed^t H^bl Servt

SAM^l H. PARSONS.

FROM GENERAL WASHINGTON.

HEAD QUARTERS, MORRISTOWN, 7th April, 1777.

Mr. Verstilee delivered me your favour of the 1st Inst.—The account it contains of the Strength of your Bat^n falls very short of the Condition I had reason to believe it was in, from what Col^o W— Livingston told me immediately on his return from you. I cannot give you the Order you have applied for, but have sent you one for 300 stand on ye Commissary of Military Stores at Springfield. The inclosed contains an order to send 3,000 immediately to that place. Be pleased to give it to an expeditious Conveyor. I must insist that you will not in a Single Instance abate your attention to the purchase of arms. The late arrivals will not supply the Continental Army. They must therefore be proportionably delivered out ; and he who depends entirely on being Supplied from these funds & omits purchasing all the arms within his reach, will not be greatly disappointed. The sooner you furnish General Parsons with the Return he called upon you for, the better—The Campaign is on the very eve of opening. A decisive blow at the beginning will leave the fortunate party very little to do for some time afterwards. Now if the officers in direct Disobedience of my repeated orders, waite at their respective homes in good quarters till they are pleased to think they can conveniently leave them, I must take the Field with little more than my family, & loose this important opportunity—My orders, therefore, to send on the Troops as they recover from the Small Pox, even by twenties, must be strictly complied with. None must be delayed for Discipline.—I am told that you have ordered Col? Livingston to you, to superintend the recruiting during your absence from Connecticut, and that the Maj^r is to come on with y^r Recruits. Will it not tend greatly to the completion of y^r Batt^n to detain the Maj^r in that country, & let Col^o Livingston command the Recruits in the field? I think it will.

Sincerely wishing you here very soon at the head of your Bat^n ,

I am, &c.,   G^o WASHINGTON.

RETURN.

A Return of the Recruits in the Battalions rais^d in the State of Connec^{tt} :

Col. C. Webb . . . No Return.	Swift Suppos^d	150
Huntington 280	Chandler, No Return.	
Wyllys 193	Col? Sam! Webb	134
Durkee. 163	Lt. Col. Meigs, 3 Comp^y .	70
Bradley. 320		
Douglass 276		1586

    Col. Angell of Rhode Island   240

The above are the Total Returns of the Non. Com. Officers & Soldiers inlisted the last of March in the Regiments before mentioned.

[Endorsed] New Haven 8th April 1777 from Gen! Parsons with Returns & Sentence of Court Martial ag^t Placey——Ans^d 19th

TO MAJOR-GENERAL HEATH.

WETHERSFIELD IN CONNECTICUT, April 12th, 1777.

MY DEAR GEN^l :

Last Evening I received a Letter from His Excellency enclosing one for You, another for Nathl. Barber, with orders to forward them as expeditiously as possible, haveing no direct conveyance, I have tho't best to forward them by express.—His Excellency informs me—the letter to your Honor contains an order for forwarding 3,000 Stand of Arms to the Stores at Springfield out of which I have orders to Arm my Men,—I shall be particularly obliged by the return of the bearer to hear what time 'tis probable the arms will be on; give me leave to congratulate you on your late appointment to the Command at Boston, in which department I hope soon to pay my respects in Person to You, my Letters from Head Quarters contains no material News,—His Excellency is really in distress for want of Men,—much I fear the Enemy will gain advantage before we can get an equal force to oppose them.

Wishing you every Happiness your Imagination can fancy, I am my Dear Sir,

Your friend and Very
Obed^t. Hum^{bl} Servt.
SAM^l. B. WEBB.

Maj^r. Huntington begs y^r.
acceptance of His most
Respectfull Compliments.*

* From the *Heath Papers* in the Massachusetts Historical Society.

BRIGADIER-GENERAL PARSONS TO GENERAL WASHINGTON.

LYME, 15th April, 1777.

SIR:

Two detachments from the Regiments of this State have march'd for head Quarters. Another will march this Week; I hope some time next week a Considerable Body May be ready to leave the Colony; the Small Pox had been very heavy upon them, they are Much reduc'd by it, and about Twenty have fail'd; this is one Reason of the delay. About 150 from Rhode Island and some from Massachusetts Bay are on their March to join your Excellency. The Languor which had seized almost all Ranks of People has Induc'd me to apply again to the Govn'r & Council of this State, for adopting some Measures, which would furnish our Quota for the present, when I am Sensible men were never more wanted; and have procured the Order contained in the inclos'd Proclamation; I think this must have the effect to fill our Regiments till Jan 7, & I believe will nearly fill up ye I[n]listments for the war. The Quotas assign'd Each Town include the Nine and one half Battalions tho ye Expression in the Proclamation extends Only to the eighth, but 'tis the Intention of the Council that ye Draft shall be Suff't to fill all; They had their particular Reasons for wording ye order as they have—a Doubt arises with me about Cloathing any of the Troops which ingage till Jan'y only: if the Year is suppos'd to expire by that Time, & ye Army are again to receive 20 Dollars in Cloathing, perhaps, it may be as reasonable to give the Cloathing to these Soldiers as Others, if not, shall they have such proportion of ye Cloaths as their Service will bear to the year? Arms I suppose will be Delivered to them indiscriminately with Others.

I have Order'd all the Recruits lately Inlisted, who have not had the Small pox, to Danbury where I shall Order those who are Detach'd in pursuance of the Inclos'd proclamation & resolve; as I suppose a Hospital open'd in that neighborhood, will be Suff't to innoculate those who Chuse to Receive the Small Pox, & the Convalescents will be a Security to our Magazine of Provisions, which is at present unguarded. On the Desire of the Gov'r & Council I have sent for 3000 Stands of Arms from Portsmouth which I suppose are arriv'd at Norwich, these with about 800 arms Rec'd at Peekskill & what can be furnish'd in this State, I hope will Arm our Troops; As these arms arriv'd since y'r Excellency's Directions to me to receive the States proportion of the public Arms, which were not forwarded to Camp, I entertained some Doubt about My Right to order them; however as they are of absolute necessity for the troops and ordering them here would be on their way to Camp if not put into the hands of our Troops, I ventured on ye advice of the Council to give the Order, if your excellency direct that any part of them shall be sent, I shall immediately Order them on; but if our Troops are rais^d (which I think will be nearly decided next week) we cannot possibly arm them without these are detain'd for that use.—The Soldiers who were prisoners in N. York are many of them in distress, for their Wage and the Friends of ye deceas^d Soldiers are calling for their pay; it will be attended with Difficulty in every Instance, to ascertain the time of their Death; and perhaps an abstract of the pay of all the prisoners, who are come out, or Dead, cannot be made at one Time; with any certainty; would it not be best either to send a Sum of Money to the several States for the payment of these debts, or that the several States should pay off those Soldiers belonging to their own State & be Reimbursed the time they advance? Some of the privates who came out on Parole are still scrupulous about ingaging in the Service until they are discharg^d I understand there are confin'd in this State, a number of Inlisted Tories, taken at Hackensack & other places, if they or any other Soldiers could be sent into N. York in exchange for those of our men who are out on Parole & will Inlist again I cant but think it would be preferable to Shuting out those from our own Service who by their Sufferings are prepar'd to be the bravest & best soldiers.

Some few of the Recruits decline having the Small Pox by Innoculation.   These I have sent forward as I suppose it is not your excellency's Intention to compell any one against their will to receive that disease.

I have yet had no Return from Col. C. Webb, or Chandlers Reg^{ts} the numbers by the last Returns from the other Reg^{ts} are annex^d

Huntingdon	301	C. C. Webb—no Return.		
Wyllys	200	Col. Chandler, no Return.		
Durkee	170			———
Bradley	320			1756
Douglass	290	Webb & Chandler say		200
Swift	270			———
S. Webb	134			1956
Lt. Col. Meigs	71			

Inclos^d^ are two sentences of a Genl. C. Martial ; the lenity shewn them by our Officers, I fear will prove of Pernicious effect, I am Inform^d^ the Court were very far from being unanimous in their Opinion.

Monies for the purchase of arms ; for the Hospital ; & many other purposes ; is much wanted ; if your Excellency, would Order 2000 or 3000 Dollars to me for these purposes, it would enable me to furnish those persons, employ^d^ in a more satisfactory manner. I am Informed forty-one Sail of Ships, 1 Skow, and 3 brigs, passed by for N. York—the Day before yesterday.

I am with Esteem,

Y^r^ Excell^cys^ most ob^t^ H. Servt.

Saml H. Parsons.

FROM ROBERT TEMPLE TO GENERAL WASHINGTON.

Ten Hills, April 21^t^, 1777.

Dear Sir :

This will be delivered you, by my good friend Mr. Russell, who is kind enough to take Charge of a letter, & an acco^t^ to General Mifflin, Quarter Master General, as that goes open for your perusal. I will not trouble you, upon the matter, farther than to beg your Excellency's Influence in procuring me, that Relief, which you, may think, I deserve. Believe me, Sir, I would not live longer, (than I can help) in sight of a once Idolized spot, where there is not the least Vestige of my Fathers, or my own, Industry to be seen, no not for a Thousand Guineas a year. It is too much for me, I must remove to some part of the World, where I can forget what I have been. Mr. Russell knows to what Straits, this horrid unnatural War, has reduced me, and my poor family, every one of whom, desire to be cordially rememberd to you, & Mrs Washington. Will not Gracious Heaven, In Mercy, to poor mankind, incline the hearts of Britain, and America, to a just accomidation, can powder and Ball, ever procure a permanent Peace, with all Submission, I think not. That Heaven may screen your Excellency, from every harm, is the Sincere wish of

Your Respectful Humble Servant

R^t^ Temple.*

To Gen'l Washington.

* "Captain Robert Temple came over in 1717, with a number of Scotch-Irish

BRIGADIER-GENERAL PARSONS TO GENERAL WASHINGTON.

HARTFORD, 11th of May, 1777.

DEAR GENERAL:

The 5th Inst I was honor'd with the rect of ye letter of ye 23d of Aprl I have order'd all the Troops in this State who are of ye Continental Army to N. Haven, & Danbury; in the western Parts of this State; Govr Trumbull desires me to post them there until he shall receive an answer to a letter he has sent your Excellency, respecting the Defence of this State, As their march to Peekskill, if they should be Order'd there will be very little retarded by it; I have directed their rendezvous at those two Places, & shall order them to New Haven, westward on the Sea Coast; & hope the Governor will soon receive yr Excellency's Answer, so that I may be able to give satisfaction to you & him.

I cannot think a Descent on the Coast of this State, very probable unless it be to distract our attention from some Capital attempt on the Post near North River, or some other Place of More Consequence, than the possession of any Post within this State; however of this your Excellency has the best means of judging. The Draft

emigrants. He was undoubtedly a descendant of Sir Thomas Temple, of Stowe, baronet, probably through his third son, the Rev. Dr. Thomas Temple, of Dublin, who had a son Thomas. Robert Temple married here Mehitable Nelson, who was grand-daughter of Robert Nelson, by Mary, daughter of Sir John Temple of Staunton-Barry. Captain Temple owned the Ten-Hills Farm. His children were Robert Temple, who married the daughter of Governor Shirley, and had three daughters,—one married to Christopher Temple Emmett, and another to Hans Blackwood, Lord Dufferin,—John Temple, and William Temple." *William H. Whitmore*, in *Winsor's Memorial History of Boston*, II, 540.

During the siege of Boston, Sullivan had raised some redoubts at Ten Hills farm, to protect his post on Plowed Hill (Mount Benedict) from assault on the Mystic side. On March 15th, 1776, Joseph Reed wrote to Washington of the arrival at New York of a packet from England, "and in her came passenger Mr. Robert Temple (owner of the late beautiful farm below our lines); he came to town [Philadelphia] last night. The report is that in papers under his buttons he has brought a letter from Arthur Lee, advising that the commissioners were coming out, instructed to settle the dispute; to get from us as much as they can: but if peace cannot be had on their terms, to make it on ours." This view of the commissioners' powers was found to be based more upon Temple's conjectures, than upon any certain authority. In August, 1776, "Lord Howe asked permission for a Mr. Robert Temple to come on shore, which has been granted." Reed, *Life of Joseph Reed*, I, 217.

ordered by the Governor & Council I fear has not been so effectual as I hop'd ; but the number of Recruits added by that measure is not yet fully known.   There are but few (as I am yet able to learn) who have Inlisted to the first of Jan'y only, most have ingaged during the War ; I have not had Certain Returns from all the Regiments, but as nearly as I can find the 3^d of May Non-commissioned officers and Soldiers were as follows :

Huntington's	 480	S. Webb's	200
C. Webb's.	 220	Lt. Col. Meigs	92
Durkee's	 299		———
Douglass'	 320		2821
Swift's	 300	Officers	· 374
Wyllys's	. . . . . . ——— 292		———
Chandler's	 268	Totals	·3195
Bradly's	 350		

On this view of the matter I have come to this Place, where the General Assembly are now Sitting, to indeavor to procure the Assembly to Pursue some decisive Measure to fill up the Quota of this State immediately : and I think there are fair prospects of their adopting Measures which will not fail of accomplishing My hopes ; at present I dont know that I can do more service in any way than by remaining here till they have gone thro their proposals for raising the Levies : Perhaps those who are still to be innoculated will be a sufficient security to this Coast if posted there in their Convalescent State.   Some of the Posts of the Enemy on Long Island I think might be surpris^d with very little Danger of Loss : if our Condition is such as we can spare a few Hundred of our Troops, for the purpose, there appears from the Situation of our Prisoners a pretty good Prospect of Succeeding in an attempt to retake & bring them off, if this should be thot proper the Measure should be adopted y^r opinion of the propriety of Bringing them off & Direction therein I shall be happy in Receiving—I shall apply to the Assembly for adopting the mode of paying the prisoners which y^r excellency has advis^d I hope they will pursue it.   I have not received the Monies sent by Col. Lee & cannot hear that he has pass^d through this State ; & therefore suppose he has been detain^d in New York or New Jersey & not yet come forward.

The Descent of the Enemy on this Coast and Subsequent Death of General Wooster has prevented the execution of Wm Stone; the Warrant for his Execution is still in My Hands. As tis sign^d by your Excellency I cannot make the necessary Alterations therein without your Directions, which I should be glad to receive and obey,

I am with the greatest Esteem,

Y^r Excellency's obed^t h^b Ser^t

SAM^t H. PARSONS.

BRIGADIER-GENERAL PARSONS·TO GENERAL WASHINGTON.

HARTFORD, 15th May, 1777.

SIR:

I have rec^d yours of ye 7th Inst. & have ordrd all the Troops who have had the Small Pox and are able to march to Peeks Kills, by the numb^r wanting still to Compleat our Battalions with those who have not yet been thro' ye Small Pox tis probable we shall soon have two or three Thousand Men who have not had that disease. As I believe our Quota will be rais^d soon in this advanc^d Season, will it be best to proceed any further in Innoculating the Troops? I have rec^d a Request from the Govr & Council of this State a Copy whereof I herewith send you; As I could not Comply with their Desire without your Excellency's Direction I have stayed those, only, who have not had the Small Pox or are in a Convalescent State; I wish to receive y^r ord^{rs} respecting this matter; In the mean time I shall continue to order all the able Bodied Men who have had the Small pox to Peeks Kills.

The Gen^{ll} Assembly have pass^d a Resolve which I think will not fail to procure our Men within Twenty Days. If I can get a Copy of the Act I shall send it by Col^n Palfry.

The last Returns I had are as Follows:

12th May,	Huntington's . .	480	13th May, C. Webb	257
13 " "	Bradly.	444	13 " " Lt. Col. Meigs .	110
1 " "	Swift	369		—
6 " "	Chandler . . .	297		2851
10 " "	Durkee	318	Col^n Douglass supp^d . . .	400
13 " "	S. Webb. . . .	205		—
15 " "	Wyllys	371		3251

This with the addition of the Officers makes us more than one half our Quota ; the prospects of Speedily compleating the Battalions are good. Nothing on my part shall be omitted which can forward this service.

Thirteen Transports have gone to New Port ; there is no Certainty of Troops being on board ; from the Information we have here, we have no Reason to believe any Considerable number have gone from thence to New York. I have no great apprehensions of a Descent on our Coast, but think we may make some on theirs to advantage.

I am y.ʳ Excellency's Ob.ᵗ H.ᵇˡ Ser.ᵗ

SAM.ᴸ H. PARSONS.

TO GENERAL WASHINGTON.

WETHERSFIELD IN CONNECTICUT, 19ᵗʰ May, 1777.

My returns up to the 16ᵗʰ Instant amount to 234 Including Dead & Deserted; upwards of 50 have already March.ᵈ for Peeks-Kill agreeable to orders received from Brigadier General Parsons, the others I shall forward on as they leave the Hospital. The Assembly of this State are now sitting—and are adopting very Spirited Measures for immediately filling the Nine and a half Battalions, as Your Excellency will see by the enclosed Act.

I have the Honor to be with Much Esteem Your Excellencies

Most obed.ᵗ Serv.ᵗ

SAM.ᴸ B. WEBB.

FROM GENERAL WASHINGTON.

HEAD QUARTERS, MORRIS TOWN, MAY 24ᵗʰ, 1777.

DEAR SIR:

I have received your favour of the 19ᵗʰ instant, in which you inform me, that by the last returns your Regiment amounted to 234, including dead and deserted. This is rather an unsatisfactory account of the matter, and admits the supposition of a very large as well as a small part coming under this description. I should be glad you would be more explicit in your next, and furnish me with as exact a return, as circumstances will permit, of the true state of your Regiment.

I am happy that the Assembly are exerting themselves to complete their quota, and I hope you will employ all your industry to bring your corps, as fast as possible, into the field.

I am, with regard, yours, &c.,

G⁰. WASHINGTON.

FROM MRS. DEANE.*

DEAR SAMMY:

I receivᵈ your very kind letter pᵣ poste wherein you acquaint me of an oppertunity to Dispose of my Carriage, which I am Determinᵈ to Embrace if it Can be Done to advantage, notwithstanding I have from Mᵣ Deane his perticular Desire not to Part with itt ; however I will hazard his Displeasure on the Occation as the Mony will alway purchase one as good if He think it necessary—but to the point, the Phaeton Coste Eighty Six pounds philadelphia Currency, and as I mean not to Set a price that is not likely to be Complyᵈ with, so neither should I be wiling to part with it For less than the Full Value. perhaps the General would give Sixty lawful, in Short it Cant be worth much less, but as Barny will be with you when this Coms to hand, wish you to Confer with Him and I will Confirm and Acquiess in what Both of you shall Judge most For my Interest—I am glad the lady you mentionᵈ is on the Recovery and I Dare Say under the Care and Inspection of So tender A master She (or any other lady) might Feele Her Drooping Spirits Revive Very Soon—I Expect to hear Ere long you have taken her on your account at the price I offerd or that you have Sold her For twenty Pounds in Either Case the Grey mare aught to be worth the money I am Dear Sammy wishing you health and happiness your Very affectionate Friend

ELIZABETH DEANE.†

* Second wife of Silas Deane, and step-mother of Colonel Webb.

† From the cabinet of the Connecticut Historical Society. It is without date, but must have been written before April, 1777. Mrs. Deane was a daughter of

Dear Sammey

I recd your very kind letter 1st poste wherein you acquaint me of an opportunity to Dispose of my Carriage, which I am Determin'd to Embrace if it can be Done to advantage, notwithstanding I have from Mr Deane his particular Desire not to Part with it. however I will hazard his Displeasure on the Occation as the Mony will always purchase one as good if He thinks it necessary —— but to the point, the Phaeton Coste Eighty Six pounds philadelphia Currency ~~~~~~ ~~~~~~ and as I mean not to Set a price that is not likely to be Comply'd with, So neither should I be willing to Part with it For less than the Full Value perhaps the General would give Sixty lawful, in short it Can't be worth much less, but as Barny will be with you when this Comes to hand, wish you to Confer with Him and I will Confirm and acquiesce in what Both of you Shall Judge most For my Interest — I am glad the lady you mention is on the Recovery and I Dare Say under the Care and Inspection of So tender a matron She (or any other lady) might Feel Her Drooping Spirits Revive very Soon —— I Expect to hear Ere long you have taken her on your account at the price Sofold or that you have Sold her For twenty Pounds in Either Case the Grey mare aught to be worth the mony I am Dear Sammey wishing you health and happiness your very affectionate Friend Elizabeth Deane

TO GENERAL WASHINGTON.

WETHERSFIELD (IN CONNECTICUT), June 8, 1777.

At the time I last wrote to your excellency it was impossible for me to ascertain the exact number of the Dead and Deserted of my Regiment,—since which I have been thro the different parts of the State promoting (as far as was in my power) the recruiting service, —and am happy in informing your Excellency that the officers of my Regiment in general have exerted themselves to their utmost.—My returns of yesterday are 282—Deserted XI, Dead 14, March'd for Peeks Kill 110—Another detachment of about 40 will march from this in two days,—the others I shall press forward as fast as possible; my Lieut' Colo. with two Captains and a proportion of subalterns are with the Men at Peekskill. Major Huntington I should immediately order on, but that I think for a little time he can be of much more service to me in the Country, than he can be (with so small a proportion of Men) in the Camp. I am in hopes soon to have a considerable addition to my Regiment.

Colonel Gurdon Saltonstall of New London, who was a prominent and active patriot, and in 1776, at the age of sixty-eight, marched with nine companies of Connecticut militia to Westchester county. He received the rank of Brigadier-General, and after the Revolution became the first State collector of customs at New London. He died in Norwich at the house of his son-in law, Thomas Mumford, 19 September, 1785. Mrs Deane never saw her husband after his visit to Wethersfield on the rising of the first Congress, and died while he was abroad. In the Wethersfield church-yard her head-stone stands, of modern make, bearing the simple inscription :

MRS.

ELIZABETH DEANE

DIED

June 9th 1777

aged 35.

Many of my officers are anxious to be ordered to Camp, but I cannot see the propriety of haveing so large proportion of officers there without men; I shall follow my present plan (unless otherwise directed by your excellency) which is to send one Captain, two Lieutenants, and one Ensign to every 64 men—Non commissioned officers included, those men that have marched, are well cloathed and accoutred.   Frocks to cover their uniform will soon be on from Boston.   Had I not met with many disappointments from the Agents, they would have been here before the troops march'd. Col. Sheldon has equiped between 70 & 100 men. He desires me to inform you they will set off for Peeks Kill the 10th Instant.   All the Regiments of [   ] raising in this State (save mine) have taken a Number of Negros into the service.   I hope my conduct in refusing them (though many have applied) will be approved of.   I am &c.

S. B. WEBB.

FROM GENERAL WASHINGTON.

CAMP AT MIDDLEBROOK, June 7th, 1777.

DR SIR:

By Mr Turnbull, who is just past this for Philadelphia, I am informed that you have lately drawn 500 Hunting shirts—500 Waistcoats—and 500 Overalls, in addn to the cloathing you obtained some time ago.   By a late return from Genl Putnam, who comds at Peekskill, dated the 31st ulto., it appears that of your Regiment, he has only 21 men at that Post—and, by a Return from Genl Parsons of the 13th of ye same M., it further appears that the whole strength of your Regiment was only 205 Rank and file ;—What is the meaning of all this?—and in what point of view am I to consider such proceedings?   Can you conceive it necessary that your Regiment is to have one Suit for parade and another to march to New Haven? Present appearances render it doubtful whether they will ever get further, or intend to leave the State of Connecticut—and, more than all this, can you think it justifiable to keep 200 and odd spare Suits by them when a numbr of poor fellows, who have been doing hard duty in the Field, have scarcely cloathing to cover their nakedness, and many of them rendered unfit for duty for want thereof, whilst the Clothier Genl knows not where to provide them.

I am sorry you oblige me to tell you in plain terms that this conduct is highly offensive to me, and you are hereby enjoined to proceed, with every man of your Regiment fit for duty, immediately to Peekskill, leaving the necessary officers, with proper Instructions to Recruit to your Establishmt

You are to carry all the cloathing to Peekskill that the Troops there may be benefitted by the superfluity of your Regimt

I well remember that you, to obviate My objections to Cloathing your men in red, propos'd Hunting shirts as a covering ; but I then observed that this could not be expected at the Public expense, nor had I any conception that you could have entertain'd the most distant thought of drawing these things from the Public Stores, where you must have known how difficult a matter it is to provide for the large demands of the Army.

It is with pain I have been induced to express My self in a language so pointed ; but your own reflection will convince you that I have but too much reason.

In am, with regard, Dr Sir, your most obed. servt .*

G? WASHINGTON.

---

* Webb's reply to this letter is not to be found; but the subject must have been satisfactorily explained, as we find that Washington gives an order on the Quartermaster-General for so much clothing as will be needed for one regiment—an order that could not have issued had Webb been guilty of what the General charged against him. See *Memoir*.

TO MRS. SIMPSON.

WETHERSFIELD IN CONNECTICUT, June 13th 1777.

MY DEAR SISTER:

I should have wrote you last week by our Brother Joe, but could not tell whether he would be admitted to go in,—however before this I suppose he is with you. And we remain in anxious hope that our B^r yourself and Peggy will come out to your many friends, —they are well and wish much to see You,—this goes by a Serjant of the 55th Regiment who was taken at Princetown; he has a furlow for sixteen days—I have requested him to call and deliver this letter; should you not come out I hope to hear from you by his return—Your friends here, and at the Mansion House in Broad Street desire to be affectionately remembered —wishing you & family Health and Happiness—I am your friend &

Affect. Brother.

SAM. B. WEBB.*

MRS. SIMPSON.

FROM THOMAS MIFFLIN.

HEADQUARTERS, June 28th, 1777.

Col. Webb has his Excellency's, General Washington's Orders to appropriate so much of the scarlet cloathing, taken from the Enemy at Sea, as will be sufficient to cloath one Regiment. The said cloathing to be set apart for his Reg^t

THOMAS MIFFLIN,

Q. M. G.

* Addressed: "Enquire of Mr. Hugh Wallace in Queen Street [New York]— or Miles Sherbrook in Hanover Square—where Mr. Simpson lives."

JOURNAL.

JULY—DECEMBER.*

NEW HAVEN, FRYDAY, July 4th, 1777.

Thro: Hurry, and my situation as Aid-de-Camp to His Excellency General Washington, I have long neglected my Journal; but as it may hereafter give me satisfaction, I am determined from this day (if possible) to continue it regularly. On the 11th of January 1777, I had the Honor of being promoted to the Rank of a Colonel (having served as Aid-de-Camp to Gen¹. Washington) and ordered to proceed to Wethersfield in Connecticut on that business, haveing authority (in conjunction with my other Field officers (Viz Wm S. Livingston Lt Col., & Eb. Huntington, Major,) to appoint the Officers to the Regiment. I arrived at Weth'd the 24th of January and proceeded to the appointing Officers,—where I continued superintending the Recruiting Service till yesterday morning—when I set off to join my Reg^t. —Arrived at New Haven, and received instructions from Brigd Gen¹. Jed: Huntington (who is now here) commanding Officer, to continue here till further orders. This morning Lieut Dawson of the 38th (British) Reg^t. arrived in the harbour from N. York with clothing for the Prisoners in this State; he was permitted to land them and return. Afternoon we went by water to West Haven where a detachment of my Regt was stationed, returned and spent the Evening w^t. Gen¹. Huntington and a number of Officers at Beers's Tavern.

* This journal is contained in the same memorandum book as that printed on p. 128.

Saturday, July 5th, 1777. This day we Received Orders to March early to-morrow morning for Camp. —I left Major Huntington to bring on the Troops, and at 7 oClock went over to Stratford, where I spent an agreeable Evening with the Miss Johnsons.

Stratford, Sunday, July 6th, 1777. This day attended Church, dined with Capt. Walker, drank tea with the Miss Johnsons—and went over to Fairfield.

Monday, July 7th. This morning General Huntington went forward to Danbury, leaveing the several detachments to proceed under my Command. Spent the day very sociably with Major Abel and Mr. Burr.

Tuesday, 8th *July.*—At 3 oClock the Revallee beat, troops paraded, order of March given out, and moved at 4—halted at Greenfields, and Brakefasted,—at Reading and Dined, arrived at Danbury, 23 Miles from Fairfield, at 6 oClock—well wet, it haveing rained all the afternoon; ordered the Men to be immediately Barrack'd, sup'd and spent the Evening w^t. Mr. Lord (Commissary).

Wednesday, 9th *July,* 1777.—Left the troops at this place under maj^r. Huntington to halt one day,—and proceeded to Peeks-Kill with Genl. Huntington, arrived at major Genl. Putnam's at 7 oClock and lodg'd—was here informed that Intelligence had this day been received that Ticonderoga had fell into the hands of the Enemy—with part of its Garrison. Some believe it, but General Putnam does not Credit it.*

---

*On June 20th a council of war determined to evacuate Ticonderoga and to take post on Mount Independence. As a siege would easily reduce them in that position, a second council, held on July 5th, determined to retreat. St. Clair was the commander in this move, which Washington thought was "among the most

Thursday, 10th *July.* After brakefast camp [came] down to my Reg^{t.} which I find in General Varnum's Brigade, encamped on a hill S. E. from Peeks-Kill landing—the other Reg^{ts} are, [Christopher] Green's— [Israel] Angell's and [Henry] Sherburne's from Rhode Island,—Sherburne's one of the Additional Sixteen. Found my Officers and Soldiers in Health, notwith-standing a very fatigueing March they have lately had from this into the Jersey's and back again,—took Quarters in Lt. Col^{o.} [Jeremiah] Olney's Tent—my Baggage not arrived.

Peeks-Kill, Fryday, 11th *July.*—Att 10 oClock this morning Major [Ebenezer] Huntington, arrived with the detachment, and barrack'd them on the Inhabitants, the weather being such as was impossible for them to encamp; confirmation on this day received of our people evacuateing Ticonderoga, and that they are retreating towards Fort Edward. What can be the occasion of this manœver no one among us can tell, but unless some-thing has happened w^{h.} we are Ignorant of,—there must be infamous conduct.

Saturday, 12th *July.*—the weather continues cloudy and Wet, close in Quarters. Spent a Sociable Evening in Company w^{t.} Lieut Colo [Henry B.] Livingston and Maj^{r.} [Ebenezer] Huntington at G. Beekmans Junr. at Cortland's Seat.

Peeks-Kill, Sunday, 13th *July,* 1777. Ordered the

unfortunate that could have befallen us." St Clair was tried by a general Court-Martial, and acquitted "with the highest honor;" and the sentence was con-firmed by Congress, only New England being in opposition. *St Clair Papers; Journals of Congress.* The proceedings of the court martial were printed by Congress, and have been reprinted in the *Collections of the New York Historical Society* (1880).

detachment from the Barracks and encamped them with the Regiment. Drank Coffee w^t. Genl. Putnam, who informs Me General Washington is on his March for this place within Thirty Miles of the River.* Glover's Brigade is ordered to hold themselves in readiness to join the Northern Army.—A report prevails that a large Fleet has sail'd from N. York—their destination unknown.

Monday, 14th *July.* The weather very good and pleasent, no further accounts from the Northern Army —'tis much to be feared our late misfortunes in that quarter will prolong this unnatural War. Orders to collect all the Boats for the more speedy transportation of the Army from the Jersey's to this shore.

Peeks-Kill, Tuesday, 15th *July.* By a Man just from N. York we have information that most of the Army have embarked, together w^t. their baggage, Artillery, Waggons, &c.; he says they are going of on some expedition, rather conjectures New England is their Object—& that about 3500 are to be left to Garrison N. York and the Islands adjacent.

Wednesday, 16th. *July*—this day a Sloop of War mounting 20 Guns two Row Gallies and a Schooner came up and anchored in Haverstraw bay.

Thursday, 17th *July.*—Field Officer of the day, dined with General Putnam, who informs that our

---

* "In consequence of the advices from General St. Clair, and the strong probability there is that General Howe will push against the Highland passes to co-operate with General Burgoyne, I shall, by the advice of my officers, move the army from hence to-morrow morning towards the North River." *Washington to the President of Congress,* 10 July, 1777. He was then at Morristown. On the 12th his Headquarters were at Pompton Plains, and on the 15th, at the Clove. See also *Putnam to Van Cortlandt,* 12 July, 1777. *Journal of the* (*N. Y.*) *Council of Safety,* 994.

people evacuated Ticonderoga, and bro't of 40 pieces of Cannon w^t. them. An Action ensued on the Retreat, when the Enemy retired w^t. great loss.

Camp at Peeks-Kill, Fryday, 18th, 1777.—Relieved this morning at 8 oClock by Lieu^t. Col^o. [Jeremiah] Olney—the Enemies shiping gone down the River, Captains [John] Hart, [Judah] Alden and [Caleb] Bull of my Reg^t. arrived in Camp. A party of about 40 Men (about a week since) landed on Rhode-Island about 4 Miles above Newport and made prisoner Major-General Presscott, commander in Chief of the Enemies troops there,—this was done by passing two of their frigates and marching 1½ Mile, & took him within a quarter of a Mile of two of his Brigades—One of his Aid-de-Camps fled by a window—which obliged the party to push w^t. the Genl & his other Aid. The whole Island was soon alarmed—but too late for them.*

Camp at Peeks-Kill, Saturday, 19th *July,* 77. No further intelligence of the Enemies movements. General Arnold is gone to join the Northern Army†—

---

* This enterprise was conducted by Lieutenant-Colonel William Barton, of the Rhode Island forces. The aid who was captured was Major Barrington.

† "Immediately upon the receipt of your first letter, concerning the distress you would labor under for want of the assistance of an active officer, well acquainted with the country, I wrote to Congress and desired them to send up General Arnold, provided the matter before them respecting his rank was settled in such a manner that determined him to continue in service. Upon my Requisition, General Arnold, waiving for the present all dispute about rank, left Philadelphia and arrived here last Evening, and this day proceeds on his journey to join you. Although he conceives himself, had his promotion been regular, superior in command to General St. Clair, yet he generously upon this occasion lays aside his claim, and will create no dispute, should the good of the service require them to act in concert. I need not enlarge upon the well-known Activity, Conduct, and Bravery of General Arnold. The proofs he has given of all three have gained him the confidence of the public and of the Army, the Eastern Troops in particular." *Washington to Major-General Schuyler,* 17 July, 1777.

Dined with Brigd^r. Varnum, the afternoon reviewing my Regiment.

Sunday, 20th *July*. This day Major Genl. Lord Sterling, with Conway's & Maxwell's Brigades, march'd from the Clove, pass'd the River, and arrived at this place early this morning. His Excellency General Washington with the remainder of the Army march'd from the Clove for New Windsor which is about 18 Miles above us on the opposite Shore, this last movement must be in consequence of a number of the Enemies Ships appearing in the Sound, off Fairfield & Compo.

Camp on the Heights of Peeks-kill, Monday, 21 *July,* 1777. This morning Brigadiers Parsons and Huntington with their Brigades march'd towards the Sound, to oppose the Enemy should they land on that Coast.

Tuesday, 22^d *July* 1777—this morning at 4 oClock Genl. Varnum's Brigade march'd from Peeks-kill about five Miles to the Rear to the left of the Road to Fish-Kills, where we encamped on a very high stony hill.— Genl Parsons has gone about 16 Miles from this— Dined w^t. Genl. Putnam.

Wednesday, 23^d *July,* 1777. Busy in seeing my Encampment regulated stones hove out, &c.—This day a number of Men are taken down with the Measels, this together with the Itch makes a number returned unfit for Duty.

Camp on y^e. Heights near Crompond, July 24th, 1777, 5 M. from P. Kills. By a spy from New York we have intelligence the Enemy sal'd from Sandy Hook yesterday—their destination unknown,—the Afternoon rode to Beverly Robinson's with Genl. Putnam about 9

Miles from this and drank Tea—returned ab.ᵗ 11 at night.

July 25ᵗʰ, 1777—This day we intercepted—or rather a letter was delivered Genl Putnam from Genl Howe to Genl Burgoyne in which he says "he shall sail the first wind for Boston." 'Tis suspected this letter was designed to fall into our hands,—so much so that Genl Washington has ordered Sheldon's Regiment of Cavalry & Generals Sullivan & Lord Sterling's Divisions to cross the river & return into Jersey.* There are many different opinions in regard to the present movements, some think the Enemy are bound to Philadelphia—others that N. England is their object.

Camp, Saturday, July 26ᵗʰ 1777—This day on duty, as Field Officer of the day. Lᵗ. Colᵒ. [Henry B.] Livingston set of as a flag of truce to New York. Dined with General Putnam; at 10 oClock set out on the Grand Rounds—this night was very stormy and dark; got back about three in the mornᵍ.

Sunday, 27ᵗʰ *July.* Capt John Wright arrived from Connecticut and delivered me a number of Letters from my friends. Genˡ. Putnam has a letter from General Silliman, who informs that a large fleet have been discovered of [f] Long Island steering to the Eastward—this is supposed to be part of the Enemy's fleet which sail'd from Sandy Hook last Wednesday—at 2 oClock Received orders to strike our Tents, at three March'd & took Post on the Heights near the Continental Village. The Brigades of Parsons and Huntington have returned to Camp—Generals Sullivan and Lord Sterling's Divisions have cross'd ye River into the Jerseys.

* See *Washington to Putnam*, 25 July 1777, *post.*

Camp, Continental Village, Monday, 28th *July,* 1777.
Orders from General Washington that the whole Army
at this Post hold themselves in readiness to march,
without their Baggage on the shortest notice,—by a
deserter from the Enemy, it appears they have got on
board the North River pilots—and some conjecture
they wish to draw our Army from this post, then return
& make a sudden stroke to gain the Highlands.

Tuesday, 29th *July*—L^t. Col^{os} [Jeremiah] Olney,
[Henry B.] Livingston & myself rode to Fort Consti-
tution to see Maj^r. [Ebenezer] Huntington, cross'd the
River with him and dined at Mr. Moores—spent an
agreeable afternoon in Company with Miss Nancy
Moore and the Miss Robinsons,* the whole a circle fo
violent Tory's—their friends and connections all being
on that side. L^t. Colonel [Henry B.] Livingston returned late last Even^g from Kings-bridge where he met
Govr Tryon—who treated him very ill. Dr. A. Leon-
ard, a gentleman who was much esteem'd in the Army,
cut his own throat Wednesday Even^g in Jersey.

Camp, Continental Village, Wednesday, 30th *July,*
1777.—General Putnam Received intelligence from
His Excellency General Washington that Seventy Sail
of the Enemy have arrived in Delaware Bay—in consequence of which the Army are moveing for Philadelphia; Generals McDougall and Huntington w^t. their
Brigades are ordered to send their heavy baggage over
the River, and be in readiness to follow on the shortest
notice.

---

* Probably Susanna and Joanna, daughters of Beverly Robinson. He commanded the Loyal American Regiment, and two of his sons, Beverly and John
held commissions in it.

Thursday, 31ˢᵗ *July,* 1777. An extream warm day —at my tent writing most of the day.

Friday Augᵗ. 1ˢᵗ. This day the General Officers of this department together wᵗ several other Gentlemen dined at my marque. The Afternoon was spent in Joy and festivity,—Dr Leonard I am told is like to live, —his wound is terrible.*

Camp, Continental Village, Saturday, Augᵗ. 2ᵈ 1777 Took an early Dinner and went to Peeks-kill in Compnʸ with B. Major Humphrey—where we embarked in the General's Barge, landed reconnoitered Fort Montgomery—from thence proceeded up the River and

---

* "In behalf of the Revᵈ Mr Abiel Leonard, Minister of the Gospel in the Town of Woodstock in the Colony of Connecticut, and by said Colony appointed Chaplain to the Regiment under my Command, who came to Cambridge with said Regiment, I beg leave humbly to represent to the President of the Continental Congress, that the aforesaid Abiel Leonard left his Family and Parish for the sake of serving the common Cause of America and likewise a private Grammar School, on which a considerable Part of his necessary support depended, and under the Peculiar Disadvantage of being obliged to provide and pay a preacher to supply his Pulpit, during his Absence. And when he came to Cambridge, finding the whole Army, except the Regiment from the County of Berkshire unprovided with Chaplains, and the Main Body depending on the Services of the Revᵈ President Langdon, a burden too great for one alone to bear, he join'd with the said President and assisted him in said Services until the celebrated Charlestown Battle; after which, as part of his Particular Regiment, was stationed at the new Entrenchment at Prospect Hill, together with several Regiments more destitute of Chaplains, and Part on Cambridge Neck of Land at the distance of a Mile and half from Prospect Hill, where he had also many more than those of his own particular Charge to attend, he attended Divine Service every Day at each Place Alternately; and went thro' the whole Labor of a Chaplain to the whole, as far as he was able, and in the new Situation since the Division into Brigades, still continues to serve four Regiments (his own included) and proposes so to do, till further Provision is made. All which extraordinary Labors, perform'd to general acceptance, may perhaps Merit the attention of the honble Continental·Congress, tho' the said Mr. Leonard would not wish to make the Distress of his Country, a plea for great advantages to himself."—*General Putnam to the President of Congress, 1777.*

drank Tea with the Miss Robbinsons,*—at Sun set mounted our Horses and returned to Camp after an agreeable Jaunt.

Sunday, Augt. 3. Removed our encampment about 400 yards further East which took up most of the forenoon, dined w^t. B. Genl. Varnum. The rain prevented divine service this afternoon,—Yesterday McDougall's & Huntington's Brigades cross'd the river with orders to proceed with all dispatch to join His Excellency General Washington.

Camp, Continental Village, Monday, August 4th, 1777. This day sat as president of a General Court Martial. Came on the Tryal of Ensign Craiger of Col^o. Livingston's, charged with robing the Inhabitants.† An express arrived this morning from His Excell^y Genl. Washington to M. Genl. Putnam informing that on Thursday morng the 31st Ul^{to} the British fleet sailed from the Capes of Delaware, in consequence of which, McDougall's & Huntington's Brigades are ordered to return—& Lord Sterling's & Genl Sullivan's Divisions to march for this place‡— an Idea prevails they will attempt this post.

Tuesday Augt. 5th. A very wet day, nothing materialy new—on Court Martial from 9 to 2 oClock.

Wednesday Augt. 6th. General Putnam has received such intelligence that he has reason to think the Enemy will turn their attention this way; two Reg^{ts} of Militia of this State have arrived in Camp this day, more ex-

---

* Daughters of Beverly Robinson.

† See *Orderly Book*, 5 August, 1777, *post*.

‡ Washington's letter dated Chester, August 1st., is printed in my *Writings of Washington*, vi, 1.

pected. A row galley and Schooner of the Enemies this day came up the River—'tis said ours are to attack them this night.

Camp, Con!. Village, Thursday, Aug!. 7ᵗʰ, 1777 Gen!. Huntingdon & Jerre Wadsworth Dined and spent the day with me,—tis [reported] Lᵗ. Colº. [David] Dimon wᵗ. his Regᵗ. has retired from the whit-Plains to Byram Bridge—900 of the Enemy haveing sallied upon him, his numbers so much inferior, it was imprudent for him to have fought them; four Lᵗ. Dragoons are missing.—a troop of Lᵗ. Horse from Connecticut arrived in Camp, Militia coming in.

Fryday, Aug!. 8ᵗʰ. This day between the Hours of 9 & twelve Edmund Palmer—a spy & Robber was executed agreeable to the Sentence of a Gen!. Court Martial.

Saturday, Aug!. 9ᵗʰ. Attended the Court Martial 'till 3 o'Clock, the Afternoon Gen!. Putnam spent a couple of hours wᵗ. me at my Marque over a social glass of Wine.

Camp near yᵉ. Continental Village, Sunday, Aug!. 10ᵗʰ, 1777. Divine service was this day performed in my encampment by Mr. [Ebenezer] David, chaplain to [Israel] Angell's Battallion of Rhode-Island, an agreeable speaker,—we have Intelligence that our Northern army are retreating, and that the Enemy are within twenty miles of Albany,—we yet hear no further Intelligence of the Fleet & Army which was off the Capes of Delaware.

Monday, August 11ᵗʰ, 1777. The Connecticut Militia are comeing in fast—but as yet we can hear nothing further from the Enemies fleet. Capt Manly of the American Frigate call'd the Hancock mounting 34 Guns was lately taken by a 64 & a 40 Gun, Ships of the British—after an obstinate engagement, and was carried in to Hallifax—he we hear is in New York.

Camp, Continental Village, Tuesday, Augt. 12th 1777. It is astonishing we can get no certain accounts from the Army under Gen^ls Howe, the morn^g of the 31st they left the Capes of the Delaware, & have not been heard of with any certainty since 'tis now near a Month since they left New York, a rumor is this day in Camp that they have been discovered of[f] Nantucket Shoals—if this is true no doubt their intentions are to go far to the Eastward, land and make a force'd March to join General Burgoyne,—should this be their real design—their intentions in going to the Southward were to draw our Army that way, to lead them further from the place where they really designed the Attack, —in which they have succeeded,—the main body of our Army is now near Philadelphia, and it must be a long tedious March for us—should they land in New Hampshire time will unfold the Secret.

Camp, Continental Village, Wednesday 13th *August,* 1777. This morning General Gates set of to take command of our Northern Army. Major Gen^ls Schuyler and S^t. Clair being ordered down to Congress to answer for the late retreat & Evacuation of Tyconderoga,—we have just Received an acc^t. of a Battle fought near Fort Stanwix—the Enemy march'd down 7 or 800 Men to cut of the communication between that & Albany—the Militia under Genl Herkamer from the German flatts attacked them & gained the ground after 6 hours engagement in which we lost 1

Colonel, 2 L[t]. Colonel, 3 Majors and 77 Rank & file,
the Enemy left dead on the Field 250 among which
were Stephen Watts* of New York, B[r]. in Law to S[r].
John Johnson and   †Bastard son to S[r]. W[m]
Gen[l]. Herkamer a brave good Man, since Dead of
his Wounds.

Camp at the White Plains, 22[d] Sept[r]. 1777.

New Windsor, West side Hudson's River, October
8th 1777 On the 16th of September I march'd from
Peeks-kill at the head of 500 Men—three nights following we made a descent from Fairfield on to Long
Island, arrived at the Fort in Satalkut ab[t]. day break,
the Enemy had previous notice of our comeing and
were prepared to receive us, as our design was a surprise (disappointed in this) we fire'd on the Fort near
three hours—and then by a council call'd by Genl Parsons concluded to retire—the Enemies shiping then
drawing near to destroy our Boats. We relanded safe
on the main without the loss of a man, Lieu[t]. Avery‡
only being wounded; from this after lying three days
at Fairfield we march'd for Norwalk—from thence to
Horseneck where we continued about a week. General Parsons then ordered down his Brigade from
Peeks-kill—we then march'd and took post at the

---

* Stephen Watts was a son of John Watts, prominent in the colonial history of
New York. At the age of twenty-two he received a commission of Major in the
" Royal Greens," a company raised chiefly in the valley of the Mohawk, and
commanded by his brother-in-law Sir John Johnson. He was wounded, not
killed, at the battle of Oriskany, and later went to England. His wife was Mary
Nugent. See Stone, *Life of Sir William Johnson*, II, 502.

† Blank in the MS.

‡ Two lieutenants of this name were in Colonel Jedediah Huntington's regiment
—Simeon and Thomas, both of Groton.

White Plains, where continued some time. In consequence of Genl. Washington's ordering a number of Troops from Peeks-kill to Head Quarters, we were directed to take their place, where I arrived after a Six Weeks tour.—Here we encamped and lay in peace 'till the morning of the 2^d Inst (Oct^r.), when Intelligence came that the enemy were comeing up the River,—the 3^d. , 4th, & 5th we were amused by their landing on the East Shore, early on the morning of the 6th they landed between Kings ferry & the Dunder barrack under a heavy fog,—Governor Clinton who then commanded the Garrison at Fort Montgomery immediately dispatch'd an express to General Putnam at Peeks-kill—the letter was sent by an infamous scoundrel who did not deliver it 'till the fireing was heard at 3 oClock p. m.—the Enemy were then attacking Fort Montgomery, reinforcements were immediately dispatch'd— the Garrison fought most gallantly against 4,000 of the Enemy 'till dark, when under cover of the night they entered the lines where no men were posted haveing only 500 Men in the Fort which would take 3,000 to Man—the darkness favor'd our Men in flying —some to the River and some to the mountains, so that in kill'd wounded and missing we have lost only 200, and happily the Governor and his B^r. Genl. James Clinton both escaped—my Lieu^t. Col^o. Wm S. Livingston unfortunately fell into their hands—haveing stayed in the Garrison by particular desire to Governor Clinton. This day I cross'd the river and encamped in New Windsor—the remaining part of the Army are at Fish-kill.

New Windsor, 9th *Octr*, 1777. This day marched

this day broke up the river and encamped — in New Windsor
the evening part of the Army are at Pish Hill.

New Windsor to N.W. N.W.
This day marched out four Miles back of Pish & and
encamp'd at of place call'd Little Mountain when
we remain'd. Till Wednesday 16th — when a float of 30 sail of
the Enemies shipping begin to put the river in consequence of
which we receiv'd orders next month — it 3 o'Clock harnass'd my
R.g 2 Miles south of Thompson. — 16th Octr Start.d at
the Runnells — when at Thompson received the agreeable
intelligence that Genls Burgoyne and his whole Army had
surrender'd prisoners of War to Genl Gates, at the same time
had orders to make a force march to Stringtown as the Enemy's
shipping now lying of that place, — the orders were strictly
comply'd with by marching at the rate of 4 Miles an hour —

out four Miles back of Hudsons river and encamped at a place call'd Little Britain,* where he remained till Wednesday 15th—when a fleet of 30 Sail of the Enemies shiping pass'd up the river, in consequence of which we received orders and march'd at 3 oClock, barrack'd my Reg^t. 2 Miles south of Shongum†—16th Octo^r. Started at the Revallee—when at Shongum received the agreeable intelligence that Genl. Burgoyne and his whole Army had surrendered prisoners of War to Genl. Gates, at the same time had orders to make a force'd march to Kingston as the Enemy's shiping were lying of that place,—the orders were strictly complied with by marching at the rate of 4 Miles an hour but unfortunately for us the Enemy landed when we were about 6 Miles of the Town and Burnt every house Barn &c—this Savage kind of War, destroying defenceless Town, and making War against Women and Children seems peculiar *to Britons* and *Savages*. We received orders & filed off to the left in hopes of falling in with the Enemy should they attempt to pass into the Country, arrived at Marble Town ab^t. 8 in the Even^g—where we encamped.

Hurly,‡ Fryday, 17th, 1777. Arrived at this place 4 Miles from Marble-Town & 3 Miles from Kingston. The Enemy's shiping are burning all the buildings up & down the river that are within their reach, such cursed Barbarity is not equalled in History, Revenge for Burgoyne's misfortunes seems their darling object.

Hurly, Saturday, 18th *October,* 1777. This little

---

* In the centre of New Windsor.

† Shavungunk Mountain?

‡ Named from the Lovelace family—they being Barons Hurley in Ireland.

Village was inhabited by the Dutch—the late burning
of Kingston occasioned many of them to remove
further back into the Country.—the inhabitants of this
country are remarkable for Hospitality, the Women in
general rather corse,—some few I have seen here, &
others that fled from Kingston that are handsome, sensible & chatty—perhaps on further acquaintance I may
be more particular.   The Enemy continue burning—
dwelling houses—Mills &c near the Shore, but carefully avoid landing where any Troops appear to oppose
them, at Evening rode ab͏ᵗ a Mile over the *Kill* (dutch
for river or rivulet) in C͏ʸ w͏ᵗ Gov͏ʳ Clinton & Governeur Morris drank Tea with the Miss Tenychs* & the
Miss Elmondoffs.

Hurly, Sunday, 19͏ᵗʰ, *Octo͏ʳ,* 1777.   We have this
day the articles of treaty between L͏ᵗ Gen͏ˡ Burgoyne
and Major Gen͏ˡ Gates, & 'tis the general opinion that
Gates has given him much better terms than he need
have done, which causes much uneasiness, nothing
materially new, the shiping—as yesterday.

Monday, 20͏ᵗʰ *Oct͏ʳ* .   A heavy N. E. storm spent the
afternoon and Evening with Governor Morriss at Col͏ᵒ
Wyncoop in C͏ᵒ with Miss Elmondorph.

Tuesday, 21͏ˢᵗ   By Col͏ᵒ Wilkinson, Dep͏ʸ Adju͏ᵗ
Gen͏ˡ of y͏ᵉ Northern department, we are informed
Gen͏ˡ Gates's situation was such, that he could not get
a surrender of Gen͏ˡ Burgoyne on better terms than he
did,—The Miss Elmendorph & Miss TenEycke's favored me with their Comp͏ʸ at tea this afternoon.

Hurly, Wednesday, 22͏ᵈ *Oct͏ʳ* , 1777.   This day the

* Matthew Ten Eyck was one of the original patentees of the Hurley tract in
1708.

shiping have been employed runing up and down the
River burning single houses—and otherways distressing the peaceable Inhabitants. The weather has cleared
off with a cold N. W. wind.

Thursday, 23 *Oct*ʳ. , at 8 oClock the Enemy's fleet
weigh'd anchor with a fair wind and stood down the
River. at 12 we heard a very heavy firing which we
supposed to be at or near Poughkeepsie. I rode
down and saw the remains of Kingston, which is situated on a plain 2½ Miles from Hudsons river, and to
appearances was one of the most beautiful Villages I
ever saw—the inhabitants are now scattered all over
the country,—pass'd the Eveng at Mʳ. TenEycke's.

Hurly, Fryday, 24ᵗʰ *Octo*ʳ. , 1777. His Excellency
the Govʳ. gone over the River. orders for us to be in
readiness to march on the shortest notice ; spent
the day riding, the Evening the Miss TenEycks &
Miss Betsy Elmondorph—with several Gentlemen—
were at my quarters—pass'd it sociable with the Band
of Music &c—&c.

Saturday, 25ᵗʰ *Oct*ʳ. , 1777. This day rode out to
Stony ridge with Governeur Morriss—at Evening received a letter from Governor Clinton with orders to
March with all the Troops here for New Windsor,
Sunday 26th. The Army march'd from Hurly at 12
oClock—I crossed Hudsons River and put up at
of Rhynebeck, spent the Evening with Capᵗ. Wooster
at Capt Sheldons—two very pretty Daughters.

Monday, 27ᵗʰ *October*, 1777. Set of in the rain about
12 oClock stop'd and dined with John Livingston, after
dinner rode to Hagermans, three Miles from Poughkeepsie—14 from Rhynebeck where we put up for the

night, the country thro: which we have rode this day is settled by the Dutch, well cultivated but very indifferent livers, their Houses small & built of logs—the extreame dullness of the weather prevented my observations on the Road.

Tuesday, 28ᵗʰ *Octobr.* . The N. E. Storm continues —the rain incessant, at 5 oClock P. M. sat of and rode to Vancleeks* in Poughkeepsie—three Miles only, where we put up for the night the storm too severe to proceed any further.

Poughkeepsie, Wednesday, 29ᵗʰ *Octobr.* , 1777. Sat off at 10 oClock and arrived at General Putnam's about 1 P. M. find most of the Army at this place, 6,000 of General Gates's Troops on the March from Albany to this post, spent the Evening with Lieuᵗ. Colonels [William S.] Smith & [David] Cobb.

Fish-kill, Thursday, 30ᵗʰ *October*, 1777. Once more by way of novelty the Sun shows us his gladdening Rays, spent the day at Head Quarters writing, my Regt not being yet arrived at New Windsor, occasioned by the rise of Water near the Polts—which prevents their crossing.

Fryday, 31ˢᵗ *Octor.* . This day we have intelligence that the Enemy had made an attempt on the Fort & Cheavaux de Frize in Delaware, & repulsed, with the loss of between of 4 & 500 Hessians kill'd & wounded, Count Donop their commander taken wᵗ. 100 more,

---

* This house was erected in 1702 by Baltus Van Kleeck, and stood on Mill Street, near the corner of the present Vassar Street. It was used for public meetings during the agitations that followed the Stamp Act of 1765. When the first legislature under the new constitution of the State was driven from Kingston, Governor Clinton called upon it to assemble at Poughkeepsie, and early in January, 1778, it convened in this tavern.

The Augusta a 64—Appollo of 32—both Burnt,—this evening on a council of War.

Sunday, Fish-kill, November 2nd, 1777. This day Lieu^t. Col^o. [Alexander] Hamilton arrived in Camp from Genl. Washington & confirms the news of yesterday,—pass'd the Evening in Company with him at Col^o. [John] Lamb's Quarters.

Monday Novr. 3^d. Received orders to join the Brigade under General Parsons at or near the White Plains—my Regiment marched immediately for Peekskill. I took the rout to Danbury—where I arrived late in the Even^g after a fatigueing ride of 35 Miles— part of it a shocking road pass'd the Evening at M^r. Lloyds.

Tuesday, 4th. Sat of at 10 oClock in Company with M^r. Lloyd and Capt. [Charles] Whiting—rode to Wilton—Norwalk & arrived at Stamford about Dusk —sup'd at Mrs Well's.

Horseneck, Wednesday, Novr. 5th, 1777. Arrived here from Stamford about 9 A. M. found General Parsons's quarters at Knapps—continued here the day not a little fatigued.

Thursday, Novr. 6th. An exceeding heavy storm from ye N. E. close in quarters till Evening—pass'd an hour or two with the Miss Bush's.

Fryday, Novr. 7th. My Reg^t. arrived yesterday at Kings street five Miles from this went there—and returned at Evening, which pass'd sociably at our Quarters w^t. Major Bigelow.

Saturday, Novr. 8th. Joined my Regiment at Kings street this Evening arrived Major General Putnam,— orders to cook two days provision, and be ready to March on the shortest notice.

Quarters in Kingstreet, Sunday, November 9th, 1777.
March'd at 1 oClock arrived at Wards Six Miles from
Kings Bridge, lay there 'till Sun set covering a For-
ageing party, then sat of for our Quarters where we
arrived about 12 at night, after a March of 24 Miles.

Monday Novr 10th.   In the course of Six days past
we have had no less than 30 Deserters from the
Enemy at Kingsbridge, they all agreed that we are
hourly expected to make an attack on their Works—
and to endeavor to take the City—many of the Inhabitants are getting their valuable effects on board the
Ships and all in great confusion.

Tuesday, Nov. 11th 1777.   Received orders and
March'd at 1 oClock—took Quarters on the Maroneck
Road 2 Miles from White Plains, Charles Webb's—
Wyllys's Meigg's & Enos's Regt on my left—General
Warner's Brigade of Militia on my right—on the road
leading via Stephen Wards to Kings-Bridge.

Wednesday, Nov. 12th.   An exceeding stormy day
—employed in writeing.   Desertion from the Enemy
continues.

Thursday, Nov. 13th.   Received orders to hold ourselves in readiness to March on the shortest notice to
join His Excellency Genl Washington in Pensylvania,
—rode to Horseneck with Majr Huntington—Lodg'd
at Knapp's.

*Quarters between Maroneck & White Plains, Fryday,
Nov.* 14th, 1777.   Returned from Horseneck with
General Parsons and dined at my Quarters—prepare-
ing for a March.

Saturday, Nov. 15th.   Cloathing arrived for my
Regt., which at this season is very welcome—the

Evening spent with decent sociability in Company with my Officers—& the Band of Musick.

Sunday, Nov. 16ᵗʰ. My Regᵗ. being much troubled with the Itch this day obtained permission and Marched them to Rye, to endeavor a cure, rode on myself in Cº. with General Parsons to Horseneck—suped with Majors Putnam and Humphrey at Mr. Bush's—lodg'd at Knapp's.

Monday, Nov. 17ᵗʰ, 1777 Returned this forenoon to Rye—took Quarters at Doughty's—the Evening a number of Ladies alias Women to hear the Band.

Tuesday, Nov. 18ᵗʰ. By much the coldest day we have had this season,—the sleet and Snow of yesterday, & the severety of this day indicates an early approach of Winter.

Wednesday, Nov. 19ᵗʰ. The forenoon rode to Maroneck from thence to White Plains in company with Major General Putnam and Brigadier Parsons— every moment indicates something speedily to be done, —large supplies of Ammunition &c &c prepareing.

Rye. Thursday, November 20ᵗʰ, 1777. This being Thanksgiving thro: the N. England States in Compʸ. with Brigadier Parsons—Majʳ. Huntington and Capᵗ. Bull of the Lᵗ. Dragoons I rode to Knapp's in Horseneck, where we found a large circle of Gentlemen & Ladies, and an elegant, rather say good, entertainment prepared, we pass'd a sociable afternoon and spent the night 'till past 12 in danceing.

Rye, Fryday, Nov. 21ˢᵗ, returned to my quarters abᵗ. 12 this day had my Regᵗ. mustered.—at Evening received a note from Brigadier Parsons informing me he had recᵈ information that the Enemy intended burning

Tarrytown this night,—and directed my Reg.ᵗ to lodge on their Arms and be ready on the shortest notice.

Quarters at Rye, Saturday, Nov.ʳ 22.ᵈ, 1777. The forenoon employed writeing afternoon went to attend the funeral Solemnities of Maj.ʳ Bound, his connections being Quakers—they requested he might not be buried w.ᵗ the Honors of War, which was complied with.

Sunday, Nov.ʳ 23.ᵈ at 1 oClock set of with General Parsons and arrived at Fairfield 34 Miles at 7 in the Evening—put up at M.ʳ Burr's—

Monday, 24.ᵗʰ Nov.ʳ—Dined at M.ʳ Burr's then rode to Stratford, spent the Evening at D.ʳ Johnsons and M.ʳˢ Walkers.

Tuesday, Nov.ʳ 25.ᵗʰ sat off very early in the morning—rode to Fairfield and brakefasted—sat of and arrived at my quarters ab.ᵗ Sunset, a report prevails that the Enemy have possessed themselves of Mud Island Fort in Delaware—they evacuated their Forts at Huntington and Satalkut on Long Island last Fryday—y.ᵉ 21.ˢᵗ Instant.

Wednesday, Nov.ʳ 26.ᵗʰ, 1877 March.ᵈ from our Quarters in Rye at Revallee beating—halted in Maroneck & cook'd three days provisions.

Thursday, Nov.ʳ 27.ᵗʰ The Army began to March at Sunrise—halted at New Rochelle and form'd in Brigade proceeded on thro: East Chester to the Brunks, Col.ᵒ Meigs was ordered over to entice the enemy out from their Works,—and to retreat in such a manner—if possible to induce them to persue, but in vain they did not choose to risk a Battle, a skirmishing happened between too small parties in which the Enemy has 4 kill'd 3 wounded—on our part two slightly wounded, at sun set we retired & took our Quarters in New Rochelle.

Fryday, Nov. 28th . continued all day at New Rochelle I find one thing in view yesterday was to favor a decent upon staten Island under General Dickenson—we have not yet heard what success he met with.

Saturday, Nov. 29th . Received orders and March'd to my old Quarters in Rye thro: a severe N. E. Storm, last night a scouting party went down to West Chester made prisoner Col? James Delancy & several others— a second party fired on the Pickquet at Cortland & alarm'd ye Enemy.

Sunday, Nov. 30th . With Brigadier Parsons rode to Horseneck—we have a rumour from the Southward that Maj. Gen! Green fell in with Lord Cornwallis defeated him & took 1200 Prisoners.

Horseneck, Monday, Dec. 1st , 1777 This day my Reg. march'd in to this place, an expedition is intended on Long Island—we expect to cross tomorrow evening.

Tuesday, Dec. 2d continued at this place—Major Huntington gone to Norwalk,—with General Parsons & Col? Delancy dined at M. Bushes.

Wednesday, Dec. 3d . My Regiment march'd at 9 this morning—at 1 P. M. Brigadier Parsons and myself set forward and arrived at Norwalk about Dusk— sup'd in C? with Col? Ely and a number other Officers at Dr. Hills tavern—spent a very sociable Evening.

Norwalk, Thursday, Dec. 4th , 1777—a day of leisure an elegant Dinner provided at Doct. Hills about Twenty officers present—the Band of Music &c &c the Wind has been too high for us to cross the Sound.

ORDERS OF MAJOR-GENERAL PUTNAM.*

HEAD QUARTERS, PEEKS KILL, 10 JULY, 1777.

Parole, *Leonard.*   C. Sign, *Webb.*

Lt Col^o [Giles] Russel
B. Major [Thomas] Fosdick   } Officers of the day for to-morrow.
Adjutant Smith

The Genl orders the Disposition of the several Brigades to be as follows, vizt :—

Brigadier Genl McDougall's Brigade to be on the Right near the old Orchard.

B. Genl Parsons on the Left between H^d Quarters and Col^o Saml Drake's.

B. Genl Varnum's on the right of the Center next to Genl Mc-Dougall's.

B. Genl Glover's on the left of the Center next to Genl Parsons.

B. Genl Huntington's in the center upon the Fish Kill road leading from Peeks Kill.

Two Cannon to be fixed at the forts Independance, Montgomery & Constitution.

The above Sentence should a come in after the next below.

The Signal to be given on the appearance of the Enemy is firing of two Cannon from Genl Varnum one Minute from each other, two ditto at the park by Genl Huntington two D^o by Genl Parsons in like Manner.

The Brigades to be as follows, vizt :—

Col^o [John] Durkee's
Col^o [Philip Van] Cortland's   } Genl McDougall's.
Col^o [John] Chandler's

* I print the "General Orders" issued at the Highlands by the commanding officer, during the service of Col. Webb under Putnam, because they present the best picture of the routine of that service. The record is taken from two sources, easily distinguished by the spelling. The earlier entries are from an orderly book kept by Major Richard Platt, of the New York Brigade, and the later from a similar book kept by Sergeant Daniel Ware, of Connecticut. For the former, I am indebted to the *New York Historical Society,* and for the latter, to the *Connecticut Historical Society.* The records from 1 June, 1777, to November, have been printed in separate form; but I include in these volumes only what pertained to Col. Webb's service.

Israel Putnam

Eng⁴ by F.H. Hill & Sons, New York

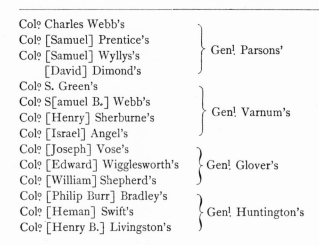

Col? Charles Webb's
Col? [Samuel] Prentice's
Col? [Samuel] Wyllys's
    [David] Dimond's } Gen! Parsons'

Col? S. Green's
Col? S[amuel B.] Webb's
Col? [Henry] Sherburne's
Col? [Israel] Angel's } Gen! Varnum's

Col? [Joseph] Vose's
Col? [Edward] Wigglesworth's
Col? [William] Shepherd's } Gen! Glover's

Col? [Philip Burr] Bradley's
Col? [Heman] Swift's
Col? [Henry B.] Livingston's } Gen! Huntington's

HEAD QUARTERS, PEEKS KILL, 11 JULY, 1777.

Parole, *England*. C. Sign, *America*.

Col? [Edward] Wigglesworth
B. Major McDougall
Adjutant Pearl. } Officers of the day for to-morrow.

The Gen! considering the Busy Season of the Year & how important it is to the public as well as to themselves that the Militia be at home in their Business at this Time, & not being now wanted, altho' he cannot say how soon they may be—The three Reg^ts of Militia viz! Col^os [Cornelius] Humphrey's, [Henry] Luddington's, & [Derck] Brinkerhoff's, who first came in are dismissed with the Gen^ls thanks for their Alertness in coming to the Defence of their Country when desired & for their good Services relying upon it that the Zeal & Ardor they have shewn in the great Cause we are engaged in, will prompt them to turn out without (*sic*) the utmost Alacrity on all future Occasions.

Col? [Samuel] Wyllys's & [William] Douglass's Reg^ts are to meet to attend prayers at five o'clock to-morrow Morning. Divine Service will be perform'd here by the Reverend Doctor [Abiel] Leonard next Lord's Day.

Fifty men to parade to-morrow morning at five o'clock without arms with the party ordered to Fort Montgomery to go on Fatigue with two Subalterns.

The Muster Master acquaints such Officers as have not delivered in their Muster Rolls properly attested that he will be under the Necessity of making out his Regimental Abstracts without inserting them unless they are immediately sent in.

HEAD QUARTERS, PEEKS KILL, 12 JULY, 1777.

Parole, *Windsor*.   C. Sign, *Park*.

Mʳ George Havens is appointed Conductor of Ordnance Stores at Fort Montgomery & the other Posts in the Highlands, in the Room of the Conductor * who is appointed an Officer in Colº [William] Malcom's Regᵗ .

The Genˡ is sorry that no more attention is paid to the Preservation of the Forage—orders that no Officer or Soldier in future will take any Forage or Feed by turning in Horses, belonging to private property, without first applying to the Qʳ Mʳ or Forage Master to have the same assigned him & such Qʳ Master &c. after finding where it may be had is to report the same to the Genˡ for his liberty, before any such forage or feed may be taken or horses turned in.

Lᵗ Colº [David] Dimon
B. Major [David] Humphreys   } Officers of the day for to-morrow.
Adjutant Selden

HEAD QUARTERS, 13 JULY, 1777.

Parole, *Boston*.   C. Sign, *Cambridge*.

Roger Alden, Esqʳ , is appointed to act as B. Major to Brigʳ Genˡ Huntington's Brigade till further orders & is to be respected & obeyed accordingly.

* Probably Daniel Neven (or Nivins), commissioned a Captain in Malcom's Regiment, 2 July, 1777.

HEAD QUARTERS, PEEKS KILL, 14 JULY, 1777.

Lt. Col? [Matthew] Mead
B. Major [Roger] Alden } Officers of the day for to-morrow..
Adjutant Barker

As Health & a respectable Appearance among Officers & Soldiers gives Strength & Dignity to an Army—and as their keeping themselves clean & neat, using proper diet well dress'd & not lying on the cold ground, & in the damp night air needlessly will contribute much to the Preservation of their Health & the Dignity of their Appearance. The Gen! expects that the Troops keep themselves clean & neat, their Hair cut decently short & comb'd & avoid using unwholesome Food or that is partially cook'd, when they have opportunity to cook it thoroughly. Also that they take Care not to lye upon the cold ground or in the damp night air when the Situation of the Army doth not make it necessary. And if any of the Officers should be so inattentive to the Preservation of their Health & Reputation as to neglect to observing these Regulations—the Gen! requests the Officers to exert their Influence by Authority & by Example to compel & induce the Soldiers to a Compliance therewith & to inspire them with every Military Virtue.

A Brigadier General of the Day will be appointed to whom Returns are to be made & by whom Complaints are to be heard & Examinations taken, who is to direct in Regulating the Affairs of the Camp & to Command in the absence of the Gen! .

The Commanding Officers of Companies at the daily Roll Calling to examine the Arms & Ammunition of the men in their respective Companies, see that they are well equipt & that they do not waste their Ammunition, note & report the Deficiencies that in case of an attack from the Enemy, we may be ready to meet them.

A Gen! Court Martial to sit to-morrow morning at 9 o'clock at the Widdow Warren's to try such prisoners as shall be bro't before them. Col? [William] Shepherd to preside. Majors [Ebenezer] Grey & [Thomas] Grosvenor,

1 C. 1 S. from Gen! McDougall's Brigade }
2 1   from Gen! Parson's   do   }
0 2   from Gen! Huntington's do   } Members
1 2   from Gen! Varnum's   do   }

HEAD QUARTERS, PEEKS KILL, 15 JULY, 1777.

Brig! Gen! McDougall
Lt. Col? [Isaac] Sherman
Major [Thomas] Fosdick } Officers of the Day.
Adj! Learned

As nothing renders an Army so formidable to the Enemy, so respectable & usefull to its friends & so internally secure in itself as being expert in War—at this Time when we expect daily to be ingaged and the ordinary Camp Duty but small, the Gen! expects the Troops that are of [f] Duty will be employed in Military Exercises, & directs that every Company shall be exercised from Revellie Beating to six o'clock in the Morning the Time of Relieving Guards, & from 8 o'clock to ten in the Forenoon & from 4 o'clock in the afternoon till seven & that each Reg! shall have two field Days in a Week for Regimental Exercises, those of B. Gen! McDougall's on Monday's & Thursday's, those of B. Gen!s Parsons', Varnum's, Glover's, & Huntington's on Tuesday's & Friday's.

The Season of the year being hot & unhealthy & the Time draws nigh, in which we may expect the Enemy will begin their Capital Operations when our whole strength may be wanted, the Gen! strictly prohibits all persons from taking or communicating the small pox by Inoculation or in any other voluntary Manner under the severest penalties.

The Gen! orders that the Q! M! provide & deliver to the Troops slings for their Canteens, Bayonet Belts.

At a Gen! Court Martial held at Phillipsburgh on Sunday, July 13th, 1777, by order of Philip Van Cortlandt.

L! Col? [Frederick] Weissenfels, President.

Thomas Powall private in Capt. [Charles] Graham's C? Col? Cortlandt's Reg! was tried for Deserting to the Enemy returning & deserting again & persuading other Soldiers to desert with him, found guilty & sentenced to be shot to Death. The Gen! approves the Sentence, & orders it to be executed on Monday next the 21st of this Instant between the Hours of ten & Eleven in the Morning.

B. Gen! Parson's Brigade hath Liberty to discharge their Pieces at Retreat Beating this Evening under the Directions of their Officers.

The Bridge Guard to be augmented to 30 privates.

Lost on the Road from White Plains the day before yesterday, a large leather pocket Book, Sam! Brown wrote on it, two 30 Doll: Bills, three 1/ N York Bills, one 6ᵈ Do a number of papers—if the Pocket Book should be found, it is ordered to be bro't to Head Quarters.

HEAD QUARTERS, PEEKS KILL, 16 JULY, 1777.

Brigad: Gen! Parsons
Col? S. B. Webb
Brigade Major [David] Humphreys } Officers of the Day.
Adjutant Hopkins.

The Gen! having been informed of Damage being done to private property by the Soldiers destroying the Fences, &c. strictly forbid the Troops taking away or burning any Fence or rails to the Detriment of any particular Inclosure & expects that the Officers will take special care that this order is observed.

Taken from Thomas Smith, Esq: , a pint silver porringer yesterday, the Handle had carv'd work upon it with a Hole in the End of it on the Back of the Porringer were the Letters T. C. T. Any persons finding sᵈ porringer are to Convey it to Col? Livingston or to Hᵈ Qʳˢ & shall receive an Honorable Reward.

Col? [Philip Burr] Bradley's Regt has Liberty to discharge their pieces this Evening at Retreat Beating under the Direction of their Officers.

HEAD QUARTERS, PEEKS KILL, 17 JULY, 1777.

Gen! Varnum,
L: Col? Olney
B. Major [Richard] Platt } Officers of the Day to-morrow.
Adj: [John] Holden [Jr.]

The Gen! orders a Picquet Guard at the Church near King's Ferry to consist of 1 M. 2 C. 4 S. 8 S. 8 C. 2 DF. 120 P. to mount this Evening & to be relieved to-morrow Morning. That the Detail for Guards & Fatigue be taken from all the Brigades indifferently—that special Care be taken to receive & communicate Gen! Orders to the Troops by the Officers, for the Plea of Ignorance is inadmissible to excuse.

The Picquet above ordered is to keep Patrols consisting of 'twelve men each, continually out patroling down the River & towards Croton to make Discoveries, & to take any Scouts from the Enemy & to Kill all tory Villains found in arms against their Country or plundering or carrying any Cattle or Goods to the Enemy & such patroles are strictly forbid to plunder or injure the Inhabitants being quietly in their Business on any Pretence whatever as they must answer it at their Peril.

The Genl. orders that the Troops have special Regard to the Preservation of their Health, now the season is approaching in which it is usually sickly in Camp owing partly to the Season ; but more to their own Imprudence.

That the Troops avoid eating unripe Fruit, going into swimming, drinking too freely of cold water when they are hot & their blood inflam'd.

At a Genl. Court Martial holden by Order of the Genl. 16th July, 1777, Colo. [William] Shepherd, President.

David Hass of Capt. Ball's Co. in Colo. Shepherd's Regt. was tried for Desertion & acquitted.

William Gordon of Capt. [Samuel] Sacket's Compy. in Colo. [Henry B.] Livingston's Regt. was tried for Desertion & inlisting into another Regt. found guilty & sentenced to receive 100 Lashes upon his Naked back.

John Whiting, alius Jo Wright in Capt. Blusdale's Company, Colo. [Edward] Wigglesworth's Regt. was tried for inlisting twice, vizt. in Colo. Durkee's Regt. after he had inlisted in Colo. Wigglesworth's found guilty & sentenced to receive 100 Lashes on his naked back.

Nathaniel Please of Capt. Ball's Compy. in Colo. [William] Shepherd's Regt. was tried for Desertion, found guilty & sentenced to receive 100 Lashes on his naked back.

The Genl. approves the sentence of the Court Martial respecting the several Prisoners afore said & orders the same to be executed to-morrow morning at Guard Mounting.

A Party for fatigue to consist of 1 C. 3 S. 4 S. 4 C. 50 P. to parade to-morrow morning at Guard Mounting with three Day's provisions.

Major Hait Field Officer of the Picquet to-night & Major Sill ield Officer for to-morrow.

BRIGADE ORDERS, 18 JULY, 1777.

The Brigade will practise the Manual & Manœuvres ordered by the King of Great Britain in 1764, for his Army till it shall be otherwise ordered by the Commander in Chief. Such Officers as have not practised in Exercise & Manœuvres will be industrious in perfecting themselves: as the Brigadier intends calling on every Commissioned Officer of the Brigade to exercise & manœuvre the respective Reg^{ts} to which they belong. Those Officers who are practised in those particulars will drill the awkward Serg^{ts} to qualify them to drill the Rank & File. The Sergeants, Rank & File of every Regiment will provide themselves with a hard stick of the size & form of a Cartridge & keep them in their pouches to go thro' the firing motions.

* * * * * *

Edmund Palmer that Noted Tory a Robber Was taken Prisoner & Confined in ye Provost Guard for Robing the Inhabitence & Leving war Against his Country : is to have his Tryal Next Tuesday at 9 o'clock in the Morning by A General Court Marshel all Parsons that Can give Evidence Against s^d Palmer are Requested & Required to Attend the Trial.*

HEAD QUARTERS July ye 19th 1777.

Brigadier General [Jedidiah] Huntington ⎫
Colo [John] Chandler † ⎬ Officers of the Day.
Adj^t [Henry] Ten Eyck ⎭

The general orders *all Sutlers and* the Sellers of Stores in Camp Except ye Comisarys of Particular Brigades (*States*) Who are Appointed to Deal out the State Stores to their own Troop at Perticulir (*certain*) Prices (*immediately*) to make a Return to him of their Names of ye Quantity & Quality of th[e] Goods the Prices they Sell at and By what author[ity] they (*suttle*) Settle in Camp. Capt [Ebenezer] Flagg is appointed to Act as Brigade Magor to *Brigadier*

* This paragraph, the first of the entries in Sergeant Ware's book, is not found in Platt's.

† Of the Eighth Regiment, Connecticut Line.

General Varnams Brigade till further orders and is to be *respected and* obayd as Such   A bourd of General officers to set on Munday Next *at 9 o'clock in the morning* at yᵉ house of the Widow Warrens to Enquire into the (*Pretensions and*) Perticular Clames of Several Candidates of the Late Vacant officers of the Late Col [William] Douglas* Who is Deceased & of the Regᵗ Lately Commanded by Colo [Jedidiah] Huntington Who is Promoted and Report to (*the Honorable*) Magor General Putnam with their appinian of the Premesis in order to Be Transmited to gena[l] Washington yᵉ sᵈ Board to Consist of Generals Mc : Dougle Varnam (*Glover*) & Huntington

a Court of inquirey to Set Next Munday at 9 ocl[ock] in yᵉ morning to Inquire into the Several Cri[mes] of the Prisoners in the Provost Guard the nature & Evidence theirof & make Report of that they Shall Find with there oppinian Respecting them

the Court of Inquirey Colo [Heman] Swift, Capt Hide [Jedidiah Hyde] Capt Mattuck [Samuel Mattocks] Capᵗ [John] Harmon

A full C[aptˢ] Company

1 Capᵗ	4 Sargᵗ 4 Corpʳ
2 Lieutenants	2 Drum & Fife & [ ]
1 Ensign	Privates †

are ordered to be Detachd from Colo. [Philip Burr] Bradleys Regiment to goe to Fort Independance & Releave the Melitia at t[hat] Post tomorrow

Brigadier General Huntington
Colonel [John] Chandler
Brigade Major [Ebenezer] Flagg   } Officers of the day to-morrow.
Adjutant [Henry] Teneik

HEAD QUARTERS, PEEKS KILL, 20 JULY, 1777.

Lost yesterday a Pᵗ of Sadle Baggs near Hᵈ Qʳˢ with Men's Clothes & Linnen in them, any Person that shall find sᵈ Baggage with the Cloathing & deliver them at Hᵈ Qʳˢ shall be well rewarded.

* "*Claims of the several candidates for the office of Colonel in the Regᵗ late Douglass's.*"—*Platt.* Douglass died of hard service, 28 May, 1777.

† In Platt's record, the figures differ from these.

HEAD QUARTERS, PEEKS KILL, 21 JULY, 1777.

Brigadier General Varnum
Lt. Col. [Giles] Russell
Brigade Major ———
Adjutant ———

The Picquet at the Church is reduced to 1 C, 2 S, 4 S, 4 C, 2 D. F., 50 P.

Lt. Col? [Jeremiah] Olney & Major [Samuel] Ward are appointed Members of the Court Martial of which Col? Shepherd is Pres? — one Cap? & one Subaltern from Gen! McDougall's Brigade, one Cap? & 2 Subalterns from Gen! Glover's Brigade to supply the vacancies occasioned by the Marching of Gen! Parson's & Huntington's Brigades.

1 S, 15 P. that are reapers to parade at Head Quarters to-morrow Morning with Sickles from General Glover's Brigade.

A dark rone Horse taken up by Major [Joseph] Hait in Camp as a stray; the owner on applying may have him.

Colonel [John] Chandler is appointed President of the Court of Enquiry upon the Prisoners in the Provost Guard in the place of Colo. [Heman] Swift. S? Court to sit to-morrow morning at nine o'clock.

HEAD QUARTERS, 22ND JULY, 1777.

Parole, *Newark.* Countersign, *Elizabeth.*

.Brigadier Genl Glover
Col? [Joseph] Vose
B. Major [Ebenezer] Flagg
Adjutant Pearl
} Officers of the Day.

The Picquet kept at the Church in future is to be taken from Lord Sterling's Division, consisting of one field officer & 120 men as at first.

The Court appointed to examine into the Grounds of Uneasiness among the Commissioned Officers of Col? [Edward] Wigglesworth's Reg? occasioned by the appointment of Major Porter, report that as Major Porter was appointed by authority which was proper and competent for the Purpose, it ought not to be drawn into Question by them.

The Gen! approves the Sentence & earnestly recommends it to all Officers of the Army not to let trifling Considerations respecting Prudence [precedence?] & Rank impede or divert their Attention from the great Object for which we are at War, viz. the Defence & Salvation of our Country, remembering that true Honor results not so much from Elevation of Rank & Place as from Sublimity of Soul & great military exploits.

At a Gen! Court Martial held by order of the Honble Major Gen! Putnam at Peekskill on the 17th Instant, Col? Shepherd, President.

The following Soldiers were tried for the several Crimes annexed to their Names respectively, viz :

Amos Rose, private in Colo. Sam! B. Webb's Reg! tried for firing a gun loaded with a Ball at Lt. [Elisha] Brewster, found guilty & sentenced to suffer the Pains of Death.

The Gen! approves the Sentence & orders that said Rose be shot to Death on Friday the first of next August between the Hours of Ten & Eleven in the Morning.

Henry Hercules Hoff, private in Col? [Henry B.] Livingston's Reg! tried at the above Court for Desertion, found guilty & sentenced to receive one Hundred Lashes on his naked back.

Sam! Fosdick of Col? Livingston's Reg! tried by s^d Court for Desertion, found guilty, & sentenced to receive 50 Lashes on his naked back.

Tho? Doyle tried by s^d Court for Desertion, found guilty & sentenced to receive 100 Lashes on his naked back.

Tho? Colvill of Colo. Sam! B. Webb's Reg! tried by s^d Court for Desertion, found guilty & sentenced to receive 50 Lashes on his naked back.

Edward Murphey of L! Col? [Jeremiah] Olney's Detachment tried for Desertion found guilty & sentenced to receive 100 Lashes on his naked back.

Henry Williams of Col? [Heman] Swift's Reg! tried for perswading Soldiers to desert, found guilty & sentenced to receive 100 Lashes on his naked Back.

The Gen! approves the several Sentences & orders them to be executed to-morrow morning at Guard Mounting on the grand parade.

The Gen! is sorry that he is so frequently put to the disagreeable Necessity of ordering Punishments to be inflicted owing to the great

Frequency of Crimes, the Perpetration of which renders punishments absolutely necessary for the Reformation of Offenders, & to deter others in order to maintain that Subordination, Order & Regularity which is necessary for the well-being of an Army—earnestly recommends it to all the Soldiers to take Warning by the Sufferings of others : for tho his Eye pities their Sufferings, his justice will not spare their Crimes, & so to behave as to give as little Occasion for the disagreeable Employment of inflicting punishment as possible & to prevent what he imagines to be one principle cause of such irregular Conduct, viz! drinking spirituous Liquors to Excess, he strictly forbids the Soldiers frequenting taverns, Tippling Houses, or Sutler's Shops where spirituous Liquors are sold & their drinking spirituous Liquors to excess.

The Provost Guard is augmented to 1 C., 2 S., 2 S, 2 C, 2 D. F., 50 P.

Gen! McDougall's Brigade hath Liberty to discharge their Pieces this Evening at Retreat Beating under the Direction of their Officers.

After Orders, 22 July, 1777.

Considering the Imperfection of Man & his liability to err ; The Inexperience & Rashness of Youth that betrays them into many criminal Imprudences & exposes often to be seduced into evil practices by the Example of false pretence & subtle Insinuations of designing Veterans in Iniquity & that in some Cases where it would be perfectly just to inflict punishment, the great End of Government will be answered, the Public Interest Secured by the Exercise of Mercy in the forgiveness of offenders—trusting that all these Reasons concur in the present case to urge & justify the Hand of Clemency in being reached out to save two unhappy young men who are justly condemned for their Crimes & trembling with the anticipation of their Punishment just ready to come upon them—

It is the Genl! good Pleasure that Sam! Fosdick & Thos. Colvin receive a pardon & a Pardon is hereby granted to each of them & it is ordered that they be discharged without receiving Punishments & join their Reg!s, relying upon it that the Consideration of this Goodness to them will more Strongly induce them to virtuous & order Behavior than the Smart & Twinges of Punishment. At the same time would caution every one against taking Encouragement from this act of Clemency to presume to transgress.

CAMP AT FRADRICKS BOROUGH JULY 22 1777

Brigade orders for genaral Parsones Brigade : the General Expects that yᵉ officers take Perticuler Care that no Ingury be Done to Indeviduals under Pretence of their being Enemys to the Cause We are ingaged in and there be no Complaints in Camp or on yᵉ March of fences being Destroyd or any Damage being Commited by the Soldiers of the Brig[ade] the Roles of yᵉ Respective Companys are to be Calld [   ] Every Day : viz Morning & Evening at Which time the Commisiond officers When off Duty are Expected to Att[end] 1 Capᵗ 2 Subaltons 4 Sargᵗˢ 4 Corᶫ & 50 Privates are to Parade tomorrow at 1 oclock at yᵉ Church with three Days Provision.

CAMP AT FRADRACKS BOROUGH Yᴱ 23ᴰ JULY 1777

Regimental orders the Regᵗ to Perade Dayly for Exercise Agreeable to the general & Brigade orders Captains & officers Commanding Company are to Make their Pay abstracts for Six Months to yᵉ Pay master Without Delay to Make an Abstract for Each Month Seperately tho officers of the Day for yᵉ Camp [will?] be for the futuer Mentioned in orders : No one is to Stray Any Distance from Camp Without Leave all the Lasure time yᵉ men have Should Be Spent in Brightning their arms till they git them Very Bright and Clean   Strict attention ought to be Paid * the Teems Which Brought provisions from thence May be Made use of for that purpose   Such Inverleads as are Scattered on yᵉ Road the general Directs should be Collected together that an attentive and Prudent officer from Each Regᵗ Be Sent to take yᵉ Charge of them & Bring on By Easy Marches Such as are able to join yᵉ Brigade

a guard from Each Regᵗ to Be kept to Prevent yᵉ horses or oxen Straying or Being Stole or Breaking into Inclosiers & Doing unnessary Damage   the unavoidable Destruction an army Makes in its Progress is But two great without yᵉ aditional Evil of Criminal Neglegence for Wanton Depradations [He] Would fondly flatter him Self of the Fealings of h[uma]nity and yᵉ Dictates of honour as to Become Plunderers and Villians as to Subject them Selves to [   ] & Punishment and Loose the fare Rep[utation] they have Alredy aquired to Presarve [   ] Carrecter will Ever give Eᵐ the greatest Pleasure and Satisfaction

* Some words omitted.

HEAD QUARTERS, PEEKS KILL, 23 JULY, 1777.

Parole, *Goshen.*   C. Sign, *Kent.*

Brig^a Genl McDougall
Lt Col^o [Henry B.] Livingston
B. Major [Thomas] Fosdick   } Officers of the Day to-morrow.
Adjut^t Larnard

The Genl strictly forbids all persons robbing Gardens or taking any thing from the Inhabitants without leave of the Owner's or wasting or destroying private property of any kind, whereby the Inhabitants may be injured or distress'd on pain of severe punishment & all officers are strictly enjoined to see that this order is observed & complied with.

HEAD QUARTERS, PEEKS KILL, 24 JULY, 1777.

Parole, *Sterling.*   C. Sign, *Durkee.*

Brigadier Genl Varnum
Major [Samuel] Ward
Brigade Major [Ebenezer] Flagg } Officers of the Day.
Adjutant [John] Remington

Genl Glover's Brigade is ordered to march to the Northward to join our Army there with all Expedition.

A Fatigue Party of Reapers from Genl McDougall's Brigade of 1 S, 1 S., 1 C., 20 P. to parade at Head Quarters to-morrow morning to have fatigue Rum & Wages.

Major [Ebenezer] Huntington 1 C., 3 S, 4 S, 4 C, 4 D. F., 100 P. to relieve the garrison at Fort Constitution to-morrow morning.

Col^o S. B. Webb's Reg^t hath Liberty to discharge their Pieces this Evening at Retreat Beating under the Direction of their Officers.

At a Genl Court Martial held at Peeks Kill by order of the Hon'ble Major Genl Putnam, 22 July, 1777, Colonel [William] Shepherd, President.

Serg^t John Smith & William White of Capt D. Dexter's Company, Col^o Angel's Reg^t were tried for Desertion & attempting to go to the Enemy, for stealing & embezzling Cartridges & carrying off their Arms & accoutrements belonging to the Continent.

The Court find the Prisoners guilty & sentence the Serg^{ts} to be reduced to the Ranks & each of them to receive 100 Lashes on their naked backs.

The Gen! approves the sentence & orders it to be executed to [morrow] morning at Guard Mounting.

Edmund Palmer was arraigned & tried upon a Charge of Plundering, robbing & carrying off Cattle, Goods, &c. from the well-affected Inhabitants & for being a Spy for the Enemy.*

The Court finds him guilty of the whole Charge alledged against him, & sentence him to suffer the Pains of Death.

The Gen! approves the Sentence & orders it to be put in Execution on Fryday, the 1st. of next August ensuing between the Hours of 9 & 11 in the Morning—by hanging him up by the Neck till he is dead, dead, dead.

Jeremiah Maybee was bro't before the Court on suspicion of being a Spy.

The Court find him to be an Inhabitant of this State & his Offence of such a Nature, that its proper to refer him to the Convention or civil Authority of this State.

L! John Waterman & Ensign Abbit [John Abbot] of Colo. Durkee's Reg! were bro't to Trial upon an Arrest by order of Col? Phillip Cortlandt for behaving in a scandalous & cowardly manner before the Enemy on a scouting Party near the White Plains on the 10th Instant & making a false Alarm in Quarters at the same time.

The Court upon maturely considering the case adjudge Lt. Waterman guilty of behaving in a scandalous and Cowardly Manner before the Enemy; but are of opinion that he did not wilfully occasion a false Alarm in Quarters & thereupon order that s⁴ Waterman be cashiered & that his Crime, Name, Place of Abode & Punishment be published in the news paper in & about the Camp and in that State, from whence he came & where he usually resided—but as for the s⁴ Charge against s⁴ Abbit they are of Opinion that he is not guilty & acquit him with Honor.

The Gen! approves the Sentences & orders s⁴ Waterman to quit his Reg! & the Army forthwith.†

* The proceedings of the Court Martial are printed in *Calendar of New York Historical Manuscripts*, II, 258.

† Abbot resigned in December, 1777.

John Smith, William White & Doctor Taller's Negro are ordered to be sent on board the Men of Warr immediately upon receiving their Punishments at Fort Montgomery.

The Person in whose Hands the marking Iron is, will return it to Head Quarters immediately.

HEAD QUARTERS, PEEKS KILL, 25 JULY, 1777.

Parole, *Crane*.   C. Sign, *Lamb*.

The following is an order issued at Head Quarters, Ramapaugh, 23^d Inst :—

The March of the Army whenever it begins will be made with the utmost Dispatch. This renders it indispensably necessary to divest it of as much Baggage as possible.

Each Brigadier is therefore immediately to cause certain Waggons to be prepared for the Tents of his Brigade, and when Orders are given to march they are to suffer nothing to be put into these Waggons but the Tents & see that they are not heavy loaded even with them—& the more to facilitate the march of the Army, the Commissaries are to leave no Means untried to procure a Supply of hard Bread to be reserved for the march—& when the Army moves they are to go forward before it & get the Provisions ready to be delivered out the moment the Army halts. The Qr Mr Genl. will have ready a proper Number of empty Waggons to follow each Brigade to take up the sick & lame. The rest of the Baggage is to be left under the Care of a small Guard to follow on after the Army accompanied by the women—None of them are to be suffered to go with the Troops.

12 Seamen to parade to-morrow morning to go on board the Boats under Capt. Buchanan.

HEAD QUARTERS, PEEKS KILL, 26 JULY, 1777.

Parole, *Kingston*.   C. Sign, *Princeton*.

Brigr Genl. Varnum
Lt. Colo [Jeremiah] Olney
B. Major [Ebenezer] Flagg   } Officers of the day.
Adjutant [John] Holden [Jr.]

A Genl. Court Martial to sit at the Widdow Warren's at 9 o'clock next Monday Morning. Colo Durkee to sit as President. 3 Capts & 3 Subs from Genl. McDougall's Brigade; 3 Capts & 3 Subs from Genl. Varnum's, for Court Martial.

HEAD QUARTERS PEEKSKILL 27 JULY ·1777

Brigadier Gen! McDougle
L! Colo [Giles] Russel* } officers of the Day.
Brigade Major Platt
Adj! [Elihu] Marvin

A Piquit Consisting of 1 Cap! 2 Subs 4 Sargiants 4 Cor! & 50 Privates is ordered to Be kept at the Church below kings fery to take 3 Days Provision & to be Releavd once in 3 Days : from the Present uncartainty of the Enemys Distination they having Saild out of hook & undoubtedly Intend to Attack Some Place South *or* East of this & *that* a Conciderable Part of the Troops at Peekskill Will Be Calld to y: Place When Ever the attact Should be made the gen orders Persuant to y: Advice Rec⁴ from Gen Washington that y: Several Brigades at this Place *be thoroughly* Aqu[ip]t and hold them Selves in Redyness to March at y: Shortest Notice

General Parsons & huntings [Huntington's] B D ˙[Brigades] are ordered : Huntingtons to Peekskill : Parsons to his former ground on y: Left   General Varnams Brigade is ordered to Incamp on the hill Back of the [   ] generals Nearer to general Huntingtons †genr! huntington's to Incamp *at Peeks Kill* on General Varnams former Ground : 2 Battallians of General Parsons Brigade to Incamp on the hill East of y: Generals *Head Quarters* Whare Colo Webbs (*Wyllys*) & Douglases was Incamed

---

HEAD QUARTERS, PEEKS KILL, 28 JULY, 1777.

Parole, *Albany.*   C. Sign, *Canaan.*

1 S 1 C 12 P from Gen! Huntington's Brigade to parade to-morrow morning at 6 o'clock with proper tools to clear & mend the Road from Peeks Kill to King's ferry.

1 S 1 C 12 P from Gen! Parsons Brigade to relieve the Cattle Guard at Crumpond to-morrow morning.

* Cumstock. *Platt.*

† " On the Hill in front of the Gen'ls near Mandevill's."—*Platt.*

HEAD QUARTERS, PEEKS KILL, 29 JULY, 1777.

Parole, *Glover.*   Countersign, *March.*

Gen! Huntington
Major [Hezekiah] Holdridge
B. Major [David] Humphreys   } Officers of the Day.
Adj! Selden

L! Col? [David] Dimon is ordered to march to fort Montgomery to relieve the Militia whose time is out.

REGIMENTAL ORDERS CAMP AT PEEKSKILL JULY 29 1777

Capts & officers Commanding Companies to make out their Muster Roles Each Capt to make 5 and to Apply to the L! Colo for a form : a Courtmarshel to Set to-morrow at 10 oclock to try all such Prisoners as Shall Be Brought Before it Cap! [John] Mills to be President all Parsons Concarnd to Attend y? Revalee to Beet for the future Emediately after the firing of the Morning gun at Which time Reg! is to Perade for y? Purpose of Exercising officers are Required to Attend : y? Sarj! Magor is Peromtoryly Ordered to Confine all those Sarj!ᵗˢ that are not Properly Attentive to their Duty and if he Omits Complying with this order he May Rest Asured that he will Be Sevearly Punished the Sarg!ᵗˢ Must be Sencable that they are Answerable for y? Least inattention the men Seem to Pay to their Duty When in their Power to Remady it & May Expect to be punished According As the Sarg!ᵗˢ are not Aproved of as yet By the Field officers those that not thorough in performing their Duty will be Reduced to do Privates Duty & those Cor! & Privates who the Commanding officer Shall think Desarving Shall be Prased for he is Determined to Reward them that behave Like good Soldiers and to punish them Who by their un Soldier Like behavour May Demand it : the L! Colo is Surpiised that After So many Repeeted orders to y? Contrary the men Should Presume to burn Fences or Destroy y? Property of any of the Inhabitence the officers are Calld upon : & Injoind to Prevent any Such thing for the Future & to Indeavour to find out those Who have Ben guilty that they May be brought to tryal and Punished y? men in general are amaising Dilatory in turning out when Required the Adjtn and Sargt Magor are to Require ye Sarj.^{ts} to turn out their Men and have them on ye Parade 'Imediately when Required : those Sarj.^{ts} Who Dont Bring on their Men Accordingly are to be Punished but if ye men Refuse to Comply with ye orders they Receive from their Non Com officers they are ordered to Be Confined & they May Rest Asured they Shall be Punished Sevearly :

As Commissioned officers of Companies Attend Role Call morning & Evening they will take Perticuler Care to Bring thoes men who Do not attend and have no Leave of Absence to a Condine Punishment

---

HEAD QUARTERS, JULY 30.TH, 1777.

Parole, *President.*   Countersign, *Hancock.*

General Varnam
Major [David Fithian] Sill
B. Major [Ebenezer] Flagg   } officers of the Day.
Adgertent [Henry] Ten Eyck

Persuant to ye orders Rec.^{d} from Genr.^{l} Washington 2 Brigades namely genr.^{l} McDougles & general Huntingtons are Emediately to Pack up their heavy Bagage & Convey it over the River and hold them Selves in Redyness to March with four Days Provision *ready drawn to march* at a Minutes Warning and all the Partys Detachd from Either of the Brigades on [*or*] any out Posts Exept the guard at Danbury & those on Bourd ye Ships and Whale boats are *ordered* Emediatly to Join their Respective Regiments.

The Garrison at Fort Constitution is reduced to a Cap.^{ts} command consisting of one Company from Genl Varnum's Brigade. Major [Ebenezer] Huntington is to return to the Reg.^{t} & all the Troops belonging to Genl McDougall's Brigade are immediately to join their respective Reg.^{ts}.

Lt. Col.^{o} [David] Dimon is to march immediately to the White Plaines with his Reg.^{t} to relieve Col.^{o} Cortlandt & the Detachment under his Command who are immediately to join their respective Brigades instead of marching to Fort Montgomery, which is occasioned by the different orders since rec.^{d} from Genl Washington.

The Bridge is to furnish 9 Centries if Necessary. The Hospital guard four, two at each Barrack.

Mr. Simeon Belding late Qr Mr of Colo [Samuel] Wyllys's Regt is appointed Qr Mr to Genl Parson's Brigade.

HEAD QUARTERS, JULY 31, 1777.

Parole, *Jamaica*.   C. Sign, *Flushing*.

Brigadier general Parsons
Lt Colo [Samuel] Printice   } officers of the Day.*
Brigd Magor Humphris [David Humphreys]

John kenis (*Kavas*) of the 3 Pensylvania Regt Commanded by Colo Ward (*Wood*) was tryd for Disartion the Court Sentance the Prisoners to Receave 100 Lashes on ye naked back Tomorrow mornig at Guard Mounting: Samuel oakley † of West Chaster County was Tryd for being an Enemy To his Cuntry & a Robber taking arms also as being Spy from the Enemy it was unnessary to Produce Any Evidence altho it Might have ben Produced ye Prisoner of his own accord Confest as Much as ye Court Could Require to be Satisfied of his guilt ye Court Judged the Prisoner guilty of ye Crimes Eledged Against him Concidering the Extraodenary & Atrotious Nature of his Crime as a Robber & Spye from ye Enemy also taken in arms Sentance him to Suffer the Pains of Death Reuben Smith Tryd as an Enemi to his Contry & a Robber of ye well Effected Inhabitance the Cort agudg the Prisoner Guilty of ye whole Crime *and* in order that the ·Examplery Punishment May Sarv to Deter other Villins from Commiting ye Like Crimes Sentance him to Receive 100 Lashes on the Naked Body the first 20 of which are to be Inflicted on ye grand Perade the tomorrow morning

Remainder to Inflicted at the head of Each Brigade Day by Day Provided the Same No of 100 Lashes be not Deminished or Lessned after which Sd Prisoner is to be Sent on Bourd one of the (*Continental*) Ships of war in ye North River there to Be kept to hard Labour at ye Same time to be Secured from Making his Escape During the Present war: John Hartstone (*Houston*) Capt in

---

* Adjutant Hart.—*Platt*.   † *Lemuel Akerly*.

Colo gansaevils* Reg? Tryd for y? following Charges first for Disurt-
ing to the Enemy While a Cap? in y? Continental Service & after he
had Rc? 500 Dollars Recruiting money and taking with him to y?
Enemi Secondly for forfiting y? Confidence Placed in him by Colo
Lamb for his going to y? Peekskill 3? for Disarting the gentlemen
under *whose* Confidence he was Put in order to be Conducted to
Genr! Putnam 4!y for Forging a Pass *signed* "by order of General
McDougle Richard Platt Magor of [Br]" as to the first Charge òf
Disarting to y? Enemy y? Court is of Appinan that the Prisoner is
not guilty *thereof. As to the Remainder of the Charges against him,
the Court is of opinion that the Prisoner is guilty of the same* as allso
Appears by his own Confession the Court therefore order & adgudg
that y? S? Hartstone (*Houston*) be Dismissed from y? army y? general approoves the Sentance & orders the BD [Brigade] Magor of
the Day to see them Put into Execution as above Directed & that
John hutson leave the Camp Emediatly   Samuel Oakerly [Lemuel
Akerly] to be Exercuted on Munday 11th Day of August next between y? hours of 9 & 11 oclock in y? fore noon y? Execution of
Edmund Palmer & Amos Rose which was to be tomorrow is Respited till munday next at y? Same time of the Day   y? Court martial of which Colo [John Durkee] Durkey was Presid[ent] President is Desolved

   Brigade orders   Colo [Samuel] Prentice Regiment to Furnish
the generals guard tomorrow all the Musick in the Brigade to attend
on the Grand Perade tomorrow morning L? Colo Prentice Regt to

---

* This record well illustrates the difficulty of tracing the persons intended.
"Gansaevil" is evidently intended for Gansevoort, and Peter Gansevoort was appointed Colonel of the Third Battalion of New York, 21 November, 1776.
Hartstone or Hutson were not found in any New York Company; but Platt
Orderly Book gave it as Captain John Houston of Gansevoort's Regiment. In
1775, Houston was a Second Lieutenant in the New York line, and when the
force was re-organized at the end of 1776, was recommended for a Captaincy, as
an "excellent officer and unprovided for." He received a commission, but the
record suddenly becomes silent as to his service. I give in parallel columns the
names of the three officers of Houston's regiments, the first column being taken
from the *State Archives, The Revolution*, I, p. 140, and the second from *Calendar
of Historical Manuscripts*, II, 49:—

John Houston, Capt.	John Houston, Capt.
John Welder, Lieut.	John Welch, Lieut.
Prentice Brower, 2? Lieut.	Prentice Bowen, 2? Lieut.

Send 1 Sarg! 1 Cor! & 12 Privates to Releave the guard at fourt Independance

Regimental Orders   Camp a Peekskill July 31 1778[1777].
the Court marshel of Which Cap! [John] mills was President is Desolved   No officer for the future will give Leave of Absence from Camp to any Soldier & None is to Be absent without Leave of one of ye Field officers & he is to have his Permition in writeing or he may Expect to be taken up and Punished   Captains or officers Commanding Com^y s are fourthwith to Make out Returns to the Lt Col^o of the men they have in their Companies & Whare they are and those that Absent and by whose Permition &c ye Lt Colo Recomends to ye Comisnd officers to turn out Every Day to inform them Selves into Every part of Exercise Nessary for an officer to understand ye Sarj^{ts} & Cor^{ls} are to turn out Every Day twice to Exersise By them Selves

---

HEAD QUARTERS AUGUST Y^E 1 1777

general Varnam
Colo [Samuel] Wyllys
BD Magr Flag *
Adj! [Elisha] Hopkins
} officers of the Day

the Court of inquirery of which Colo [John] Chandler was President is Desolved the general has been informd that Much Damage has ben Done by the main guard in ye housé whare it has ben kept By Cuting ye Pillars of the Peazza Pulling up the flore &c he therfore Strictly Injoins it upon ye Main Guard and all other Guards to take special Care not to Injure the Houses in which they are kept or the ajacent Buildings *under severe Penalties.*

HEAD QUARTERS PEEKS KILL 2 AUGUST 1777

Parole, *Cowardice.*   C. Sign, *Death.*

Brigadier Gen! Parsons
Lt. Col^o Sherman
B. Major [David] Humphreys
Adjutant Holden
} Officers of the Day.

* Box—*Platt.*

Camp Peeks July   Camp Peekskills August 4 1777 Brig^d. Gen^rl
Parsons Lt Col^o Olny Brigade Maj^r Omppres [David Humphreys]
Adj^t [Henry] Ten Eyck Officers of the Day   Gen^rl Putnams Guard
to Consist of 24 Privates the Gen^rl has Reason to know that the
attention of the Enemy is turned towards the North River and the
passes on the high Land Dayly and hourly Expects an Attack Recommends and enjoins it upon all Officers in this Department
Emediatly to Examin the state of the arms & amunition of their
men and See that they are Put in the Best Condition   the Surgeon
of Several Reg^ts are Directed to Make Dayly Returns of the Sick
under their Care to Doctr Burnet Surgeon & Phisition Genr^l   Colo
[Charles] Webbs Regt to Furnish ye generals guard tomorrow.

HEAD QUARTERS PEEKSKILL AUGUST Y^E 5TH 1777

Parole, *Barry.*   C. Sign, *Burk.*

General McDougle
Colo [Heman] Swift
BD Magor [Richard] Platt   } officers of the Day.
Ajertent Royce [Nehemiah Rice]

a Fatigue Party To Consist of one Capt 1 Sublt and 150 men to
Perade tomorrow morning at 6 oclock *to bring up the Boats from
Kings Ferry to Fort Montgomery.* A subalterns party of thirty men
to parade to-morrow morning at 6 o'clock with their arms & with
Six Days Provision from genr^l McDougles BD the officer of ye Party
to wait on ye general for orders ye four Brigades in this Department
are to form 2 Divisions : Brigadier McDougle & Brigadier Genl
Huntington to form one Intire Division Bd gen^l Parsons & general
Varnams Brigades to make another Division to Be Commanded By
the Senier Brigadier of Each Division
    The Detachment that lately returned from White Plains with
Colo Cortlandt have liberty to discharge their Pieces this Evening
at Retreat Beating under the Direction of their officers.
    Brigade orders the Senior Field officer of General Parsons Brigade
to Command : Colo Wyllys to Command till Further orders in order
more Effectually to Prevent any Reledation of Disipline and Loss of
arms   one Company of Each Reg^t in ye Brigade is to [be] off Duty

Every Day & to Be Peraded with their arms & Accutrements and a Carefull Examination to be made at which time all ye officers in the Camp are to be Present the Duty required of the Reg^t are to be Done By the other Companyes and Defeerances are to be Carfully noticed the Companies Deficiancys & Names of ye Soldiers to be Returned to ye Commanding officer of ye Reg^t a Coppy theirof to be kept by the Commanding Officer of Companies Which is Carefully to be Examined with ye Deficiances found and the next Examination for all which the Soldiers Will Be Charged and Stopages Made from his Wages unless they arise from unEvitable Providence or in ye Way of his Duty a Report to Be made Every Eight Days By ye Commanding officer of the Reg^t to the Brigadier General as it is perticularly ye Duty of the Sarjeants to See the orders of ye officerr Carryed into Execution it is Recomended that they make Dayly Reports of the State of the Company to the officers & that Every officer make him Self thoroughly Aquainted With State of the Companys to which they Belong and at all times to Be able to Render a Particular Account thirof

Detales for Guard	Colo Charles Webbs Regiment				
	C	S	S	C	DF	P^r
Colo Webb for Guard . . .	o	I	I	I		8
for Piquit						4
Fatigue for the boats . . .	I	o	o	o		8
for Common Fatigue . . .	o	o	o	o		2

Capt [David] Parsons * Company 1 Sarjt 4 men for Main Guard August ye 6th 1777

HEAD QUARTERS AUGUST 6TH 1777

Brigadier General Huntington
Colo [Philip Burr] Bradley
Br^d Magor [Roger] Alden   } Officers of the Day
Adj^t [Elihu] Marvin

Colo Charles Webbs Regimen in general Parsons BD is to Be Mustered tomorrow morning at 8 [*five*] oclock and the Com^y of Light Dragoon † at Eight [*six*] oclock Do that the Workmen of the Ar-

---

* At this time a prisoner in the hands of the British.

† A part of Sheldon's Regiment.

moury Be Subject to the orders of Colo Allen the Superintendant. the Commanding officers of the Respective Reg^{ts} are to give orders for Repairing the Defective arms in their Respective Regts With A Cartifycate how the arms Come Defective those that are Cartifyd to Want Repairing by unEvitable Exident the armours are to Repair without Chargeing to ye Reg^t those that are Cartifyd to be So through the Deficiancy of Soldier are to Be Chargd to the Reg^t An Account of Cost and the Names of the Soldiers are to be monthly Transmited to the Comnding officer of the Reg^t Who is to Deliver the Same To the Pay Master of Reg^t and he is to Stop Such Cost out of the Defitiant (*defaulting*) Soldiers Wages

the Signal to be given by ye Sub^{ltn} and his Party (*of thirty*) gone towards Harvestraw & (*on*) their Discovering the Enemy fleet to be Coming up the North River is a Large *fire &* Smoke on ye hill

BRIGADE ORDERS AUGUST Y^E 6TH 1777

all the Men belonging to Colo Demons Reg^t who have been Releavd from Duty Sence the Reg^t Marchd or who have recovered from Sickness So as to be able to do Duty are to joine the Reg^t at White Planes without the least Delay Lt Colo Reg^t * to Releave the guard at fourt Independance with A Sarj^t Cor^l & 12 men Colo [Samuel] Wyllyses Reg^t to Releave ye guard at Robinsons Mills with the Like Number Each Party to Carry 3 Days Provision Colo Webbs Detales for guard S C D F P

	S	C	D	F	P
	1	1	1	1	8
for Piquit				2	

HEAD QUARTERS AUGUST 7TH 1777

Parole, *George.*   C. Sign, *Clinton.*

General McDougle †
Colo [John] Chandler
BD Magor Box   } Officers of the Day tomorrow.
Adj^t Leonard

Colo Angels and Colo Samuel B Webbs Regiments are to Be Mustered tomorrow Morning at 5 oclock all ye Brigades are to Perade

* Varnum—*Platt.*   † Regnier?

to morrow morning on yͤ hill By the gallows to Attend the Execution of Amos Rose & Edmund Palmor * at a genrᶦ Court Marshel held at fourt Muntgumery on yͤ 5ᵗʰ of august 1777 By order of Genrᶦ Putnam Lt Colo Meggs [Return Jonathan Meigs] Presedent Samuel Gray a Soldier in Capt Hautrimacks Company Colo Douglases Regt Was Arained for Trͮal for Desartion found Guilty and ordered to Be led to yͤ gallows with A Rope Round his Neck and their to Receive 100 Lashes on his Naked Back and Drͮumd out of garrison.†David Smith A Soldier in Capᵗ Goodens [Henry Godwin] Comͽ Colo Deboys [Dubois] Regᵗ Was tryed for Disartion and Sentanced to Receive 50 Lashes on his naked Back. Isaac Dolelson [Donaldson] A Soldier in Capᵗ [Thomas] Lees Company Colo Deboys [Dubois] Regt Was tryd for Sleeping on his Post found Guilty and to Receive 50 Lashes on his naked Back yͤ General Approves of the Sentances of the Court Martial & orders yͤ Prisoners to Receive their Punishment as Respectively ordered Excepting that Part only Respecting Samuel Grays being Drͮumd out of garison : that Instid of that he be Confined (*to service*) on bourd the Ship

at A genᶦ Court Marshel held at Peekskill August 5ᵗʰ 1777

By order of General Putnam Colo Samuel B Webb Tryd Lt Samuel Cringeon (*Simeon Cregier*) ‡ of Capt [Benjamin] Walkers § Company yͤ 4 New york Battallion Was arained and tryed on a Charge

---

* It was in this case that Putnam wrote the curt letter to Clinton that is so often quoted as an example of his energy. Clinton had sent a flag to Verplanck's Point, demanding Edmund Palmer, then in the hands of the Americans, as a lieutenant in the British service. Putnam wrote in reply:

HEAD QUARTERS, 7 AUGUST, 1777.

Edmund Palmer, an officer in the enemy's service, was taken as a spy lurking within our lines; he has been tried as a spy, condemned as a spy, and shall be executed as a spy, and the flag is ordered to depart immediately.

ISRAEL PUTNAM.

P. S.—He has been accordingly executed.

A very fanciful account of this incident may be found in Bolton, *History of Westchester County*, I, 72.

† It was Samuel Gray, of Captain John F. Hamtranck's Company, of Colonel Lewis Dubois' Regiment.

‡ His name is not on the New York Revolutionary rolls.

§ He was later Aid to Baron Steuben, and in 1782 to General Washington.

brot Against him for Steeling from & Plunder the Inhabitents of Many Valuable Articles when he Was Sent out with a Party With Express orders to Protect them from being Plundered upon full hearing the Evidence & the Prisoner the Court find him gudge (*and adjudge*) him guilty of the Vialation of ye first Article 13 in Section 9th 16th Article Sec^{t} 13th and the 21 Ar^{t} Sect 14 of ye Martial Law & there upon orders S^{d} Ensign Gray (*Cregier*) to be Cashiered and the name Place of Aboad Crime & Punishment of S^{d} Ensn be Published in ye Publick New prints of ye State of New york and that S^{d} Cringeon (*Cregier*) Be Confined on bourd the Ships at fourt Muntgumery till Restitution be made by him to ye Sufferers the Genl Approves of ye Doeings of ye Court Martial Exepting his being Confined on bourd the Ships and there upon Sentance S^{d} Ens^{n} Cregeon to be Confined (*cashiered*) and to (*be*) Sent under guard to the Convention of this State to be by them Further Punished and held till Restoration Be Made By him to Whome he has Plundered as ye Convention Shall Judg Proper the Commanding officer of the Train of Artillery & Light Dragoon are ordered to Make Returns of their Respective Companies at this and the ajacent Posts Emediately

---

Division Orders, August 7, 1777.

One hundred and twenty men from Genl Huntington's Brigade properly officered to parade at Gen'l McDougalls Encampment tomorrow morning at six o'clock with one days provision without arms, there to take orders from Col^{o} Durkee. Ensign Cole who has charge of the Intrenching Forts will see them collected every Evening. He will also at the same time return all axes to the Reg^{ts} that are borrowed of them.

The Service has been greatly injured by the Delay of making up the Pay Rolls & Abstracts in due Season. Genl McDougall therefore expressly orders that the Pay Rolls of each Reg^{t} for every Month be punctually bro't to the respective Brigadiers the first day of every Month after Pay becomes due, ready to be attested; in Order that they may be put into the Hands of the Pay Master, to enable him to receive the Money for the Regiment, whenever the Military Chest shall be in Cash. Whoever fails to obey this Order, will be put in Arrest.

HEAD QUARTERS AUGUST Yᴱ 8ᵀᴴ 1777

Parole, *Hanover*.   C. Sign, *Square*.

General Varnam
Lᵗ Colo [Josiah] Starr
Brigade Mᵣ [David] Humphris   } officers of the Day
Adjᵗ Smith

Colo Bradleys Regt to Be Mustered tomorrow morning at 5 oclock are Directed to be Prepared Accordingly

And the unreasonable prices extorted from the soldier by the market People for want of a Rule or Standard to regulate the Prices of Articles sold in Camp shall be as follows: Butter, 2 / pᵣ lb. Mutton & Lamb at 8*d*—Veal 6*d* Milk 6d pᵣ Quart. Potatoes 6 / pᵣ Bushel—Squashes 1 / pᵣ Peck Beans or Peas in the Pod 1 / 6 pᵣ peck. Cucumbers 1 / pᵣ Dozen Pig for roasting 1 / pᵣ lb. Turnips Carrits & Beets 6 / pᵣ Bushel. The above Prices in New York Money & no Person or Persons in Camp may give or take for the above enumerated Articles more than the Stated Prices & so in proportion for greater or lesser Quantities on pain of forfeiting the Article or the value thereof.

The Provost Guard is reduced to 1 C 1 S 1 S 1 C 2 DF 34 P.

DIVISION ORDERS, 9 AUGUST, 1777.

One Hundred & twenty men properly officered from Gen'l Huntington's Brigade to parade to-morrow morning at' six o'clock at Genl. McDougall's Encampment—there to take Orders from Colo. Durkee.

HEAD QUARTERS, PEEKS KILL, 10 AUGUST, 1777.

Brigᵣ Genᶫ Varnum
Lᵗ Colᵒ [Giles] Russel
B. Major [Roger] Alden   } officers of the Day.
Adjutant [Thomas] Converse

At a Genᶫ Court Martial held at Peeks Kill by Order of the Honᵇˡᵉ Major General Putnam on the 9ᵗʰ August, 1777, Samᶫ B. Webb, President:

Cornelius Bradley of Capt Humphrey's Company in Lt. Col^o Prentice's Reg.^t was tried for Desertion, carrying off his gun & inlisting again in Capt Meads Comp.^y —found guilty and ordered to receive 100 Lashes on his naked back.

Thomas Spencer of Capt Mansfield's Comp.^y in Lt Col^o Prentice's Reg.^t was tried for Desertion, found guilty and ordered to receive 50 Lashes on his naked back.

George Cook tried for sleeping on his post, found guilty & ordered to receive 50 Lashes on his naked back, but as he had been unwell for several Days & kept awake two or three Nights before, by his Distemper, was then unfit for Duty & was standing up when found asleep,—The Court recommend him to the Genl for a Pardon.

The General approves the Proceedings & Judgment of the Court Martial against the several Prisoners aforesaid & gives Sentence against them respectively to receive their several Punishments ordered by the Court Martial to-morrow morning at 6 o'clock.

BRIGADE ORDERS AUGUST Y.^E 8TH 1777

Colo Wyllyses Regt to furnish ye generals guard tomorrow the Same fatigue tomorrow as usal

---

HEAD QUARTERS AUGUST 9TH 1777

Parade, *Ulster*.   C. Sign, *Orange*.

Brigadier gen.^l Huntington
Magor Hart [Hait]
Brigd Magor [Richard] Platt   } officers of the Day
Adj.^t Marshel

Colo Swifts & Colo Livingstones Regts to be Mustered tomorrow morning at 5 oclock   the general is Surprised at the averices of the Contry

Regimental orders Camp at Peekskill August ye 11th 1777

the Reg.^t officers and men to Be upon the Perade Emediatly after ye firing of the Morning Gun

A Very Perticuler attention to Be Paid to this order the arms to Be Bright and Clean

HEAD QUARTERS AUGUST Y^E 11TH 1777

General Huntington
Lt Colo [Matthew] Mead   ⎫
Brigad Magor Box   ⎬ officers of the Day
Adjt Hart   ⎭

Amos Rose and Samuel Oakerly (*Akerly*) are Respited from Execution till Munday after Next   a hogshead of flower was found
buryd in the Ground in the Reer of Colo Wyllyses Incampment
Any Parson Claiming the Same Will Appear and Make Evident their
Property in S^d Flour within four Days or it will be liable to Be used
for the Publick

two barrels of good tobacco to be Sold (*at 7 o'clock*) tomorrow
Morning at Vendue on the grand Perade Which Was taken from
ye Enemy

	C	S	S	C	DF	P
Colo Webbs Detals for Guard	o	o	1	1	2	11
For Piquit	o	1	1	1		4

Colo Wyllys Reg^t to Furnish the generals Guard tomorrow Colo
Webbs to Furnish ye Guard at the Commisarys Colo Wyllys Reg^t to
furnish the Cattle guard this Evening

HEAD QUARTERS AUGUST 12TH 1777

General Varnam
Magor Johnson   ⎫
B^r Maj^r [David] Humphries   ⎬ officers of the Day
Adj^t [Elisha] Hopkins   ⎭

Colo Hughs D. Q. M General of this Department presents his
Most Respectfull Complements to the Genr^l officers and Colos
Commanding *or commanders of* Regts and others Who have had
Clothing at the Q^r M General Store in Either or both of Preceading
Campaigns and Begs Leave to Aquaint them the Accounts that Re-
main Unsettled are in his hands   the Regimental & Brigade Q M^r
and Deputy Q M^r genr^l of Divisions are forbid to take or Give any
orders for forage without Permition from Capt *Thomas* Campbell
Forage Master for this Department at the Continental Villiage Colo
Durkeys and Cortlands Reg^t in Genr^l McDougles Brigade are to be

Mustered tomorrow Morning at 6 oclock and Colo Chandlers Reg.
with Cap. Lees Com. of Artillery are to be Mustered Next Day
after tomorrow morning at 6 oclock   2 Subs 4 Sarj. 4 Cor.ls & 50
men Saylors if to be got to Perade tomorrow Morning Opposit to
y.e generals in order to Man the Shark and Campden Galleys

   Detales for guard &c

	S	C	DF	P
for the Galleys	I	I		II
for fatigue				2

   Colo Prentice Regt to furnish the Generals guard tomorrow Colo
Wyllys Reg. to Releave the guard at the Comisary Store   the Same
fatigue tomorrow as today

HEAD QUARTERS AUGUST Y.E 13.TH 1777

Perole *Gates*   & Countersn *Troop*.

General Huntington ⎫
Maj. Sedgwick   ⎪
                   ⎬ officers of the Day
BD Magor [Richard] Platt ⎪
Adj. [Henry] Ten Eyck ⎭

   as the Enemys fleet have Disappeared for Some time with Evident
Design to Supprise Some Part of this Continent and there is the
Greatest Reason *to suspect* that they will Supprise this Post and that
Very Soon.   the general is greatly Pleased at the Sperit Discovered
in the Millitia in turning out so Chearfully in Defance of their Rights
& Privaledges Against our Cruel Enemy in this busy time of the
year and that they *may* be able to Render the Best Service to their
Country : the gen.l Directs the Commanding offiers of Reg.ts to Mus-
ter & Examin their Respective Reg.ts and Companies of Mellitia
Respecting their Arms Accutrements and Aminition and See that
they are Put in the best Condition and Report there Deficiencies
Also that they Exercise there men from Six Oclock Untell ten in the
Morning and four till seven In the After noon *every day*.   Whereas
the Gen.l is Enform.d that the Enhabitents Refuse to Sell their Milk
to the Troops at the Staited price for Six pence per Quart which is
a veary high price and Considering that it is of the Last Importance
that the Troops be supplyed. and willing that the Enhabitents should

be paid a Risonable Price for what they supply the Trops with   The Gen! Orders a brave and Prudent Officer with thirty men to be De-tach^d from Each Brigade to Collect the Cows from these who Refuse to sell there Milk at the stated price in the Several Brigades s^d Offi-cer is to take An Account of the Cows *their* No Marks Natural and Artificial. and the Owners names this to Be Done this After noon and S^d Cows to be Milked to Supply s^d Troops and kept under Guard till the Owners Engage to Sell the Milk what they Can Spare from there *own families* to the Troops at the Stated price   the Gen Directs the general Directs the Commanding officers of Regts Emediately to Cause Every Soldier in their Regts that Shall be found taking or Robing Any Guardian of the Fruite or Burning Rails *or fence* Be-longing to Private Property to be Whipt on the Naked Back at the Discretion of the Commanding officer According to the Demerit Not Exceading twenty Lashes without the formalty of Tryal By A Court Martial   A Serj^t Cor! & 12 men is ordered to perade tomor-row morning at 6 oclock to guard A Number of prisoners to Sapours [Esopus]   Colo Webbs Reg^t to furnish the generals Guard tomorrow & Cattle grd this Eveng

HEAD QUARTERS AUGUST 14TH 1777

Parole, *Danbury*.   C. Sign, *Litchfield*.

Brigadier gen! Ward
Lt Colo Wesenfield*   ⎫
BD Mag^r [Roger] Alden   ⎬ Officers of the Day
Adj^t Selden   ⎭

the general hereby Acquaints the officers of the Army that ye Barachs at No. 3 are thoroughly Clensed and to be Improoved as a general horspatal for the Reception of the sick and Wounded   the officers and Regamental Surgeons in this Department are Directed Strictly to observe & follow ye Directions of Congress Respecting the Sick & Wounded   Phisition & Surgeon gen! May know how to Dispose of them & Doct Burnet is Directed to Report Any that Shall Neglect or fail of this Necessary Part of their Duty to the Commander in Chief of this De Partment or the Director Gen! of

* Weissenfels.

this Department that they May Be Duely Punished : the Genr! orders that all yᵉ Drumers in this Department Make Returns of the State of their Drums to the Commanding officers of Regts who is hearby Directed to Cause those wanting *repairs* to be *immediately* Repared & in future yᵉ Drumers are to keep their own Drums in Repare at their own Expence the Commanding officers of Regts & Companys are to See that they Doe it and in Case of neglect the officers are to See it Done and Stopages are to be made out of their Wages to Pay the Same

The Regimental Returns of the sick to Docʳ Burnet Physician & Surgeon Gen! have of late been very deficient.

The Regimental Surgeons are enjoined punctually to observe & perform their Duty in that Respect agreeable to the Resolutions of Congress that the

1 S 2 S 2 C 30 P to parade to morrow Morning at 6 o'clock with axes & spades to mend the Road from Kings Ferry to Peeks Kill. The Party will receive the Tools at Qʳ Mʳ Gen!ˢ Store at Continental Village.

HEAD QUARTERS AUGUST Yᴱ 15ᵀᴴ 1777

Parole, *Adams.*   C. Sign, *Wyllys.*

BD General Varnam
Colo Samuel B Webb *
Brigade Magor Box   } officers of the Day
Adjᵗ Waterman

found By one of Colo Swifts Regᵗ in Last June A large Pack Containing A Regimental Coat faced with Brown with A Book & Sundry Articels in it which the owner may have By Aplying to the Adjᵗ of Sᵈ Regᵗ and making Evident his Property   the Commanding officer of yᵉ Militia Regts and Companies are to take Spetial Care that their *men* Dont go off without Being Regulerly Discharged and *that* none to go without Returning *all* their Camp utentials flints Cartreges & Every thing Drawn out of the Store on Pain of Paying for those articles *themselves*   the Melitia in general Wards Brigade have leave to Discharge their Pieces this Evening at Retreet beeting under the Direction of their officers

* Colo Durkee, *Platt.*

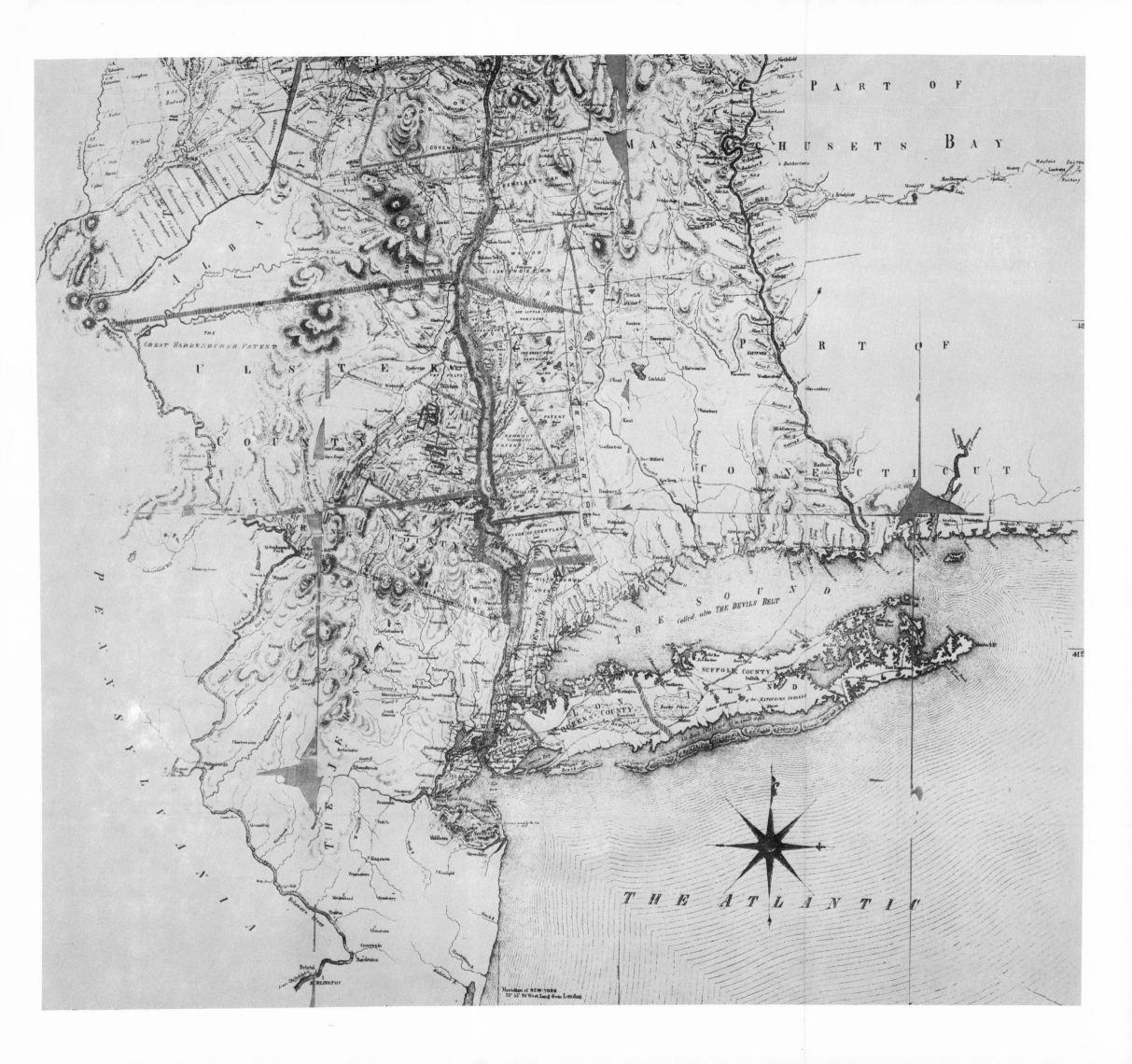

HEAD QUARTERS AUGUST 16.TH 1777

General Huntington ⎫
Mag.r Holdrey [Hezekiah Holbridge] ⎪
BD Maj.r [David] Humphris ⎬ officers of the Day
Adj.t Royce [Nehemiah Rice] ⎭

Colo Mosely Lost on y.e 14.th Instent A Large Spyglass Shagreen Case that might be taken Apart   Any Parson finding the Same and *will* Return it to the owner or to head Qrs Shall Receive 3 Dollers Reward and no Questions Asked

the Soldiers Who are Ingaged in y.e Eight Month Service Either By Inlistment or otherwise Allso those of the 2 Battallion Raised by the State of Connecticut untill the first of January [*June*] next as well as those of the Melitia have Liberty to List into the 3 year Sarvice or During the war Returning the Premiams they have alredy Recd from that State in Part towards y.e Premeum to be Paid by that State as (*to the*) Soldiers Inlisted in to the Continental Service as Above S.d : and those of the Eight Month men and of y.e 2 Battalion[s] and those Inlisted as teemsters or Waggoners Must Return the Premeams Recd from the State *of Connecticut*. a general Cortmarshel is Apointed to Set next Munday at 9 oclock at the Widow Warrens Colo Durkey President

L.t Col.o Wyllys, Majors Huntington & Stanley, 1 C, 2 S from McDougalls, Parsons and Huntington's Brigades, members.

HEAD QUARTERS AUGUST 17.TH 1777

Parole, *Tappan.*   C. Sign, *Bay.*

General Ward ⎫
Lt Colo [Samuel] Prentice ⎪
BrD Major Box * ⎬ Officers of the Day
Adjt [Elihu] Marven ⎭

* Platt.

HEAD QUARTERS AUGUST 18TH 1777

Parole, *Burlington*.   C. Sign, *Slip*.

General Hunting[ton]

Colo [Israel] Angel

BD Magor Box   officers of the Day *

Adjt Rogers

the general orders that all the Drum & Fife Magrs Make Returns Emediately of the Drums & Fifes in the Respective Regts also how many are wanting that they May be Furnished and Repared & after that the Drumers and Fifers are to keep them in Repair *at their own expence.*

HEAD QUARTERS AUGUST 19TH 1777

Parole, *Putnam*.   C. Sign, *Webb*.

general Huntington

Colo [Israel] Angel

BD Magor Box   Officers of the Day

Adjt Rogers

the general takes notice that the greatest Loads Drawn in Carts and Wagons are of hearty & well men Whereby the Teams are greatly Woryed he orders that no Soldier Ride in Carts or Wagons Except the Drivers and Sick Who are ordered to be Carryd on Pain of Being Whipt 20 Lashes on the naked Back   Such officers as have not Carryd in their Muster Roles to ye Deputy Muster Master Genrl. Will take Notice that unless he is furnished with Em by tomorrow morning 8 oclock they Can not be Included *in* the Abstracts *that* are Emediately to Be Sent to Hed-Qrts

---

PEEKSKILL AUGUST 20TH 1777

Regimental orders Capts & officers Commanding Comys to Make a Return to ye Qr Mr of the number of men & of Tents and how Desposed of in their Respective Companies ye Qr Mr will make a Regimental Return of the Same kind & Deliver it to the Colo.

* Platt gives as the officers of the day: General Varnum, Colo Wyllys, Brigade Major Alden, and Adjutant Convers.

Prayers to be Attended at 6 oclock in ye morning & Emediatly after Retreet beeting at Evening   officers as well as men will Punctually Attend

the men are ordered to Cook nowhare But in the Rear of the Reg^t at ye Distance of 20 or 30 Rods from the Tents   the fires on the Sides and front of the Incampment are to Be Put Emediatly   all the men off Duty Exipt those Imployd in Cooking to turn out to Clean the Perade & Streets of the Incampment   the officer of the Day in future to See that the Tents are Struck Every Day if the Weather will Admit of it and See that the ground is Properly Dryed

----

HEAD QU^{RTS} AUGUST Y^E 20TH 1777

Parole, *Hempstead.*   C. Sign, *Plains.*

Colo [Charles] Webb
B^r D Maj^r [David] Humphris   } officers of the Day
Adj^t [Henry] Ten Eyck

at A gen^l. Cort Marshel held at Peekskill August 19th 1777   Colo Durkey President Lt Roger More and Ensign David Russel [Resco] *of Capt. Roger's company in Col^o.* [Roger] *Enos's regiment* Was Arained and Tryed for Mutiny & Disobaying orders and Refuseing to March and Secure [succour] this Post when ordered upon ye 7th of this Instant Both found guilty of ye Charge and ordered to be Cashiered the general Aproves of the Sentance & orders Lt Moure & Russel [Resco] to be Cashiered and to Deliver up their Commissions Emediately and Quit the Army   the Regimental Pay Master and [*or*] Commanding officers of Com^{ys} are Directed [*desired*] to Send Emediately to the Deputy Muster Master for their Muster Roles as he Expects to Leave this Post within a Day or two   the general orders that no officer or Soldier Presume to Ride any of the Wagon horses on any Pertence Whatever without A writen order from A general officer or ye Deputy Quarter Master General of this Department   one Capt 2 Subs from general Parsons Brgd to be Returnd on genr^l. Court marshel tomorrow morning at 9 oclock in the Room of those Who are gone on Comd

one Capt 2 Subs 2 Sarg^t 2 Cor^l. & 30 men to be taken from general Parsons BrD to go to Fishkill tomorrow morning to Releave

Capt. Catlin and his Party Imployd in making Cartriges & the men Should Be Such as have ben used to Such Business Colo Webb one Subalton and Six Privates

---

HEAD QUARTERS AUGUST YE. 21ST. 1777

Parole, *White Plains.* C. Sign, *Rye.*

Colo Swift
BrD Magor [Richard] Platt } Officers of the Day
Adjt. Royce [Rice]

if a Parson or Parsons of the Like [*following*] Description Should Make their appearance ye. General orders that they be taken up and Brought to Hed Qrs namely A lad About 17 years old 5 feet 3 Inches high Slim built Pock marked has the Apearance of a Creeold Light brown hair & Eyes &c Colo Printice Regt to furnish the generals gard tomorrow Colo Wyllyses Regt to furnish the Comisarys Guard tomorrow

Regimental Orders the officers Commanding Comy. are to Account to the Colo Emediatly of the arms Lost at the time When Capt. Parsons was taken

---

HEAD QUARTERS AUGUST YE. 22 1777

Parole, *Baltimore.* C. Sign, *Yates.*

Lt Colo Butler
BD Mager [Roger] Alden } officers of the Day
Adjt. [Elihu] Marvin

at a general Court Marshel Wharof Colo Durkey was President William Davis of Capt Barleys [Bardsley] Comy Colo Swifts Regt was Brought to Tryal for Steeling the 3d time the Prisoner Confesses him Self guilty & Beggs the Court to have Compasion on him the Cort Sentance him to Receave 100 Lashes on the naked Back and further order that he Be Sent on bourd one of the Continental Guard Ships in the north River (*at Fort Montgomery*) their to Be kept to hard labour During the war

John Benson of Capt. Bettses Company Colo C Webb Regt was Tryd for Disartion and Steeling Some good[s] the Prisoner pleeds guilty as to Disarting & as to the Rest [*theft*] he Confesses he had 5 Black Silk Hankerchiefs and 6 Check Linen D̄ọ that he gave 14 Dollars for and that the Same was taken from by one Heart by Virtue of an Advertisement the Cort adjudges the prisoner Guilty of the whole Charge and Sentance him to Receive 100 Lashes on the Naked Back and then Sent on bourd one of the Guard Ships [*Continental Frigates*] and their kept to hard Labour During the Present war the genr̄ḷ Aproves of the Above Sentances and orders them to Be Put in Execution tomorrow morning at Guard Mounting

GENERAL ORDERS HEAD Q̄ᴿ AUGUST 23ᴰ 1777

Parole, *Huntington*.   C. Sign, *Belfast*.

Colo Chandler   ⎫
BD Maj̄ṭ Box   ⎬ officers of the Day
Adj̄ṭ Convearce   ⎭

the general is very Sorry to See A Set of men in Camp Determined to Destroy the Morals & Lives of the Troops as well as the order and Disipline of yͤ army by Selling Spiritous Liquers he positively forbids any Parson Selling any kind of Spiritous Liquors Exept the State Comisarys to any Soldier without leave in writing from his Commanding officer and in Case any (*Inn Keeper*) Setler or Retailer Presume to transgress this order all his Liquers are Emediately to Be Seazed for the use of the hospatol the general thinks it Strange that there is Need of his Mentioning in order that it is yͤ Q̄ᴿ Masters Duty to Receave take Care of and Deliver out aminition to the Troops as their is Ocation

John Chilson of Col̄ọ Webb's Reḡṭ has lost a light brown Mare, 5 year old, 14 Hands high, trots & paces, main the off-side, short tail, tapering &c., & offers a Reward of 3 Dollars & Necessary Charges paid by him on Lieu̇ṭ Trowbridge of s̄ḍ Reḡṭ .

Strayed from the Stables at Head Quarters, a small chestnut colored mare of the Naraganset Breed, full of Spirits, tho' very low in flesh, small thin neck, with thick Bushy long main & Tail, trots & paces, & gallȯps off—formerly owned by M̄ṛ Bacon of Woodbury & perhaps gone that way. The Gen̄ḷ will give 3 Dollars reward to have her bro't into him.

HEAD Q^{RS} AUGUST 24.TH 1777

Parole, *Trumbull.*   C. Sign, *Wadsworth.*

Lt Colo Starr
BD Magor Humphris   } officers of the Day
Adjertent Ten Eyck

the General Court marshel Wharof Colo Durkey was President is
Desolved a General Court marshel to Set at Fort mountgumery on
Munday next at 8 oclock in the morning   Colo Deboice President
the Prisonrs under the Sentance of Death now under the prevost
guard have a further Restbit from their Execution untill the 2.^d Munday of September *next.*

HEAD Q^R PEEKSKILL AUGUST 25 1777

Parole, *Willet.*   C. Sign, *Stark.*

Magor Heart [Hait]
BD Maj.^r Platt   } Officers of the Day
Adj.^t Rogers

Pursuent to orders Rec.^d from general Washington the Train of
Artillery at this Post and their Dependant are Directed to make
Returns Weekly to general Putnam that he may Be able to make a
general Return to General Washington of the Artillery at this Post
upon the Present Prospect it is Probable the Troops will Remain
hear Some time   the Commanding officer of Each Reg.^t are Directed to Cause an aker of ground to be fixed for Turnups
the Seed the general has Sent after and will be hear Soon—
which Turnips will be for the use of the respective regiments.

A Detachment of 500 men Properly officered to Perade tomorrow
morning by the main Guard *at five o'clock* under the Command of
Colo Swift * and Lt Colo Mead and then and their to Receave their
orders to have two Days Provisions Cooked &c   Regimental orders
Peekskill August 25.th 1777   those men that have not taken the oath
of Fidelity to the States are to be Sworn tomorrow at 10 oclock
officers Commanding Companies will make a list of the Men that
have not taken the oath to Deliver to the Judg advocate Who is to
Sware them

* Platt says *Webb.*

HEAD Q^R AUGUST Y^E 26TH 1777

Lt Colo Russell
BD Maj^r Alden } officers of the Day &c
Adj^t Rogers *

Strayed from Genl Putnam's Stable a small brown Horse, about 14 hands high, Star in his forehead, snip Nose, trots & Canters well, has a Bunch on one hind leg just above the Hoof; any person finding him is to return him to Head Quarters & shall receive Six Dollars reward & all necessary Charges paid.

Thomas Sales [Yates] Esqr is Apointed Ad C to Magor Gen Putnam and is to be obayd and Respected acordingly the officer of the Prevost guard from time to time are to take Care that the Barrocks at No 2 are kept Clean

a number of Blanks for Regimental Returns are at head Q^{rs} Redy for the use of the Regiments

---

HEAD Q^{RS} AUG^T 27TH 1777

Parole, *Varnum.* C. Sign, *Angel.*

Magor Johnson
BD Maj^r Box } officers of the Day
Adjt Marvin

Lately strayed from Genl McDougall's Encampment a large dark sorrel Mare, well built, no brand, or Mark, trots well, has two Quirls in her forehead, is four years old—Whoever shall take up & return s^d Mare to David Lauret Junr in Col^o Chandler's Reg^t shall receive 5 Dollars Reward from said Lauret.

General McDougles † Brigade has Leave to Discharge their Pieces this Evening under the inspection of their officers

---

HEAD QUARTERS AUG^T 28TH 1777

Parole, *Plymouth.* C. Sign, *Salem.*

Magor Sedgwick
BD Magor Humphris } Officers of the Day
Adjt Waterman

* Platt says *Rice.* † Platt says *Varnum's.*

To be sold to morrow morning at 8 o'clock at the House of Capt William Drake at public Vendue five Oxen, seven Cows & seven Horses which were taken from the Enemy by Major Blagden's light Dragoons, near Fort Independant on Fryday last.

Major Blagden's light Dragoons have liberty to fire their Pieces this Evening at Retreat Beating under the Direction of their Officers.

HEAD QUARTERS AUGT 29TH 1777

Parole, *Davenport.*   C. Sign, *Eno.*

Colo Durkey
BD Magor Platt   } officers of the Day
Adjt Converce

a genl Court marshel is apointed to Set tomorow morn at 9 oclock at the Widow Warrens Colo Angel President

2 Capts and 2 Subalterns from Genl McDougalls Brigade.

1	"	2	"	"	Varnum's	"
1	"	2	"	"	Parson's	"
1	"	1	"	"	Huntington's	"

Genl Varnams Brigade Excused from Duty tomorrow for Brigade Exercise & Scurmishes by firing Field peacs and Plattoons and Each of the other Regiments will have the Same Indulgence in their Turns

---

HEAD QUARTERS AUGT 30TH 1777

Parole, *Green.*   C. Sign, *Yates.*

Lt Colo Levingston
BD Magr Alden   } officers of the Day
Adjt Johnson

Colo C Webbs Regt to furnish ye Genl Guard tomorrow

HEAD QUARTERS AUGT 31ST 1777

Parole, *Norwalk.*   C. Sign, *Stratford.*

Magor Th[a]yer
BD Majr Box   } officers of the Day
Adjt Marshel *

* Rogers, *Platt.*

Major Ward is apointed a member of the Court marshel that is to Set tomorrow in the Room of one *of the Captains* in General Varnams [*McDougall's*] Brigade

Taken up a stray & bro't to Head Quarters: a brown or bay Horse, about 14 Hands high, four years old, a large Starr in his Forehead, white on his Nose, both hind Feet white, some white on his Forefeet above his hoofs, trots & canters.

Any Person that can evince his Title to him, may [have] him.

HEAD QUARTERS SEPTEMBER Y^E 1 1777

Parole, *Maryland.* C. Sign, *Baltimore.*

Major Huntington
BD Maj^r Humphris } officers of the Day
Adj^t Royce

the Quarter masters of the Several Reg^ts are ordered to Carry in their Bill for Back Rations to the Comisary to the first of September Inclusively that they may be alowed & Settled According to their former Establishment

---

HEAD QUARTERS SEPTR 2 1777

Parole, *Franklin.* C. Sign, *France.*

Lt Colo Printice
BD Magor Platt } officers of the Day
Adjt Marvin

the time for Mustering ye Troops in this Department is again arived the Commanding officers of Comys of artillery Light Draggoons foot & Artificers will Emediately Prepare their Muster Roles to the first of Sepr agreeable to the Usal form & as the honourable Continental Congress Will Dispence with only three Roles for the future it is Expected that all 3 will Be acutely Drawn and Produced upon the Perade at the time of Mustering Compleetly finished no Excuse Will be taken for any Defetiances in the Roles Such officers as have not Recd their Muster Roles of the Last muster are

Directed to Send to the muster master at Colo Sam! B Webbs * for the Same

1 Cap! 2 Subs 3 Sarj^{ts} 3 Cor! & 50 Privates to Perade to Morrow with Tools Proper for mending the highway between kings fery and Peekskill the Duputy Q^r Master will See them Properly furnished with Tools

Colo Webbs Reg! to furnish the gen! guard tomorw

	HEAD QR^{TS} SEP^T 3^D 1777
Parole, *Philadelphia*.	C. Sign, *Chester*.

L! Col? Cumstock
B Major [Roger] Alden } Officers of the Day.
Adjt [Henry] Ten Eyck

the Price of Cyder this year made in Camp Shall be 6^d York money or 4^d Lawfull Pr Quart and no more   and Every Parson who Shall give or Receive more for Cyder than the Price aforesaid Shall for the first offense forfit the Same given or Re^{cd} for S^d Cyder and for ye Second offence Shall Be punished at the Descretion of a Court Martial

General McDougle Brigade is Excused from Duty tomorrow for Brigade Exercise Scurmishing and Firing Field Peaces and Plattoons those Soldiers that have Inlisted from the Melitia are Emediately to Join the army   the Season Being advanced and the Days Shortned the time for Releaving guards in fut[ure] is to Be at 8 oclock in the Morning and *the Gen! orders that the Troops* Exercise from Revalle Beeting till 8 oclock and from 10 till 12 oclock & from 2 to 3 [5] oclock in ye afternoon

at a general Court marshel held at fourt muntgumery by order of general Putnam on the 29 of August 1777 Colo Duboice President Capt Lee Garner [Capt. Lt. Gano] of Colo Lambs Reg! of Artillery was try[d] upon a Charge of Insulting [*assaulting*] Lt Colo Clory [McCloughry] by Confineing his Waiter *and* for taking [*making use of*] his own Property the Court upon Mild [*maturely*] Concideration of the Eviden[] Against Capt Lee garner Do Judg him not guilty of the Charge   Cap! Thomas Betts an asistant Deputy Q^r

* Platt says Col? Sam! Drake.

Master Genr! was tryd on a Charge of greatly [*grossly*] Abuseing Capt Gooding [Godwin] by [*of*] Neglecting his Duty and Exposeing his Property and the Property of the united States to the Inclemency of the wet[her] and for Publickly Expressing him Self in a maner unbecoming a man in his Place in the Continental Service and a friend to Liberty the Court upon Marsh [*maturely*] Considering the Evidence Judg Capt Betts to be greatly guilty of grossly Abuseing Capt Gooding of Neglecting his Duty and Expressing him Self unbecoming an officer in the Continental Service and a friend to the Cause of Liberty and that he Be therefore Discharged from ye army the general Aprov[s] the Preceading Judgments of the Court marshel aforesd and orders Capt Thomas Betts Deputy Qr Master Genr! to Quit the Continental army and that Capt Garner Be Discharged from his Arest

Strayed from the Pasture of Capt Wm. Drake a yoke of Oxen, one a brindle bug Horned ox with a white tail—the other a black ox with a large white Spot under his Throat about Midling size—the Brindle ox the largest. Any Person who will return sd Oxen or give Information of them to sd Capt. Wm. Drake shall be generously rewarded.

Stolen in the Evening of the 1st Instant out of the Holsters on the Horse, a pair of very genteel Pistols, brass mounted, black Walnut or Mahogany Stocks. A Hook in one to hang to the Belt more than midling in Length, which pistols belonged to Colo Eno. Any Person that will return said Pistols to Colo Eno or Head Quarters shall receive 5 Dollars Reward & no Questions asked—& the Troops in this Department on discovering the aforesaid Pistols are to seize & send them [to] Head Quarters.

HEADQRS SEPTR 4TH 1777

Parole, *Wentham.*   C. Sign, *Mendam.*

Major Holdridg
B D Magr Box   } officers of the Day
Adjt Waterman

No Parson is to take orders at Hedqr But Brigade Magors Adj!s and Comisiond officers. General Putnam Perceiving that *the orders of* his Exelency Gen! Washington granting to Scouting Partys as a reward to there Extreordnery Fatigue & hard Ship & Dangers : the Plunder taken from the Enemy *to* Be Devided for their Benefit through unacquaintedness of those orders or some other Causes : has not Rightly Ben Attended to   the Intention of those orders are not that any of the men (*our own*) or Enemys Stores Disarted (*discovered*) *at any evacuated Post be considered the Property of those who first marched in, or that any public Hous discovered* by Scouting Partys are to be Apropriated to them unless they find the Enemy in actual Persesian of them and Disposed (*dispossess*) them throff all Plunder taken under Such Surcomstances as by S⁰ orders is to Divided amongst the Corps (*captors*) ither by Contenen Troops or Melitia it is to be Disposed of (*reported*) by the Commanding officer of the Party to yᵉ General *or* Commanding *officer* at s⁰ Post Who is to Cause all Provision and Millitery Stores to be Aprised By the Comisary or Qr Master Gen! for use of the army and the Value thereof to be Paid to S⁰ Party and Such Articles as are not nesisary for the Use of the army are to be Sold at Publick Vendue under the Direction of the Quarter Master Gen! or his Deputy for the Benefit of the Captures (*captors*) S⁰ Plunder to be Advertised in general orders 3 Days Before the Sail & A Perticuler Description of the thing taken and Perscribed (*preserved*) by the Qʳ Master General or his Deputy that Any Parson Claiming Write to S⁰ Plunder may have oppertunity to Evince the Same.

HEAD QRᵀˢ SEPTR 5ᵀᴴ 1777

Parole, *Sweden.*   C. Sign, *Denmark.*

Lt Colo Shearman
B D Magor Humphris   } officers of the Day
Adjt Holding

Persuant to a Requestation of Governor Trumble the Command officers of the Respective Battallions Raised in the State of Connecticut to Serve in the Continental army Are ordered Emediately to Cause Compleet Returns to be made of their noncomisioned officers & Soldiers Inlisted or Detached to Serve in the 9 and half Battaln ordered to be Raised in that State Containing their Ranks & Names

& Names of the town in which they belong the time their Inlistment or Being Detached and the term of time for Which they are ingaged With a Perticuler account of those who have Disarted and [*or*] have *not* joined: also those who are hired for 3 years or During the War According to the Recomendation of Congress and by Whom they were hired to be Sent to Governer Trumble that the Cause of the Defetiancy of those Battallions may Be found out and Steps taken to fill them Up

the gen! is Suprised to find the orders of y<u>e</u> 16 of August Last Respecting the Melitia and 8 months men Inlisting into the Continental army for 3 years or During the war are Misstaken & Missaplyd the genr! had No Idea or intention that any in the Continental Service Should or Could Be *excused or* Released on Such Inlistments Nor that the Regulations of Congress Respecting two men hiring one to Be Ingaged in the Continental Service for 3 years or During the war Could be Extended to those who are allredy Ingagd in Service of (*for*) the war (*or*) for any shorter time to Excuse them till the Expiration of their service and all officers are hearby notifyd to take Care at their Peril Not to Prevart those Regulations of Congress and Perticuler States whare (*and*) the generals orders given out.

all Calculated for the Biseness (*benefit*) and advancement of the army to *the Detriment of the Army and the Diminution of* its uumbers by Excuseing Any who are Actually *engaged or* Inlisting others and all those soldiers Who have ben Excused and others Inlisting are ordered Emediately to Join their Respective Reg! and Both they and those and they that have *newly* Inlisted to Be holden till the Genr! See fit to order otherwise.

at a general Court marshel held at Peekskill By order of General Putnam Sept y<u>e</u> 4<u>th</u> 1777 James Duggins [Duggan] of Colo Charles Webbs Regt was tryed for fireing his gun at a party of fatigue men as they was Coming from Work and uncaping another Cartradg to fire again are found Guilty of the Charge But are of Appinan that the Prisoner Ment to fire at one Barns Who had thretned to kill his wife the Court therfore Sentance the Prisoner to set upon the gallos half an hour with A halter Round his neck and then to receave 50 Lashes on his naked Back at the gallos the gener! aproves the Sentance and orders it to be Put in Execution tomorrow at 9 oclock at which time and Place General Parsons BD is ordered to attend at a genr! Court marshel held at Peekskill Sep! 2 1777 Colo Angel President Serg! *John* Dunbar Serg! W̲ᵐ Pack Park Sarj! Aaron Buck Sarj! John Peterson Paterson Sarj! Newel Sabin [Noel Tabor] Sarg! Josiah [Joseph] Brown & Francis Baptist W̲ᵐ Hardin Asa Luis [Lewis] *Corpl.* John Goold Gideon Cary W̲ᵐ Lane W̲ᵐ Davis Drumer[s] all of Colo Greens Reg! was tryd for Raising a mutiny and on Tryal the Court is of apinan that the Prisoners are not guilty of the Crime of Raiseing a muteny But that they are guilty of behaving in a Disorderly maner   the Court therefore orders that the *six* Sargts be Suspended During the Pleasure of the Colo[s] or Commanding officer[s] of the Regt̲ˢ to which they belong   they further order that the *others of the* above Prisoners be Repremanded *at the Head of their Regiments by the Col?̲ or* the Commanding officer of the Reg! all Exept Cor! John Brown* and he is Aquited   Henery Foresides† of Cap! Flaggs Company Colo Greens Regt Tryd for Disarting his Reg! and Inlesting again into Colo Webbs Regt the Court on Consideration of the Prisoners Crime and his Bad Conduct (*character*) Sentance him to Receave 100 Lashes on the naked Back and then to Be Sent on bourd the Continental guard Ship of war there to Be kept to hard Sarvice During the war   John Flitcher (Fly) of Cap! Barnards Com̲ʸ Colo Wyllys Regt was Tryed for Disartion & found Guilty and Sentanced to Receave 100 Lashes on his Naked back   the gen! Aprooves of the Proceadings and and Judgment of the Court marshel above s̲ᵈ and orders them to be Put in Execution at 9 oclock tomorrow morning   W̲ᵐ Taylor Provost Master (*martial*) was tryd for Disobaying gen! orders in Riding the Wagon horses belonging to the army   the Court is of Appinian that the Prisoner is guilty of a breech of general orders But *not* knowingly & willingly (*wilfully*) Do Aquit him from *further* Punishment the gen! aprovs of the Judgment and orders s̲ᵈ (*William*) Taylor to Be Releasd from his Confinement

at a gen! Court marshel held a Peekskill Sep̲ᵗʳ 5 1777 Colo Angel Prsd Samuel Sturdavent‡ was Tryd for Inlisting into Cap! Grangers Com̲ʸ Colo Charles Webbs Reg! after he had Inlisted in Colo Swifts

* Platt says it was John Gold who was acquitted.

† Forsy.

‡ Hardwant.

Reg! after he had Recd the Bounty the Court being Convinced of his Villiany and that he Deserves an Examplery Punishment Sentance him to Recv 100 Lashes on his Naked Back to be Inflicted on three Differant Days and then to be sent on bord one of the Continental Guard Ships there to be kept to hard Labour During the Present war the Gen! aproves of the Judgment By whiping him 34 Lashes tomorow morn at 9 oclock 33 next Morning & 33 on Munday morning the general Court martial whare of Colo Angel was President is Desolved

---

HEAD QRTS SEP! 6TH 1777

Parole, *Christeen.*   C. Sign, *Elk.*

Colo Angel

BD M! Alden *   } officers of the Day

adjt Converce

the general observing some Inconvenianceys (*indiscretion*) in granting Furloughs to the Determent of the army orders that for the future No Furloughs Be granted to *any of* the Troops in this Department Exept by a general officer the Commanding officers of the Respective Reg! are Directed to make Returns of all the Desarters from the British army in their Respective Reg! and Cause them to apear tomorrow morning on the grand Perade

---

REGIMENTAL ORDERS PEEKSKILL SEP! 7TH 1777

the Regiment is to move tomorrow at 2 oclock on to the ground Whare Colo Swifts Reg! formerly Incamped the orderly sarjts are ordered to Perade the Sick Every morn before Doct Colmans tent at the time he shall apoint

---

HEAD QRTS SEPT 7TH 1777

Parole, *President.*   C. Sign, *Hancock.*

Colo Charles Webb

BD Maj! Alden   } officers of the Day

adjt Johnson

* Platt says the Brigade Major was Platt.

the Deputy Paymaster Gen! has Rec^d a form for General and Company Pay abstracts   he Directs the Regimental Paymasters to Call at his office for Copies   a Sarjt and 12 men are ordered as a guard over the Store at Peekskill to go on tomorrow morning the orders of yesterday Respecting those that Disarted from the British army are not fully understood   the general orders the Commanding officers of the Respective Regts to Cause their Capts to Examin their Companis and Report the number of British soldiers theirin and Cause them to apear on the Perade tomorrow morning at 8 oclock in order for their being Inlisted and Embodyed into one Regt agreeable to the orders of his Exclency general Washington that they may have an oppertunity to Distinguish them selves *pursuant to the noble spirit they have discovered by coming over to us.*

HEAD Q^{TRS} SEP^T 8TH 1777

Magor Ward
B D Maj^r Humphris   } officers of the Day.
Adj^t Rogers

HED Q^R SEP^T 9TH 1777

Parole, *McDougall.*   C. Sign, *Greene.*

Colo Swift
B D Maj^r Box   } officers of the Day.
Adj^t Rogers

The troops in the Several Brigades in this Department are ordered to Perade on the hill whare the gallous Stands at 9 o'clock to attend the Execution of Amos Rose and Samuel [Lemuel] Ackerley   the Troops in the Several Brigades are to Be Mustered Sucsessively in there order viz general McDougles BD to morrow at 2 oclock afternoon General Parsons on Wednesday at 2 o'clock afternoon Gen! Huntingtons on Fryday 2 oclock afternoon   to Be Sold at Publick Vendue on Friday next on the grand Perade 21 Cows and one Calf and Six horses taken from ye Enemy by Colo Denmon [Dimond] the Vendue to begin at 10 oclock in morning

Division Orders.

As Gen! Huntington's Brigade is near Commissary Else, it will furnish him with four men every Day, if they should be wanted to assist him in the store and to cover the offal—and they will be allowed for those men in Detail of the Division.

Gen! Huntington will cause the Gen! Orders respecting the sutlers to be executed in the Neighborhood of his Camp—the Landing at Peekskill will require attention.

HEAD Q^{RS} SEP^T. Y^E 10TH 1777

Parole, *Bradley.*   C. Sign, *Chandler.*

Colo Bradley
BD Maj^r. Plat   } officer of the Day
Adj^t. Marven

the Commanding officers of the Regts are to Cause Emediatly A Return to be made to the gen! of all those who have Disarted from the British Troops or Navy Since the Battle at Lexington and had never Ben in the Service of the united States Before they Disarted from the British army or navy who have Inlisted with Capt fallon from their Raspective Reg^{ts} in order that the Continental Bounty they have Red [received] may be Paid Back into the hands of William Bedlow Eng^n Deputy Paymaster gen! in this Department Who is to Lodg his Receit with the Paymaster gen! * no Soldier who has Inlisted with Capt Fallon and has Cloths Suffitiant to Cover him til they get (*to*) Philadelphia without their Regimental Coats are to take their Coats with them those that have not are to take them the Sevear Season of the year is aproaching upon us and Many of the Troops ar Distitute & Stockens and other nesesary Cloathing which to suply one Commisiond officer of a Company is ordrd to go Emediatly home to Recrute and Procure those articles for their Companies and Return to Camp by the first of october next the Paymasters of the several Reg:s are ordered to Pay those men who have Inlisted with Capt Fallon from their Respective Reg^t to the time of their Inlisting with Capt Fallon or to give Proper Cartiycates for their wages Due and that Same has not been Paid Before they Marched from hear

* Platt says " with the Gen! "

HEAD QR.^{TS} SEP.^{TR} Y.^E 11.TH 1777

Parole, *Oronoko*.   C. Sign, *Firm*.

Colo [John] Chandler
BD Maj.^r [Roger] Alden   } officers of the Day
Adj.^t [Henry] Ten Eyck

HEAD QR.^{TS} SEPT.^R 12.TH 1777

Parole, *Liberty*.   C. Sign, *Property*.

Lt Colo [Josiah] Starr
Brd Magor Box   } officers of the Day
Adjt Waterman

the Reason of *some* Regiments being ordered to the northward *from the Brigades here* and *for* Some other Reasons A New Aragment is becom Nesery the Genrl orders therefore that the Regiments of Colo Durkeeys Chandlers and Bradleys form one Brigade and be Commanded by General McDougle and that the Regts of Colo Green Angel and Sherbourn form one Brigade and be Commanded by Colo [Genl] Varnam and that the Regiments of Col Charles Webb Wyllys & Samuel B Webb & Demmon [Dimond] form one Brigade and Be Commanded by BD General Parsons and that the Regts of Lt Colo Prentice & Colo Swift form one BD and be Commanded by BD Genr.^l Huntington

HEAD Q.^R 13 SEPT.^R 1777

Maj.^r Hait
BD^{mr} Scott *   } officers of the Day
Adj.^t Selden

The Genl orders the following Resolutions of Congress to be publishd in orders, vizt :

IN CONGRESS, SEPT. 6TH 1777

the Committee and Treasurer (*on the Treasury*) having taken into Consideration the Letter from General Gates of the 28th of August as Neeting (*respecting*) Cloathing for the army under his Command aforded (*referred*) *to* them *by* the Congreass Reports that it appears from the Cloathier Genr.^l Report that he has ordered Considerable Suplys of Cloathing to be forwarded to the *army in the* Northern Department from *Boston* and he has Little Doubt of being

* Platt says Major Sedgwick and B. Major Platt.

able to in *the* Cource of 3 years (*the year*) to furnish the (*specific*) Articles of Cloathing Directed to be given as a Bounty to the Troops and as it will Be Equilly Disadvantagus to the Soldier as to the Searvice, Should they Receave the Money in Stead of Such Cloathing, the Bourd Disaproves of Stopages Made by the Deputy Paymaster General in the northern Department out of the Pay of the Troops in that Department on account of the Cloathing and Directs that the money Be Returned Exept in Case whare a Regt has Ben furnished with more Cloathing then their Bounty and that the greatest Care aught to Be taken to Doe Justice to the Soldiers as well as the Publick in this Asential Point it is the appinan of this Bourd it is not Suffitiant that *the* Clother Genrl. Charge *the Regiment with* the articles Delivered and taken (*takes*) *the receipt* of the *Colo. or Commanding* officer *and that the Colo or Commanding officer* on Delivering the Cloathing to the Captains or Comnding officers of Each Company takes his Rects Every Commanding officer of A Company aught moreover Strictly to be Required to keep A Cloathing Account with his Company Distinguishing the Several Articles Deld to Each Non Commisiond officer and Soldier and take Rects for the Same as his Vouchers and when Each Non Comsd officer & Solder Respectively Shall have Recd his Bounty of Cloathing ye Comisd (*commanding*) officer of the Company to whch he belongs Shall Deliver the Account to & Rects to the Commanding officer of the Regt to Enable him to settle the Cloathing Account with the Clothier Genrl. as well as to Descover Whether Equil Justice has Ben Done to the Companies that Such Troops as have not Ben furnished with Clothing Aught to Be furnished with their Whole Bounty without Delay Which the Bourd have Earnestly Recommended to the Attention of the Cloather Genrl. and he on his Part has Ingaged to Exeart Every means in his Power to Accomplish (*That*) Such of the Troops as have on their own Expence Provided any of those Articles of Cloathing alowed as a bounty or Shall Not have Drawn their Cloathing in the Cource of the year Shall be Intitled to Receave the full Value thereof at the Everage Price which the Clothing Shall Cost the Publick & Whereas when the Bounty of Clothing was Provided by Congress it was Conceived that it Might be Impractable to obtain A Suffitiant Quantity *of cloath* for Regimental Coats for the Troops and for that Reason two hunting Shirts were Substituted but in the Event So Considerable a Suply has ben Provided that Clother Genrl. has Ben Enabed to furnish more of the Troops with Regimental Coats and with hunting Shirts & Experience having Shewn that a further alteration of the articles of Cloathing as a Bounty may be made to the Advantage of the Soldiers & without Loss to the Publick therefore it is the apinan of the Committee that it Be Resolved that the Clothier genrl. Be Directed to as far as he Shall have it in his Power to furnish all Non Comsd officers and Soldiers in the Service of the United States who have not Recd their Bounty of Cloathing at their Election Either with the Several Articles Allowed by Congress in the Resolution of the 8th of October 1777 (1776) or in Lue thereof the following articles Viz

  1 Regtl Coat at 8 Dollars & 60 Ninths [ninetieths]

  1 Jacket with (*out*) Sleaves at 2 Dollars & 60 Ninths

1 Pr Buckskin & 2 Pr of W or Linnen Breeches 8 Dollars
1 hat or Leathern Cap at 2 Dollars & 60 Do

2 Shirts	8 Do	
1 Pair overhalls	6 Do	First Cost
1 hunting Shirt	4 Do	Estimated at
2 Pair Stockens	4 Do	56 Dollars
2 Pair Shoes	6 Do	
1 Blanket at	6 Do	

But as the Cost of the Articles Last Specifyd exceeds that of the *cloathing al-lowed as a* Bounty for the troops *by* 8 Dollars and & 30 Ninetieths of a Dollar So much Shall be Stoped out of the Pay of Every Non Comsd officer and Soldier who Shall Be Suplyed in the manner Last Directed as will make the amount of Cloathing they Shall Receave Equil to the Valley (*value*) of the Bounty of Cloth-ing which Upon an Everidg of the Price of the Several articles is Estimated at 47 Dollars & 60 Nintiths of a Dollar the sd Report Being twice Read on the Questian put Resolved that Congress Agree to the foregoing Report & Resolves By order of Congress Septr 6th 1777

JOHN HANCOCK Presd *

HEAD QTS SEPTR 18TH 1777

all disarters and Prisoners are to be Sent to hed Qrs for Exami-nation   whenever Scouts are Sent out Notice is to be given, they are to be under the officer of the Day   the officer of the Day is to visit all guards & Piquits by Day and Night and make Returns Patroles are to be kept out & Sentinals advanced in the frunt of the Incampment & allso be under the Direction of the Day   the whole army is to keep 2 Days Provision by them Constantly and be Every way Equipt for Action   A Return of the State of the Respective Regts to be made

WHITE PLANES HEAD QTS SEPTR 21 : 1777

officer of the Day tomorrow Colo Ludenton   the Same No to go on Piquit to night as Last Night & one the Same roads great Care to be taken not to Put any on this Piquit But Such in whose Fidelity the greatest Confidence May Be Placed   Colo Ludington & Magor Gray will guard the Same Roads as Yesterday

Patroleing Partys are Constently to be kept up

A Detachment from the whole lines to Consist of 1 Colo 1 Lt

---

* With the entry of this day's orders the record of Platt ends, as he was or-dered to the main army.

Colo 1 Magor 6 Cap.t 18 Sub.ts 24 Sarj.ts 6 Musitioners and 100 Rank
& File to Perade tomorrow morning at 9 oclock in the frunt of the
Incampment With two Days Provision officers of this Detachment
Colo Charles Webb Lt Colo Butler Maj.r Huntington

REGIMENTAL ORDERS

the Cap.ts of the Several Companies in this Battallian are forthwith to make returns of the Non Coms.d officers & Soldiers taken
with Capt Parsons with their Names & the Names of those Disarted
& the time when also the Names of those Decd and the time when
Died Porter Walbridge is Apointed Fife Maj.r & is to be obayd
accordingly

REGIMENTALORDERS 22 ND SEP.TR

the Reg.t to Perade y.s afternoon at 1 oClock at which time the
arms & amunition is to be Examined no officers or Solder is to be
out of Camp on any account But to be redy to march on the Shortest notice the roasters to Perade with the Reg.t at y.e above mentiond time

---

WHITE PLANES SEPT.R : 22   HEAD Q.TS

the out Piquit to Consist of 50 men only great Care is to be
taken that the Troops are kept in Constant Rediness to march with
2 Days Provision which is to be Constantly on hand
the Paroles are to be Constently kept up as the Safty of the Camp
much Depends on it the guards & Piquits are to be kept up also
Maj.r Gray & Colo Ludington as has Ben kept Before
officer of the Day Lt Colo Shearman

HEAD Q.RTS y.E 23.RD SEP.TR WHITE PLANS

the advanced Piquit to be the Same as yesterday till further orders
frequent Complants having Ben made of Plundering the Inhabitent
Robing gardings &c the Genr.l in the most Positive terms forbids
any practice of this sort we aught to Consider the Inhabitence already too much Distressd & that we Come for their Protection &
not for their Distruction Small Scouts are to be kept out on Mild

Square & towards Stephen wards Patrooling towards yͤ Enemy to Perade at 9 oclock in the morning 2 Sarjͭˢ & 18 men they are to Return in the Evening & the Ranging Companies their amunition to be Made tomorrow morning to the officer of the Day

HEAD QRͭˢ SEPͭᴿ 19ͭᴴ 1777 WHITE PLANES
C S S C DF
A Detachment of 2 3 4 4 0 and 80 men Likewise 1 Field officer to Perade at four oclock and advance on toward Stephen Wards & Mild Square and Patroole as Last night   Colo Ludington to furnish guards and patroles from the Camp to the North River Majͬ Gray to Send a guard and patrole on the road between Stephen Wards and the North River on the Aproach of the Enemy 3 Canon will Be fired in the frunt of the Incampment on which the Tents are to be Struck and all the Bagage Loaded the Troops to be prepared at their Several Posts as ordered

HEAD QRͭˢ AT WHITE PLANES SEPͭᴿ 20ͭᴴ 1777
the Troops are all to Perade at their Incampments at 10 oClock tomorrow morning all Regͭ and Companies to apeare at their several alarm posts at Revalee beeting their Posts will Be asined them by the Commanding officers of Regͭˢ   Scouts are to be Carefull to make Returns on their Return
C   Subs Sarjts
A Detachment of one Field officer   2   3   5   and 90 men Rank & File from Colo Wyllyses Colo Webb & Colo Samuel B Webbs Regiments are to Perade at 4 oclock this afternoon
officer of the Day Colo Wyllys the waggons & teems are to Perade tomorrow with the Troops   a line of Cartrige to Be Placed a Round the Incampment on Every Side and Every Person Attempting to Enter is to be taken up and Examined   Lt Colo Butler to Command the Detachment

HED QRͭˢ AT WHITE PLANES SEPT 24ͭᴴ 1777
Notwithstanding the orders of yesterday as well as Positive orders Against plundering the Inhabitence Some Soldiers in direct opersi-

tion to orders and Contrary to Rules of humanity did plunder from
Mᵣ Burts a Calf the only Substance of the Distressd Family yᵉ
officers of Every Rank & and Soldiers are Calld upon in the Strict-
est Positive terms to Exrt themselves in Detacting the offenders that
Justice may be Done to the Ingered Inhabitents and the Camp
Clensed from the Imputation of Robery and Theft a Party of 105
men Properly officered to perade at 9 oclock with 2 Days Provision
Majᵣ Grosvener to Command the Party

Colo Butler
Adjᵗ Ten Eyck ⎰ officers of the Day

Regimental orders the Colo is perfectly willing to Indulge Every
officer in the Regᵗ as Much as is Consistant with Duty & the good
of the service but he is perfectly sencable as Every officer of the
Least Consideration Must be that Every order General and Regimental must be Punctually attended to and Complyd with yᵗ order
is absolutely asential to be attended to in Camp and what alone
gives life and Sperit to an army & Could wish he Could be So happy
as to find that the officers by their Practice would make it Evident
that they are not Insenceable of it

he Cannot But Imagin that yᵉ officers by their Inatention in Di-
siplining their Comʸ and keeping up yᵗ order So nesary that they
Doe not Desire to attend or have no ambition of Exelling by their
Puntual attendence to Duty and is very Sory that he is under the
Disagreeable nesesity of Issuing orders to Compell yᵐ therefor the
Colo Recomends it to the officers to Examin the genrˡ and Regimental orders yᵗ have Ben Issued & Espetially in Exerciseing yᵣ
men Calling yᵣ Roles &c and faithfully Complying with Eᵐ the Colo
Expects that the officers Strictly Attend Role Calling & they are re-
quired to Punish all non Comsᵈ officers and Soldiers who Do not
attend to yᵣ Duty

Enos Fountain is apointed Dᵣ Majᵣ to Doe Drum Majʳˢ Duty till
further orders & is to be obayd accordingly & is to take Perticuler
Care that the Several Beets beet in Camp are beet in their Proper
Season Sarjᵗ Lee in Capᵗ Hinckleys Comʸ for his missdemenier is
orderd to Doe Privates Duty

HEAD Q^{RTS} SEPT^R 25TH 1777

Maj^r Huntington   }
Adj^t Hunt   }   officers of the Day

the Genrl Directs that the utmost attention be Paid to Prevent the Soldiers Strgling from y^r Regts that the Roles be Calld three times a day at which time Some of the Coms^d officers will attend it is Expected that all officers in their Several Ranks will be very attentive to the Disipline of those under y^r Command Every Extreordinary occurance must be Reported Emediately to the Commanding officer of the Corps in which it happens and by him to the genr^l A neglect of not Giving Intelligence of Disarters may be attended with ye Most Disagreeable Consequences

---

HEAD QUARTERS SEPT^R 26TH 1777

the genr^l is happy to Inform ye officers & Soldiers of the Success of our arms in the Northern Department on the 18th Instant Colo Brown with his Reg^t Attacted a Part of the Enemy at the Landing Place Northward of Lake George and in a few minute from Whence without Loss of time he Detachd A Party to the Mills between the Landing and Tiantarague whare A great Number of the Enemy Was Posted who were all made Prisoners a Block house near that Place & Mount independence fell into our hands and were in Prosesion of ye old French Lines and had Surrounded the fourt at Tye and mount independence which by Later accounts are Surendered on the 18th Capt Brown took 2 Capts 9 Sub^{lts} 2 Commisarys & 262 non Coms^d officers & Soldiers & 18 Artificers

282 in the whole he took 105 Battoos in Lake Champlane & 50 above the falls Including 17 Gun Boats and one Armed Sloop 293 Arms and Retook more than 100 of our Prisoners

on the 19th genr^l Burguin with his whole force Attacted the Left wing of Genl Gates Army But were Bravely Repulsed

---

PEEKSKILL HEAD Q^{RTS} OCT^R Y^E 1 1777

Colo [Samuel] Wyllys officer of the Day

the Honourable Generable Asembely of the Stace of Connecticut having ben Pleased to Appoint Return gun Meggs Colo of the

Reg! Latly Commanded by Colo David Dimon he is orderd to Join s! Reg! Emediatly & is to be obayd & respected accordingly officers Commanding Reg!s and Cap!s are Directed to See the teems anexed to their Several Comd!s are Imployd in Drawing wood for their Several Corps to Prevent the burning of fences the Melitia at the Barocks who have no Waggons will Aply to the Q! master Gen! for A Suffitiant Suply to Draw their wood

3o of the Melitia to Perade Every morning till further orders for fatigue they will Receave their orders from Cap! Buckingham who will be on the Parade & Recv : them y! Black Smiths armourers & Carpenters Wheelrites & majours Who are well Acquanted with' the Business are to Perade at Head Qr!s tomorrow morning at 7 oclock

---

HEAD QR.TS PEEKSKILL OCTO.BR Y.E 2.ND 1777

Colo Webb
Adj! Barker
} officers of the Day

A Court marshel to Set at Fort M.ntgumery to try Such Prisoners as Shall be Brot before it Colo Lamb President the members genr! Clinton will Apoint the Commanding officers will make out y! Returns of the field & Staff officers & of the Sarj! & Drum & Fife Maj!s & Qr!r Master Sarj! Agreeable to the form heartofore given by the Eldest Capt in making Such Roĺes the Roles are to be Cartified on the Back under the Proof of the Effectives By the Commanding officer of the Reg! in the following Manner

I hearby Certify the above Role to be a true State of the Field and . Staff officers & of the Sarg!s Drum & Fife Maj! & Quartermaster Sarj!

Commanding officers of Companies will take Notice that no Return are to be made of the not Joind for the future unless they are well asured that such will Cartainly Join in a few Days and Even in that Case they not to be Reconed among the affective untill they Join their Respective Corps No Injury occurs to them therefor when they Join their Corps their time of Inlistment is to be mentioned and they will Draw Pay for the whole time genr! Parsons BD has Leave to Discharge their Pieces at Retreet beeting

PEEKSKILL OCTO^{BR} 2ND 1777

Regimental orders Peekskill octo^{br} 1777   as the genr! has given Promition to the BD to Discharge their Peaces this Evening the Colo orders Every Non Coms^d officer & Soldier to attend on the Peiade at the beeting of the Long Role one half an hour before the firing of the Evening gun*

TO GENERAL WASHINGTON.

CAMP AT PEEKS KILL, 14TH JULY, 1777.

Two days since I Received from Jerre Wadsworth, Esqr. , Four Quarter Cask of Cane Spirits, One Q^r. Cask of Madeira Wine, and One large Cheese for your Excellency, and shall be much [pleased] to know what to do with them. They are at present in Store at this place. Enclosed is a New Map which I lately purchased, supposing it might be of use, in case the Seat of War should continue in this part of the Continent.

I arrived at this place the 9th. Inst, having March^d. 254 Men, including Non-commissioned officers,—and have left proper officers in the Country to forward on the remainder.

I am with Esteem y^r. Excellency's Most obed^t. & Very Hum^{bl} Ser^t.

SAM^L. B. WEBB.

---

* This is the last of the orders which concerned Colonel Webb. The stirring events of the next few days seem to have prevented Sergeant Ware from making the proper entries, and when he again began, Webb was in a separate command —under Governor Clinton—and Ware's company had marched to join the main army under Washington.

Clove July 15th 1777.

Dear Sir,

Your favour of yesterday,
date is just come to hand. — You have
my thanks for your care of the Spirits,
and Cheese, which I could wish to have
sent forward to me at this place, or
wherever I may be. — Col: Trumbull
went from hence to day, to Peekskill;
if you could get it into his care
he will, I am persuaded, put it into
hands that will not suffer it to be
stolen or adulterated on the way —
but as his stay there will be very
short I must request your attention
to this matter if he should become
of. — I have also to thank you Sir,
which I do very sincerely, for the
map which will, if we should have
occasion to Manœuvre about in the
parts described by it be very useful to me. —

I was led to believe by
Genl Parsons that the Connecticut Regiment would average abt.
600 Men each your having been
put upon the same footing with the
right of that State I was in hopes to
have found stronger than you have
mentioned. — I am with sincerity,

Yr obed: & affect: Serv.t
G. Washington

FROM GENERAL WASHINGTON.

CLOVE, July 15th, 1777.

DEAR SIR:

Your favour of yesterday's date is just come to hand.—You have my thanks for your care of the Spirits and Cheese, which I could wish to have sent forward to me at this place, or wherever I may be.—Col? Trumbull went from hence to day to Peeks Kill; if you could get it into his care he will, I am persuaded, put it into hands that will not suffer it to be stolen or adulterated on the way—but as his stay there will be very short I must request your attention to this matter if he should be come of [f].—I have also to thank you Sir, which I do very sincerely for the Map, which will, if we should have occasion to Manœuvre about in the parts describ'd by it be very useful to me.

I was led to believe by Gen'l Parsons that the Connecticut Regiments would average abt 600 Men each yours having been put upon the same footing with the Eight of that State I was in hopes to have found stronger than you have mentioned.—I am with sincerety

Y? obed! & affect. Serv!

G? WASHINGTON.

MAJOR GENERAL PARSONS TO GENERAL WASHINGTON.

PEEKS KILL, 15th July, 1777.

DEAR GENERAL:

Col. S. Webb is apprehensive he has fallen under your Excellency's displeasure from the Misrepresentations of his Conduct by Persons who designed him an Injury & has desir'd Me to inform your Excellency of his Conduct as far as I have been acquainted, Since he went into Connecticut to raise his Regiment—

If My Memory Serves me he came into the State about the first of Feby, Soon After which I had Orders to Assist in forming the Regiments to be rais? in that State which led me to a knowledge of his Situation early after his Arrival there; the State had extended their Additional Bounty to the Eight Battalions only which gave him little Hopes of Soon filling his Regiment; however under this discouraging circumstance he exerted himself with unwearied Diligence to raise & equip a Regiment with little Success—About the Beginning of March the Council of Safety extended the State Bounty to that Regiment, on which their Prospects brightned & their Inlistment increas^d : but other difficulties arose to retard that Regiment. As all the Officers were Young Men in the Vigor of Youth, the People of the County were in general oppos^d to them & tho', I believe, they universally were as diligent & attentive to the recruiting Service as any Officers in the Army their Success was not equal to that of some other officers of less Merit. I have had Occasion very frequently to call upon Col. Webb & his Officers in the Course of the Winter & Spring and in Justice to him, I ought to say, I have never found any Officers more Attentive to their Duty, or More Anxiously Concern^d & industriously imploy^d to recruit their Men & prepare them to March than Col. Webb & the Officers of his Regiment— Major Huntington I always found Attentively Assisting in this Business : and I do not know an Instance in which Idleness or Dissipation has taken Place in Col. Webb or his Officers during their Continuance in the State—and Altho' the Number recruited in that Regiment is not so great as in Some other Regiments, yet Considering the Prejudices of the People & many other Difficulties he had to encounter I believe no Man could have done better. The Officers of that Regiment without Exception I flatter Myself will do Honor to them selves & convince the World of the Propriety of their Appointment whenever cal^d into Action—

The Two Regiments lately Commanded by Genl. Huntington & Col. Douglass are vacant, of [ ] Colonels—I wish the Appointments could be made when your Excellency can attend it. Lt. Colonels [Zebulon] Butler, [Samuel] Prentice, [David] Dimon & [Return Jonathan] Meigs I Suppose are the only Candidates. The Two last are Officers which will do Honor to Any Appointment. Col. Butler is an experienced good Officer & Col. Prentice has been long in Service. Prentice & Dimon are the Lt. Colonels of the vacant Regiments—

I am Your Excellencys Obed^t. hb^le Servt ,

SAM^l. H. PARSONS.

FROM GENERAL WASHINGTON.

CAMP AT THE CLOVE, July 17, 1777.
DEAR SIR:

I have been favoured with yours of the 16th and am much obliged by your care and attention in forwarding the spirits and wine.

I am happy to hear you entertain hopes of recruiting your regiment. It is a desirable object; and I shall be well pleased, as I am persuaded you will when it is effected.

You will make out an exact list of your officers and the dates of their appointments, and transmit it to me, after which, commissions will be made out and'sent. Be particular as to the Times of their appointment, that the Commissions may be filled up as they should be, otherwise there will be confusion and complaints.

I am, Dr Sir, your afft H'ble Servt *

Gº WASHINGTON.

MAJOR-GENERAL PUTNAM TO MAJOR-GENERAL HEATH.

HEAD QARS, PEEKS KILL, JULY 25TH, 1777.
DR SIR:

last evening came in here, who left New York last Tuesday, one Henry Williams about 18 years old, was taken prisoner when the Enemy landed on York Island Septr last, his parents fled to Mamaronecks—he has had his liberty, upon Mr Dean's Security till about three weeks ago—when he was put into the Provost for Speaking ill of the King & well of the Congress—

Monday last Col. Shereff sent to have him released & to come to him—when he came to Col Sheriff he told him he must Carry a letter from G How to G Burgoine, he made Sundry excuses but to no purpose

he then asked liberty to Consult his friends— Shereff told him he might not for the business required Secrecy & despatch—accordingly he got ready & Set out Tuesday morning with the letter of a Small Compass Sewed in the fold of his Coat— he received Six half Joanns & a promise to be well rewarded & directions for passing their & our lines—

he came & delivered the letter to Col Courtland who Commanded at white plains—& by him sent with the young man here

* The body of the letter is in the writing of Robert Hanson Harrison.

in the letter G How "acknowledges the recp! of one of y.̣ 14.ᵗʰ of "may—& acquaints him that he shall be at B—n soon to Cooperate "with & Support G Burgoine—that the demonstrations he has given "of a Southern Expedition he thinks will have their desired effect "that Gen! Clinton will be sufficient to amuse G Washington & Put- "nam" &c*—although the manuveres of the Enemy have been cal- culated with great art to perplex, I think their real intention is now more evident—G Clinton is to Command at Kings bridge where are about 5000 men that one Taylor of middling stature dark com- plexion Short brown hair, blue camblit coat faced with white is con- stantly employed as an Express from N york to G Burgoine

I have now received an Express from Gen! Washington who is of Opinion that their destination is Philadelphia & the dispositions of the army are ordered accordingly tho' not altogether without regard to a possibility of mistake—thinks it adviseable to take Such meas- ures & make such a disposition as not to be surprised in case the Enemys destination is to the Eastward   the Enemy when they sailed out of the Hook stood directly out without inclining to the East or west—

I hope & trust to see the day when this Country will be so hot for them that they will be glad to stand off most directly not for our de- ception but their own Safety

with esteem & regard am your
Obedient humble Serv!
Israel Putnam.†

JOSEPH WEBB TO GOVERNOR TRUMBULL.

WETHERSFIELD, 25 July, 1777.

MAY IT PLEASE YOUR EXCELLENCY:

I wou'd inform you that Cap! William Griswold Col. Chester &

---

* "To me a stronger proof could not be given, that the former [Howe] is not going to the Eastward, than this letter adduces. It was evidently intended to fall into our hands. The complexion of it, the circumstances attending it, &c., evinces this beyond a doubt in my mind." *Washington to Putnam*, 25 July, 1777. Howe's letter is printed in full in my *Writings of Washington*, V., 514.

† From the *Heath Papers* in the Massachusetts Historical Society.

Several of us propose seting up the Salt Work's in So Strong a Manner as to be of real Service—provided it will in any shape answer—I take the Liberty to say this that we may meet with your Excellency's Approbation Smiles, & Assistance to Encouragement as far as is consistant—my Worthy Friend M: Holmes I think will let you Know the Circumstances & do us every favor in his power—I have the Misfortune to tell you of the loss of the Brig Generous Friends, M: Sebor, that was bound to *France.* He was unhappy Enough to run two days after He was out into a fleet of Britons bound from Hallifax to Newyork at one oClock in the morning, and after a chace of [—] Six hour's was taken carried into Newyork, & by Gov: Brown's influence He with Capt. Sam. Stillman has come out upon parole—brings nothing new—tells me that he understood Cap: Raymond was Exchanged for one Cap. Bebee—but I trust this is a mistake for if I recollect right you Expected Cap: Trowbridge—M: Chew has sent to me to know if your Excellency has Received an Answer from General Washington about his Exchange *—

I am your Excellencys

Most Ob: H Serv:

Jos: Webb.

Yesterday an Express passed thro this Town with a Mail from Portsmouth—its Seams a packet from france as late as the 27th May has arrived brings Letters from M: Deane—one to y:s Exelly which

---

* "Mr. Loring, Commissary of Prisoners, has by a message by Mr. [Joseph] Webb, of Weathersfield, lately returned from New York (whither he went with a flag, to transact some business of great importance to him), acquainted me that he is ready to give in exchange for Mr. [Joseph] Chew and Mr. [George] Bell, Deputy Commissaries of Forage, any two of our subaltern officers; or for Mr. Chew, any committee-man in their power. If any exchange of prisoners can now be made, and you have no material objection against it, I should be glad of your permission to exchange Captain [James] Raymond, Mr. Chew, and Mr. Bell, prisoners in this State, taken on Long Island by Colonel Meigs, for Captain [Caleb] Trowbridge and Lieutenants [Thomas] Fanning and [Jabez] Fitch [Jr.], who were all made captive on Long Island last summer [*i. e.* at the battle of Long Island]. We rather wish Mr. Chew's exchange, as he is a gentleman of sense and address, acquainted with gentlemen in every part of this State, and capable of doing as much hurt—much more, I believe by his residence here, than he could do in arms against us." *Governor Trumbull to Washington,* 27 June, 1777. The General replied that such an exchange was "entirely agreeable" to him. *Writings of Washington,* V., 456.

we Now forward—if you want to write the Packet goes from there in 15 days from this *—

FROM THOMAS MUMFORD.

GROTON, 4 AUGUST, 1777.

DEAR SIR:

I have not had the pleasure of a line from you since you left this state, it will ever be agreeable to me to hear of your welfare and all the officers of your Regiment, particularly while my son † is one of them. I will thank you to inform me if you have raised the officers of your Regiment, in whose company you have placed my son. I wish you may not have too mnch trouble in instructing him in his Duty (as he is but a boy). I flatter myself as far as he has knowledge, he will endeavor to perform your pleasure.

I have sent him sundry things he wrote for (packed in a Tierce) to be forwarded by Cap![Jerre Wadsworth from Hartford, among which is a good Marke tent with Flyer; I mean to spare no pains or expense for his Comfort while he acts the officer and behaves well.

We cannot hear a word where How's fleet & army are gone, you will oblige me when you get intelligence where they are &c. to give me your information. We have no intelligence from our northern army except that they flee from before the Enemy whenever they appear, leaving them their strong Holds &c. &c. &c. I think to satisfie the Publick there must be an enquiry into the Conduct of the Commanding officers.   *   *   *

THO.S MUMFORD.

GENERAL WASHINGTON TO SILAS DEANE.

CAMP IN BUCKS COUNTY, 13 AUGUST, 1777.

SIR:

I have had the pleasure of receiving several of your fav.rs by the hands of Gentlemen coming to America with a desire to enter into our Service, but as they were merely introductory, I hope I shall be excused for not answering them in regular order.

---

* From the *Trumbull Papers* in the Massachusetts Historical Society.

† Giles Mumford, a second lieutenant in Col. Webb's regiment.

The difficulty of providing for those Gentlemen in a manner suitable to the former ranks of some, and the expectations of many, has not a little embarrassed Congress and myself. The extravagant Rank given to the Officers who first came over from France, most of whom have turned out but little better than Adventurers, made those of real Merit and long Service, who came over with proper credentials, naturally conclude that they should enjoy the highest posts in our Army ; indeed it could not be expected that they would consent to serve in this Country in an inferior station to those whom they had commanded in France. Had not this difficulty been in the way, it would have been in a great measure impossible for us to have provided for them all in the line of the Army, for the following Reasons. When Congress at length determined to establish the Army upon a permanent footing, the Regiments and Field Officers Commissions were naturally given to those Gentlemen in the different States who had stepped forward and distinguished themselves from the beginning of the contest. All that could then be done was to give those that came well recommended, Commissions in the Continental Army, from whence they derived Rank & Pay, but as they were assigned to no particular Corps, they were in a great measure excluded from any real command. This, to those who came over upon Motives of interest only, was not unsatisfactory ; but it was very irksome to men of real spirit who wanted to distinguish themselves, and who could not brook the thoughts of drawing pay without rendering Service for it. From this state of the Case you will plainly perceive, that had applications for employment in our Service been but few, it would not have been easy to have granted them in a proper manner, but when they have been so extremely numerous (and scarce a Man willing to accept of any thing under the degree of a field Officer) it has been really distressing, especially when it is considered that many of the Gentlemen are men of Merit, and who have come from home out of a desire of serving our Cause.

I have often expressed my Sentiments to Congress upon this head, and have wished them to take some measures to make Doctr Franklin and yourself acquainted with our difficulties. If the Gentlemen in France were properly informed that our Army was fully officered and that all Vacancies are filled by Succession, none would come out but those in particular Branches with whom particular Stipulations are made. I make no doubt but you are sufficiently importuned for Letters of recommendation, which I am confident you will grant to none but those whom you think worthy of them. But I hope you will in future let the Gentlemen who apply for them into a true State of the nature of our Service and of the difficulty of getting into it in any but an inferior Station; if, after that, they chuse to come over upon a Risque, they cannot complain if their expectations are not answered. Altho' letters of recommendation are not binding, yet if the parties that bring them have not their wishes fully com-plyed with they are apt to attribute their disappointment to slight of them and want of attention to the Gentlemen recommending.

I have laid this matter thus fully and candidly before you that you may endeavor to prevent the fruitless applications and great Expence that these Gentlemen must incur who cannot be provided for.

I am, &c

G? Washington

FROM BRIGADIER-GENERAL PARSONS.

16 August, 1777.

Sir:

You will have your Command paraded in the Street in Front of Col. Wyllys's Reg^t at 12 o'Clock provided with Arms 30 Rounds of Ammunition & 3 Days Provision & march them to Crumpond where you will open the inclos^d which will give you further Directions. These you will communicate to no man untill you march forward

Y^r h^l Servt

S. H. Parsons.

Details.

Col.	Maj^r	Cp^t	Subs.	Serg^ts	Corp^ls	Privates	Mu	
		1	3	3	3	50	0.	C. Webb
	1	1	3	3	3	60	2.	Wyllys
	1	2	5	8	8	100	2.	Prentice
		0	3	3	3	50	0.	Durkee
1	0	1	2	3	3	40	0.	S. Webb
01.	0	1	2	3	3	40	0.	Angell
1. 1.	2.	6.	18.	23.	23.	340	4	Total

FROM COLONEL CALEB GIBBS.

HEAD QUARTERS, CROSS ROADS, BUCKS COUNTY, 16 August, 1777.

DEAR WEBB:

I cannot tell the reason of your so soon dropping the correspondence between us. I am confident it is not my fault, for I think you are indebted to me, if I am [not] very much mistaken; but be that as it may, we should not be so ceremonious when we consider the many agreeable hours we have pass'd together, and in a family so happy & agreeable as the Good General's. Our Good Friend Cary I have not heard from, by letter, since he left us. I shall write him by the next Post & to desire him to let me know the reason. If any one had told me it would have been so long I would have been very angry; however, I intend acting a generous part with all my old acquaintances in the letter way.

I have nothing here to write you. Gen'l Howe with the fleet, has not been heard of to our knowledge since the ninth, and then they were seen off Cenepucken, standing to the Southward. This Manœuvre of Gen'l Howe's occasions many conjectures, and I believe those who were so sanguine of his making this movement to the Southward as a finesse, give up the point, & they can not think the North River is his object. Many may yet think that the Delaware is his object, but let the world say what they will, I never will alter my opinion that is of his going up the North River; for he can have nothing of so much Consequence to British Arms in View as that, at this Juncture.

His Excellency would be glad to know if you received any money of his for the use of the family when at White Plains or after you left York Island until you came to Hackensack, or while you remained with the Family, for he has been making up his accounts, and he thinks he has spent moneys out of his own private purse, & no charge made to the publick of it.

It is his wish that you would let me know as soon as possible, & to make the letter come more safe to me, you will direct & enclose it to him for fear it should miscarry.

The Lads are all well, & desire to be remembered.

I am, yours sincerely,

C. GIBBS.

P. S. In haste. My regards to Livingston & all acquaintances.

FROM DAVID HUMPHREYS.

DANBURY, 17th Augst, 1777.

DEAR SIR:

I am directed by Gen! Parsons to inform you that 60 Men properly Officer'd, from Co! Cook's * Reg! of Militia, are to be annex'd to your Detachment : it is not possible they will be in readiness to March, when the Continental Troops leave this Town, if they are not you will please to leave a prudent Judicious Officer with such directions as you think proper, who will give them their work, & conduct them in such a manner, as to give as little room for speculation, & make as little alarm as possible.

This party, & Your Own detachment, the Gen! thinks, had better be supplied with four or five days hard bread from the Commiss? Store in this Town, which cannot probably be procur'd at Fairfield, if other provisions may be had, fatigue Rum may likely be Obtain'd from the Store likewise, so that making your Troops Comfortable & bringing them on by easy Marches, the Gen! Wishes you An agreeable Time, &

I am, with the greatest esteem
Your Very humble serv!
D. HUMPHREYS.

FROM DAVID HUMPHREYS.

FAIRFIELD, 18 AUGUST, 1777.

DEAR SIR:

Upon our Arrival at Fairfield, we found affairs not in exactly the same situation we expected, in Consequence of which, General Parsons desires you will Order your March so as not to arrive at the place before Wednesday Night. On this plan, the Detachment from Col. Cook's Reg! will be able to join your Troops when they move from Danbury.

As there is no issuing Store at this place, by the Gen!s Direction I have wrote to M! Lloyd upon the subject, who will doubtless supply you, as desired.

In addition to the surgeon you already have, Gen! Parsons would

* Co! Thaddeus Cook.

wish you to apply to Doct. Turner for another surgeon and a suitable Quantity of Bandages.

Your Prudence will suggest every precaution to prevent suspicion & conjecture from raging to the extreme degree, it is to be feared, they otherwise will. I am, Dear Sir, with sincere respect,

Your most ob't Hum! Serv!

D. HUMPHREYS.

P. S. Since writing the above, I am informed your Troops are much nearer than was expected. Tho' the Gen! is gone to New Haven, I am persuaded it will be most agreeable to him to halt at some distance from Fairfield. The Gen! , I imagine, will be back this evening.

BRIGADIER–GENERAL PARSONS' ORDERS.

FAIRFIELD, 21t Augt , 1777.

On the present Expedition tis of ye first Importance to the Success of the Enterprise & the Credit Honor & Safety of the Troops that the most exact order & Discipline be observd : and the Honor of our Arms & the Righteousness of our Contest will be made manifest to the World & our Enemies by the regular & orderly Behavior of the Officers & Soldiers, tis not from base & mercenary motives, tis not to distress the helpless Women or honest Citizen we draw our Swords, but from the noble & generous Principle of maintaining the Rights of Humanity & vindicating the Liberties of Freemen. The officers & Soldiers are therefore most earnestly exhorted & Strictly Commended to forbear all Violation of Private Property ; not the least Article is to be taken but by Orders ; we are to convince our Enemies we despise their Practices & Scorn to follow their Example. But should any Person be so lost to all Virtue & Honor as to infringe this order He or they may depend upon the most exemplary Punishment.

No Officer is to suffer a Soldier to leave his Ranks on any pretence whatever & the greatest Silence on ye March is to be observd .

[SAM : H. PARSONS.]

FROM BRIGADIER–GENERAL PARSONS.

NORWALK, Aug.t 29th, 1777.

SIR :

You are to proceed with the Detachment under your Command to Horseneck or Sawpitts as you think most Safe and Convenient for Securing your Boats, Protecting the Country & carrying into Execution the Designs the Detachment was sent out for ; take Care that the Whale Boats are kept safe under a good Guard when they are not in Use : You will Send Parties to Hempsted Harbour, Great Neck or such other Parts of Long Island as you find safe, to destroy the Forage & other Things collected for the Enemy's Use. It appears to me probable you may in Conjunction with Col. Dimon Clear all the Stock from Frogs Neck & the Parts adjoining, in which Perhaps your Whale Boats will be very Useful Observing the Proper Tides to go on, that your Boats may return on the Ebb with Safety.

I desire you to write to Gen'l Putnam for the Howitzer & Some of the Artillery Officers, who are Skillful in Using it : inform him of the Difficulties we meet with from the Reports of the Country & that t'will be necessary to postpone the Second Descent upon the Island untill these Rumors have Subsided, & in the mean Time I am gone to the Gov.t to have things Settled there in the best Manner I can.—Every Method you can devise to deceive the Enemy & blind the People, may be advisable to pursue. Perhaps t'will be best to dismiss the Vessells (except the Ferry Boat), with private Orders to the Capt.s to return in four or five days. If in any Thing you can co-operate with the Troops already at y.e plains, you will Do it & let your Guards & Patroles be kept vigilantly & with great Care.

I am Y.r Hb.le Sev.t ,

S. H. PARSONS.*

TO MRS. JOHN SIMPSON.†

HEADQUARTERS, September 5, 1777.

MY DEAR SISTER :

It is extremely disagreeable that our Situation is

* From the collection of Dr. John S. H. Fogg, of Boston.

† Addressed " Mrs. John Simpson from Boston, now living in New York."

such that we are debarred the pleasure of seeing each
other, and to be deprived of a little social Conversation in the Epistolary way adds greatly to the Misfortune. However, 'tis necessary it should be so in general, and adds much to the pleasure when now and
then an Opportunity offers in which we can write more
freely. Miss ——, who I fell in Company with this
morning at breakfast, has very politely offered to convey a letter immediately to your hands. So good an
Opportunity I could not let pass without acquainting
you of my and your other friends being in a State of
Health which renders them happy.—Joe and his lady
live at the old Mansion House as happy as heart can
wish. Hetty & Abbey are their companions. A few
families which are genteel and cleaver make up an
agreeable Circle. I spent five Months with them,
which I shall count among the number of my Happy
days—Hetty and myself used frequently to ramble
where our sister Sally had been before and with us,
much we wish'd for her good Company. Hetty says
she should be as happy as this world could make her,
if her Sister and Friend (Peggy) was with her. They,
I have reason to suppose, would be equally pleased in
her Comp'y. Whose fault has it been that they are
not all together, now at Wethersfield? This I leave
with you to answer. This I can with truth say—no
pains on my part have been wanting—witness my former letters when at Cambridge.

Busy Imagination yet paints to me a future day that
we shall meet and spend many social, friendly hours
together. Be it so. I wish it most fervently. Of this
be assured—that the Sons of America will reign Mas

ters of the Land which God gave them. The combined powers of Europe can only Distress, not Conquer her free born Sons. Of this I trust Britain is, or soon will be convinced. But I must stop my pen; it leads me to a subject which I did not intend to mention. Rest easy, my friend & Sister, on my Account, 'tis in the Cause of *Virtue* my *Country* and the rights of Man, I am engaged, and He who ever has in the greatest dangers preserved me can continue his protection. If I fall, it shall be gloriously. Remember me with the warmest Affection to Br. Jack, Miss Peggy and other friends, if such there are who may enquire after your friend and Bro.

S. B. WEBB.

Mr. Jack W[ebb] is at or near Peeks-Kill in Health.

TO THOMAS MUMFORD.

HORSE NECK, Sept! 6, 1777.

DEAR SIR:

Long since I should have acknowledged the Receipt of, and thank'd you for your several friendly letters, but very continual hurry and moveing situation has prevented, nor have I time at present to write you so particular as I could wish. I have the pleasure to acquaint you your Son bids fair to make a good and great Officer. He is exceedingly attentive to his duty and gives universal sattisfaction both to superiors & Inferiors of the Reg.t I recollect your mentioning something about his keeping a Horse, to which I have not the least objection. It will be at his own expence, as no forage is allowed by the Public. It is the Custom in all other Armies for each Officer to have a Bat Horse, on which he carries his Portmanteau with Cloathing—by which means they are more comfortable on a March and not so liable to loose their Baggage. I am much obliged for your very friendly attention to my Regiment. I am told by Capt. Buckley you are providing Shoes which will come reasonable. You could not do the Reg^t. greater Service. I am yet out with the Detachment commanded by Gen'l Parsons, and am in hopes for many reasons to be annexed to his Brigade.

Time will not permit me to add. You shall hear more particularly from me soon. In the Interim I beg a continuance of your letters which will be acceptable to, Sir, your friend & most humble Servt.

SAM'L B. WEBB.

My most Respectfull Compliments Wait on Mrs. Mumford, and my other friends.

I think the Cause of America never before wore such pleaseing aspects as it does now.*

MAJOR-GENERAL PUTNAM TO GENERAL WASHINGTON.

PEEKS KILL, September 13th, 1777.

DEAR GENERAL:

I should rejoice to have a line from you but I know in your Situation your attention is engaged in transactions of the greatest Moment. We have intelligence from the Northward that Supplies of Men & Stores Come in fast to General Gates that he has Moved up to Stillwater—that General Lincoln & Stark with Seven or Eight thousand Men are Marched from Bennington to get into the rear of G. Burgoine.

I have for Some time been Meditating an Expedition towards

* From the Ford collection of *MSS.*

New York & expect to be able to Attack the Enemy at Staten Island Powles Hook York Island & long Island at one time * for by Information from one quarter & another I have gained Knowledge of their Strength very Nearly at their different posts, & that an enterprize of that Kind might be Undertaken with good prospects of Success—enclosed I send a return of the Troops Under My Command at this & the adjacent posts—in case I Should go upon the proposed Expedition Gov! Trumbull has encouraged me a large reinforcement from Connecticut which together with the Continental Troops here & what assistance I shall be able to Obtain from this State & the Jersies, I Immagine I shall have a Sufficiency of men : Wishing, dear General, that by the blessing of heaven, all your Measures may be taken in Consumate Wisdom & the enterprizes of your Arms, against our Cruel Enemies, may be Crowned with glorious Success & Victory I remain with great esteem & respect Most Sincerely your Obedient humble Servant

ISRAEL PUTNAM.

MAJOR–GENERAL PUTNAM TO GENERAL WASHINGTON.

PEEKS KILL, Sept. 16th, 1777.

DEAR GEN! :

I am extreamly Sorry to hear that you have been unfortunately obliged to retire and leave Gen! How in possession of the Ground. I hope Providence will yet so smile on your Efforts, which I Know will be to your utmost, as to put Gen! How and his force in your power, the disadvantages of being Attacked are very great, the Enemy chuse their Mode of Attack, oppose their greatest strength to your weakest part besides the Spirit of the Assailants, is almost Universally Superior to those, who act only on the defensive.

I Received an order of Congress to hold fifteen Hundred Troops ready to Cross the North River, which were to Succour the Jerseys in case they should be wanted, as the Militia from that State were call'd to your Assistance—about 1000 of the Enemy Crossed from Staten Island to Elizabeth Town last Friday & Marched through

* It was in fulfilment of this plan that Col. Webb was sent to Fairfield, as detailed on page 229, *ante.*

New Ark towards you—A considerable Body of the Enemy by the best information two or three thousand Crossed about the same time from Kings Bridge to Fort Lee and Marched towards Hackensack—last Sunday Morning Genl. Mc Dougal with about fifteen Hundred Men Crossed the North River to oppose the Enemy below & Succour the Jerseys—

After this I Received another Resolve of Congress ordering Me to send fifteen Hundred men immediately to your assistance.

Now I cant Suppose the Congress mean I should leave the Jerseys to be raveaged and the Enemy to March where they Please or this Post Exposed to fall into their Hands—

Genl. Parsons is at white Plains,* by being there he Answers A double purpose, to protect that part of the Country from the incursions of the Enemy & is in My opinion equally or a greater Security to this Post then if they lay here, as he is under advantages to learn their first Movements—I have sent to Govr. Trumbull Genl. Wallcot & Silliman & to Govr Clinton for the assistance of the Melitia to be forwarded with the utmost dispatch—Under these Circumstances I wish to be directed whether the fifteen Hundred men shall be forwarded at all adventures to your assistance especially as I am well informed that a Considerable reinforcement has arrived at N York and am with great Esteem and respect—

Your Excellencys obedt. Humble Servant,

Israel Putnam.

P. S. This Moment one Colin Chapman belonging to Col. Bradlys Regiment who was taken at Danbury & enlisted with the Enemy came in. He says that the News at the Bridge was that 10,000 recruits had arrived at New York, that the Enemy in Jerseys Consist of four or five Thousand, that he came over with them to Fort Lee last Friday—that few of them were taken from the Bridge, that they Marched to Sanbreskers Mills between Peramus & Hackensack & there he Deserted from them, that they had Collected a great Many Cattle & Horses.

* See page 229, *ante*.

GENERAL WASHINGTON TO MAJOR-GENERAL PUTNAM.

CAMP, ON SCHUYLKILL, 34 MILES FROM PHILADELPHIA,
23 September, 1777.

DR SIR,

The situation of our affairs in this Quarter calls for every aid and for every effort. Genl Howe, by various manœuvers and marching high up the Schuylkill, as if he meant to turn our Right Flank, found means by countermarching to pass the River, several miles below us, last night, which is fordable almost in every part, and is now fast advancing towards Philadelphia   I therefore desire, that, without a moment's loss of time, you will detach as many effective rank and file, under proper generals and other officers, as will make the whole number, including those with Genl McDougall, amount to twenty-five hundred privates & non-commissioned fit for duty.   The corps under Genl McDougall, to my great surprise, by a Letter from him some days ago, consisted only of nine hundred & Eleven.   You will direct the Officers, commanding the Detachment now ordered, to proceed as expeditiously as they can to reinforce me.   The Rout through Morris Town and over Coryell's Ferry will be best for them to pursue.   Before they arrive at the ferry, they will hear where I am ; but that they may know their destination, when they are in Two days' march of It, they are to advise me by Express, and I will write on the Subject.

I must urge you, by every motive, to send on this Detachment without the least possible delay.   No considerations are to prevent it.   It is our first object to defeat, if possible, the Army now opposed to us here.   That the passes in the Highlands may be perfectly secure, you will immediately call in all your forces now on command at outposts.   You must not think of covering a whole country by dividing 'em ; & when they are ordered in & drawn together, they will be fully competent to repel any attempt, that can be made by the Enemy from below in their present situation.   Besides, if you are threatened with an Attack, you must get what aid you can from the militia.   The Detachment will bring their Baggage, but I wish 'em to come with no more than will be absolutely necessary.   That you may not hesitate about complying with this order, you are to consider it as peremptory & not to be dispensed with.

Colonel Malcom's regiment will form a part of the detachment. I am, dear Sir, &c.*

P. S. The Troops now ordered need not bring any artillery.

MAJOR-GENERAL PUTNAM TO COLONEL MALCOM.

HEAD QUARTERS, PEEKSKILL, 27 Sept., 1777.

SIR:

I have just Receiv'd, a Letter from General Washington Dated 34 miles up Schuylkill wherein he informs me that Genl. Howes Army had found means to cross Schuylkill, several miles below his Army; upon which He has ordered a further reinforcement from this Post, of which corps you must join. You will therefore upon the rect of this prepare to join Genl. Parsons Brigade, whom I have ordered up from the White Plains. I shall endeavor to send some militia to guard the stores Remaining in the Clove. Your Baggage must go with you.

I am Sir &c

ISRAEL PUTNAM.†

FROM THOMAS MUMFORD.

GROTON, 27 September, 1777.

DEAR SIR:

Your very kind & agreeable fav? of 6th Inst I duly Rec?d, the Contents Respecting my Son afford me very sensible Pleasure, my most ardent wish is that he may continue to merit your approbation, he informs me he has quite Recovered from his late indisposition. I hope when Opportunity offers for a young subaltern to Distinguish himself, my son will properly step forth, & Trust in him who Cannot Err for Success on his best endeavours. As I consider him but eighteen years of age I must repeat to ask the fav? of your wholesome Advice & Direction to him, which I am very sure he often stands in need of.

---

* The above order from General Washington put an end to the project, General Putnam had formed for separate attacks on the enemy at Staten Island, Paulus Hook, York Island, and Long Island, at the same time.

† From *Fragments of Revolutionary History*, edited by Gaillard Hunt, p. 140.

We have no inteligence from Gen! Washington since he Recrossed the Schuylkill to face Gen! Howe anew. My Hearts desire and earnest Prayers are for his success even to Compleat Victory. I think he was rather out General'd in the late Action at Brandywine (which has not been common). Our successes to the northward appear Rapid, the Last Advices (but not from Authority) are that our Troops are again in Possession of Ticonderoga. Shou'd that prove True, I am in Hopes M! Burgoine & his army will not be able to return to Canady.

General Spencer is like to have an Opportunity to display his Talents, an attack upon Rhode Island, being Determin'd on & is to take place in Ten or 12 Days. Had you force enough at Peeks Kill &c to drive the Scoundrels from New York it wou'd near compleat their whole Ruin.

I had a Line from Cap! Bulkley on the affair of Shoes & Stockings. His Excellency & Council of Safety having requested all the Towns in this State to furnish their non-commission'd officers & Soldiers with those articles &c. at the stipulated Prices, I wou'd advise you to get all you can from that Quarter, and what I can furnish (which you may depend on) may remain as a Body Reserve. I hope to be able to furnish your Regiment with a p! of each. Please let me know in Season how I can convey them to you. My Constant Studdy is to exert my utmost interest & influence in Support of American Independence, & particularly to make our Armies as comfortable as possible. I shall be at New Haven by the Ninth of next Month to attend our General Assembly—shall be there some time. Hope for the pleasure of Corresponding with you while the warr lasts, at least. I congratulate you on the Remove of your Regiment into Gen! Parson's Brigade. My son says now he with your other officers are Happy. I think you have a better Opportunity to display your Talents than before.

Whenever I can render you any acceptable Service it will give me pleasure, and I take the Liberty to subscribe myself (as I really am) my dear Sir

Your sincere & affec! friend

THO! MUMFORD.

MAJOR-GENERAL PUTNAM TO PRESIDENT HANCOCK.

PEEKS KILL, Septr 29th, 1777, 8 oClock P. M.

PLEASE YOUR EXCELLENCY:

I have the pleasure to Acquaint you that the ten pieces of Cannon with fixt Amunition, ordered from Springfield, Arrived Safe this day at this place.—but with Sorrow I am obliged to inform you that by Authentick intelligence received from Lt Fanning A prisoner of ours who is exchanged & came out from N York last Saturday, & divers other ways, Sixty Sail of Transports Arrived there last Thursday with three thousand british & German Troops under gen : Robertson being part of a larger detachment not yet arrived—*

That the preparations Making & their dispositions Most clearly indicate Some Capital expedition Speedily to be Set on foot—& he conceives its against this post & Fort Mt gomery—their guides are called in from Croton—their bakers ordered to work Night & day to furnish bread.

The Ships hauled into the North river—Ammunition taken on board—the Troops have evacuated Pawlis Hook & Crossed to Harlem—and the Troops at Kings Bridge have been Under Marching Orders for Some time—The late recruits with the Troops before in New York &c amount to Nine or ten thousand—The large detachments lately drawn from this post have reduced its Strength to about one thousand effectives Continental Troops & four hundred Militia Two hundred of whom are from this State one half of them without Arms, and what is worse it would be deem'd unsafe to trust them Notwithstanding my repeated urgent Applications to this & the State of Connecticut for the Assistance of the Militia No more has come in partly owing, I conceive to the large drafts for the Northward—

This is all the Strength left me, exclusive of the Forts & Ships

---

* " I make no doubt but some troops have arrived at New York from Europe, but I am pretty certain they are not any thing like so numerous as your informant mentions. I know it has been their custom thro' the whole Campaign to swell their reinforcements much beyond what they really were. If Genl Burgoyne is defeated, or hindered from making any further progress, as we may reasonable infer he is, from the last accounts, the North River will be no object for the Enemy. I rather think if Genl Clinton moves at all it will be thro' Jersey to form a junction with Genl Howe." *Washington to Putnam*, 1 October, 1777.

which are but poorly Man'd—to protect the Stores & defend these extensive important passes—this post I am Sensible is of the last Consequence to the Continent, & I will exert Myself for its defence weakened as it is—but permit me to tell you Sir, that I will not be Answerable for its Safety with the strength left Me against the force I am Sensible the Enemy are able, & I believe will Speedily Send against it—besides the fifteen hundred with Gen! Mc Dougal Gen! Washington has ordered Another detachment of one thousand which are Sent on. We have Nothing Material from the Northward More than is Contained in the printed hand bill I Sent you—With Esteem & respect I am Sincerely Your Excellencys Most

Obed! humble Servant,

ISRAEL PUTNAM.

P. S.   desire direction with respect to the Cannon—as I have Not Now Artillery Men Sufficient to Manage them all at this Post.

MAJOR-GENERAL PUTNAM TO GENERAL WASHINGTON.

HEAD QUARTERS, PEEKS KILL, 2^d October, 1777.

DEAR GEN^L :

Yours of the 28th Ul^{to} and a Copy of one the 23^d I was Duly Honour'd with, Gen! Varnum with his Brigade crossed Kings Ferry the Day before yesterday, and the Same Evening Gen! Parsons Arrived from the White Plains.

Last Night Major Hughs (son to Colonel Hughs D Q M Gen! to this Department) Arrived here with an express from General Gates, by which I learnt that the Army under his Command was likely to be in the Most Deplorable Situation for the want of flour, as he had but twenty Barrells with him, & only one Hundred at Albany, he also Adds, that he has twenty Thousand head Daily to feed, if so, I am fearful they will suffer greatly before any Supply can possibly be convey'd em ; I have had for some time past, a number of hands baking hard Bread at Fish Kill, which I have ordered with the Utmost Dispatch to be sent up, & in order to be Sure of a More Speedy Transportation, I thought proper to Order as Many Small Craft as Possible, Properly Man'd, with Oars, so that if the wind should be unfavorable they May Make Tolerable Dispatch with Rowing.

There is a further advantage in Sending these Small Crafts, as they can with great ease, take them up to the half Moon which is but about Sixteen Miles from Gen! Gates' Army—

There appears to be (in all parts,) the utmost Confusion with the Commissarys Department; had I not exerted Myself in Procuring Cattle from Connecticut, we must have used all the Salt Provisions at this Post, which I think ought to be preserved as Much as Possible, I hope to god that some better Regulations will Soon take Place, & Proper Commissarys of Purchases Sent to the Eastward, or our Troops in General will Suffer greatly.

I Must still repeat & inform you, that from the best and Clearest Intelligence I am able to get, the Enemys Strength in, & ab! N. York amounts to at least Nine Thousand, they are without Doubt preparing for Some Important Attack from the last accounts I am Inform'd, that the Officers from Kings Bridge Remov'd the greatest Part of there Baggage to N. York,—I have Made Such Applications for the Connecticut Militia, as I hope in a little time will Afford me sbme small Assistance, but at Present this Post is very Weak, the Militia from this State will not Turn Out—Since General Parsons Brigade Left the White Plains, the Enemys L! Horse has Made an Excursion up to the Saw Pitts and drove off a Number of Cattle, Another Party of the Enemy Crossed into the Jerseys, but upon Gen! Varnum approaching that way they thought proper to take their Departure.

The various accounts, I receive from the Southward respecting the Situation of your Army & the Progress of the Enemy Makes Me very Anxious to hear the particulars from you, which will be Thankfully Acknowledged by D! General.

Your Much Esteem'd & Most Ob! H!ble Serv,

ISRAEL PUTNAM.

FROM JOSEPH WEBB.

4 October, **1777.**

We are still at a loss where General Howe is. If you know, for Heaven's sake send us word. Report says he's in Philadelphia. I deny it, arĩd think I do right untill I have a greater certainty.

Hetty & Sally Chester are returned from Doct! Johnson's. I am in hopes she's on the mend, but much weaker than we cou'd wish.

Mr. Mumford, the last time I saw him, complain'd much of your not writing ; perhaps you may find your accompt in doing of it. Tell M.ʳ Rogers I have rec.ᵈ his letter & will forward it by the Post. Little Sally is as merry as a Cricket & plays enough for Ten ; says U. Sam very plain.   Harriet B. is well.

Hetty & Mrs. W. are gone out a riding.   I am,

Your aff.

[JOSEPH WEBB.]

Saturday, 3 oClock.

Be thankful for these short Letters, for that's the way to get more. What's become of Bailey, the Cutler?

God bless Livingston & Hunting[ton]—Adieu.

MAJOR–GENERAL PUTNAM TO PRESIDENT HANCOCK.*

HEAD QUARTERS, PEEKS KILL HEIGHTS, October 6th,
5 oClock A. M.

SIR :

On the Morning of the fourth Ins.ᵗ a party of the Enemy came up this River, in a Number of Transports and between thirty and forty flatt Bottom.ᵈ Boats, under Convoy of Some Ships of War, Some Gally's and Tenders—the Weather being Foggy they were not discovered till they had got as far as Tarry Town, about 20 Miles below this place, where they Landed about 2,000 of their Men, and March'd five Miles into the Country, but finding the people had principally drove off their Cattle and being harrass'd by our Parties, they Reimbark'd at 5 cClock on the Morning of the 5ᵗʰ Ins.ᵗ —and after being Join'd by some Transports, and about 20 Ships of force they proceeded up to Kings Ferry, about five Miles from Peeks Kill, and Landed a Considerable Body there, at the Same time Sent

---

* In his *Journal*, Col. Webb has sketched the movements of his regiment while Clinton and Vaughan were on their marauding expedition on the Hudson (p. 231, *ante*).   As these manœuvres were the leading events in Col. Webb's military service, after the battle of Bunker's Hill, I print a number of letters to fill in his outline with detail.   Many of these letters have never been in print, and are taken from various collections.   I regret that the letters in the *Trumbull Papers* were denied me by the Massachusetts Historical Society; but the Gates, George Clinton, and Sparks collections were freely opened to my inspection and copies granted without question.

a party in Boats, under Convoy of two Ships and a Gally, and took possession of Fort Independence (where there is but one Small Cannon Mounted), without Opposition,—I Detach⁴ a party of about 500 Light Troops to Watch the Motions and Harrass the March of those at Kings Ferry, and about 150 Melitia to Oppose them which Landed at Fort Independance.

The remainder of the Troops (which is but few) I have arranged on the Different passes in the Highlands, to Oppose them—

Notwithstanding my Repeated applications for Melitia from Connecticut and this state, there has verry few Join'd Me—Governor Clinton has in Consequence of this Movement prorogued the Assembly, and Arrived Last Evening at Fort Montgomery—he has Issued Orders for Calling in the Malitia, and I hope his personal Attendance will Animate them to turn out with more Spirit—

The force we have here is very inadequate, to that which the Enemy can bring to act against us, but sensible of the Importance of this Post I shall Exert every Nerve for the Defence of it—and I hope we shall be able to prevent their possessing themselves of the Passes, till we can be Reinforc⁴ by the Melitia—But (as I wrote you before) with the force Left me to Defend the Post (which is Less than 1,000 effective Continental Troops) I cannot Warrant it, Neither do I think Myself Answerable for it—I have order'd all the Sick and Unnecessary Baggage and Stores in our Rear, which I believe are Safe—

I have the Honor to be Sir &c

ISRAEL PUTNAM.*

* On the 4ᵗʰ Gates had written to Governor Clinton: "By Accounts received from Deserters, I am confident G. Burgoyne expects a Great Effort will be made by G. Clinton, to open a Passage through the Highlands, to facilitate his (G. Burgoyne's) approach to Albany. Your Excellency and Genᶫ Putnam, will be prepared to defeat that attempt." And on the 5th, he wrote to the President of Congress: "By all the Intelligence I can procure from Spies, Deserters from the Enemy, & such of our own men who escape from captivity, I am convinced; that General Burgoyne's principal hope of getting to Albany, is on General Clinton's forcing the pass of the Highlands, and defeating General Putnam. Of this, I advertised Governor Clinton in my Letter of yesterday. Too many precautions cannot be taken to prevent the Enemy Forcing their way up the North River; the Conquest Even of Rhode Island is of infinite less Importance than the Securing the Pass of the Highlands."

LIEUTENANT–COLONEL OSWALD TO COLONEL LAMB.*

6 October, 1777.

Heaven preserve you all, my dear Colonel ! I feel for you, and lament that I can't assist you. I have made application to General Putnam, that a reinforcement of artillerymen and myself, might be sent off to your support, but to my mortification, he absolutely refuses. By the next express let him know if more artillery[men] are needed, and that I might be ordered to join you. A large reinforcement is on their march to your assistance.

Yours, affectionately,

E. OSWALD.

GOVERNOR CLINTON TO THE NEW YORK COUNCIL OF SAFETY.

NEW WINDSOR, 7 October, 1777.

GENTLEMEN :

The extreme fatigue I have undergone the three days past, and the want of rest for an equal number of nights, renders me unfit to write you on matters of so serious consequences to this State, as I have to communicate. I am able only briefly to inform you, that yesterday about 10 o'clock A. M. our advanced party was attacked by the enemy at Doodle Town, about 2½ miles from Fort Montgomery : they consisted of but 30 men ; the enemy by appearance and accounts, so far received, of 5000. They received the enemy's fire and returned it, and retreated to Fort Clinton ; soon after we received intelligence that the enemy were advancing on the west side of the mountain, with design to attack us in the rear. Upon this I ordered out Lieut. Colos. [Jacob] Bruyn and [James] McClaughry, with upwards of 100 men, towards Doodle Town, and a brass field piece, with a detachment of 60 men, on every advantageous post on the road to the furnace. They were not long out, before they were both attacked by the enemy with their whole force ; our people behaved with spirit, and must have made great slaughter of the enemy. I strengthened the party on the furnace road to upwards of 100, but they were obliged to give way to so superior a force as the enemy brought against them. They kept their field piece in full play at them, till the men who worked it were drove off

* Colonel Lamb was at Fort Montgomery.

Painted by Ames.

PUBLISHED BY JOSEPH DELAPLAINE.

Engraved by P. Maverick.

GEORGE CLINTON.

with fixed bayonets, then spiked it, and retreated with great good order to a 12-pounder, which I had ordered to cover them, and from thence to the fort. I immediately posted my men in the most advantageous manner for the defence of the post, and it was not many minutes before, [it] as well our post at Fort Clinton was invested on all sides, and a most incessant fire kept up till night; and soon after dusk, when the enemy forced our lines and redoubts at both posts, and the garrisons were obliged to fight their way out, as many as could, as we were determined not to surrender, and many have escaped.

I was summond, sun an hour high, to surrender in five minutes, and thereby prevent the effusion of blood. I sent Lieut. Col. [William S.] Livingston to receive the flag, who informed them that he had no orders to treat with them, except to receive their proposals, if they meant to surrender themselves prisoners of war, in which case he was empowered to assure them good usage. About 10 minutes after, they made a general and desperate attack on both posts, which was resisted with great spirit, but we were at length overpowered by numbers, and they gained the possession of both posts. Officers and men behaved with great spirit, as well Continental troops as militia. Our loss in slain can not be great, considering the length of the action. My brother, Gen'l [James] Clinton, is wounded, and I believe made prisoner. This is the case with Major [Samuel] Logan. The number of missing I can not ascertain. The ships are both burnt and Fort Constitution demolished, by our people, without my orders; but I cannot, as yet, condemn the measure. The officers all say it was right. I am clear it was as to the fort, after removing artillery and stores, which has not been done. The ships I hoped might have been saved. Gen'l Putnam will retreat to near Capt. Haight's, about three miles from Mrs. Van Wyck's, and I mean to rally my broken but brave forces, and advance to-morrow on Butter Hill. Gen'l Putnam is to send Colo [Samuel B.] Webb's regiment to join me.*

I beg you will give the substance of this account to Gen'l Gates in answer to his letter to me. I have only to add that I greatly re-

---

* "Yesterday morning Col. Samuel B. Webb, with the baggage of the whole, & some stores, set out for Fishkill." *Col. H. Hughes to General Gates,* 8 October, 1777.

gret the loss of those posts ; but I am consoled with the full persuasion that they have bought them dear, and that I have done the most in my power to save them.   I beg you to excuse incorrectness, and am with due respect,

Your most obed! servant,

GEO. CLINTON.

P. S.   Major [Stephen] Lush * is, I believe, their prisoner.†

GENERAL WASHINGTON TO MAJOR-GENERAL PUTNAM.

HEAD QUARTERS, Octobr 8th, 1777.

DEAR SIR:

Your Favor of 2ᵈ Inst I receiv'd yesterday & I understand that General Varnum with his Brigade got as far as Coryells Ferry last Night—I expect Such Measures will be taken as not to let the Army under General Gates suffer at present for want of Flour, & that things May be put in Such a Train that a Circumstance of that Kind can not possibly happen in future.   I Sincerely wish with you that a better Regulation could take place in the Commissary Department, As, either by a fault in its Constitution or an unpardonable neglect in the Executive part, this Army has been Clogg'd & retarded in Some of its Most important & interesting Marches, untill the opportunity of doing what was intended, was entirely lost—I expect your Exertions in Calling out the Connecticut Militia May have its proper Weight, Tho' I cannot be of Opinion that the Enemy have left any thing like the Number of Men at New York which your intelligence informs you of.

In pursuance of a Concerted Plan we March'd on friday Night last to attack Genl Howe's Army which lay at 12 or 13 Miles distance—We drove in their Picketts about 6 in the Morning the Men pursued with great Eagerness & Bravery & Surmounted every opposition ; the Enemy were routed in the greatest Confusion Several Miles, we pass'd thro' their Encampments & took Some pieces of Cannon, in short we were flatter'd with every appearance of a Most glorious & decisive Action when to My great surprize Our Men began to give way, which when the Line was once broke became pretty

* Aide-de-Camp to Governor Clinton.

† From the *Journal of the Council of Safety*, I, 1063.

General, & could not with our utmost Exertions be prevented, & the only thing left was to draw them off in the best Manner we could— which was effected without Any very Considerable Loss as we brought off our Cannon &ꞔ   In this Action Brgᵗ Genᶦ Nash (of the Carolina forces) was Mortally Wounded & several others of great Bravery but inferior Note were Wounded Some dangerously & Some Slightly— General Agnew on the Side of the Enemy I believe is Kill'd on the Spot & report says that one or two other General Officers are Wounded.   Upon the Whole I have no doubt but their loss was at least equal if Not Much greater than Ours, & it has Serv'd to Convince our people that when they Make an Attack, they can Confuse & Rout even the Flower of the British Army with the greatest Ease, & that they are not that Invincible Body of Men which many Suppose them to be—The Accounts Coming in hourly from Philadelphia Make the Loss of the Enemy Much greater than we Imagin'd ; they Say that More than 200 Waggons came in Loaded with their Wounded that Genᶦ Agnew is Kill'd & Genᶦˢ [Sir William] Erskine & Grant badly Wounded beside—Several Colonels & Officers of Note.*

I have Spoke to Mr. Boudinot about Some Flour which was to be Sent into our prisoners at New York, this May be Applied to any uses of the Army which you think Necessary—

By a Letter from Mr. Hawkes Hay I understand the Enemy have push'd a Number of Men up the North River & landed on the East Side in Expectation I Suppose of finding few or No Men at your Post—I am fully Satisfied that every thing in your power will be done towards Calling in Reinforcements & Making a Vigorous defence, Assuring you, that the Number of the Enemy Cannot possibly be great even Should they leave N. York Staten & Long Island quite bare.

GOVERNOR CLINTON TO THE NEW YORK COUNCIL OF SAFETY.

[8 October, 1777.]

GENT:

I wrote to the Legislature yesterday, giving them as particular an account of the loss of forts Montgomery and Clinton as I was then

* This was the affair at Germantown. It is fully described by Washington in his letter to the President of Congress, 5 October, 1777.—*Writings of Washington*, VI, 93.

able; since which, I have the pleasure to inform you, that Gen'l [James] Clinton is got in, and his wound does not appear to be any ways dangerous. Many other of our officers have also arrived, who we had reason to believe, were made prisoners. Not more than eleven officers of Colo. [Lewis] Duboys's regiment are missing; two hundred of his men, including non-commissioned officers, have already joined me at this place; many more of them may be hourly expected, as we have heard of their escape. Many also of the two artillery companies, who were at those posts, have escaped and joined us, and more of them are hourly expected.

The night I left Fort Montgomery, as my escape was effected by crossing the river, I waited on Gen'l Putnam at Continental Village, in order to concert the proper measures to be pursued after this unfortunate event. The general officers there agreed in opinion with me, that the intention of the enemy, under Sir Henry Clinton, was to relieve Burgoyne's army, by effecting a junction with him; that as they had carried the forts, their next object was to pass the chevaux-de-frize, so proceed up the river. The posts at Peekskill and Tydman's, by the loss of those which commanded the navigation, have lost their importance; it was therefore agreed that Gen'l Putnam should retreat with his army to a very defensible pass in the mountains, about three miles from Fish Kills, where he is, in the most speedy manner, to get in the Eastern Militia. I am to rally my forces near this place, call on all the Militia of Orange and this end of Ulster; also to be furnished with a Continental regiment from Gen'l Putnam's army to defend the chevaux-de-frize in the best manner I can; and that as soon as we find the enemy can raise or pass it, both armies to move northward, so as to keep pace with the enemy, covering those parts of the country, which will be their greatest object, until they shall think proper to land.

As soon as ever I find the shipping are likely to pass the chevaux-de-frise, I will by a forced march, endeavor to gain Kingston and cover that town. I shall have one brass twenty-four pounder and six small brass field pieces which will make a formidable train.

I am persuaded if the Militia will join me, (which I have reason to hope,) we can save the country, (a few scattering houses along the river excepted,) from destruction, and defeat the enemy's design in assisting their northern army.

A deserter, who had been taken and forced to Enlist in Col. Fanning's regiment, came in to us yesterday, from the enemy at Fort Montgomery : he deserted immediately after it was taken, and informs me that the enemy's loss was very great ; that Gen'l Sir Henry Clinton commanded in person ; had three general officers with him ; their force was 5000—three thousand of them British troops and Hessian yaegers, the remainder new levies—commanded by Brig?. Gen'l Beverly Robertson [Robinson] and Colo. [Edmund] Fanning. I have only to add, that though the country esteem the posts lost of the greatest importance, yet the manner in which they were defended, has given such general satisfaction as to elate and not depress their spirits.   I am with esteem, gent'n,

Your most ob! h^{ble} servant

GEO. CLINTON.

N. B.   I am this moment informed by Gen'l Putnam, that the Eastern Militia come in very fast ; that he is confident that he will soon have ten thousand men with him ; in which case he will keep posts up as far as Poughkeepsie and Rynbeck to head the enemy, should they push up the river.   We shall save considerable of the stores at Fort Constitution, and perhaps some of the artillery, as the enemy has not got up that high yesterday.*

MAJOR–GENERAL PUTNAM TO GENERAL WASHINGTON.

FISH KILL, 6 o'clock, Wednesday Morning, 8 October, 1777.

DEAR GENERAL :

It is with the utmost reluctance I now sit down to inform you, that the enemy, after making a variety of movements up and down the North River, landed on the morning of the 4th instant, about three thousand men at Tarrytown ; and, after making an excursion about five miles up the country, they returned and embarked.   The morning following, they advanced up near King's Ferry, and landed on the east side of the river ; but in the evening part of them reembarked, and, the morning after, landed a little above King's Ferry, on the west side ; but the morning being so exceedingly foggy concealed their scheme, and prevented us from gaining any idea what number of troops they landed.   In about three hours we dis-

---

* From the *Journal of the Council of Safety*, I, 1065.

covered a large fire at the Ferry, which we imagined to be the store-houses; upon which it was thought they only landed with a view of destroying the said houses.

The picket and scouts, which we had out, could not learn the exact number of the enemy that were remaining on the east side of the river; but, from the best accounts, they were about fifteen hundred. At the same time a number of ships, galleys, &c, with about forty flat-bottomed boats, made every appearance of their intentions to land troops, both at Fort Independence and Peeks Kill Landing. Under all these circumstances, my strength, being not more than twelve hundred Continental troops and three hundred Militia, prevented me from detaching off a party to attack the enemy that lay on the east side of the river. After we had thought it impracticable to quit the heights, which we had then possession of, and attack the enemy, Brigadier-General Parsons and myself went to reconnoitre the ground near the enemy; and, on our return from thence we were alarmed with a very heavy and hot firing, both of small arms and cannon, at Fort Montgomery, which immediately convinced me that the enemy had landed a large body of men at the time and place before-mentioned. Upon which I immediately detached off five hundred men to reinforce the garrison; but, before they could possibly cross the river to their assistance, the enemy who were far superior in numbers, had possessed themselves of the fort. Never did men behave with more spirit and alacrity, than our troops upon this occasion. They repulsed the enemy three times, which were in number at least five to one. Governor [George] Clinton and General James Clinton were both present; but the engagement continuing until the dusk of the evening gave them both an opportunity, together with several officers and a number of privates, to make their escape.

The loss of the enemy in this affair, Governor Clinton thinks must be very considerable. Our loss, killed and wounded, is by no means equal to what he might have expected. General James Clinton was wounded in the thigh, but I hope not mortally. Governor Clinton arrived at Peeks Kill the same evening, about eleven o'clock; and, with the advice of him, General Parsons, and several other officers, it was thought impossible to maintain the post at Peeks-kill with the force then present, against one that the enemy might, in a few hours, bring on the heights in our rear. It was, therefore, agreed that the stores ought to be immediately removed to some secure place, and the troops take post at Fish Kill, until a reinforcement of Militia should come to their aid.

I have repeatedly informed your Excellency of the enemy's design against this post; but, from some motive or other, you always differed with me in opinion. As this conjecture of mine has, for once, proved right, I cannot omit informing you that my real and sincere opinion is, that they now mean to join General Burgoyne, with the utmost dispatch. I have written General Gates, and informed him of the situation of our affairs in this quarter. Governor Clinton is exerting himself in collecting the Militia of this State. Brigadier-General Parsons I have sent off to forward in the Connecticut Militia, which are now arriving in great numbers. I therefore hope and trust that, in the course of a few days, I shall be able to oppose the progress of the enemy. Time will not permit me to add any thing more respecting the engagement, only that our loss (I believe, from the best information,) does not exceed two hundred and fifty, killed, wounded, and taken prisoners. This evening I intend writing you again, but am now very busy. I am, dear General, with sincere regard,

Your very obedient, humble servant,

ISRAEL PUTNAM.

MAJOR—GENERAL PUTNAM TO GENERAL WASHINGTON.

FISHKILL, 8 October, 1777.

DEAR GENERAL:

Since I wrote you this morning, I have waited on Governor Clinton, to consult about our present circumstances, and fix upon the most effectual measure that could be pursued against the enemy, who are now landing a considerable number of troops at Fort Constitution, and proceeding up the river with their ships, galleys, flatbottomed boats, &c. They will, from all appearance, be at the chevaux-de-frise in the space of an hour. They will know the situation of our troops, and I sincerely believe that their intentions are to make all expedition to get above us. I do not think weighing the chevaux-de-frise is a matter of great moment to them.

If they cannot effect it with the greatest ease, they will proceed up the river with the flat-bottomed boats, and such small vessels as can convey the baggage of the troops, stores, &c., to Half-Moon. If they attempt to march by land, on the west side the river, Governor Clinton will annoy them as much as possible with about four hundred Continental troops which I yesterday detached over, and the Militia, which he is now collecting. If this side should be their route, I will, with the remainder of the Continental troops and the Connecticut Militia (which, I am happy to inform your Excellency, are coming in very fast), oppose them to the utmost of my power. All our stores, baggage, &c., except a few barrels of flour and bread, are removed from Peekskill. I have now a small guard at that place, and, if I can with any safety remove it from thence, I shall be glad. All the ordnance stores, which are not immediately wanted, I have ordered to the eastward. All our baggage, except what is absolutely necessary, I shall send off in the morning to some place of security; after which my troops will be light, and I flatter myself will either be able to fight them, or keep pace, should they keep upon the water.

I have the pleasure to inform you that many more of our troops made their escape than what I was at first informed of. Colonel Dubois, who is one of the number, this day collected near two hundred of his regiment, that got off after the enemy were in the fort. About five o'clock the enemy demanded a surrender of the fort; but, to their surprise, and the honor of our commanders, they had an answer that it should be defended to the utmost of their power. This renewed the action with double ardor, which continued till quite dark, when the enemy (who, we have since learnt, were five thousand in number) forced our lines; after which, our troops would not surrender, but fought with bayonets, swords, &c., in such a manner as reflects the highest honor on our noble garrison. General James Clinton was wounded with a bayonet in his thigh, and a number of other officers and men with the same weapon.

Yours of the 1st. instant I have this day received. The ten pieces of artillery you mention were ordered from Springfield by Congress, two of which, from a request of General James Clinton, were sent to Fort Montgomery; two I have with me; and the other six are

on the other side the river, with Governor Clinton. I am, dear
General, with great regard,

Your obedient, humble servant,

ISRAEL PUTNAM.

P. S. General [Sir Henry] Clinton commands the enemy in
person, with two other General officers.

GOVERNOR CLINTON TO GENERAL WASHINGTON.

NEW WINDSOR, 3 miles from the River, 9 October, 1777.

DEAR GENERAL:

I have to inform you, that, in consequence of intelligence received
by General Putnam from General Parsons (who lay with his brigade
at White Plains), of the enemy's having received a reinforcement
from Europe at New York, and that by their movements there was
reason to believe they intended an attack on Peekskill, and to possess themselves of the passes in the Highlands, the General immediately wrote to me these circumstances; and, to prevent if possible
the disagreeable consequences, that might arise if the army at the
different posts was not timely reinforced, I ordered that part of the
Militia of this State, that had not already marched to the northward,
to move, and part of them to join General Putnam, and the remainder to reinforce the posts of Fort Montgomery and Fort Clinton;
but, it being a critical time with the yeomanry, as they had not yet
sown their grain, and there being at that time no appearance of the
enemy, they were extremely restless and uneasy. They solicited
General Putnam for leave to return, and many of them went home
without his permission. Urged by these considerations he thought
proper to dismiss a part of them.

As I thought it essentially necessary, that they should remain in
the field for some time, in order to check the progress of the enemy,
should they attempt to put their designs in execution, I issued another
order for one half of them immediately to march, part of them to
join General Putnam, and a sufficient number to reinforce the forts
and the pass at Sydman's Bridge, at the mouth of the Clove; and,
in order to induce them to turn out with the greater alacrity, I
thought it necessary to fix their time of service to one month, at the
expiration of which time they were to be relieved by the other half.

While this was in agitation, and before a proper arrangement could possibly be made by the respective officers, as to what part of them could serve for the first month, they were not so expeditious as was absolutely necessary, which the event has fully evinced. A number of the enemy's ships made their appearance on the 3d. instant in Tarrytown Bay, where they weighed anchor the next day, being joined by several ships of war and transports from New York. They proceeded up the river as high as King's Ferry, and at daybreak on Sunday the 5th landed a considerable body of men on Verplanck's Point.

As I was apprehensive from many circumstances, that an attack on the forts was intended, I despatched Major [Samuel] Logan, an alert officer, who was well acquainted with the ground, on Sunday evening through the mountains to reconnoiter, and if possible gain intelligence of the enemy's motions. The Major returned about nine o'clock on Monday, informing me that from the best intelligence he could procure, and the rowing of the boats, he had reason to believe they had landed a considerable force on the west side of the river at King's Ferry, and between that and Dunderberg; but, as the morning was foggy, it was impossible to discern them, so as to form any judgment of their numbers. As soon as I had obtained this intelligence, I immediately despatched Lieutenant Jackson with a small party to discover the enemy's movements; but they had not proceeded more than two miles on the Haverstraw Road, when they were attacked by a party of the enemy, who had formed an ambuscade at a place called Doodletown. They immediately retreated after returning the fire. As soon as the firing was heard, I detached Lieutenant-Colonel [Jacobus S.] Bruyn * with fifty Continental troops, and as many of the Militia under Lieutenant-Colonel McClaughry, to sustain Lieutenant Jackson; the garrison being at that time so weak, that we could not afford them greater aid on that road, and I imagined it would be necessary to send out a party likewise on that road, which leads to the Forest of Dean. The detachments under Colonels Bruyn and McClaughry were soon engaged, but, being too weak to withstand the enemy's great force, retreated to Fort Clinton, disputing the ground inch by inch. Their gallant opposition, and the

* Of the Fifth regiment.

roughness of the ground, checked the progress of the enemy for some time.

While matters were in this situation in the neighborhood of Fort Clinton, a large body of the enemy were advancing on the road, which leads from the Forest of Dean to Fort Montgomery. As I had only one field-piece at the above fort, I ordered Colonel Lamb of the artillery to send it off to an advantageous post on that road, with a covering party of sixty men, and another of the same number to sustain them, in order to give the enemy a check, and retard their movements till I could receive a reinforcement from General Putnam, to whom I had sent an express for that purpose.* This order being immediately complied with, the piece had hardly reached the place of its destination, and the covering party been posted on strong ground, when the enemy were seen advancing with hasty strides : but being unexpectedly annoyed by discharges of grape-shot from the field-piece, and a well-directed fire from the muskets, which made great havoc among them, as we have since been informed, they were repeatedly driven back, till, filing off through the woods upon the right and left with a view of surrounding our men, and the handful of brave fellows being alarmed at their critical situation, they were constrained to abandon the field-piece, after rendering it useless to the enemy by spiking it. In order to cover the men who were retreating, and to check the farther progress of the enemy, I ordered out a twelve-pounder, which, being well served with grape-shot annoyed them greatly, and gave the men an opportunity of retreating into the garrison with very little loss on our side, except that of Captain Fenno, who commanded the field-piece, and was made a prisoner.

This was about two o'clock in the afternoon ; and the enemy approached the works and began the attack, which continued with few intervals till about five o'clock, when an officer appeared with a flag. I ordered Lieutenant-Colonel [William S.] Livingston to meet him without the works and know his business. Colonel Livingston having demanded his rank and business, he was told by the bearer of the flag, that he was Lieutenant-Colonel Campbell, and that he came

---

* See page 230 *ante*. Lossing says the name of the messenger was Waterbury, who "treacherously delayed his journey, and the next day deserted to the enemy." *Field Book*, I, 735.

to demand the surrender of the fort to prevent the effusion of blood. Colonel Livingston replied that he had no authority to treat with him, but, if they would surrender themselves prisoners of war, they might depend upon being well treated ; and if they did not choose to accept of those terms they might renew the attack as soon as he should return within the fort, he being determined to defend it to the last extremity. As soon as Lieutenant-Colonel Livingston returned, the attack was renewed with great violence ; and, after as obstinate a resistance as our situation and the weakness of the garrison would admit, having defended the works from two till the dusk of the evening, the enemy, by the superiority of numbers, forced the works on all sides. The want of men prevented us from sustaining and supporting every part, having received no reinforcement from General Putnam.

Our loss, killed, wounded, and prisoners, is not so great as might have been expected, when the strength of the enemy and our weakness are properly considered. My brother was wounded with a bayonet. Many officers and men and myself, having the advantage of the enemy by being well acquainted with the ground, were so fortunate as to effect our escape under cover of the night, after the enemy were possessed of all the works. I was so happy as to get into a boat, crossed the river, and immediately waited on General Putnam, with a view of concerting measures for our future operations, to prevent the designs of General Clinton, and impede his progress in facilitating the movements of Burgoyne from the northward. I can assure your Excellency, that I am well convinced, if night had not approached too fast to correspond with our wishes, the enemy would have been disappointed in their expectations ; as a reinforcement of five hundred men from General Putnam's army were on the east side of the river, ready to pass for our relief, when the works were forced ; and many of the Militia were in the mountains on their march to join us, had not the communication between us and them been cut off.

I have to add that by some fatality the two Continental frigates were lost, they having been ordered down by General Putnam for the defence of the chain ; but, being badly manned, they could not be got off in time, though I ordered the ship Congress to proceed to Fort Constitution the day before the attack, lest she should meet with a disaster ; and the ship Montgomery, which lay near the chain, having neither anchor nor cables to secure her, it being the ebb of tide and the wind failing, fell down so near the chain, that Captain Hodge was constrained to set her on fire to prevent her from falling into the hands of the enemy. The Congress, unfortunately getting aground on the flat near Fort Constitution, shared the same fate. Fort Constitution, being destitute of troops to defend it, was evacuated, after bringing off part of the stores.* I am now about three miles from New Windsor, with Colonel Samuel B. Webb's regiment of Continental troops, the remains of Colonel Dubois', about one hundred of Colonel Lamb's regiment, who escaped from the fort, and some Militia ; and I intend to collect what force I possibly can to oppose the enemy, should they land on this side of the river.

Sir Henry Clinton commanded in person. Governor Tryon, General Vaughan, and two other general officers, were with him. The army who attacked us, by the lowest account, consisted of three thousand, chiefly British and Hessian troops. The garrison of both our posts did not exceed six hundred men, and many of these unarmed Militia. The ordinary garrison was thus reduced by detaching Major Moffat with two hundred men to the post at Sydman's Bridge, and Colonel Malcom's regiment being ordered from thence, and sixty men on Anthony's Nose by General Putnam's orders, received the day before the action. I have only to add, that where great losses are sustained, however unavoidable, public censure is generally the consequence to those who are immediately concerned. If in the present instance this should be the case, I wish, so far as relates to Fort Montgomery and its dependencies, it may fall on me alone ; for I should be guilty of the greatest injustice, were I not to declare, that the officers and men under me of the different corps behaved with the greatest spirit and bravery. I am, &c.,

GEORGE CLINTON.

---

* Captain Gershom Mott was in command.

SIR HENRY CLINTON TO SIR WILLIAM HOWE.

FORT MONTGOMERY, 9 October, 1777.

SIR:

In the last letter which I had the honor to write to your Excellency, I mentioned my intention, with the small force that could be spared from the important post you had left under my command, to make an attack upon Forts Clinton, Montgomery, &c. Your Excellency recollects the situation of these forts, that they are separated by a creek which comes from the mountain, and communicate with each other by a bridge.

In my opinion, the only way of effecting it was by a coup de main in the unguarded state they then were. The Commodore and I having made our arrangements, and every proper jealousy having been given for every object but the real one, the little army, consisting of about 3000 men, arrived off Verplanks point, preceded by the gallies under the command of Sir James Wallace. On our appearance the enemy retired without firing a shot, leaving a twelve pounder behind them ; and Sir James moved up to Peekskill Neck to mask the only communication they had across the river on this side of the Highlands.

At day-break on the 6th, the troops* disembarked at Stony-point. The avant guarde of 500 regulars and 400 Provincials, commanded by Lieutenant-Colonel Campbell, with Colonel [Beverly] Robinson of the Provincials under him, began its march to occupy the pass of Thunder-hill. This avant guarde, after it had passed that mountain, was to proceed by a detour of seven miles round the hill, and debouchee in the rear of Fort Montgomery, while Gen. Vaughan with 1200 men,† was to continue his march towards Fort Clinton, covering the corps under Lieutenant-Colonel [Mungo] Campbell, and aportée to co-operate, by attacking Fort Clinton, or in case of misfortune to favour the retreat. Major-General Tryon, with the remainder, being the rear guard,‡ to leave a battalion at the pass of Thunder-hill, to open our communication with the fleet.

---

* 52d and 27th regiments, Loyal Americans, New York Volunteers, and Emerick's Provincial Chasseurs.

† Grenadiers and light infantry, 26th and 63d regiments, one company of the 71st, one troop of dismounted dragoons, Hessian Chasseurs.

‡ Royal fuzileers, and Hessian regiment of Trumbach.

Your Excellency recollecting the many, and, I may say, extraordinary difficulties of this march over the mountains, every natural obstruction, and all that art could invent to add to them, will not be surprised, that the corps, intended to attack Fort Montgomery in the rear, could not get to its ground before five o'clock ; about which time I ordered General Vaughan's corps, àportée, to begin the attack on Fort Clinton, to push, if possible, and dislodge the enemy from their advanced station behind a stone breast-work, having in front, for half a mile, a most impenetrable abbatis. This the General, by his good disposition, obliged the enemy to quit, though supported by cannon, got possession of the wall, and there waited the motion of the co-operating troops, when I joined him, and soon afterwards heard Lieutenant-Colonel Campbell begin his attack. I chose to wait a favourable moment before I ordered the attack on the side of Fort Clinton ; which was a circular height, defended by a line for musquetry, with a barbet battery in the centre of three guns, and flanked by two redoubts. The approaches to it through a continued abbatis of 400 yards, defensive every inch, and exposed to the fire of ten pieces of cannon. As the night was approaching, I determined to seize the first favourable instant. A brisk attack on the Montgomery side ; the gallies with their oars approaching, firing, and even striking the fort ; the men of war that moment appearing, crowding all sail to support us ; the extreme ardour of the troops, in short, all determined me to order the attack ; General Vaughan's spirited behaviour and good conduct did the rest. Having no time to lose, I particularly ordered that not a shot should be fired ; in this I was strictly obeyed, and both redoubts, &c., were stormed. General Tryon advanced with one battalion to support General Vaughan, in case it might be necessary, and he arrived in time to join in the cry of victory.

Trumbach's regiment was posted at the stone-wall to cover our retreat in case of misfortune. The night being dark, it was near eight o'clock before we could be certain of the success of the attack against Fort Montgomery, which we found afterwards had succeeded at the same instant that of Fort Clinton did, and that by the excellent disposition of Lieutenant-Colonel Campbell, who was unfortunately killed on the first attack, but seconded by Colonel Robinson of the Loyal American regiment, by whose knowledge of the country

I was much aided in forming my plan, and to whose spirited conduct in the execution of it I impute in a great measure the success of the enterprise.

Our loss was not very considerable excepting in some respectable officers, who were killed in the attack.

About ten o'clock at night the rebels set fire to their two ships, Montgomery and Congress, some gallies and other armed vessels, with their cannon, stores, &c., in them.

I have the honor to send your Excellency a return of the cannon, stores, &c., taken.   That of stores is very considerable, this being, I believe their principal magazine.

The Commodore has assisted me with his advice, and every effort. We sent a joint summons to Fort Constitution, but our flag meeting with an insolent reception, unknown in any war, we determined to chastize, and therefore an embarkation under Major-General Tryon, and Sir James Wallace, with the gallies, was ordered.   They found the Fort evacuated in the greatest confusion, their store-houses burnt, but their cannon were left unspiked.   The Commodore immediately ordered Sir James Wallace up the river, and if it should be possible to find a passage through the chevaux de frize, between Polypus [Pollopel's] Island and the Main, he may probably do essential service.

In justice to Captain Pownal, who commanded the flat boats, and the officers under him, I must mention to your Excellency that that service could not have been more zealously or punctually attended to.   I have the honour to be, &c.,

H. CLINTON.

OCTOBER 9, 10 o'clock at night.

P. S.   Major-General Tryon, whom I detached this morning with Emerick's Chasseurs, 50 Yagers, the Royal Fuzileers and regiment of Trumbach, with two three-pounders, to destroy the rebel settlement called the Continental Village, has just returned, and reported to me that he has burned barracks for 1500 men, several store houses and loaded waggons.   The extreme badness of the weather making it necessary to be as expeditious as possible, no account could be taken of the stores, but I believe them to have been considerable. I need not point out to your Excellency the consequence of destroying this post, as it was the only establishment of the rebels in that part of the Highlands, and the place from whence any neighboring body of troops drew their supplies. Fanning's and Bayard's corps marched from Verplank's Point to co-operate with General Tryon, but finding he met with no opposition, they were ordered back to their post.

COMMODORE HOTHAM TO LORD HOWE.

ON BOARD H. M. S. PRESTON, OFF PEEKS-KILL CREEK,
9 October, 1777.

Sir Henry Clinton having thought it adviseable to make a diversion at this juncture up the North River, and the necessary arrangements being made in consequence, the flat boats and batteaux on the 3d instant proceeded to Spikendevil-creek in three divisions, under the Captains Pownall, Jordan and [John] Stanhope : * Captain Pownall having the direction of the whole.

A body of about 1100 troops were embarked in them that evening, and the same night proceeded to Tarry Town, where they landed at day break, and occupied the heights adjoining. A second division, nearly of that number, marched out at the same time from Kingsbridge, and formed a junction by land with those who passed by water. The squadron under Captain Ommanney had moved up the day before to receive them, the smaller part of it, namely, the galleys and armed vessels, (as they might be to act separately) I thought it adviseable on this occasion to make a distinct command, and could not place them better than under the direction of Sir James Wallace, whose knowledge of the river, as well as Captain Ommanney's, we fully experienced the advantage of.

The third division of troops were embarked in transports, and on the 4th in the morning left New York, under convoy of the Preston, and in the course of the same tide arrived off Tarry Town.

The general embarkation was that night made, and the wind being still favourable, the whole, preceded by the squadron under Sir James Wallace as an advanced guard, reached Verplanks Point at noon the day following, and those in the flat boats landed with appearance only of an opposition. Sir James Wallace was immed -

* Commanding the sloop *Raven.*

ately despatched higher up the river to cut off the enemy's communication by Peeks-Kill ferry.

The 6th at daybreak the general debarkation took place, and all the troops, except about four hundred, who were left to secure Verplank Neck, were soon landed at Stony Point, upon the opposite shore, from whence they had about twelve miles to march through a mountainous and rugged road to Fort Clinton and Montgomery.

The ships and transports then moved higher up, and anchored opposite Peeks-Kill landing.

In the afternoon the advanced squadron and the two frigates got under sail and opened [fire on] Fort Montgomery, with a view only to make an appearance, and thereby to cause a diversion in favour of the attack, which we observed had now begun. Sir James by the help of his oars got near enough in with the gallies to throw some shot into the fort. The cannonading and the fire of musquetry continued 'till night, when, by a most spirited exertion, a general and vigorous assault was made, and the two important forts of Clinton and Montgomery fell by storm to his Majesty's arms. On which I have the honour to congratulate your Lordship most sincerely. The rebel frigates are both burnt, with a galley, and a sloop of ten guns is taken.

The loss on the enemy's side is not yet exactly known, but they are supposed to have had about 100 killed and 250 taken prisoners. The greatest loss on the side of the King's troops are about 40 killed, among whom are some valuable officers, namely, Lieutenant Colonel [Mungo] Campbell, Major Sill, Major [Alexander] Grant, and Captain Stewart, and about 150 wounded.

A summons signed by Sir Henry Clinton and myself was the next day sent up to Fort Constitution, by a flag of truce, which being fired at, returned, and determined the General immediately to correct the insult by an attack. An embarkation was accordingly made on the morning of the 8th, and proceeded up the river for that purpose, under cover of the galleys.

We found upon our arrival the Fort had been abandoned in great confusion, their barracks burnt, but all their artillery left. The whole number of cannon taken in three forts amount to 67, with a large quantity of provisions, ammunition, and stores of all kinds to a very considerable amount. I have directed such part of the chain and bomb as cannot be saved to be destroyed : the construction of both gives strong proofs of labour, industry, and skill.

Sir James Wallace, with his flying squadron, is gone still higher up the river, and if he passes the chevaux de frize at Pellipus [Pollopel's] Island, he may do essential service, as there can be nothing to give him any interruption.

When it is considered that this attack was made after a most fatiguing march over precipices, and through roads almost impenetrable, which made it impossible for the troops to avail themselves of the use of cannon so necessary for such a purpose, and the little assistance they could therein promise themselves from the ships ; the access through the highlands to the forts, rendering the approach to them so precarious, it redounds the more to the credit of an enterprize, which was formed and executed with equal judgment, valour, and success.

The Captains, officers, and men under my command have been so strenuously zealous in their exertions upon this occasion, that every testimony is due from me in approbation of their conduct during this service of fatigue, of which Capt. Pownal had his share, and is well able to inform your Lordships of every particular. * * *

I have the farther pleasure to acquaint your Lordship, that General Tryon is just returned from Continental Village, where he has destroyed barracks for 1500 men, with stores to a considerable amount.

GOVERNOR CLINTON TO THE NEW YORK COUNCIL OF SAFETY.

HEAD QUARTERS, MRS. FALLS,* 10 October, 1777.

GENTLEMEN :

When I wrote you last, I was in great hopes of being able to have collected and embodied so many of the Militia of this and Orange County, as with the two small Continental regiments now with me, and the reinforcements promised me by General Putnam, I should have such a formidable force as to enable me to prevent the enemy's penetrating the country, by throwing myself in between them and the most important places as they move up the river.   I am sorry to

* Mrs. Alexander Falls, who resided at the *Square,* about four miles west of New Windsor.

inform you I am greatly disappointed in my expectations, the Militia do not join me as I could wish; they are well disposed, but anxious about the immediate safety of their respective families (who for many miles back are yet moving further from the river,) they come in the morning and return in the evening, and I never know when I have them or what my strength is. The reinforcement I had reason to expect, and was promised by Gen'l Putnam, I am now informed by a letter from him, is only to consist of [Dirck] Brinckerhoof's regiment of Militia, which I am sure will not pass the river, and indeed it is unreasonable to desire them. This being my situation, I thought it my duty to advise you of it, as my only hopes now are, that my force may not be known to the enemy, and that this may deter them from doing what, if they should attempt, I could not prevent.

I have 7 field pieces with me; 5 of the heaviest I have ordered on the west side of the Walkill, towards Shawangunk, which is the route I mean to take to Kingston, the moment the enemy move up the river.

I wish some small works were thrown up towards the Esopus Landing to cover it and secure the defiles leading to the town. Every man that can fire a gun should be immediately embodied and employed at those works. I rejoice with you on the most agreeable accounts from the northward, and thank you for the early communication of it. I know of no enemy on this side Butter hill clove. The 4 armed vessels that were near Pollepen's [Pollopel's] Island, fell down out of sight yesterday evening. I am with much esteem,

Your most obed. Servant,

GEO. CLINTON.

P. S. Yesterday my guards took two persons from Fort Montgomery; one of them, Daniel Taylor, charged with a message to Gen'l Howe, the contents enclosed in the letter to Gen'l Gates, which I have left open for your perusal, then to be sealed, and forwarded by express.* The enemy's own accounts are, that they lost 7 field officers and upwards of 350 rank and file killed; a young nobleman, a volunteer, mortally wounded; Colo. Bruyn, Livingston, and Major Hammell Logan are prisoners, the last only wounded.

* The other prisoner was probably Isaac Van Vleck.

[From *Gaine's Mercury*, 11 October, 1777.]

October 6.—This day the fortresses Clinton and Montgomery, on the North River, in New York, fell into the hands of the British, under the command of Sir Henry Clinton. A gentleman who was in Fort Montgomery when it was taken, gives the following particulars of the event :—On Saturday night, we had advice that a large number of ships, brigs, armed vessels, &c., had arrived at Tarrytown, where they had landed a considerable body of men, supposed to be about one thousand, and had advanced towards the plains. Colonel Lutlington [Henry Luddington] being posted there with about five hundred Militia, they sent in a flag to him requiring him to lay down his arms and surrender himself and men prisoners of war. Whilst he was parleying with the flag they endeavored to surround him, which he perceiving, ordered his men to retreat. The British then returned to their shipping, and the next morning we had advice of their being under sail, and coming up as far as King's Ferry. In the afternoon they landed a large body of men on the east side of the river to draw our attention that way, but they re-embarked in the night, and next morning landed on the west side.

On Sunday night his Excellency Governor Clinton, who then commanded at Fort Montgomery, sent out a party of one hundred men, under the command of Major Logan, across the Dunderberg, to watch the motions of the enemy. This party returned in the morning, and reported they had seen about forty boats full of men land below the Dunderberg. The governor sent out another small party of about twenty-eight men, under the command of Lieutenant Jackson. On the road that leads to Haverstraw, two or three miles below Fort Clinton, they fell in with a concealed part of the enemy, who ordered them to club their muskets, and surrender themselves prisoners. They made no answer, but fired on the enemy and hastily retreated. They returned the fire and pursued our people half a mile, but they all got back to the fort without losing a man, though within five rods of the enemy before they were discovered. Upon this intelligence one hundred men were immediately sent off, under Colonel Brown, who fell in with the enemy about two o'clock in the afternoon, when a smart engagement ensued, but the enemy being of much superior force, our people were forced to retreat.

At the same time it was thought proper to send some of the

artillery, with a field piece, to occupy an eminence commanding the road that leads to Orange Furnace, with a party of men to defend it. They were attacked soon after, and our field-piece did great execution ; but it soon bursting, our men retreated, and an engagement of small arms was kept up a good while. Most of our men got within the breastworks, when the attack became general on both forts. At the same time the enemy's shipping came in sight, but the wind being light, and the tide against them, none of the vessels could come up, except the galleys and armed sloops, which fired upon us, but did no execution ; we, in return, fired upon them, and believe did them some damage.

The enemy continued a vigorous and incessant attack upon the forts : but notwithstanding their utmost efforts, they were many times repulsed and beaten back from our breastworks with great slaughter. But the smallness of our numbers (being in both forts but about five hundred), which required every man to be upon continual duty, and obliged him to unremitted exertions, fatigued our people greatly ; whilst the enemy, whose number was supposed to be at least four thousand, continued to press us with fresh troops.

About four o'clock they sent in a flag, demanding in five minutes a surrender of the forts, and ourselves prisoners of war ; or that they would put us all to the sword. An answer was returned by Colonel Livingston, acquainting them that we were determined to defend the forts to the last extremity. The action was renewed with fresh vigor on both sides, and continued till the dusk of the evening, when they stormed our upper redoubt, which commanded the fort, which after a severe struggle, and overpowering us with numbers, they got possession of ; and we were obliged to give way. At the same time they stormed and got possession of Fort Clinton, in which were none but militia, who nobly defended it, till they, like the garrison at Fort Montgomery, were obliged to give way to superior force. The darkness of the evening much favored the escape of our people, the greatest part of whom, with almost all the officers, by some means or other got off, and joined our army, or returned to their places of residence. How those who were so unfortunate as to fall into the hands of the enemy were treated by them, we have not heard, but have reason to think it was with a cruelty suitable to the wickedness of the cause in which the British are engaged.

ACCOUNT BY A BRITISH OFFICER.

[From *Gaine's Mercury*, 11 October, 1777.]

I have now the pleasure to felicitate you on our taking the forts Montgomery and Clinton by storm. It was effected last night. The garrisons in both places consisted of twelve hundred rebels. Of our detachment, we lost Mungo Campbell, Lieutenant Colonel of the 52d, and Major   Sill of the 63d. Major [Alexander] Grant of the New York Volunteers, was killed a little before the attack, which was commanded by Colonel Mungo Campbell. My old acquaintance, George Turnbull, late captain in the Royal American Regiment, was ordered to take the command of Grant's corps. He has acquired great honor, being the first that entered Fort Montgomery, after losing one officer and eight privates. Sir Henry Clinton, who himself narrowly escaped the enemy's grape-shot, in consideration of his very gallant behaviour, has appointed him Lieutenant-Colonel Commandant of the New York Volunteers, in the room of the brave Major Grant. The gallant Count Gabrouski, lately arrived from England, has died of his wounds. Amongst the prisoners is Colonel William Allison, of the Drowned Lands, whose son was killed in the fort.* This person is a member of the provincial congress for the State (as it is termed) of New York. Also young William Livingston, late of New York, in the profession of the law. A great part of the twelve hundred rebels, who garrisoned the forts Montgomery and Clinton, or were not killed or prisoners, made their escape, as it was very dark when the forts were taken. The forbearance and humanity shown by all the troops to the rebels after they became their conquerors, was astonishing ; and savored of that benign temper which ever characterizes the army of Great Britain.

GENERAL WASHINGTON TO MAJOR—GENERAL PUTNAM.

SKIPPACK CAMP, 11th October, 1777.

DEAR SIR:

I rec⁴ a line from Col⁰ Fay dated the 4ᵗʰ instant in which he informed me that the Enemy had landed at Verplanks point. The

---

* William Allison was a member of the New York Provincial Congress of 1775, representing Orange county; Colonel of the Goshen regiment of militia in 1776, and brigadier-general in 1782. The son I am unable to identify.

Express who was stationed at Kings Ferry came off and also informs me that a party landed at the same time upon the West side of the River. I have not rec^d a line from you respecting the Matter which Makes me conclude that your dispatches have been intercepted by Some of the disaffected upon the Road. If this reaches you, I beg I may hear from you immediately. I have just rec^d a letter from Govr Livingston of the 8th inst in which he informs me that he had, in consequence of my request, ordered three thousand Jersey Militia to March immediately to the Highlands and I am not without hope that part of them will arrive before the Enemy have Made too great progress—

I am &c

G^o Washington.

GOVERNOR CLINTON TO THE COUNCIL OF SAFETY. (?)

Headquarters, Mrs. Falls', 11 October, 1777.

Dear Sir:

I am this moment favored with your letter of yesterday, with a letter from Mr. Morris (by a second express) containing the most agreeable accounts from the northward. By a copy of a letter from Gen'l Sir Henry Clinton to Burgoyne now enclosed you, you will observe that Clinton is in no way confident of their being able to form a junction of their armies, though there are nothing but bars between them. I wish nothing more than that Clinton may attempt it. I am persuaded that though the chance of war may at times occasion our prospect to appear gloomy, when the enemy push hard, yet it is in that way their ruin must and will be effected ; and I greatly hope that Clinton, not wise enough to improve by example, will, like Burgoyne, (flushed with his late success,) give stretch to his forces, or at least send parties out to try the affections of the inhabitants ; in either case, I have not a doubt but he will meet with the same fate. Should this not be the case, I hope in a few days to have strength enough to be the assailant.

We have nothing new here since I wrote you yesterday. I have sent a flag to Gen'l Clinton for a list of our prisoners, &c., which is not yet returned.

The letter from Clinton to Burgoyne, taken from Daniel Taylor, was enclosed in a small silver ball of an oval form, about the size of a fusee bullet, and shut with a screw in the middle. When he was taken and brought before me he swallowed it. I mistrusted this to be the case from information I received, and administered him a very strong emetic, calculated to operate either way. This had the desired effect; it brought it from him; but though close watched, he had the art to conceal it a second time. I made him believe that I had taken one Capt. Campbell, another messenger who he knew was out on the same business; that I learned from him all I wanted to know, and demanded the ball on pain of being hung up instantly and cut open to search for it. This brought it forth.

I have been particular in this little matter that you may in future understand this new mode of conveyance. I am, in great haste, with high esteem,

Your most obed! serv!

GEO. CLINTON.

FORT MONTGOMERY, OCTOBER 8, 1777.

Nous y voici, and nothing now between us but Gates. I sincerely hope this little success of ours may facilitate your operations. In answer to your letter of the 28th Sept. by C. C. I shall only say, I cannot presume to order or even advise, for reasons obvious. I heartily wish you success.   Faithful yours

H. CLINTON.

THE SILVER BULLET.

In the *Reminiscences of General Samuel B. Webb*, his son, General James Watson Webb, stated that it was to Webb's regiment that Sir Henry Clinton's spy came, and thus fell into the hands of the Americans. The story, in brief, was as follows: On the 10th of October, a horseman was challenged by a sentinel of the American force, who inquired for General Clinton, and desired to be conducted to that officer's quarters. Escorted by the guard into the presence of Governor Clinton, the messenger saw at once that he had blundered into the camp of the American General Clinton, instead of reaching that of Sir Henry Clinton. He was seen to swallow a bullet, which aroused suspicion ; and Dr. Moses Higby gave him an emetic, compelling him to disgorge, as described in the Governor's letter. The bearer of the bullet was one Daniel Taylor, of New York, a lieutenant or Sergeant in the British service. He was tried at New Windsor on the 14th, Colonel Dubois being the President of the court, condemned as a spy, and, four days later, was hung at Hurley.* It was noted by a witness to the execution, that Taylor "did not appear to be either a political or a gospel penitent."

The bullet and letter passed into the keeping of General James Tallmadge, the executor of the will of Governor Clinton, and was by him exhibited before the New York Historical Society on February 7, 1843, and shortly after was presented to the American Institute.

General Webb printed a letter from Pierre Van Cortlandt, dated at Peekskill, February 28th, 1845, in which he said :

"When I see you, I will relate to you the particulars of Gov. George Clinton detecting the spy from Sir Henry Clinton to Gen. Burgoyne in 1777, at New Windsor; of which Jas : Tallmadge made such a great display in presenting the silver bullet to the American Institute. Your father was an efficient agent in detecting the spy, the particulars of which I have very frequently heard Gov. Clinton repeat."

In 1860 these relics appear to have again passed into the possession of the Clinton family, but I have been unable to trace the present owner.

I was inclined to doubt the accuracy of Mr. Van Cortlandt's memory on this incident, as an event of such picturesque importance, would surely have been mentioned in Webb's journal, had his agency in the capture been direct. Yet a number of circumstances point to his having been immediately connected with it. The uniform of his regiment, captured in a British vessel, and only slightly modified in color from its original condition, was calculated to mislead a tory or Englishman. Taylor was doubtless as much mislead by the color of the guard's uniform, as he was by the confusing the two Generals of the name of Clinton. Nor was he alone in this. In the report of the main guard to Governor Clinton, at Hurley, on

---

*The proceedings of the court, and Taylor's confession, are printed in *Ulster Historical Society*, 158.

October 18th, mention was made of John Hole, a Tory, "confined for being a guide to a party of Col? Sam! B. Webb, thinking they were British regulars, and piloting from his own house." In March, 1778, when Washington proposed to Brigadier-General Parsons to attempt the surprise and capture of Sir Henry Clinton, then at Captain Kennedy's house in New York, he wrote : "I will add a thought which has occurred since the writing of it ; and which, if the scheme is practicable at all, may add not a little to the success ; namely, to let the officers and soldiers employed in the enterprise be dressed in red, and much in the taste of the British soldiery. Webb's regiment will afford these dresses."

Then, Colonel Webb was with the Governor at Little Britain, where Taylor was captured, arriving upon the very day of the capture. A march of four miles could have been accomplished in the morning, and was not of so fatiguing a nature as to prevent a detail of guards from the regiment—a service that in such a critical period would more naturally be entrusted to regulars than to militia. A statement, positively made, that Taylor was captured by a party of Webb's regiment, under the command of Lieutenant Howe, is puzzling, as there was no Lieutenant Howe in the regiment. A slip of memory on a name could, however, be more easily made, than one on the main events of the capture.

There is a third kind of evidence, of high value, and almost conclusive. In the *Washington MSS.* in the Department of State, the copy of the intercepted letter from Sir Henry Clinton contained in the bullet, that was sent to the Commander in Chief, is in the writing of Colonel Webb. The copy of Clinton's letter that was sent to General Gates is also in the writing of Colonel Webb ; and he wrote out for transmission to Gates, the confession of Taylor, as well as wrote for the Governor's signature, the letter from Governor Clinton to Gates, dated 11 October, 1777, and enclosing the facts of Taylor's capture. As Colonel Webb could not have been acting as the Governor's aid or Secretary, the conclusion is just that he was given these duties in recognition of his having been instrumental in the taking of Taylor. The omission to mention it in the Journal, may be attributed to the pressure of service at that period.

GOVERNOR CLINTON TO THE NEW YORK COUNCIL OF SAFETY.

LITTLE BRITAIN, 3 miles from N. Windsor
12 October, 1777.

GENTLEMEN:

Yesterday evening an armed schooner, two row galleys and a small brig passed the chevaux de frize, and are out of sight up the river this morning. They can have very few, if any, men on board, but they may be able notwithstanding, to destroy effects which may be found in stores on the banks of the river. Therefore give you this early notice of this movement, that you may order out small parties to such places on the river at which rum or any public stores or other valuable effects are deposited. This, I am sure, will secure them. I would advise that proper care be taken to defend Kingston Landing. The few pieces of artillery you have, ought to be taken to the most suitable place for that purpose. Our galley moved up the river a few miles before the enemy.

If we had round shot for our 24 pr. we might make this small fleet very uneasy in the river; but this we have not, nor do I know of any nearer than Albany, to which place I beg you would send for 100 of that size, and 200 for 4 prs. Three wagons will bring the whole. I wish to know how soon I may have them. They are essentially necessary; indeed I may venture to say Sir James Wallace, who commands this mosquito fleet, would not have ventured to pass the chevaux-de-frise had we been able to use our 24 pr. whose axletree was broken at the time but is now repaired.

I have no late accounts from the enemy below. Gen'l Putnam just now writes me that he hears they have landed, and are moving up the river; his letter implies on this. I sent a party out yesterday, to look into Forts Montgomery and Constitution; they are not yet returned. Captain Wooster, who went in with a flag, returned yesterday evening. He was received on board a ship, about a mile this side Fort Montgomery. He thinks they are destroying the works there and at Fort Clinton, as from the smoke he judged them to be on fire. Gen'l Vaughan commands there. Gen'l Clinton was absent. Vaughan's aid-de-camp answered my letter by informing the prisoners were sent to N. York; that any thing I wanted to send them might be sent on board the advanced ship, and from thence would be forwarded to them, directed to Mr. George Clinton, Fishkill. No list sent me, but all Colo. Duboys's officers missing are prisoners, with Major Lush, Colos. Ellison [Allison] and McLaughry. The latter has severe wounds, but none dangerous.

I am distressed for want of horsemen. The duty is too hard for Captn. [Ebenezer] Woodhull's small company. Captn. [Silvester] Salsbury's company (a few to attend you as expresses) must immediately join me, for which please to give him an order, as I have not at present time to do it. The communication being now cut off between Gen'l Putnam and me, before I had a proper supply of ammunition, I must beg you will forward me to the artillery Park, at Shawangunk, 10,000 cartridges for small arms, of different sizes.

I am this moment favored with your letter of yesterday. The militia of Shawangunk are now with me. I have sent a proper guard there from another quarter, for the artillery; which in my opinion, is much better than to leave men of the neighborhood for that purpose. Col. [Johannis] Snyder's regiment may continue at Kingston, to throw up the necessary works to defend the landing and town. The rest of the reinforcement from the Northward must immediately join me. Were the whole to continue with you, they would not be able to meet the enemy should they pass by and land near Kingston; and should they take their route by land, which is most likely, with my present force, which consists only of the militia of this quarter of the country, two small Continental regiments, and Colo. [David] Southerland's regiment, consisting of 130 men. Out of these, I have strong guards along the river shore, who have orders to keep pace with the vessels now in the river, and throw themselves between them and Kingston Landing, should they go that high up. I am persuaded it is not only for the safety of Kingston, which I have much at heart, but for that of the country in general, that I should have my whole force collected to one point; as in that case I shall be able to meet and oppose the progress of the enemy, or at least throw myself in between the enemy and such places as may be an object with them to gain, which shall be my constant care to do. I am, with much esteem, gentlemen,

Your most obed⁺ servant,

GEO. CLINTON.

P. S. From many circumstances, I am persuaded the enemy are about moving. Gen'l [Sir Henry] Clinton's being out when my flag went down yesterday—this small fleet coming up the river, con-firms me in this opinion ; and I believe it will be by land, against some of our stores, and to ravage the country.*

LIEUTENANT-COLONEL OSWALD TO COLONEL LAMB.

FISHKILL, 13 October, 1777

G[eneral] Parsons is at Peekskill. This morning, old Put came and ordered me to send off Capt. Lockwood, with his two pieces to join him, and I am told we are all to go down to the White-plains.

This morning, G. Parsons sent intelligence, that Clinton had been reinforced from New York, and is determined to push up the river.†

THE BURNING OF KINGSTON.

[From the *New York Packet*, 23 October, 1777.]

October 14.—Yesterday, General Vaughan, having under his com-mand a large body of British, who have committed various acts of vandalism, in their passage up the North River, landed a number of men at Esopus, marched up to the defenceless town of Kingston, about two miles from the river, and immediately set it on fire. The conflagration was general in a few minutes, and in a very short time that pleasant and wealthy town was reduced to ashes; one house only escaped the flames. Thus by the wantonness of power the third town in New York for size, elegance, and wealth is reduced to a heap of rubbish, and the once happy inhabitants (who are chiefly of Dutch descent) obliged to solicit for shelter among strangers ; and those who lately possessed elegant and convenient dwellings, obliged to take up with such huts as they can find to defend them from the cold blasts of approaching winter. We learn that the inhabitants saved the best part of their movable property ; but some lost the greater part of their temporal all. 'Tis said the enemy took little

* From *Journal of the Council of Safety*, I, 1069.

† From the *Life of John Lamb*, p. 186.

" Dislodging the enemy at New York is certainly an object worth our attention, and if they really do approach up the river, and you think yourself able to stand them, I think I ought immediately to proceed down to New York." *Major-General Putnam to Major-General Gates*, 13 October, 1777.

plunder, being told that Governor Clinton was at hand with fifteen hundred men, but unluckily not so near as to save the town. They burnt several houses at Rhynbeck Flats, and proceeded as far as Livingston Manor, where they burnt a few more. Our troops are now up with them. It is hoped they will be able to put a stop to these depredations. Britain, how art thou fallen ! Ages to come will not be able to wipe away the guilt, the horrid guilt, of these and such like deeds, lately perpetrated by thee.

GENERAL WASHINGTON TO GOVERNOR CLINTON.

HEAD-QUARTERS, 15 October, 1777.

DEAR SIR:

I was this day honored with yours of the 9th, containing a full account of the storm of Forts Montgomery and Clinton. General Putnam had given me information of the loss two days before, but not in so full and ample a manner. It is to be regretted that so brave a resistance did not meet with a suitable reward. You have however the satisfaction of knowing, that every thing was done, that could possibly be done by a handful against a far superior force. This I am convinced was the case. This affair might have been attended with fatal consequences, had there not been a most providential intervention in favor of General Gates's arms on the 7th instant ; but I am fully of opinion, that Sir Henry Clinton will not advance much farther up the river, upon hearing of Burgoyne's defeat and retreat. Nothing but absolute necessity could have induced me to withdraw any further part of the troops allotted for the defence of the posts up the North River ; but such was the reduced state of our Continental regiments, after the battle of Brandywine, and such the slowth and difficulty of procuring reinforcements of militia from the southward, that without the troops from Peekskill we should scarcely have been able to keep the field against General Howe. I had the greatest hopes, that General Putnam would draw in as many Connecticut militia, as would replace the Continental troops, and I make no doubt but he did all in his power to obtain them in time. I am sorry that you were under the necessity of destroying the frigates. The only consolation is, that if we had not done it ourselves, the enemy would either have done it for us, or have carried them down for their own use.

Since the battle of Germantown, upon the 4th instant, the two armies have remained in a manner quiet. The enemy have made several attempts to remove the obstructions in the Delaware, but hitherto without effect. They are now making preparations to raise batteries in the rear of Fort Mifflin, which commands the uppermost chevaux-de-frise. If we can maintain that post, and one opposite upon the Jersey shore, I am in hopes our ships, galleys, and floating batteries will be able to keep their stations and repel any force, that can be brought by water directly in front. I most earnestly expect further news from the northward, which I hope will bring us accounts of the total ruin of Burgoyne's army.

It is not unlikely that one of Sir Henry Clinton's objects will be to destroy the boats and small craft in the North River. Should this be the case, and he succeed, I think it will be advisable for you to set a number of workmen to building flat-bottomed boats at some secure places within three or four miles of the water, from which they may be easily hauled. They are so exceedingly useful, and so frequently wanted, that I think the business cannot, in such case, be too soon begun or carried on with too much expedition. I have written to General Putnam upon the same subject. I am, dear Sir, &c.

G? WASHINGTON.

GENERAL WASHINGTON TO MAJOR-GENERAL PUTNAM.

HEAD QUARTERS, 15th October, 1777.

DEAR SIR:

I am fav^d with yours of the 8th and 10th instants giving me the account of the loss of Fort Montgomery and the evacuation of Peekskill in consequence of it, but I am very glad to find that you had previously removed the greater part of the Stores. This stroke would have perhaps proved fatal to our Northern affairs in its consequences, had not the defeat of Gen! Burgoine so providentially taken place upon the 7th instant, I can scarcely think that Sr Henry Clinton will pursue his Rout now the object of it is disappointed, I mean a juncture with Burgoine. But I hope if he should attempt to penetrate further, you will be able, with the Militia from Connecticut and New York and the reinforcements sent down by Gen! Gates, to stop his progress. Gen! McDougal has just suggested a matter to me which he thinks of importance. He imagines that the Enemy, supposing they are obliged to fall down the North River again, will destroy all the Boats they find or carry them down with them; in either Case we shall have no means of crossing. He therefore advises that the Boat Builders in the Peekskill department be immediately set to work to make a number of Boats, which may be built some distance back from the water and brought down upon Carriages. But If the Enemy go down again they may be built convenient to the water. If our Boats are destroyed the sooner this work is set about the better. Since the Battle of Germantown both Armies have remained quiet. The Enemy have been endeavouring to remove the obstructions in the Delaware, but they have not yet made much progress.

I am &c:

G.º Washington.

LIEUTENANT-COLONEL OSWALD TO COLONEL LAMB.

Fishkill, 15 October, 1777

Dear Colonel:

The whole army are paraded, and wait orders for marching to Peekskill, or perhaps farther down, just as the maggot may bite; however, I am ordered to send for a number of shells, &c., prepared for the two inch mortars, and to have them in readiness when called for.

I hope to have the pleasure of spending the remainder of the campaign with you. If we move on towards New York, I suppose that part of the army with you, will join us.*

GOVERNOR CLINTON TO THE NEW YORK COUNCIL OF SAFETY.

Head Quarters, near New Windsor,
15 October, 1777, 9 o'clock a. m.

Dear Sir:

I am this moment informed by a light horseman from my guard at New Windsor, that twenty sail of the enemy's shipping (two of them large vessels) are in the river below Butter Hill. There was a heavy

---

* From the *Life of John Lamb*, p. 187.

fogg on the river in the morning when they were discovered, so that the officer of the guard could not be particular as to the size of the vessels; he thinks it highly probable that more may be near at hand and might be seen were it not for the fogg. Had it not been for this movement of the enemy, I intended this day or tomorrow to have drawn my few troops from this place towards the rear of fort Montgomery but I must now desist and watch their motions; and should they land and march against me with any considerable force, I shall be constrained with my present numbers to retreat before them, annoying them only if favorable opportunities shall offer. I was in hopes ere now to have received the reinforcement from the northward which you mentioned; not a man of which are yet arrived. I wish Col. Pawling with his regiment was with me. Since writing the above, the enemy's fleet consisting of 30 sail have passed Newburg with crowded sail and fair wind, are moving quick up the river; the front of them are already at the Dance Caamer. There are eight larger, square rigged vessels among them, and all appear to have troops on board. My troops are parading to march to Kingston. Our route will be through Shawangunk to prevent delay in crossing the Paltz River.* I leave Colo. Woodhull's, McClaughry's and part of Hasbrouck's regiments as a guard along the river.—Hathorn's is gone to the southward to guard a quantity of arms towards headquarters. When he returns he is to join this guard. I have neither time to copy or read this scrawl; the substance must be communicated to Gen. Gates. Let the militia be drawn out ready to oppose the enemy. I will be with you if nothing extra happens, before day;† though my troops cannot.

I am yours &c.

GEO. CLINTON.

* "They crossed the ferry where now stands the Rosendale bridge, making a hurried march and few halts; in fact it was too rapid to leave the troops in any condition to fight should they reach the enemy's position. The route of the column was on the Green Kill road, but only a portion of the advanced guard arrived at Kuy Kuyt, overlooking Kingston, to behold the village in flames, and the enemy nearly retired to his shipping." Pratt, in *Ulster Historical Society.*

† The governor arrived at Kingston at nine o'clock that evening.

COMMODORE HOTHAM TO VISCOUNT HOWE.

PRESTON OFF PEEKS KILN CREEK 15 October, 1777.

MY LORD:

Since I had the honour to write you by the Apollo, not anything material has happened here ; but Sir Henry Clinton having occasion to write to the Commander in chief, I take the same opportunity to acquaint your Lordship, that the number of men which would be necessary for the Defence of the more extensive Garrison of Fort Montgomery, has induced Sir Henry to destroy it, and to add some works to that of Fort Clinton which commanding the first, effectually removes all apprehension from thence, and reduces the Force necessary to maintain it to about 800 men.   This has enabled him to send a Detachment of about 1600 men up the North River under General Vaughan ; Sir James Wallace who has already explored the River as high as Pakepsy, directs the Naval Part consisting of the Gallies & small vessels as before ; and Captn Stanhope under him commands the Detachment of Flat Boats appointed for the occasion.

They sailed yesterday, & are now above the chevaux de frize off Pollipus Island, where I have placed the Mercury to secure that Passage against their return, & the Cerberus being reported to me as only fit for River service takes her station off Stoney Point to scour that neck, & to give her assistance at the same time to the Camp at Verplanks.

The Tartar flanks approaches to Fort Clinton, & the Preston lies between the two, within signals of either.

The principal object of the move up the River is to facilitate the motions (whatever they may be) of the Northern Army, and by the alarm which it will occasion to cause a Diversion in their Favour.

The Unicorn was to sail today with a Convoy of victuallers for Rhôde Island.   The Galatea's rudder was dropping off and has been obliged to be unhung & the Brunc's standing as well as running Rigging mostly condemned by survey.   I have the honour &c

W. HOTHAM.

GOVERNOR CLINTON TO MAJOR-GENERAL GATES.

KINGSTON, 16th Octr , 1777, one o'clock.

D^R SIR:

I am to inform you that the Enemy's Fleet consisting of upwards of thirty sail anchored last Night about six Miles below the Landing

Place of this Town, which they now lie directly opposite to, and appear to be making Dispositions for Landing. I have so few Men with me that I cannot say I have the best Prospect of making so good a Defence as might be wished. A Reinforcement is on the way which I left last night, and which I believe will not come up in Season, and at any Rate must be exceedingly fatigued. I am just informed that the Enemy are coming to the Land. I think it necessary to give you this Information that you may take such steps as may to you appear Necessary to render their Acquisition of this Town of as little Importance as possible. I have the honor, &c.,

GEO. CLINTON.

P. S. I most sincerely congratulate you on your Success to the Northward.*

FROM GOVERNOR GEORGE CLINTON.

KINGSTON, 16th Octbr , 1777.

GENTLEMEN :

You are to forward the Heavy baggage, Quarter-Master's, and Commissary's Stores, & such Ammunition, as may not immediately be wanted, to Hurly or Marble Town by the shortest Route ; as the Enemy are making a Disposition, to Land, below this Town, you will see the necessity of this measure, and lose no time. I need not urge the hastening your March. As we cannot possibly Man the whole of the Artillery, I would have you bring forward, only 3, Four-Pounders, and the 24, with a sufficient quantity of Ammunition.

I am Y^{rs}

GEO. CLINTON.

All the Artillery Men, are to come forward, & a proper Guard of the other Troops, are to be furnished for the security of the Stores &c .

TO COL? DUBOIS & WEBB.

* From the *Gates Papers* in the New York Historical Society. The letter was written by Gouverneur Morris.

Kingston 16th October 1777

Gentlemen

you are to forward the Heavy baggage
Quarter-Master's, and Commissary's Stores &
such Ammunition, as may not immediate-
ly be wanted, to Hurey ~ or Marbly town by the shortest Route
as the Enemy are making a Disposition
to Land, below this Town, you will see the
necessity of this measure, and lose no time
. — I need not urge the hastening your March
. — As we cannot possibly Man, the whole
of the Artillery, I would have you bring
forward, only 3, Four-Pounders, and the
24, with a sufficient quantity of Ammunition. — I am

yr   Geo Clinton

All the Artillery Men, are to come forward & a proper
guard of the other Troops, are to be furnished for the
security of the Stores &c —

To Cols Dubois, & Webb.

MAJOR-GENERAL PUTNAM TO GENERAL WASHINGTON.

FISHKILL, 16 October, 1777.

DEAR GENERAL:

I have been honored with the receipt of your two favors of the 8th, and imagine before this you have received mine of the same date, containing the disagreeable intelligence of the loss of Fort Montgomery, after a most spirited defence, and of our evacuating Peekskill in consequence thereof. I congratulate you on the bravery of your troops in attacking and putting to flight the British army, and regret the unfavorable circumstances that prevented its terminating in a complete victory.

Last Monday, General Parsons, with about two thousand troops marched down and took possession of Peekskill and the passes in the Highlands. He has taken a number of cattle, horses, and sheep, that were collected by the enemy. The enemy have burnt the buildings and barracks at the [continental] village, and several dwelling houses at Peekskill. They have demolished Forts Montgomery and Constitution, and are repairing Fort Clinton. Yesterday, about forty sail passed up the river, crowded with troops, and are now at anchor above Poughkeepsie, the wind not favoring. We were on our march after them, when I met the agreeable intelligence of the surrender of General Burgoyne and his army, as prisoners of war, a copy of which is inclosed ; and thereupon I do most sincerely congratulate your Excellency.

I have halted my troops, and am now considering what ought to be my next movement. I have sent to General Clinton for his opinion on the subject, and ordered General Parsons to spare no pains to find the situation and strength of the garrison at King's Bridge, in order to direct my future operations most advantageously.* I have about six thousand troops, who are chiefly militia. I understand that General Campbell † was killed at Fort Montgomery, and several field-officers, and others of inferior rank.

The enemy's loss, by the last accounts I have been able to get, is

* "Dislodging the enemy at New York is certainly an object worth our attention, and if they really do approach up the river, and you think yourself able to stand them, I think I ought immediately to proceed down to New York." *Putnam to Gates*, 13 October, 1777.

† An error. It was Lieutenant-Colonel Mungo Campbell.

very considerable ; not less than a thousand. The two Continental frigates, and the row galley, which lay above Fort Montgomery, were burnt, to prevent their falling into the hands of the enemy, for which I am very sorry, as one, I believe, might have been saved.

I have the unhappiness to inform you, that Mrs. Putnam, after a long and tedious illness, departed this life on Tuesday night. With the highest esteem and respect, I am, dear Sir,

Your most obedient, humble servant,

ISRAEL PUTNAM.

MAJOR-GENERAL PUTNAM TO PRESIDENT HANCOCK.

FISH KILL, Octr 16th, 1777.

PLEASE YOUR EXCELLENCY :

I was this Moment hond with the receipt of your Favour of the 5th with the inclosed resolves of Congress—previous to which I receivd the Agreable Intelligence from the Northward that Genl Burgoine & his whole Army Surrendered prisoners of War last Tuesday a Copy of which intelligence I enclose & there upon most heartily Congratulate Your Excellency—

The Enemy's Fleet about forty Sail ; great & small, Crowded with Troops, passd by here up the river yesterday & now lye above Poughkeepsie wind & tide not favouring—we were on our March Northward when I met the Acceptable News—I halted the Troops & am considering what ought to be My future Movements—The Enemy have demolished all the Forts on the river Except Fort Clinton, they have burnt All the Buildings & barracks at the Contitinental Village & some buildings at Peekskill—Genl Parsons is in Possession of Peekskill with about Two thousand Men, & has taken upwards of one hundred Cattle & horses & a Number of Sheep from the Enemy—

I have the Misfortune to acquaint you that Mrs Putnam after a long & Tedious illness departed this life last Tuesday Night—

The Deputy Pay Masters fund of Cash in this department is exhausted—& there is No Money to purchase provision—desire Some may be ordered as speedily as possible With great Esteem & respect I have the Honr to be &c

ISRAEL PUTNAM.

GOVERNOR CLINTON TO MAJOR-GENERAL PUTNAM.

MARBLE TOWN, 17 October, 1777

DR. GENERAL:

Yesterday afternoon about four o'clock, the Enemy took Possession of and burned the Town of Kingston. For want of a proper number of troops no effectual Resistance could be made. I have now the Body of men under my Command which marched from New Windsor to my assistance, and shall immediately proceed to the Ruins of Kingston which the Enemy have abandoned. I have sent off a Party of Light Horse to reconnoitre and shall act in such manner as the motions of the Enemy may direct. I heard that General Burgoyne had surrendered and am very sorry to find by your Letter that Nothing had been done but an interchange of Proposals, but I hope that matter is by this time concluded. I have the honor &c

GEO CLINTON.

P. S. A prisoner who is by no means intelligent says that the enemy are two thousand strong commanded by Gen. Vaughan.

REPORT OF MAJOR-GENERAL VAUGHAN.

ON BOARD THE FRIENDSHIP OFF ESOPUS
Friday, October 17, [1777] 10 o'clock, morning.

SIR:

I have the honor to inform you, that on the evening of the 15th instant I arrived off Esopus; finding that the rebels had thrown up works, and had made every disposition to annoy us, and cut off our communication, I judged it necessary to attack them, and the wind being at that time so much against us that we could make no way, I accordingly landed the troops, attacked their batteries, drove them from their works, spiked and destroyed their guns. Esopus being a nursery for almost every villain in the country, I judged it necessary to proceed to that town. On our approach they were drawn up with cannon, which we took and drove them out of the place. On our entering the town they fired from their houses, which induced me to reduce the place to ashes, which I accordingly did, not leaving a house. We found a considerable number of stores of all kinds, which shared the same fate.

Sir James Wallace has destroyed all the shipping except an armed galley, which run up the Creek with every thing belonging to the vessels in store.

Our loss is so inconsiderable that it is not at present worth while to mention.   I am, &c.

JOHN VAUGHAN.

SIR JAMES WALLACE TO COMMODORE HOTHAM.

GALLIES AND ARMED VESSELS OFF ESOPUS CREEK,
17 October, 1777

SIR:

We proceeded up the river, destroying a number of vessels as we sailed along, without stopping till we arrived at Esopus Creek, where we found two batteries; one of two guns, the other of three guns erected, and an armed galley at the mouth of the creek, who endeavored to prevent our passing by their cannonade.   General Vaughan was of opinion such a force should not be left behind.   It was determined to land and destroy them, and immediately executed, without retarding our proceeding up the river.   The General marched for the town and fired it.   The boats from the armed vessels went up the creek, burnt two brigs, several large sloops and other craft, with all their apparatus that was in store upon the shore. Lieutenant Clark of the Dependence, with two or three others, in firing the stores were blown up, but we flatter ourselves not dangerously.

The officers and men upon this occasion behaved with the greatest spirit.

GOVERNOR CLINTON TO MAJOR-GENERAL PUTNAM.

HURLEY, Oct. 18th, 1777

DEAR SIR:

I am this moment favored with yours of this morning.   There is nothing new happened in this Quarter since I wrote you yesterday. The Enemy is 8 or 10 miles above this burning away, but as there are no Capital settlements there on this side of the River and the situation of the Country such as with my present Force I can't advance opposite to them with safety to my artilliry,   I mean at present to continue where I now am, in Front of the most valuable settlements and where the Stores and Effects from Kingston are removed. I imagine the Enemy will not proceed much higher up the River and that on their return they will attempt to lay waste the places they have passed going up, after our Troops are drawn from them. This induces me to think some more Troops ought to be left at Poughkeepsie and Fishkill, but of this you can best judge. Adieu You shall hear of me frequently.

Your most obed^t serv^t

GEO CLINTON.

GENERAL WASHINGTON TO MAJOR-GENERAL PUTNAM.

CAMP, 20 MILES FROM PHILA., 19 October, 1777.

DEAR SIR:

Your favor of the 16th I received yesterday morning, and was much obliged by the interesting contents. The defeat of General Burgoyne is a most important event, and such as must afford the highest satisfaction to every well-affected American breast. Should Providence be pleased to crown our arms in the course of the campaign with one more fortunate stroke, I think we shall have no great cause for anxiety respecting the future designs of Britain. I trust all will be well in His good time. The obvious intention of Sir Henry Clinton was to relieve General Burgoyne, and being disappointed in that by his surrender, I presume he will make an expeditious return. I am happy to find you at the head of so respectable a force, and flatter myself, if he should land with a view to action, though I do not expect it, you will give us a happy account of him. I believe, from the bravery of the garrison of Fort Montgomery, he purchased victory at no inconsiderable expense. General Campbell was certainly killed. This they mention in their own printed account, but call him colo. of the fifty-second regiment. He was a general on the American establishment, so declared in one of the orderly books, which fell into our hands.

I have but little to add respecting the situation of affairs here. They remain much as they were, when I wrote you last. To remove the obstructions in the river seems to be a capital object with the enemy. Their attempts hitherto have not succeeded, and I hope they will not. I am extremely sorry for the death of Mrs.

Putnam, and sympathize with you upon the occasion. Remember-ing that all must die, and that she had lived to an honorable age, I hope you will bear the misfortune with that fortitude and com-placency of mind, that become a man and a Christian. I am, dear Sir, with great esteem, yours, &c.

G? WASHINGTON.

GOVERNOR CLINTON TO MAJOR-GENERAL GATES.

HURLEY, TWO MILES AND A HALF FROM KINGSTON,

21 October, 1777

DEAR SIR:

I have repeatedly done myself the honor to inform you of my situation, and think it my Duty again to do so, that if any of those consequences should happen, which may now be easily foreseen, the blame, if any, may not lie at my Door.

When I undertook at the request of Gen'l Putnam, to put myself at the head of a body of men to protect the Western Shores of Hud-son's River, and to throw myself between the enemy and your army, should they proceed up the River, I represented to him in strong terms the situation of this part of the Country thinly inhabited, and the interior part unsettled, and separated from all assistance by a chain of mountains. In consequence of which representation, he agreed to let me have three thousand men, if the Eastern Militia should come in, as he expected they would, of which number how-ever he hath not sent four hundred. I then clearly saw that it would be impossible for me, to protect the country, unless I could be reinforced from the Northern Army, which from your letter I had reason to expect. I wrote also to Governor Dickenson of New Jer-sey upon the same subject, and I am inform'd, that he, notwith-standing the exposed situation of his own State, has ordered six Hundred Men, to my Brother's assistance, at New Windsor. Kingston hath been destroy'd merely because I have been so de-ceiv'd in my expectations of Assistance, that it was impossible to take measures, for its Security.

I am now, Sir, at the Head of a little more than one thousand Men, to cover the most valuable Part of the County of Ulster.

The Enemy have lain still yesterday, and the Day before, with a strong southerly Wind, from whence it is evident, that a knowledge of Burgoyne's Fate hath changed their intentions, against Albany. If they land in Force, I must either Retreat, or sacrifice my few men, and loose seven very valuable Pieces of Field-Artillery. If I retreat, this whole Country will be ravaged, and destroy'd ; and that, at a season of the year, when the Inhabitants, (who are warmly attached to the American Cause,) will want time to provide Cover, for their Families, against the inclemencies of the ensuing Winter.

While we act merely on the defensive, two thousand Men, on the River, will find full Employment for twelve, or fifteen : But if four thousand are left to cover Albany, two Thousand here, and two thousand, on the other side of the River, it will be by no means impracticable, to recover the Passes in the Highlands, in which Case, the greater part of the Army, now along the Banks of the River, may be brought to act offensively against the Enemy ; and perhaps render the present Campaign decisive in our favor.

Col? Malcolm, who is the bearer of this Letter, will do Himself the Honor, of stating and explaining to you my Ideas, upon this Subject ; and you will do me a particular favour, if in Answer to this, you will inform me, what I am to expect, and what is expected from me. I am Dr Genl. with particular Esteem your most obedt Servt

GEO CLINTON.*

COMMODORE HOTHAM TO LORD HOWE.

St. Albans, New York,
21 October, 1777

My Lord :

My Letters of the 15th instant which you will herewith receive were intended to have been sent by the Bristol, who is stopped to proceed with the Convoy directed by your Lordship's Letter of the 10th. In consequence of it I have left the command up the North River with

* From the *Gates Papers*, in the New York Historical Society. Gates acknowledged the letter on the 24th, and requested the Governor to meet him at Queeman's, on the following Monday; but on the 25th, he notified him of a "noble reinforcement" sent to his assistance, which was to be "solely under your [Clinton's] command," and yet to be held "subordinate to the orders I may hereafter give." It was Col. Learned's brigade that was sent on, under the command of Col. Bailey. General Poor's brigade, with some artillery, were sent to reinforce Putnam.

Captain Symonds until the return of General Vaughan, when it is intended to evacuate Everything there, as Sir Henry Clinton for the defence of this place will now stand in need of every man left under his command.

The proceedings of the second expedition up the River your Lordship will see by the inclosed copy of a letter from Sir James Wallace, and one also to Sir Henry Clinton from General Vaughan. The wind having hung to the Southward ever since, has prevented our hearing any thing farther from them : but as it last night shifted & now blows strong from the North West, it is reasonable to think we shall have them down, the object of their going up the River seeming to be now over, without giving credit to the whole of what we hear respecting General Burgoyne's army. The two Battalions of Anspach were embarked before Sir Henry Clinton and I left Verplanck's Point, and with the wind may be hourly expected down. The 17th Dragoons, with the Convalescents, Recruits, Chasseurs, and Artillery, will be embarked without loss of time, and shall proceed (as they are ready) in separate convoys, which from the experience I have had of large ones, I consider as the securest and most expeditious way for them to join you. The 7th, 26th and 63d regiments are embarked with General Vaughan. * * *

W. HOTHAM.

COUNCIL OF SAFETY OF NEW YORK TO THE NEW YORK
DELEGATES IN CONGRESS.

October 22, 1777.

* * * * * * *

The loss of Fort Montgomerie, after a gallant defence, and for want of a proper and seasonable reinforcement, having opened Hudson's River to the enemy, they improved the opportunity, advanced to Kingston, and on the sixteenth instant about two hours before the Governor's Troops, who made a forced march, could arrive, gained the Landing ; and faintly opposed by about 150 militia only, marched immediately up to Kingston, and reduced the whole town to ashes. You can easily conceive the consternation and dispersion of the inhabitants of the town and its environs on this lamentable occasion. Mr. Livingston's family being among the refugees, it will be impossible for him to attend Congress, until things wear a more settled aspect in this part of the country, and he shall have properly provided for his family. He assures the Council that as soon as this can be affected, he will repair to Congress to relieve Mr. Duer.

The enemy now lie opposite to Sagherties. As their design to extricate General Burgoyne has proved abortive, we apprehend they are waiting for orders from General Clinton, at New York, respecting their further destination. In their passage from Kingston to that place, they landed and destroyed several buildings and improvements; among others those of the chancellor and his mother. The Governor now lies with his little army at Hurly, waiting for expected succors from General Gates, and determined to move with the enemy in such a manner as will best serve the purposes of annoying them, should they land, and covering the country against their further attempts. Notwithstanding the depredations of the enemy along the river, the total reduction of their northern army affords us great comfort. We wait impatiently for an account of something as decisive from the southward, which will most amply compensate for all our losses.

We are gentlemen, &c.*

GENERAL WASHINGTON TO MAJOR–GENERAL PUTNAM.

HEAD-QUARTERS, 25 October, 1777.

DEAR SIR:

I have your favor of the 20th, enclosing a copy of General Burgoyne's capitulation, which was the first authentic intelligence I received of the affair. Indeed I began to grow uneasy and almost to suspect that the first accounts you transmitted to me were premature. As I have not received a single line from General Gates, I do not know what steps he is taking with the army under his command, and therefore cannot advise what is most proper to be done in your quarter. But I should think, if a junction of your forces was formed, part to proceed down upon one side of the river and part upon the other, that Sir Henry Clinton would be obliged to retreat immediately before you; or, if he suffered you to get be-

* From the *Journal of the Council of Safety,* I, 1072.

tween him and New York, you perhaps might in its weak state get into the city. I mention this merely as a matter of opinion, taking it for granted you will pursue the most proper and efficacious measure. Whatever may be determined upon, I beg it may be constantly communicated to me, as the operations of this army may depend much upon the situation of yours. * * * I am, dear Sir, &c.

G? WASHINGTON.

GENERAL WASHINGTON TO GOVERNOR CLINTON.

25 October, 1777

D? SIR:

Your favor of the 20th I received yesterday Afternoon and feel Much for the Havoc and devastation committed by the Enemy employed in the North River. Their Maxim seems to be, to destroy where they cannot Conquer, and they hesitate not to pursue a conduct that would do dishonor to the Arms of Barbarians. I Know your feelings upon the occasion, and regret, that you were not in a Situation to check their progress. This promised aid, I hope, will call forth the exertions of all, and that in the course of Events, we shall have more Solid Grounds for triumph. A copy of the Articles respecting Gen! Burgoyne's Surrender reached me this Morning for the first time.

When Gen! Putnam informed me of the capture of Fort Montgomery, he wrote the Congress upon the Subject. By the first opportunity I shall transmit them a Copy of your Letter now before me. I am happy you detained Col? Markham, as you found him so Serviceable, and consent to his remaining as long as you shall think him of essential use. As to his Regiment, it is now here. Had I been apprized of the circumstance you Mention, before it Marched, I would not have ordered it to join this Army.

In the afternoon of the 22? a detachment of Hessian Troops, amounting to about Twelve Hundred, under the command of Count Donnop, attempted to storm our Fort at Red Bank, and were repulsed with the loss of between four & five Hundred men in Killed—wounded and prisoners—Among the prisoners is Count Donnop himself who is badly wounded. We only lost 32 in Killed & wounded —chiefly the latter. The Next Morning Several of the Enemy's Ships of War, Warped thro the lower tire of Chevaux de frize and Attacked Fort Mifflin on Mud Island & our gallies & Armed Vessels which were posted near it.   The Canonade was Severe and of long Continance, but Without Other damage to us than the loss of three or four men Killed & wounded.   The Enemy on their part lost Two Ships —one said to be the Augusta of 64 guns—the other a Frigate of 32. The first in returning, got Aground, and fearing that she would fall into our hands, they burnt her themselves.   The latter accidentally took fire and was consumed.   According to report, the Roebuck also suffered considerably.   They Seemed much determin⁹ to carry these posts.   I hope these disappointments they have met with will prevent their further Attempts—However they are not done, there having been a Canonade this Morning.

G⁹ WASHINGTON.

FROM GOVERNOR CLINTON.

POUGH KEEPSIE, 25 October, 1777.

DEAR SIR:

I arrived late last night, where I had hoped to find Gen! Putnam, but was greatly disappointed and marched through this for Fish Kill yesterday forenoon, and I cannot learn that he has left any order concerning our small army.

I am informed the enemy's shipping pass'd the chevaux-de-Frize at New Windsor yesterday evening, and are gone down out of sight from thence ; wherefore I think it best you move down towards New Windsor, that we may be nearer to the enemy, observing the same order as to your march as when you came to Hurley.   If Col. Malcom should have returned from Albany charged with orders from Gen'l Gates, contradictory letters, you will advise me thereof before you leave Hurley.

I shall continue at this place this day, and, as I am exceedingly unwell with a violent cold, perhaps to-morrow.   The next day I hope to have the pleasure of seeing you at New Windsor.

No news here.

I am, Dear Sir, with great esteem,

Your most obed! Serv!

GEO : CLINTON.

I will leave it to Maj. Fell to see that the Quartermaster and Com? of Forage replace everything we have taken from Wm. Livingston, and also please remind him of my baggage.   It is so small that it is almost impossible to forget any of it.*

MAJOR-GENERAL PUTNAM TO GENERAL WASHINGTON.

FISH KILL, 25 October, 1777.

DEAR GENERAL:

I have been honored with the receipt of your two favors of the 15th and 19th instant ; and have the pleasure to acquaint you that, after a tedious march, we are returned to this place ; the fleet passed down by here yesterday, and did but little damage on their return.

Some heavy artillery, and a reinforcement of Continental troops, I am informed by General Gates, are on their way to join me.   By a deserter, and two of our people who escaped from the enemy at Verplanck's Point, day before yesterday, I am informed that four regiments are gone from New York to reinforce General Howe, which caused General Vaughan's hasty return down the river, probably to increase the reinforcement, as fifteen hundred of the York militia are ordered to be drafted, to supply their place at New York. I trust and hope the succor they are sending will arrive too late to relieve General Howe.

We have collected twenty-three boats that escaped the enemy, some of which want repairing, besides the boats supposed to be left up Esopus Creek, and the new galley, which have not been reconnoitred.   I shall order the boats that want repairing to be repaired, and some new ones to be built immediately.   With esteem and respect, I am, affectionately,

Your most obedient, humble servant

ISRAEL PUTNAM.

MAJOR-GENERAL PUTNAM TO GENERAL WASHINGTON.

HEAD QUARTERS, FISH KILL, 27th Octo., 1777.

DEAR GENL :

I have the pleasure to acquaint you that yesterday morning the Enemy evacuated both Forts Montgomery & Clinton (but not with-

---

* From the *Reminiscences of General Samuel B. Webb*, p. 402.

out laying the same into ashes) and destroying every work about them. All their shipping, large & small, with all the sail they could possibly crowd, proceeded down the river yesterday. They have certainly some secret expedition in view, and from ev'ry account I am able to procure, They mean to reinforce Gen! Howe. by several Deserters & they are very intelligible, I am told four reg^ts embarked last week for the Southward & these Troops that's been up the river are intended for the same purpose.

I am informed the greatest part of our heavy cannon which the Enemy took at Fort Montgomery &c are since sunk in the creek betwixt Montgomery and Clinton—but with great care may be raised, so that I intend with the utmost [haste] to re Building Fort Clinton and make such other dispositions as will, (I hope) effectually secure this part of the Country—Gen! Poor with his Brigade I expect will join me in Two days. I have therefore upon repeated applications from the Connecticut Militia tho't proper to discharge them this Morning—When the Enemy's shipping lay up the river, I wrote Gen! Gates for some heavy cannon upon Travelling carriages (in order to annoy them) which is coming down with Gen! Poor's Brigade. Am in haste

Dr Gen!

Your very hum. Servt
ISRAEL PUTNAM.

FROM BRIGADIER-GENERAL PARSONS.

PEEKSKILL, 27 October, 1777

DEAR SIR:

The Two weeks pas^d have been disagreeably spent in a dead port at Peekskill : but I am now reliev^d from the disagreeable Necessity of continuing longer here. Oysters & Blackfish will soon be my Lot. I hope to take a comfortable napp to-morrow night, or beat the Bush in which dwell some of the fairest Birds. I want nothing now but my Brigade. If Col. Webb could find Means to join it, it would be very agreeable to see him. I am, Dear Sir,

Y^r Obed^t h. Servt
S. H. PARSONS.

P. S. Remember my Hat, being now destitute of a decent one.

JOSEPH WEBB TO JOSEPH TRUMBULL.

WETHERSFIELD, Octr 27th, 1777.

DEAR SIR:

I am in great want of choice Potatoes which I take the Liberty to send to you for & as you Engage I'll pay. I have not time at present to Collect the Corn— perhaps you may persuade him to take the Mony and have it done with. The affair I mentioned to you at Hartford is finaly Settled between General DeRochefermoy Erklen & myself thus "He's to purchase in Martinico a Vessel ab^t 150 Tonns Man & Compleatly fix her—Load her with a Cargo of Molasses & other Goods—½ on his Own Acc^t & friends in Martinico— Erklen one Quarter You, J. Sebor, Self the other Quarter I was to procure the Commission from His Excellency your father; but on Examining [ ] find it can't be done on Acc^t of not knowing the Captain, &c, &c but I have since General DeRochefermoy departed found out that one Mr Bingham is Agent for the Congress at Martinico & we must Obtain the Commission there. Are you acquainted wth him? or had I best to write Col Dyer or Mr Hancock, or what is best to be done? I should b^e glad of a line from you as Early as possible

I am Sir

Your most Ob^t H Servt

JOS. WEBB

the Ladies have Just given me a rapt over the fingers for not mention theirs & my Complements to y^r Lady & family

I suppose you have heard that our Assembly have ventur'd to Nominate some other persons for Congress I was in hopes you & Jerry Wadsworth wou'd have a Chance *

GENERAL WASHINGTON TO LIEUTENANT–COLONEL ALEX– ANDER HAMILTON.

HEAD QUARTERS, 30 October, 1777.

DEAR SIR:

It having been judged expedient by the members of a council of war held yesterday, that one of the gentlemen of my family should be sent to General Gates, in order to lay before him the state of this

* From the Cabinet of the Connecticut Historical Society.

army and the situation of the enemy, and to point out to him the many happy consequences, that will accrue from an immediate reinforcement being sent from the northern army, I have thought proper to appoint you to that duty, and desire that you will immediately set out for Albany, at which place or in the neighbourhood, I imagine you will find General Gates.

You are so fully acquainted with the two principal points on which you are sent, namely, the "state of our army and the situation of the enemy," that I shall not enlarge on these heads. What you are chiefly to attend to is, to point out in the clearest and fullest manner to General Gates the absolute necessity that there is for his detaching a very considerable part of the army, at present under his command, to the reinforcement of this; a measure that will in all probability reduce General Howe to the same situation in which General Burgoyne now is, should he attempt to remain in Philadelphia without being able to remove the obstructions in the Delaware, and opening a free communication with his shipping.

The force, which the members of the council of war judged it safe and expedient to draw down at present, are the three New Hampshire and fifteen Massachusetts regiments, with Lee's and Jackson's, two of the sixteen additionals. But it is more than probable, that General Gates may have destined part of these troops to the reduction of Ticonderoga, should the enemy not have evacuated it, or to the garrisoning of it, if they should. In that case, the reinforcement will vary according to circumstances; but if possible let it be made up to the same number out of other corps. If, upon your meeting with General Gates, you should find that he intends, in consequence of his success, to employ the troops under his command upon some expedition, by the prosecution of which the common cause will be more benefitted than by their being sent down to reinforce this army, it is not my wish to give any interruption to the plan. But if he should have nothing more in contemplation, than those particular objects, which I have mentioned to you, and which it is unnecessary to commit to paper, in that case you are to inform him, that it is my desire that the reinforcements before mentioned, or such part of them as can be safely spared, be immediately put in march to join this army.

I have understood, that General Gates has already detached

Nixon's and Glover's brigades to join General Putnam ; and General Dickinson informs me, that by intelligence, which he thinks may be depended upon, Sir Henry Clinton has come down the river with his whole force.   If this be a fact, you are to desire General Putnam to send the two brigades forward with the greatest expedition, as there can be no occasion for them there.   I expect you will meet Colonel Morgan's corps upon their way down ; if you do, let them know how essential their services are to us, and desire the Colonel, or commanding officer, to hasten their march, as much as is consistent with the health of the men after their late fatigues.   Let me hear from you when you reach the North River, and upon your arrival at Albany.   I wish you a pleasant journey, and am, dear Sir, &c.*

G? WASHINGTON.

GENERAL WASHINGTON TO MAJOR—GENERAL PUTNAM.

HEAD QUARTERS, PHILAD^A COUNTY,
30 October, 1777.

SIR :

I am informed by Gen! Dickinson, that he has intelligence, which he thinks may be depended upon, that S? Henry Clinton, with all the troops under his command, has returned down the River.   If this is so, and the Brigades of Nixon & Glover should have joined you from the Northward, I desire they may be immediately put under March to reinforce this Army.   Col? Hamilton, who will deliver, or send you this, will inform you of the necessity there is for dispatch.   In my last I desired that the detachments belonging to Varnum's and Huntingdon's Brigades Might be sent forward ; if they have not Marched before this reaches you, order those belonging to Varnum which now consists of Green's Angell's Chamber's & Durkee's, not to cross the Delaware but to proceed by the shortest

* Gates resented this method of conveying orders to himself, and wrote a letter to Washington, in which occurred this paragraph, which he struck out before sending :

" Although it is customary and absolutely necessary to direct implicit obedience to be paid to the Verbal Orders of Aids de camp in Action, or while upon the Service, & with the Army upon the Spot—yet, I believe it is never practiced to delegate that Dictatorial Power to one sent to an army 300 miles distant."   *Gates to Washington,* 7 November, 1777.

Route to Red Bank upon the Jersey Shore, where the Brigade is stationed. I refer you to Col? Hamilton for all particulars relating to the Situation of this Army and that of the Enemy and am
    Dear Sir
        Y? most ob! Serv!
           G? WASHINGTON.

GOVERNOR CLINTON TO MAJOR—GENERAL GATES.

        FISH KILL, 30th Octobr 1777
          ten o Clock at night
DEAR SIR:

 I arrived here about noon, when I met your favour of the 25th Inst—My Letter of the 26th informing you of the enemies fleet having fallen down below New Windsor, must have reached you before this—I have therefore only to add that the enemy have demolished Fort Montgomery, and all the other posts in the Highlands, and moved down with their whole force towards New York, and to ask how I am to dispose of the Troops belonging to your department which you have been so good as to place under my direction. As it is probable Gen! Putnam may think it prudent to make an Attempt against New York, I am the More anxious to have your directions in this respect, that I may govern myself accordingly—I am with the highest esteem and respect
      Your affect? Humb!e Serv!
         GEO. CLINTON.

 P. S. Your troops had not reached N. Windsor yet. The last I heard of them, they were at Kingston; since which, to this day, I believe the weather has prevented their Moving.

GENERAL WASHINGTON TO MAJOR-GENERAL PUTNAM.

      HEAD QUARTERS, 31st October, 1777.
DEAR SIR:

 I am fav? with yours of the 25th from Fish Kill. Although you Say that the Enemy have passed down by that place, you do not Say whether they have gone entirely down and evacuated the Forts upon the River; but from the tenor of your letter, I imagine they have.

I shall be glad to be particularly informed of this in your next, and also whether you have heard with certainty of the reinforcements having gone from N York to Gen! Howe. We have a report that the Enemy have evacuated Rhode Island and returned to New York; but as it comes from No Authority, I shall be glad to be ascertained of the fact. If the Enemy have left the Forts, be pleased to let Me Know whether they have carried off or damaged the Cannon.

I was glad to hear that Gen! Gates was Sending down a reinforcement to you. As they will not now be wanted by you, they will be so far upon their way towards this Army; and I beg they may be sent forward with as much expedition as possible for the reasons given you in Mine of yesterday.

I am &c

G? WASHINGTON.

MAJOR-GENERAL PUTNAM TO GENERAL WASHINGTON.

FISH KILL, October, 31ˢᵗ,1777.

DEAR GEN!

I congratulate your Excellency on the Success of your arms against the Enemy, in the attack made on Red Bank, which Comes by letter from Col. Bidle—I have Already informed you, by former letters, of the return of the Enemy's fleet down the river—their having evacuated Peeks Kill, Fort Montgomery, & their adjacent posts, after destroying the Cannon & demolishing the Forts, with an Evident design, as I conceive, to Send as Strong a reinforcement to Gen! Howe as they possibly can.—

Gen!ˢ Poor's, Warner's, Learnard's, Patterson's Brigades, Col. Van Schaick's Regt. & Col. Morgan's Riflemen, Amounting in the whole to five thousand & Seven hundred men, inclusive of Col. Morgan's Riflemen, who are directed to March immediately to join you, are on their way here from the Northward—which with the Troops, I before had amount to about nine thousand men exclusive of Col. Morgan's, the Artillery men, & the Militia from Connecticut & this State, the greater part of which are dismissed—I understand likewise that a considerable quantity of artillery is Coming down—Inclosed is a Copy of the proceedings & advices of a Council of war held this day with respect to the disposition of the Troops here & that are expected Soon to arrive, which is Submitted to your future direction. To Crush Gen! How I consider a Most Capital object—think it my duty to give you a particular account of the Strength & numbers of the Troops here & Expected, that you may be enabled to make Such regulations & orders as you shall Judge necessary, in the best manner to Subserve our Important Cause—& annoy the Enemy —Gen! Wind with Seven hundred Jersey Militia are included in the above Computation. With the highest esteem & respect I have the Honor to be, your Excellency's most obed!

humble serv!

Israel Putnam.

COUNCIL OF WAR.

Head Quarters, Fish Kill, Oct! 31st 1777

Att a Council of War convened by Order of the Hon'ble Major Gen! Putnam—

Information being given to the Council by Gen! Putnam that the Enemy's Fleet had gone down the River to New York; that they had demolished The Forts Clinton, & Montgomery, in the Highlands, and destroyed the Barracks, and other public Buildings at Peeks Kill. That by Deserters and others from the Enemy 4.000 men are ordered from New York to Reinforce General Howe. That a Considerable Reinforcement from General Gates's is near, together with several other articles of Intelligence Respecting our own, and the Enemy's Strength and Situation.

The General then there Requested the Council to give their opinion what steps will next be necessary, Keeping in Views three particular points viz: the Speedy Reinforcing his Excellency Gen! Washington, in case of need, Defending and Repairing the Posts in the Highlands, and as far as in our Power diverting the Enemy's from Reinforcing Gen! Howe, likewise to be Ready if call'd, to act· offensively against the Enemy.

The Council are unanimously of opinion that 4000 move down the West side of Hudson River and take Post at or near Harrestraw— that 1.000 Remain in the Highlands to cover the Country or repair the Works as the Gen! may direct;—the Remainder to March as soon as possible towards King's bridge for the purposes before mentioned

—and that Col. Morgans Core of Rifle men which is Considered as part of the 4.000 to move down the West Side of Hudsons River, be Immediately ordered to March with all expeditiion to join his Excellency Gen! Washington.

> GEO. CLINTON.
> JAMES CLINTON B. G.
> WILLIAM WINDS B. G.
> WILLIAM MALCOM Col.
> SAM^L WYLLYS Col.
> JOHN LAMB Col.
> LEWIS DUBOYS Col.
> SAML B. WEBB Col.
> DAN^L MORGAN Col.

GOVERNOR CLINTON TO PIERRE VAN CORTLANDT.

FISHKILL, 31 October, 1777, 4 o'clock, P. M.

DEAR SIR:

I am this moment favored with yours of yesterday. With respect to Colo. Wimple's and Livingston's regiments, I can only say they were ordered down by Gen'l Gates to reinforce the little army under my command, when the enemy's shipping were at Saagertys, to enable me to invest Fort Montgomery. The situation of the enemy is since very different; they have demolished and evacuated Fort Montgomery, and all the other posts in the Highlands, and have drawn their whole force to New York, I suppose with intention to reinforce Howe, at Philadelphia. I have attended here since yesterday noon, in a council of war, to determine the measures most proper to be pursued by our army in this quarter; what they will be, is yet unknown. Gen'l Gates considers the troops sent down on the west side of the river as belonging to his department. I cannot, therefore, discharge them; it is to him they must make their application for this purpose. If they join me they shall be well supplied with provisions and every other necessary in my power to command. We shall either attempt New York or reinforce Head Quarters, and between this and 15th November, much may be done.

I enclose you the last accounts from Head Quarters, which, though not so well authenticated as I could wish, I believe to be true, and congratulate you on the important success. Excuse great haste.

Yours, sincerely

GEO. CLINTON.

MAJOR-GENERAL GATES TO " OLD PUT."*

ALBANY, 2 November, 1777

DEAR SIR :

Governor Clinton will present you my letter to him of this date, which contains my unalterable sentiments of the measures that ought to be taken, should Sir Henry Clinton attempt to succour, or rein-force Sr William Howe. I will not again repeat them here, but only take the Liberty earnestly to recommend the profoundest secrecy in whatever you determine to do ; for depend upon it, that, that con-summate artful woman Mrs. Robinson will do all in her power to be acquainted with your *Secrets.*

* So endorsed by Gates. From the *Gates Papers* in the New York Historical Society.

On November 3d. Colonel James Wilkinson, an aid of General Gates, attended Congress, and laid before that body the papers respecting the Convention made with Burgoyne. A committee of three was appointed to take steps for " directing the future operations of General Gates," and its members were Richard Henry Lee, John Adams and Elbridge Gerry. A report presented on the following day proved unsatisfactory, and was recommitted, William Duer, of New York, being added to the committee. Again was a report laid before Congress on the 5th, and was adopted. The first and last paragraphs read :—

" *Resolved*, That General Washington be informed that it is the earnest wish of Congress to regain the possession of the forts and passes of Hudson's River, and to secure the communication thereof; and for that purpose, that General Gates should remain in command in that quarter; and that General Putnam be called upon to join the main army with such a detachment from the army under the command of General Gates as General Washington may think can be spared, not exceeding the number of 2500 men including Colonel Morgan's corps.   *   *   *

That if General Washington, after consulting with General Gates and Governor Clinton, shall be of opinion that a reinforcement exceeding the number above mentioned can be detached to the main army consistent with the attainment of the objects specified in the preceding resolutions, in such case he be directed to order such further reinforcements to the main army as may be thought conducive to the general welfare, anything in the preceding resolutions to the contrary not-withstanding." *Journals of Congress,* 5 November, 1777.

As to any attack upon N. York, I utterly disapprove of it : for while the Enemy's ships of war can act in the North and East Rivers, the taking that City would be Doubtfull ; & if taken could not be held ; & be assured that all Stores of any Value to us, are, or will be afloat before any large Detachments can leave that City—and I see no good in taking an Empty Town, we cannot hold ; of course it is not an Object to Divert the attention of the King's Generals from their important Designs.   I am &c

H. GATES.

TO JEREMIAH WADSWORTH.

[November, 1777.]

Friend Jerre.—My Humble Service to you to be harrass'd for ever I believe ; just cross'd Hudsons River tomorrow to March to White Plains,   I rather think Horseneck will bring me up—fine Girls—Black fish and Oysters in plenty,—my Regt is bare foot— Bulkley sets of in persuit of Shoes this day,—Enclosed

These resolutions are of interest, because they were the result of a concession by those who were seeking to advance Gates at the expense of Washington. The committee, as first constituted, was distinctly hostile to the Commander in Chief, and it is probable that a too strong expression of that feeling led to the recommitment of the report, with Duer, a friend of Washington, added. When the last paragraph quoted above, came to be considered in Congress, it was sought to limit Washington's action by making the " concurrence " of Gates and Clinton necessary, and the two Adams, Gerry and Dyer, known partisans of Gates, voted in its favor. Lee was absent, and his brother, Francis Lightfoot Lee, voted against this limitation. Washington, in receiving the resolutions, merely wrote : " Their [Congress] proceedings of the 5th, I presume, were founded on a supposition, that the enemy were still up the North River, and garrisoning the forts they had taken. This not being the case, and all accounts agreeing that reinforcements to General Howe are coming from York, I hope the aids I have required will be considered expedient and proper. Independent of the latter consideration, I think our exertions and force should be directed to effect General Howe's destruction, if it is possible." *Washington to the President of Congress,* 10 November, 1777.

" For your comfort I can tell you that old Daddy Putnam is ordered on to the main army, and a trial is inevitable. God speed it." *Major Richard Platt to Colonel John Lamb,* 29 November, 1777. Platt was aid-de-camp to McDougall.

is good news from the Southward.—Lets hear from you—Love & Compliments to our friends—take good care of the Little Girl you Lately run away with—
Yours Affectionately
Sam⸻. B. Webb.*

MAJOR—GENERAL PUTNAM TO GENERAL WASHINGTON.

Fish Kill, November 3ᵈ, 1777.

Dear Genˡ :

I am Sorry that I am under the disagreeable Necessity of Acquainting you that there is the greatest Necessity of Money in this Department, the Troops Suffer for Want of Pay, the Commissary, and QuarterM's Department are exceedingly embarrass'd and perplexed, in their Business, greatly involved in debt, and the Public Faith will be prejudiced unless a Considerable Supply of Cash is Speedily Sent— I Must Request you to order Some to be forwarded with as Much Dispatch as possible.

The large Spy Glass I took from Col. Morris last year, and which your Excellency had, I exceedingly want, as I have none, neither can I get any. Mrs Morris Wrote Me the other day, and Requested I would take it, I should be extreamly obliged if it Might be sent by the Bearer.

Col. Hamilton Arrived here yesterday, and in Consequence of your orders, I have directed the Detachments of the Several Regiments with you, to March and Join their Corps—Genˡ Winds I have ordered to March to Red Bank, Lt. Colonels Cobb and Smith, with the Detachments from Colos Jackson and Lee's Regiments— Genˡs Poor, Learned, Patterson and Warners Brigads I have ordered to March and Join You and have only Genˡ Parsons' Brigade, and three York Regts of Continental Troops left—Yours of the 26th Ultmo came to hand after Writing the above.

I am Dear Genˡ
Verry Respectfully
Your Mot Obt Humble Servt
Israel Putnam.

* From the Cabinet of the Connecticut Historical Society,

P. S. B. Gen! Parsons is Now in the Neighborhood of White Plains; last Thursday he Detach'd a party into West Chester took about 40 of the Horse Theives, four of Delancy's Lt Horsemen & thirty horses besides Several other articles—Burnt three Vessels of about 50 Tons Burthen Laden with Butter & Cheese for New York.

MAJOR-GENERAL PUTNAM TO GENERAL WASHINGTON.

FISH KILL, Novem^r^ 7th 1777.

DEAR GEN^L^

Your's of the 31st Octr and 1st Novem^r^ I have been favor'd with, and have taken the necessary precautions, that Your Army should be Supply'd with provision.

In My last I informed You that Gen! Warner's Brigade were order'd to Join You, but as they are rais'd only till the first of Decem^r^ the Officers and Men think it exceeding hard, that they should be obliged to Make that long March and their times out soon after they could reach You—I have in Consequence of their request detain'd them here to make Obstructions in the River—Governor Clinton & Myself have been down to view the forts, and are both of opinion that a Boom thrown across at Fort Constitution, and a Battery on each side the River, would Answer a Much better purpose than at Fort Montgomery, as the Garrison would be reinforced by Militia, with More expedition and the Ground Much More defensible—All these Circumstances Considered, we have concluded to obstruct the Navigation at the former place, and shall go about it immediately.

The cannon that were left at the forts are rendered entirely useless--except six 12 pounders at Fort Constitution, and these are spiked, and the Trunnions broke off, but May be stack'd so as to Answer the purpose tolerably well.

I yesterday rec^d^ a Letter from Col^o^ Hamilton, dated at Albany, ordering Me to send forward 1000 More Cont! Troops, than was proposed when he was here, this will leave me with About 300 Cont! Troops, and no Militia, except those whose times are out the first of Decem^r^ to cover all this distressed Country—I don't think I can justify Myself in this, without first acquainting You, and if I then have Your Excellency's orders, I will with pleasure immediately and punctually comply with them.

I am Sorry to inform You that for the want of pay, Gen! Poor's Brigade of Cont! Troops have refused to cross the North River—The Troops Mutined, the Officers endeavouring to Suppress them, and they So determined to go home, that a Cap! in the execution of his Duty, run a Soldier thro' the Body, who Soon expired, but not before he shot the Cap! thro' who is Since dead—I have got several of them in Provost Guard, and a Gen! Court Martial sitting for this Tryal, About 20 of them have Made their escape and gone home, I have sent off some Light Horse, and Officers of the Brigade to bring them back—In order to Make peace and reinforce You as soon as possible, I am endeavoring to borrow about £1000 or £1500 to give them a Month's pay—in the mean time they are Curing themselves of the Itch, as soon as this operation is over they will March immediately—This I acknowledge is a bad Precedent, but it is a worse one to Keep Troops ten Months without pay.

This Department is absolutely in distress for Money, and the necessary Business cannot be carried on, without a Supply is immediately Sent.—

I am Dear Gen!

Very Respectfully

Your most obed! Serv!

ISRAEL PUTNAM.

P. S. I have just rec! informa! from Gen!s Dickinson & Parsons, that Sir Henry Clinton has embark'd about 6000 Troops, as a reinforcement for Gen! Howe, they have not yet sail'd. I shall go down to White Plains this afternoon to make a show there, possibly this will prevent their going so soon as they would otherwise—if at all.

MAJOR-GENERAL PUTNAM TO GOVERNOR CLINTON.

HEAD QUARTERS, KING'S STREET,

10th Nov! , 1777.

DR. SIR,

The night before last I arrived at this place, and shall this day proceed down towards the Plains; yesterday General Parsons and myself was down at East Chester, and within three miles of King's

Bridge ; from every appearance the enemy seems much frightened. They have called in all their outguards, and collected their main force at the Bridge. Deserters come in very fast, and from every acct. I am able to procure, their strength at the Bridge are about 2500. The inclosed you have a late paper (which in my opinion) paints their distress in many particulars, I shall be glad to see you down here ; my compts. to your brother and am,

Dr. Sir, your very hble. Servt.

ISRAEL PUTNAM.*

GENERAL WASHINGTON TO MAJOR-GENERAL PUTNAM.

HEAD QUARTERS, WHITEMARSH,
11 November, 1777.

DEAR SIR:

I have your favr of the 7th and am glad to find that you had determined to detain Warner's Militia. At whatever place Gov. Clinton and yourself determine to throw Obstructions and Batteries upon the River, I imagine it will prove Satisfactory, for no person is Supposed to have a better Knowledge of that Country than the Governor.

For the very Same Reasons that Genl. Howe is reinforcing himself strongly, ought we to reinforce also, and I therefore beg that you will comply with My request of the 9th instant which is nearly the Same as Colo. Hamiltons Namely to Send all the Continentals except Colo. Sam : Webb's and Sherburne's and the New York Battalions, and I entreat they may be forwarded as quick as possible, for should Genl. Howe's reinforcement Arrive before them, Consider what a Situation this Army will be in.

It is very evident that the Enemy, in order to Secure their remaining Army under Genl. Howe, are drawing every man from New York, to what purpose, then, would it be to keep a force up the North River when there is no enemy Near, for we have Certain accounts of the fleet's having left the Hook. I know the people are apt to be alarmed and to think themselves deserted when they see troops drawn away from them, but I am Confident they will Soon find the good effects of it.

* From the *Sparks MSS.* in the library of Harvard University.

GENERAL WASHINGTON.

I am extremely Sorry to hear of the Uneasiness that has happened in Gen! Poor's Brigade on Acct. of their pay ; and am amazed to hear that they have ten Months due to them. This is indeed a very great hardship, and there Must be a fault Some where, but I hope from the prudent Measures you have taken, they will be contented. I have wrote to Congress, in the Most pressing Manner for Money for your department and I have no doubt but you will be Soon Supplied.

G? WASHINGTON.

FROM COLONEL TALLMADGE.

UPPER DUBLIN NEAR GERMANTOWN,
Nov. 13, 1777

DEAR SIR,

Retired from Duty for a moment, I am set down to give you the Current news of the Day, the whole of which summed up amounts to but little ; so that on the whole this letter will contain subject matter for *expectation*, rather than of past occurrences.

The noble Defence lately made at the important Post on *Redbank*, you have doubtless been apprized of—By a Gentleman just from Philad? I am told that nothing could equal the mortification & disappointment of the Enemy on that repulse, as they expected but little resistance would have been made ; & on setting down & counting the Cost it has been about the amt of 500 men to them.

The greatest preparations are making by the Enemy to attack our forts both by land & sea. They have cut down sundry small sloops, which are to carry 1 or 2 heavy Guns, & float over the *Chevaux de frize*. These are preparing below, near Chester—Above the fort & at the City they have built Floating batteries, which with the Delaware Frigate is to fall down & attack the Gallies on that Qr —A 6 Gun battery of 32 pounders has been lately opened on Province Island, which fired about 200 shot the first Day, without wounding a man of ours. The plan proposed (if accounts be true) is that the Shipping & batteries should play on the fort incessantly & if possible dislodge our people ; this failing they are determined to storm it.—How difficult a Job this may be, they will be better able to judge when they make the tryal, but I rest in hopes that they will 'not succeed—Every thing almost depends on our maintaining those forts, & unless they can obtain them, it is evident their visit in Philad.ª can be of but short duration.

In front of their Camp is a Chain of Redoubts, connected together by a continued *Piquett* or *Abatis* from River to River. Though formidable, I mean their Redoubts, if they draw off much of their force to act below, I think & hope the Gen'l will try the strength of them.

A constant firing is kept up below & we in turn are almost every Day taking off their Piquetts advanced in front of their works. Gen'l *Pottar* with one Brigade is on the other side Schuylkill, Gen'l Varnum has crossed the Delaware, & lies on the Jersey side, & the main body of the Army with his Excellency is in the rear of Germantown. Thus you have the Disposition of the army, which in this part is encamped in two lines, on airy high commanding & advantageous Ground, from which we defy Gen! Howe with double his number of *invincibles*, to drive us.

Col.º Livingston I am told is a Prisoner—Unfortunate Man, I pity him much, but his amiable Lady more, because I really believe She will be more concerned for him, than he for himself. His Zeal for our Cause, & determination not to hear it ridiculed may perhaps bring him into trouble, but his Connexions in N. York & the British Army will be of great service to him.

Make my Compliments to Major Huntington & all the Officers of your Reg.ᵗ —If my old friend David Humphrey is with you, give him also the benedictions of

Your friend & h.ᵇˡᵉ Servant

BENJ.ᴺ TALLMADGE.

17ᵗʰ Novʳ

I am sorry to inform you that we have just rec.ᵈ intelligence that our People were yesterday obliged to evacuate fort Mifflin, having sustained a very heavy Cannonade for many days both from the Enemy's Batteries and Shipping. I am told that we bro't off most of the Cannon & Stores—wish I could give you the particulars, but am not able as the news has just reached us.—*

* From the collection of Dr. John S. H. Fogg, of Boston.

MAJOR–GENERAL PUTNAM TO GENERAL WASHINGTON.

HEAD QUARTERS NORTH STREET Novemb 14th 1777

DEAR GENl

I am favd with yours of the 4th 5th & 9th Inst & you will see by Mine of 7th that I have detain'd Genl Warner's Brigade.

The New York Regiments being Annex'd to General Poor's Brigade, they are exceeding unwilling to be Seperated, and I Knowing the disadvantages that would arise from their being here, have presumed in Some Measure to deviate from your Excellencys orders— Those Regiments are principally Composed of Men whose former Residence was within the Enemy's Lines—and the little time they were down in this Quarter last Summer, there was upwards of one hundred Deserters from them; Mostly to the Enemy—that we should soon loose the principal part of them here—Add to this they have lately got Some Cloaths and Money which puts them in a Much better Situation to March, than Most of the other Continental Troops here, besides all this they began their March before I Recd your Letter—This, Sir, has Induced me to let them Continue their Rout, and in their stead I have detain'd Wyllys's and Meigs's Regiments, whose Situation will by no Means admit of their Marching with that expedition which is necessary Near one half of them without a Shoe, or Stocking but a Supply is Soon expected.

Col. Charles Webb's Regt Marchd yesterday. I have directed him to advise you of his Rout by Express before he arrives. I shall be happy to find this step meets your Excellency's Approbation.

The Inclos'd is a Copy of a Letter from Col. Hamilton to Me— by which you will See that I am positively Ordered to Send all the Continental Troops from here. This Letter Contains Some Most unjust and ungenerous Reflections, for I am Conscious of having doné every thing in My power to Succour you as Speedily as possible.*

* On Colonel Hamilton's return from Albany, after executing his mission to General Gates, he found, when he arrived at New Windsor, that General Putnam had not sent forward such reinforcements to General Washington, as were expected. General Putnam seems to have had a special reluctance to part with these troops, probably in consequence of his favorite project against New York. Colonel Hamilton's letter was pointed and authoritative.

"I cannot forbear confessing," he observed, "that I am astonished and alarmed beyond measure to find, that all his Excellency's views have been hitherto frus-

I shall go to New Windsor this day to See Col. Hamilton and untill I have your Orders, I cannot think of Continuing at the Posts Myself and Send all the Troops away. if they Should go Now I am Confident Gen! Howe will be further reinforced from this Quarter. for by Deserters, Spies and Every Other Coroborating Intelligence there is Now on York Island the 35th 45th 52d and 57th British four Regts of Hessians and one of Waldee—Browns, Fannings, Byards, Robinsons, Hirlehy's and Delancys 1st & 2d Battalions of New Levies— Some Say Fannings is at Powles Hook tho' that is Immaterial—On Long Island there are None but Militia, by Information from Gen! Dickinson there is about 1000 on Staten Island.

trated, and that no single step of those I mentioned to you has been taken to afford him the aid he absolutely stands in need of, and by delaying which the cause of America is put to the utmost conceivable hazard. I so fully explained to you the General's situation, that I could not entertain a doubt you would make it the first object of your attention to reinforce him with that speed the exigency of affairs demanded; but I am sorry to say he will have too much reason to think other objects, in comparison with that insignificant, have been uppermost. I speak freely and emphatically, because I tremble at the consequences of the delay, that has happened. Sir Henry Clinton's reinforcement is probably by this time with General Howe. This will give him a decisive superiority over our army. What may be the issue of such a state of things, I leave to the feelings of every friend to his country capable of foreseeing consequences. My expressions may perhaps have more warmth, than is altogether proper, but they proceed from the overflowing of my heart in a matter where I conceive this continent essentially interested.

" I wrote to you from Albany, and desired you would send a thousand Continental troops, of those first proposed to be left with you. This I understand has not been done. How the non-compliance can be answered to General Washington, you can best determine. I now, Sir, in the most explicit terms, by his Excellency's authority, give it as a positive order from him, that all the Continental troops under your command may be immediately marched to King's Ferry, there to cross the river and hasten to reinforce the army under him. The Massachusetts militia are to be detained instead of them, until the troops coming from the northward arrive. When they do, they will replace, as far as I am instructed, the troops you shall send away in consequence of this requisition. The General's idea of keeping troops this way does not extend farther, than covering the country from any little irruptions of small parties, and carrying on the works necessary for the security of the river. As to attacking New York, that he thinks ought to be out of the question for the present. If men could be spared from the other really necessary objects, he would have no objection to attempting a diversion by way of New York, but nothing farther."—*MS. Letter, New Windsor, November 9th.*

I had previous to the Rec! of your Letter Wrote Governor Trumbull for a Number of Militia, but I have My Doubts whether they will Come in or not, as they have been Much Fatigued this Summer already. The Rhode Island expedition has been of No Service to us ; you have doubtless heard that is drop'd and 'tis said ab! 3,000 Troops Remain there—

M! Colt has accepted of his appointment as D. Commissary Gen! of Purchases, I have Seen him this day, he Informs me there are a Number of Cattle purchas! which I Shall See Immediately forwarded to you—

Since I came here we have had near 50 Deserters, Some from all Cores—

I am Dear Gen!

With Much Respect

Your Mo!! Ob! Serv!

ISRAEL PUTNAM.

GENERAL WASHINGTON TO MAJOR-GENERAL PUTNAM.

HEAD-QUARTERS, WHITEMARSH, 19 November, 1777.

DEAR SIR,

I am favored with yours of the 14th. I could have wished that the regiments I had ordered had come on, because I do not like brigades to be broke by detachment. The urgency of Colonel Hamilton's letter was owing to his knowledge of our wants in this quarter, and to a certainty that there was no danger to be apprehended from New York, if you sent away all the Continental troops that were then with you, and waited to replace them by those expected down the river. I cannot but say there has been more delay in the march of the troops, than I think necessary ; and I could wish that in future my orders may be immediately complied with, without arguing upon the propriety of them. If any accident ensues from obeying them, the fault will lie upon me and not upon you. I have yet heard nothing of Poor's or Patterson's Brigade—or of Colo. Chas. Webb's Regiment. Scammel's Brigade will be at Coryells ferry tonight or tomorrow and Lee's & Jackson's Regiments arrived here this day. Be pleased to inform me particularly of the corps, that have marched and are to march, and by what routes they are directed, that I may know how to despatch orders to meet them upon the road if necessary. I am, &c.

G? WASHINGTON.

BRIGADIER-GENERAL PARSONS TO GOVERNOR TRYON.

21 November, 1777

Sir:

Adding to the natural horrors of war, the most wanton destruction of private property are acts of cruelty unknown to civilized nations, and unaccustomed in war, untill the servants of the King of Great Britain, have convinced the impartial world, no acts of inhumanity, no stretch of Despotism, are too great for them to exercise towards those they are pleased to term Rebels.

Had any apparent advantage been derived from burning the houses on Phillips's Manor, last Monday night, there would have been some appearance of reason to justify the measure, but when no benefit can result from destroying those buildings, and striping the women and children of necessary apparel to cover them from the severity of a cold night, and leading off the captivated heads of those families in Triumph to your lines, in the most ignominious manner, I cannot assign a justifiable cause for this act of cruelty; nor can I conceive a reason for your further order to destroy Tarry Town.

'Tis not my inclination, Sir, to war in this manner against the Inhabitants within your lines who suppose themselves within the protection of the King. But necessity will oblige me to retaliate in kind, upon your friends, to compel the exercise of that Justice which humanity used to dictate; unless your explicit disavowal of the conduct of your Captains Emrick and [Joshua] Barns, shall convince me those houses were destroyed without your knowledge and against your order.

You cannot be insensible 'tis every day in my power to destroy the buildings belonging to Colo. Philips and Mr Delancey; each as near your lines as these burned by your Troops were to the guards of the Army of the United States, nor can your utmost vigilance prevent the destruction of every building on this side King's Bridge.

'Tis not fear, Sir, 'tis not want of opportunity has preserved these buildings to this time, but a sense of the injustice and savageness of such a line of conduct, has hitherto saved them; & nothing but necessity will induce me to copy the example of this kind so frequently set us by your troops.

I am, Sir, your obedient humble servant,

SAM. H. PARSONS.*

* On the night of the 17th, a part of British under command of Captain Em-

GOVERNOR TRYON TO BRIGADIER-GENERAL PARSONS.

KINGS BRIDGE CAMP, 23 Nov: 1777.

SIR:

Could I possibly conceive myself accountable to any revolted subject of the King of Great Britain I might answer your letter received by the Flag of truce yesterday, respecting the conduct of the party under Captⁿ Emmerick's command, upon the taking of Peter and Cornelius Vantassel. I have however candour enough to assure you, as much as I abhor every principle of inhumanity or ungenerous conduct, I should were I in more authority, burn every Committee Man's house within my reach, as I deem, those Agents the wretched instruments, of the continued calamities of this Country, and in order the sooner to purge this Colony of them, I am willing to give twenty silver dollars, for every acting Committee Man who shall be delivered up to the King's Troops. I guess, before the end of the next campaign, they will be torn to pieces by their own Countrymen whom they have forcibly dragged, in opposition to their principles and duty (after fining them to the extent of their property) to take up arms against their lawful Sovereign, and compelled them to exchange their happy Constitution for Paper, Rags, Anarchy and distress.

The ruins in the City of New York, from the Conflagration of the Emissaries of your party last year, remain a memorial of their tender regard for their fellow-beings, exposed to the severity of a cold night.

This is the first correspondence I have held with the King's Enemies, in America, on my own part, and as I am immediately under the Command of Sir Henry Clinton, your future Flags, dictated with decency, would be more properly directed to His Excellency.

I am, Sir, your humble Servant

W:ᴹ TRYON.*

merick surprised the Van Tassels, burnt the house, and carried back to New York Peter and Cornelius Van Tassel with halters round their necks. Peter, known as the Indian King, was a committeeman. On the 25th some patriots, under the command of Abraham Martlingh, passed the enemy's guard boats in safety, landed and burned the house of General Oliver de Lancey, after plundering it of its contents. This expedition was supposed to have been in retaliation for that against the Van Tassels.

* "By the inclosed correspondence between me and Gen! Parsons, your Lordp

FROM GOVERNOR GEORGE CLINTON.

NEW WINDSOR, 24th Novr , 1777.

DEAR SIR:

I enclose you a copy of a memorandum I lately received from Lieut. Col. Livingston,* agreeable to which you will please to dispose of his Horse and Baggage, and remind Major Huntington about sending him the *Hard Cash* he got at Sagertyes, if he has not yet done it.

Has Van Vlack been paid the money took from him? if not, I wish to have it, as Col. Lamb advanced him a part of it. If he has received the whole from you, this must be returned by him to Colo Lamb.

I think you have a bundle of my papers, which I wish to have by the first safe hand. Excuse haste, and believe me, Dear Sir, with great Regard, your most obedt servt

GEO. CLINTON.

MAJOR-GENERAL PUTNAM TO GENERAL WASHINGTON.

NEW ROCHELL, 28 Nov., 1777.

DR GENERAL:

Since I wrote My Last Nothing particular has happened in this Quarter,—Some days ago I had made a Desposition to Cross over to Long Island, and attack the Forts Huntington & Setauket, but before Matters could be got Ready for the Expedition, they Evacuated both Forts and Are Now Making very strong Works at the Upper End of the Island.

I Recd a Letter the other Day from Genl Dickinson, acquainting Me that his Intention Was Yesterday to Make a Descent Upon Staten Island, upon which I ordered Genl Parsons & Warner's Bri-

may judge of the tone I think should be held towards the Rebels." *Tryon to Lord Germain*, 1 December, 1777. In February, 1778, Tryon was appointed one of the Commissioners for restoring Peace! His Colleagues were: Sir William Howe, Sir Henry Clinton, Governor Patrick Tonyn, and the Commanding Officer at Rhode Island.

* Lt. Col. Wm. S. Livingston, now a prisoner in the hands of the British.

gades to March down towards Kings Bridge to Make a Diversion in his favour, which I hope had the desired effect—I am in haste

Dr Gen!

Your Most obed! H^{ble} Serv!

ISRAEL PUTNAM.

FROM MRS. JOSEPH WEBB.

WETHERSFIELD, November 30, 1777.

Often, my dear Brother, has my inclination led me to my pen in order to write thee, and as often has my design been frustrated. I have at this time too additional inducements knowing you cannot at this time have a Line either from Mr. Webb, or our dear Hetty— the former you have doubtless heard has left us, in hopes of obtaining leave to go with the Flagg into New York. God grant he may obtain it that he may Console and bring from thence our afflicted Widdow'd Sister. We this day had the Melancholy Intelligence from Mrs. Hubbard, who had the same from Mr. Jownson that Mr. Simpson and his Sister Peggy are no more. My heart bleeds for the dear Girl : who in a situation like hers must if possible feel double affliction. I am happy to think her Brother is with her (as I trust by this he is), & I have not a doubt but he will bring her with him when he returns. How happy shall we be to have it in our power to Contribute to her happiness, and in every possible Way to Lighten her sorrows. * * *

A. WEBB.*

COLONEL WEBB'S ORDERS.

ON BOARD THE SCHUYLER,

TUESDAY EVENING, 9 December, 1777.

The several Vessels under Convoy and in Company with the Schuyler are carefully to keep company— never to be out of hail ahead. The Schuyler will take care to shorten sail as occasion may require.

---

* She was Abigail Chester, a sister of Colonel John Chester.

The signal for landing by night will be a false fire—by day, setting the Ensign ; immediately the troops to be ready as fast as possible to step into the boats.

Capt. Wooster of the Grenadiers, with the three right hand divisions to disembark and cover the landing of the detachment. He will take care to advance double sentinels in front.

Capt. Hart on landing will form on the right; the others in course. Capt. Moseley at the left of the Line.

So soon as the signal is given a profound silence to take place, none but the commanding officers of Divisions to be suffered to speak a loud word.

After landing, the Adjutants will see that they are properly formed in subdivisions ; the Artillery will form in front between the Grenadiers and the Column ; no man then to leave his ranks on any pretence.

The Colonel has the greatest confidence in the Troops he has now to command, and doubts not that they will do Honor to their Officer as well as themselves, for which it is absolutely necessary there should be a strict compliance with orders. Those that do it will receive the treatment due to good soldiers ; but on the least variation, necessity will oblige the commanding officer to make public example of the offenders.*

---

* From the *Reminiscences of General Samuel B. Webb*, p. 150.

" I was at General Putnam's Headquarters when your Favour of the 4th Inst. came to Hand. General Parsons was then embarking 5 or 600 men, in 3 Divisions for Long Island, in order to bring off a Number of suffering Prisoners, who were waiting to be relieved." *Hugh Hughes to Gates*, Fishkill, 13 Dec., 1777.

From the [London] Public Advertiser of Dec: 12th, 1777.

To the Printer

Sir.

You deserve the thanks of the Public for a Paragraph in your paper of this day, discrediting the fallacious report of two or three deserters who imposed on Gen! Carlton (who is but a Simple and credulous Man) by saying that Gen! Burgoyne and his Army had laid down their Arms, the following extract of a letter which I have just received, will undeceive the Nation, raise the Stocks and the Spirits of my Countrymen and intimidate the House of Bourbon, and therefore beg you will Publish it as soon as Possible.

PHILADELPHIA Nov: 15th, 1777

My Dear Friend

We have just fired a feu de Joy for the safe arrival of Gen! Burgoyne and his Army. Sir Wm Howe on hearing of his Distress detached Sir Wm Erskine with a Detachment of 5000 Men mounted on the Horses which the Loyal Inhabitants of the Delaware County's had furnished. Sir Wm crossed the, Delaware, Galloped thro' the Jerseys; Swam over Hudson's River and reached General Burgoyne's Camp between Fort Edward and Fort Ann, and found the troops drawn out ready for Action. The General was harranging them in the Dress of a Roman Consul (which was the only part of the Theatrical Wardrobe which he had saved on the Retreat from Boston). Sir Wm waited very respectfully 'till the General had finish'd his Speech, which was so Pathetic that it drew tears even from the Indians, he ended his Oration with these lines, which he had set up the whole night before to Compose.

> Allons—*mes Heroes*—Mince your Scoundrel Foes,
> Arnold this day shall have a bloody Nose,
> Go General Phillips, see our Guns well Ram'd
> My Boys, we'll Die like Soldiers—or be Damn'd
> No food these three days—true—we lost the Battle
> But yet we'll have our Bellies full of Cattle.

It is impossible to describe the Exultation of the Soldiers on hearing the General pronounce these Heroic Sentiments. They insisted on being instantly led to the Combat. Sir Wm Erskine then produced positive orders that the Northern Army should Mount *En Croupe* and proceed to Philadelphia.—Rage, Grief and indignation was visible for a moment on every Countenance, but on Sir William's whispering Gen! Burgoyne, he instantly mounted behind him, and the whole Army followed his Example, in the mean time Arnold Advanced with a strong Corps, to intercept the March; Sir Wm Charged them with the greatest bravery and broke through them, halted at fifty Yards distance with Horses' Rumps to the Enemy. The Soldiers who were mounted behind faced about and gave the Yankies such a Fire as obliged them to run in the greatest confusion, it was a rapid movement and executed with the greatest intrepidity and coolness.

Sir W^m then proceeded at full Gallop; The Troops observed the strictest Discipline : a number of Pillions were taken from the Inhabitants in the Jerseys, but Receipts were given (at General Burgoyne's request) and Sir Wm Howe has since drawn on the Treasury both to pay for the Pillions and a large quantity of Dyaculum which the Loyal Quakers have furnished.   The Ladies have sent in a Waggon of Old Gloves, and all the Surgeons and Mates of the Army are now employed in spreading plasters.   The poor Highlanders have suffered most, and the Gen! has ordered them to wear Breeches 'till they are perfectly recovered.   I am happy to be able to give you this Intelligence and wishing you a merry Christmass

I am my Dear Friend Yours

JOHN VAT. ASS. Maj^r 10th *

PAROLE.

NEW PORT RHODE-ISLAND Decr 14th 1777

I Samuel. B. Webb Esqr Colonel in the Continental Forces, Prisoner of War being permitted by Major Gen! Pigot to depart this place, do promise upon my Parole of Honor to go from hence to Providence in this Province and endeavor to procure the effecting an exchange between Lt Col^o Campbell of His Majesty^s , 71st Regiment of Foot and Me in failure of which I do affirm that I will in the space of two Months repair to

* The copy is in Colonel Webb's writing.

New York (unless otherwise Exchanged) and Submit myself to any General of His Majesty's Forces who may command there.

SAMᴸ. B. WEBB.

Colº. in the Continental Army.*

TO MAJOR GENERAL HEATH.

PROVIDENCE Decʳ. 16ᵗʰ 1877.

DEAR GENᴸᴸ

On Tuesday Evening the 9ᵗʰ Instant I embarked on board the arm'd Sloop Schuyler—haveing under Convoy—three other Vessels with abᵗ. 400 Men for Long-Island—the night being dark and blustering we parted Company, at the dawn of day on Wednesday morning we were off Satalkut—when we discovered a Ship crowding all Sail for us, being to Leeward we had only one chance to escape, which was by running the Vessel ashore, no time was lost, the Vessel grounded on a Beach about 200 Yards from shore, the boat was hove out, before we could get her from the Vessel the Surf ran so amazing high that she fill'd and Sunk,—with much dificulty we regained the Vessel—by this time the Ship had come to within half a Mile of us and was pouring in her Broadside—in this cruel Situation we were obliged to Strike,—The Ship proved to be the Falcon commanded by Capᵗ. Harmond, who bro't Us to Newport, haveing a number of friends there I made interest to come out and endeavor to effect an exchange, as you will see by the enclosed Parole.

—Your former politeness and attention, leads me at

* From the *Heath Papers* in the Massachusetts Historical Society.

this time to request your influence in this matter, consider my Dear Sir—that I am a young Man just entering on the Stage of life,—my Reg^t. now happily formed, and should I remain in a State of Imprisonment long, not only personaly, but my Reg^t. must suffer much; the former objection of Col^o. Campbells exchange must now be at an end, he was then an Officer of the highest Rank of any in our hands, was therefore detained for Genl. Lee, since which Major Genl. Prescott has been made a Prisoner—I do not suppose it in your power to settle the exchange, but a letter from you to the General & another to the Massachusetts members of Congress will I am persuaded have a happy effect,—time will not permit or I should write Genl. Hancock—be pleased to shew him this letter—I cannot but hope he will favor me with Letters on the Subject.—

I hope my unhappy situation, and State of anxiety, will plead the necessary excuse for my troubling you on this Subject, I set of from this for Wethersfield in Connecticut this afternoon,—being now desstitute of a second Shirt.—I hope to hear from you on this Subject by the earliest conveyance, and wish most ardently the letters from you & Genl. Hancock may be enclosed Me.

With the warmest Sentiments of Esteem I am Dear General your friend &

Most Hum^{bl} Servt.

SAM^L B. WEBB.

N. B.   The offer is now a Col^o for a Lieu^t. Col^o which I obtained by the Influence of my friends.—*

* From the *Heath Papers* in the Massachusetts Historical Society.

RETURN OF PRISONERS TAKEN ON THE LONG ISLAND EXPEDITION.*

Col. Webbs' Reg!		Col. Ely's
Col	1	1
Capt.	1	
Adj!	1	
Sub	2	2
Sargts	4	Adjt. 1
R & F.	16	35
	25	39
Sub. of the Train		1.
Total	65.	

MAJOR-GENERAL PUTNAM TO GENERAL WASHINGTON.

SAW PITTS 16th Decem! 1777

DEAR SIR

I was last Evening fav⁴ with your two Letters of the 28ᵗʰ Ult? and 2ⁿᵈ Inst with a Remonstrance from M! Drake Inclosᵈ That piece I do own is Made up of Fatuity and Misrepresentation, at least what has ever Come to My Knowledge—

I have ever acted as Near your Excellency's orders of last Winter as was in My power—Nor has any property been dispos⁴ of for the Benefit of the Captors, Unless such as was taken in the actual Possession of the Enemy—General Parsons, and the Sequestrators have had some dispute Respecting Cattle that was taken from the Enemy while they were at Verplanks Point and up the River, which I Suppose has occasioned this Remonstrance—I could give you M! Drake's Character in full, but Refer you to Major Yates My Aid-de-Camp who is on his way to Baltimore—

The Troops at this place shall be Removed to Fish Kill Agreeable

* Enclosed in General Putnam's letter to General Washington, 13 January, 1778. I have attempted to make a full list of the officers captured from Webb's regiment, with the following results:—

Colonels Webb, and Ely; Captain Edward Bulkley; Adjutant Elisha Hopkins; Lieutenants John Riley, and Giles Mumford; Quarter Master's Sergeant Jehosaphat Starr; Sergeants Jonathan White, and Aaron Abercrombie.

to your Orders as Speedily as possible, and Nothing in My power shall be wanting to Secure the River against Any further attempts of the Enemy, but Works without Men will Answer but little purpose— I am Sorry to inform your Excellency that I have Reason to fear Col⁰ˢ Samˡ. B. Webb, & Eli are prisoners with the Enemy, and Some Men, the Numbers as yet Uncertain as the Expedition was on Long Island, and Numbers of the Men have gone to the East End— Major Yates can give your Excellency the particulars, of this Affair— and what Objects we had in View—

I Beg Leave to Refer you to him, for every particular Respecting this department—

I am Dʳ Sir
Your Most Obedᵗ Servᵗ.

Israel Putnam.

P. S.   Since I had the Misfortune to Loose Mʳˢ Putnam the Circumstances of My Family are Such as Makes it absolutely Necessary—that I Might have a Little time to go home, to Settle My Affairs, if you think it not inconsistent with the Service, I shall be glad of your Approbation—

Yours &c

I. P.

Your Letter of the 19ᵗʰ Ultᵒ is Just come to hand.

JOSEPH WEBB TO GOVERNOR TRUMBULL.

19 December, 1777.

May it please your Excellency,

This will be handed you by Capᵗ Trowbridge who was to have been Exchanged for Capᵗ Raymond—but from a hint from your Excellency that it was not best to send for Raymond out, but have Trowbridge have the Next first Vacancy—& from a proposal you made to Bigelow, I have broᵗ Him out on parole to send in a Captain Keating which Bigelow tells me will be agreeable to his Orders.

I have also thro the influence of Colᵒ Sheriff to General Clinton set the affair of Lieut. Fitch's right—and further did compleat the Exchange of two privates I carried in—I trust Major Welles has allready spent much time in painting the horrid Situation of our unfortunate Countrymen that are Prisoner's in York, more particular the privates that are in the Hospitals—tho' I may venture to say I know much more about it than an Officer that has been confin'd— I was permitted to view the whole Round's, to mention with freedom their greivances

and I trust I was of some Service—but to Return to the Hospital, I found it dismal—Death seam'd to be in Every counternance, they that was not Dead & dieing told me they wanted for fresh provision, Vegetables, Cloathing &c—the latter I acquainted Mr Pintard with who promised me to supply 'em the very Next day—for the most of the Time the flour was Sour—but of late the flour was better being supply'd by Our agent Mr Pintard—but for fresh Meat & Roots— General Jones the Town Governor said it was not in their power to supply—no not Even to their own Hospital's. something seriously ought to be done, or they will all die—I was in york abt 12 days I believe there was at least Sixty buried—we ought to send in some faithful tenders, a faithful Person to examine the Whole wretched Situation—indeed I wish a General Exchange might take place upon Honor! terms—but I must now do my duty to acquaint you that un-less something is immediately done, Newyork will be their Grave

and what is more perhaps both sides to blame—I wish I was able to wait on your Excellency in person for its [*torn*] for me to Write, what I could tell you—The Provost Situation I trust was painted by Major Welles who has taken a degree there

The officer's that was on parole on Longisland while I was in York was put on Board Ships which I complain'd of, but General Jones told me Our people was going on Longisland, that they was to be attacked in a few days, as soon as that was over they shou'd Re-turn to Longisland he beg'd I wou'd see that affair in a Just light as Capt Trowbridge can acquaint you—I wish to hear of a fine Spireted Commisary of our's going to york & there do his duty without fear, or affection—unless the General Exchange may take place which is realy the Duty of the people at home to push—you may depend the people that have been prisoners along time, think themselves in part Neglected by their Country

I did my best Endeavor's to make 'em satisfied, & that it cou'd not be help't—unless we consented to dishonor! Term's which they most readily said they cou'd not wish—

Ethan Allen begs me to represent his Situation to You "that he

has been a most Attachd friend to America." & He say's he's forgot
—He's spending his Life, his very prime

& now is confind in the Provost—& they say for breaking his parole without he own's it in part—I cou'd wish Some of 'em wou'd
be more prudent—

M.ʳ Langdon had many private Conversations with me, after Three
days being in the Provost

He was set at Liberty that is on parole of the town—He's Anxious as you can conceive a mortal to be begs he may be tho.ᵗ by your
Excellency of equal Consequence to Gov.ʳ Franklin as its his only
hope's, they will take no other in Short He's had much difficulty to
Obtain that—He's much in the down's as they look with an evil Eye
on him as a Committee Man, & a Man to be Chosen Gov.ʳ of New
Hampshire—The Bearer is waiting which prevents me saying what I
cou'd wish—but

I shall do all in my power to crowd an Exchange—

I am Sir

Your Excellencys Most Ob.ᵗ H Serv.ᵗ

JOS. WEBB.

19.ᵗʰ Decem.ʳ 1777

I have bro.ᵗ out my Sister with her Furniture, the Good Womans
lost Her Husband & her Sister which She followed both to one
Grave, & I found her Melancholly & dejected enough ; I was happy
enough to get permition for her to come out with her Effects—The
latter they wan't quite so willing, for they s.ᵈ we refused any Effects
going to them—I plead the Liberty allow'd the Landamain*—&
they finely granted the Effects—

I wish you knew the Anxiousness of my mind about these affair's
—I believe I ought to write lengthy to Gen.ˡ Washington? or what is
to be done?

I shou'd be happy to hear from y.ʳ Excellency by one line if its
agreeable & Convenient—If I can be of any service to my Country it
gives me pleasure—the Prisons[ers] was much affraid I shou'd forget them when I was out but its not the Case.†

* Perhaps *Sandemanians.*

† From the *Trumbull Papers* in the Massachusetts Historical Society.

GOVERNOR CLINTON TO GENERAL WASHINGTON.

POUGHKEEPSIE, 20th December, 1777—

DEAR SIR,

I was not honored with the Receipt of your Excellency's Letter of the 3d before Friday last—I am truly Sensible that the Security of the North River is a Matter of the Utmost Importance to the United States in the present War & that the Safety of this State in a More particular Manner depends upon it—It gives me real Concern therefore that so little has been yet Done to effect it—Works are laid out & began to defend the Cheveaux de Frize & Something done towards finishing & sinking such of them as were not completed when the Enemy came up the River and these are the only steps that have hitherto been taken.

When the Enemy left the River it was My opinion that Many of the Troops from the Northern Department should be sent to reinforce the Grand Army under your Excellency's more immediate Command as cou'd be possibly spared—That no greater Number shou'd be left in this Quarter than what wou'd be barely Sufficient to cover the Country which is more immediately exposed to the Ravages of the Enemy to amuse them from sending large Reinforcements to Gen! Howe & to Carry on the necessary works for the Security of the River. One Brigade of Continental Troops with the Militia then in service & such of this State as I shou'd be Able to call out I conceived fully sufficient for these Purposes—Two small New Hampshire Militia Regiments which were sent down from the Northward by Gen! Gates about 70 Connecticut Militia and those of Col? DuBois? who escaped from Fort Montgomery—& a Regiment of Militia of this State were assigned for the Works The rest of the Troops consisting of General Warner's Brigade of Militia (which arrived earliest) General Parson's Brigade and some Connecticut Militia were drawn off to King's Street and the adjacent neighborhoods on the Sound under the immediate Command of General Putnam—It was late before the Militia from the Northward arrived, and they were worn out with the Fatigues—of the Campaign and their long March hither—The Time for which they were engaged in the Service expired the first of this Month—and of those of this State the 15th and while they were with us—The Want of Tools and Materials was such as to prevent their being employed to any degree of

Advantage—DuDois? Regiment are the only Troops on thè Spot at present which are by no means Sufficient to Mount the necessary Guards—Of course the works are entirely neglected.

The Resolutions of Congress of the 5th of November for regaining the Forts and Passes on Hudson's River & securing the Communication thereof vested General Gates with such Ample Powers for drawing supplies of Men & Materials from New Jersey and the different States Eastward that something essential might yet have been done towards the Completion of this Important Business before the opening of the Spring would he take upon himself the direction of it ; But as (I understand) that Gentleman proposes taking his Seat at the Board of War Agreeable to his late Appointment those Resolutions as they Apply to him particularly will loose their intended Effect, and tho I learn by a Letter I received from General Putnam accompanying that from Your Excellency that he is directed to turn his Views in Future to this object yet (however capable he may be for the Task)—I fear he will fall short in the Execution of it unless he shall be able to Command the Same Aids at least which Gen! Gates was impowered to do—

I am clearly of Opinion that a strong Fortress ought to be erected either on the opposite Side of the Creek from where Fort Montgomery stood or at the West Point opposite Fort Constitution. The latter I prefer as the most defensible ground and because the Navigation of the River there is more difficult & uncertain and the River some thing narrower than it is at the former Place—A new Chain should be procured (if possible) and with the Boom which is nearly Compleated stretched across the River. This With a Floating Battery or two & Some Gun Boats I am persuaded woud answer the purpose effectually and in this opinion I am confirmed as the Enemy chose to risque every Thing for the Reduction of Fort Montgomery rather than to Attempt passing it with their Shipping while in Our Possession. If West Point should be the place fixed upon it might be of great advantage to erect a small strong Work on the high Point on the opposite shore a little above Fort Constitution.

As to the Management in this Department of which your Excellency desires my Sentiments, I am Constrained to Say, (but I wish it may be considered as in Confidence) we have either been very unfortunate or it has not been as wise as Might be wished—prudent

Management of our Small Force, in my humble Opinion woud have Saved the Forts; tho' perhaps with the far less Important Loss of the Continental Village by loosing the Forts The Village fell of course. it is true a few Stores were Moved from thence & saved but I dare Say not of equal Value with those lost at the Forts, exclusive of the Shipping; besides had we held the Forts we shoud have commanded the Navigation of the River and drove the Enemy to the Necessity of attempting to releive Burgoine (for it is Evident that this was their Intention) by Land, in which Case it Might have been in our Power by calling the Militia to our Assistance to have destroyed Clinton's whole Army. Indeed without opposition they coud not have effected a March In Season for the intended Purpose, and I am Confident they never woud have Attempted it—I never considered Peeks' Kill or the Village Posts of great Importance only as they stood Connected with the Defences of the River; for without the latter the Enemy could by landing above come in the Rear of the Former in which Case they must fall of course (The Event has fully proven this) Notwithstanding the chief Part of this Department was kept idle at Peeks' Kill and the Village, while the Forts were left without a sufficient Number of Men to carry on & compleat the Works or defend them.

If the shipping had been properly Man'd and this was often Solicited, the Congress at least might have been Saved; and even after the Loss of the Forts by a prudent disposition of the Force in this Quarter, which was Soon greatly increased by the Coming in of the Militia, Kingston Might have been Saved & the greater Part of the Mischief Committed by the Enemy along the shores of the River prevented—A Constant Intercourse which has been permitted between the Country & City by Flags has I fear been very Injurious, as well by frequently enabling the Enemy to learn our Strength as otherwise, without our being able to derive Similar Advantages from Such Correspondance. I have heard that there has been a Weekly exchange of News Papers with Gov.ʳ Tryon & that the Printers Gaine & Loudon are permitted the like Liberty. The latter I have no doubt of—An over share of Complaisance & indulgence to the disafected which tho Arising from Principles of Benevolence and Humanity will always create Jealousies & unfavorable suspicions especially among the Common People and often even reach the

Army, and shoud therefore be carefully Avoided in these Respects I can't help thinking there has been a want of Common Prudence. I have taken the Liberty of hinting my Sentiments of these Matters to Gen! Putnam, and I woud fain hope that there may be More Circumspection used in future.

The Legislature of this State is to Meet at this Place the fifth of Next Month. The variety of important Business to be prepared for their Consideration and other affairs of Government will imploy so great a Part of My Time, that I should not be able to give that Attention to the Works for the Security of the River as their Importance and the Short Time in which they ought to be Compleated require ; But you May rest assured Sir that every Leisure Hour shall be faithfully devoted to them & My advice and assistance shall not for any Consideration be witheld from The Person who shall be entrusted with the Chief Direction of them—I have the Honor to be with the Most Sincere Esteem & Respect

Your Excellencys

Most Obed! Serv!

Geo. Clinton.

TO GOVERNOR TRUMBULL.

Wethersfield Dec! 23ᵈ 1777.

My anxiety is so great that I cannot but again trouble your Excellency on the Subject of my exchange, I early embarked in my Country's cause, nor have I attended dureing this War to any private business,—and nothing can make me more unhappy than the tho't of remaining an Idle Spectator of her sufferings, and cannot but hope thro : the influence of my friends I may soon be at liberty again to join my Regiment and stand or fall with my Country.

I have not yet wrote Congress or General Washington on the Subject of my exchange with Lᵗ. Colᶥ. Campbell rather wishing my letters may be accompany'd

with one from your Excellency,—with others from
Boston &c which I am in hourly expectation of—should
you honor me with one to Congress and to The General on the subject you will greatly oblige me,—In the
interviews your proposal, of writeing Lord Howe,
offering Cap.ᵗ Furneaux for me may be attended with
happy consequences, at the same time if agreeable I
wish the Lieu.ᵗ of the Navy you mentioned might be
offered for Cap.ᵗ Bulkley. Should Lord Howe acceed to
the proposed exchange with Cap.ᵗ Furneaux, I am confident it will please the General. Wishing Health and
Happiness may attend your Excellency, I am with respect & Esteem.

Your Most Obed.ᵗ Serv.ᵗ

Sam.ᴸ B. Webb.*

Gov.ʳ Trumbull.

> Endorsed 23.ᵈ Decem.ᵇ 1777
> Col.ᴸ S. B. Webb
> re his Exch.ᵉ —rec.ᵈ p his Brother 26.ᵗʰ

MAJOR-GENERAL HEATH TO GENERAL WASHINGTON.

Boston Dec.ʳ 25.ᵗʰ 1777

Dear General

Not long Since I received a Letter from Col.ᵒ Samuel B Webb
informing me that the fortune of War had Thrown him into the
Hands of the Enemy, that He was admitted on Parole, and was
very Desireous if Possible to Effect an Exchange for Some British
Officer in our Hands, as Col.ᵒ Webb is an active and Good Officer, I
beg leave to recommend him to your Excellencys particular attention, and as an Exchange might I imagine be very easily made for
Some Officer out of the many that are Here I beg leave to Sollicit
the favor in behalf of Col.ᵒ Webb, but Submit the propriety or Ex-
pediency of the Measure to your Excellencys Determination—

---

* From the *Trumbull Papers*, in the Massachusetts Historical Society.

General Burgoyne has not as yet Sent to Rhode Island, to have the Transports ordered round, altho He has been talking of it ever Since He was Informed of the resolve of Congress restricting him to the Port stipulated by Convention—He is very uneasy that He does not hear your Excellencys Determination, as to himself and sute which He Daily Express—

I have the Honor to be
with great respect
your Excellencys
most obt Servt

W. HEATH.*

FROM MAJOR-GENERAL HEATH.

HEAD QUARTERS BOSTON
Decr 25th 1777

DEAR SIR

Yours of the 16th Instant Came duly to hand   I most Sincerely regret your Misfortune, and Hope an Exchange will be Soon effected, I have wrote to His Excellency General Washington on the Subject this Day and have shewn your Letter to Mr Hancock and requested of him to write also.   He has assured me that He will.   I shall be Happy if I can in any Degree be Instrumental in facilitating your Exchange or in any other way affording you assistance and be assured my Dear Sir That I am

Yours Sincerely—

W. HEATH.†

TO GENERAL WASHINGTON.

WETHERSFIELD IN CONNECTICUT,
Decr 29, 1777.

Before this I suppose your Excellency must have heard of a late decent on Long Island and the objects General Putnam had in View by ordering on the

* From the *Heath Papers* in the Massachusetts Historical Society.

† From the *Heath Papers* in the Massachusetts Historical Society.

Troops. The detachment under my command left Norwalk in four Transports the Evening after the 9th Instant, the weather proved very blustering by which means we parted Comp^y —on the Morning of the 10th at dawn of day we found ourselves within two Miles of a British Ship, every effort was made to clear her, but was forced on shore near Satalkut,—the Surf running high fill'd and Sunk our Boat directly after we hoisted it out, the Ship came too very near Us and began a heavy fire. In this unhappy Situation, no mode of escape left, nor any chance to defend ourselves we were obliged to submit Prisoners to Capt. Harwood of the Falcon Sloop of War, from this we were carried to Newport, where thro' the influence of some old acquaintance I obtained a Parole of which the enclosed is a Copy. I had with Me one Captain, Adjutant, two Sub's and about 20 privates of My Regiment together with about 40 of the Militia. I should without loss of time waited in Person on your Excellency but am unable to ride. The particulars relative to the Expedition General Parsons told Me he would inform you. I have dispatched Mr. Gibbs (a Volunteer in My Reg^t.) with this letter, by his return I hope to know whether Lt. Colonel Campbell can be given in exchange for Me. I Confess from the Letters which passed between your Excellency and General Howe I have little reason to flatter Myself of its taking place —but knowing at the time they were wrote Col^o. Campbell was one of the Officers highest in Rank of any in our possession, and since Major Genl. Presscott being Captivated, I could not but flatter Myself the objections were at an end. Should it be otherways I must beg your Excellency to get Me from My present unhappy Situation as early as possible, the State of My Regiment, My Accounts with the Public (which thro' necessity have been neglected) demand My earliest Attention—besides which My ardent wish is, again to be in the Field in My Country's cause, anxiously waiting your Answer

I am with the warmest Esteem

Your Excellency's Most Obed^t. &

Very Hum^{ble} Servt.

SAM^L. B. WEBB.

BRIGADIER-GENERAL PARSONS TO GENERAL WASHINGTON.

LYME IN CONNECT^T 29th Decr 1777.

DEAR GENERAL

Col. Webb's falling into the Enemy's Hands the 10th Inst. you have doubtless before this been made acquainted with.

The Descent on Long Island was design'd to destroy the Timber & Boards prepar'd at ye East End of ye Island for Barracks in New York, to destroy the Fleet there from Rhode Island for Wood. Attack a Reg^t Station^d about Eight Miles Eastward of Jamaica & remove or destroy whatever Public Stores should be found on the Island; for this Purpose Col. Meigs was to have landed at Hempstead Harbour to attack the Regiment near Jamaica, Col. Webb near Huntington to Sustain Meigs & aford Such aid to the Division Eastward as should be Wanted & destroy whatever was collected in that Part of ye County of Suffolk for the Use of the Enemy; the Easter-most Division with which I was landed at a Place cal^d Hockaback about forty Miles from the East End of ye Island with Design to destroy ye Fleet, Timber Boards &^c Col. Meigs who was to have cross^d from Sawpitts through the Roughness of ye Water was unable to pass over in his Bcats; the other Two Divisions Sail'd from Norwalk the Evening of ye 9th Inst. with fair Prospects but Unfortunately the Arm'd Sloop in which Col. Webb was on ye 10th in Morning fell in with the Falcon Sloop of War in her Passage from New York to Newport, & was forc^d on Shore at so great Distance from the Beach as render'd their Escape so hazardous as Most of them fell into the Hands of the Enemy.

Upon the Inquiry I have been able to Make, I believe they were more unfortunate than guilty of any criminal Neglect, and the falling in with that Ship was perfectly accidental as None were Station^d within Many Miles of that Place. The Eastern Division landed Safely. The Fleet (except the Swan & Harlem Sloops of War & four other Vessels) had Sail'd : One Sloop had taken in her Cargo of Timber & Boards the other three had taken none but being light hal^d into the Bay under Cover of ye Arm^d Vessels, the loaded Sloop we took & we destroy^d all the Timber & Boards prepar'd for New York & a large Quantity of Wood cut for another Fleet expected from Newport. Cp^t Hart with about forty men was so fortunate as find Capt Ascough's Boats within about twenty yards of the Shore ; and on their Refusal to Surrender gave them Several well directed Shots which did great Execution ; Capt Ascough, of the Swan, having his Thigh broken Two other Officers badly Wounded Eight Kil'd & about the Same Number wounded whose Rank are unknown ; this we have from one of the Inhabitants on Board the Swan.

When the Boats came alongside, the ships kept a constant Fire but without Execution. Immediately on this the ships weighed anchor & sailed for Newport.

The Troops except those taken with Col. Webb are Safely landed on the Main again with about Twenty prisoners taken there.

Col. Webb is now out on his Parole to endeavor an Exchange for Lt. Col. Campbell of ye 71st Reg^t & to return in Two Months unless this is effected or he is otherwise exchang^d . If there is no Special Reason to prevent the Exchange of Col. Campbell I would beg your Excellency's Permission to send in Col. Campbell, but if any objection arises against his Exchange Col. Laurence taken at Staten Island or any other of like Rank will I suppose Answer his Parole if sent in Season.

If either of these Ways or any other can procure Col^o Webb's Exchange he will be made happy & his Reg^t greatly benefitted as the Affairs of that Regiment are so Circumstanced that no Man can do Justice to them if he is confin'd.   He has always conducted himself as a good Officer & as Such Merits the Esteem of his Superior Officers.

I should at this Time have requested your Excellency's Permission to have left the Service of My Country in the Army ; was I not apprehensive the Example would have too extensive an Influence amongst the Officers of My Brigade already so discontented as to have produc⁴ very Many Applications for Dismissions.   I have endeavour'd with Some Success to give Satisfaction with Assurances Congress would pay that Attention to their Case as would do Justice.   The general Sentiments & Practice of the Country are Such as give too Much Cause for their Complaints—When the Officers are calm'd & have laid aside their Present Intentions, I hope I shall not be consider⁴ in a Disagreable Light if My Application for a Dismission should be nearer the Opening another Campaign than the close of This—

I am now by Gen! Putnam's Permission in the Country for a few Weeks with My Family—As our Assembly Sits next week at Hartford & not again till May, I could wish Measures to be adopted this Session for filling the Quota of Troops from this State and as I know your Excellency's Opinion is of great Weight, I am Satisfied an early attention will be paid to the Subject if recommended by your Excellency—

I intend to Spend Some Days at Hartford where if I can Contribute any Thing to furnishing an Army at the Opening of another Campaign I shall think Myself happy in rendering Some Service to the Cause of My Country tho' I should quit the Field Myself—

I am dear Gen! with esteem
Yᵣ Obed! h Serv!
SAMᴸ H. PARSONS.

The following accounts are taken from the newspapers of that day :

N. London, Dec. 19.   A plan having been formed to bring off or destroy a magazine of military stores which the enemy had at Setauket, on L. I., and to destroy some shipping loaded with timber at Southold, on Tuesday night of last week, part of 2 battalions of troops embarked from this State, under convoy of the sloop Schuyler, and Spy and Mifflin, schooners. Unfortunately next morning, just before light, the Falkland [Falcon], a British Frigate, in her passage from N. Y. to Newport, came across the Schuyler and 2 smaller vessels, when the latter run ashore on the Island, but the former in attempting to get in with the land, run on a spit of sand (called Old Man's) and was taken with about 60 troops on board, among them Cols. [John] Ely, and Sam'l B. Webb, &c. On Thursday, a party of men under Capt. Hart, marched to Southold, and were very near making prisoners of Capt. Ayscough and upwards of 20 men belonging to the ship Swan, who were in a house in Southold, but they getting intelligence of Capt. Hart's approach hasted to their boats. They were closely pursued, and as they were getting on board, were fired upon, when most of them were killed or wounded : 7 marines and seamen were made prisoners. Our troops after tarrying several days on L. I. returned to the main, without opportunity to effect anything considerable—the shipping having left Southold, and we learn the magazine at Setauket has been removed. *Connecticut Gazette,* 24 December, 1777.

December 15, 1777. Three rebel sloops (one a Privateer) made their appearance off Setauket last Wednesday. The Privateer was soon driven ashore and taken by one of His Majesty's ships at Old Man's (7 miles east) and the crew with all the rebels on board made prisoners of war, consisting of 64 privates and some officers, among them Cols. Webb and Ely. The same day the other two ships run into Stony Brook (4 miles west of Setauket) and being unacquainted got on a bank. They then landed two hundred men, who immediately marched to Setauket and returned the same evening to get off their sloop, but their utmost efforts were ineffectual. The next day the whole body went down the Island, and about 12 o'clock passed Wading River (18 miles from where they first landed).

Col. Hewlett with a party of Gen. Delancey's brigade, Col. [Archibald] Hamilton with a troop of horse from Newtown and Capt. [Benjamin] Hewlett with his troop of horse from Hempstead, are gone in pursuit of the rebels, and it is hoped will give a good account of them. *Gaine.*

Last Wednesday morning, a party of rebels landed at Setauket, in Suffolk county, Long Island, where they proceeded to plunder the well affected inhabitants; in our next, we expect to give the public further particulars. *Rivington's Royal Gazette,* 13 December, 1777.

Three rebel sloops, one of them a privateer, made their appearance last Wednesday off Setauket, in Suffolk County, on Long Island, and about 60 miles from this city. The privateer was soon drove ashore, and taken by one of his Majesty's ships, at a place called the Old Man's, 7 miles to the Eastward of the place first mentioned, and the crew with all the rebels on board, made prisoners of war, consisting of 64 privates, and some officers, among them an officer with the rank of Colonel, named Webb. The same day the other two sloops run into an harbour called Stoney-Brook, 4 miles to the Westward of Setauket, and being unacquainted, got on a bank : They then landed 200 men, who immediately marched up to the town of Setauket, and returned the same evening in order to get off their sloop, but their utmost efforts proving ineffectual, the next day the whole body went down the Island, and about 12 o'clock passed Wading River, which is about 11 miles from the place where they first landed.

A straggler in their rear having been asked by an inhabitant what they wanted on the Island, gave for answer, "that they intended to oblige the people of Suffolk County to swear allegiance to the Congress, and those that refused to take the oath were to be plundered, and carried off prisoners to Connecticut."

Col. Hewlet, with a party of General De Lancey's Brigade ; Col. Archibald Hamilton, with a troop of horse from Newtown, and Capt. Hewlet, with his troop of horse from Hempstead, are gone in pursuit of the rebels to the Eastward and we hope will give a good account of them. *Rivington,* 15 December, 1777.

Last Wednesday afternoon a reinforcement of troops were sent to Col. Hewlet in Suffolk county.

By the latest advices from Long Island, we are informed that the party of 200 rebels, which were lately driven ashore in Suffolk county, had not been able to get away, as, it is said, through the vigilance of the commanders of his Majesty's ships, all the boats have been secured, and the invaders betaken themselves to the woods.—Major Green marched on Thursday, with a reinforcement of 100 men, and 200 of the Hempstead militia are likewise gone down to augment the advanced body of horse and foot under the command of Col. Hewlet at Huntington. *Rivington,* 20 December, 1777.

It is reported that Colonel Samuel B. Webb, taken prisoner with Col. Ely, in the late attempt to land on Long Island, has been released on his parole, and is gone to Boston, in order to negotiate an exchange of himself for Colonel Campbell, of the 71st regiment, who has suffered a very long and painful durance in the Massachusetts government. Colonel Webb went up to Rhode Island with Col. Ely, Capt. Bulkley, Adjutant Hopkins, Lieut. Reiley, Ensign Mumford, and some other rebel officers ; with about 67 privates, prisoners, in a sloop of war. *Rivington,* 27 December, 1777.

New London, December 26 [1777] Last Monday part of Col. Webb's battalion, which arrived here from Long Island, marched for Peeks-kill.

Col. Webb, after being taken as was related in our last, was carried to Newport, where after remaining a few days, he was allowed to come out on parole, and is gone to Weathersfield. *Rivington,* 31 January, 1778.

ROLL OF WEBB'S REGIMENT.

Names of Men Enlisted in the year 1777 into a Regiment Commanded by Colonel Sam! B. Webb, known by the name of one of the 26 Additional Regiments, afterwards the 9th and then the 3d Connecticut Regiment.*

* This list is taken from one of the Webb *MSS.*, and differs in some respects from that printed in the Connecticut rolls, as published by the State.

Jonathan Arnold *	Joseph Bacon	34	Felix Curtiss	68
Abiel Allen	Thom.ˢ Barns		Samuel Cole	
John Allen	Peter Butler		James Chadwick	
Eusebius Austin	Isaac Browne		William Chapman	
Ezra Andrus	John Bennet		John Chapman	
Lewis Anjevine	John Barnum		Jesse Chalker	
John Andrus	Wᵐ Beeden		Benjamin Circum	
Christopher Avery	Josiah Burrows		Cotton Chittenden	
James Anderson	John Bassett		Adam Cramer┤	
Jacob Acor	Joel Beers		William Circum	
Aaron Abercrombie	John Beers		Phineas Cadwell	
Theodore Andrus 12	Samˡ. Blackman		Willᵐ Chadwick	
	David Blackman		David Covil	
Edward Browne	Charles Bulkley		Levi Crowell	
Thomˢ. Bidwell	Ebenezer Bradley		Gideon Chittenden	
Jared Bunce	Daniel Brewer		Timothy Cole	
Stephen Bulkley	Daniel Bostwie		Robert Colefax	
Abraham Blinn	Amherst Bartlet		John Circum	
Elijah Boardman	Hosea Birge		Amaziah Chappell	
Jabez Bennet	John Burrows		Brewster Chappell	
Hezekiah Blinn	Timothy Bevins		Moses Clarke	
Justus Blinn	Daniel Butterfield		James Clarke	
Abraham Belding	Joseph Bently		Joshua Cone	
Timothy Brainard	Daniel Bushnell		Thomas Case	
Caleb Benjamin	Samˡ. Brooks		Joshua Carpenter	
Joseph Brewer	Noah Barnum		Willᵐ Clarke	
Stephen Butler	Richard Bacon		James Christie	
Nathˡ. Browne	John Burnham		Mathew Cadwell	
Zebedae Brown	Asa Butler		Reuben Cadwell	
Jonathan Butler	Jacob Browne		David Chapin	
Samuel Beaman	John Barnes		Joel Couch	
Allen Bradley	Willᵐ Browne	32	Curtiss Crane	
John Benham			Malichi Corning	
Solomon Buck	Charles Churchill		Elisha Cole	
Walter Booth 22	Caleb Curtiss	2	Timothy Chapin	35
	34		68	103

† Afterwards Jonⁿ Stuben.

Thomas Colvin	103	Ithuriel Flowers	136	Eliphalet Hills	170
Joel Clarke		Remembrance Filly		Wᵐ Hooker	
Daniel Curtiss		Gershom Fay		Samuel Hanson	
James Charleton	4	William Fay		Timothy Hurlburt	
		Asa Fox		Ebenezer Hoadley	
Benjamin Dix		John Frazier		Prosper Hosmer	
Zebulon Dudley		Vaniah Fox		Samᴸ Hull	
Westbrook Day		John France	8	Hiland Hall	
Joseph Day				Roderic Hopkins	
Stephen Dormant		Moses Griswould		George Hopkins	
Martin Dibble		Icabod Goodrich		Joshua Howe	
David Day		Gideon Goff		Timothy Higgins	
Thomas Doyle		Jacob Griswould		Titus Hubbard	
Daniel Davis		Thomas Gerall		Daniel Hamlin	
Nathan Dunning		Azariah Grant		Elisha Hubbard	
Ebenezer Davis		John Graves		John Hopkins	
Waitstill Dickerson		John Gaylor		Joel Hoyt	
Alexander Dorchester		Joseph Gilbert		Samuel Helmes	
	13	Theodore Gilbert		Asa Hall	
Diarcha Elderkin		Josiah Gaylor		George Hayward	
Samᴸ Easton		Solomon Goodrich		Walton Harris	
Ezra Edgecombe		Alexander Graham		Willᵐ Hall	
James Earle	4	Simon Griffen		Icabud Hawley	
		James Goodrich		Stephen Hurlbut	
Thomas Fitch		Joseph Goldsmith		George Hills	
John Forbes		Gurdon Geer		Alexander Hoy	
Stephen Fox		Daniel Gilmore		Bazaleel Hamlin	
James Foster		John Goodrich		Edward Harwington	
Isaac Ford		Samuel Grant	20	John Harrison	
Elijah Flowers				James Hiskett	
John Fay		Simeon Holmes		John Hall	31
Jacob Ferris		Jonathan Hand			
Alexander Fulton		Thomas Holmes		Stephen Ingham	
Ebenezer Frothingham		Moses Hatch		Samᴸ Ingham	
Ebenezer Forquar		Joseph Hand		Eppa Jones	
Timothy Bay	12	Arunna Hackley	6	Richard Jones	4
	136		**170**		**205**

Frederick Jackson	205	William Martin	238	Gamaliel Olmsted	272
William Jepson		Leonard Munroe		George O'Bryan	
Aaron Jones		John Book Miller		John F. Ockerman	
William Jones		Zebulon Mygatt		William Oaks	
Thomas Johnson		Benjamin Mack		Francis Olmsted	5
Ebenezer Judkins		Cyperian Merrill			
Jonathan Johnson	7	Roger Merrill		Wyman Parker	
		Benjamin Mix		John Parker	
Stephen Kellogg		Comfort Marks		Richard Price	
Seth Kellogg		Benjamin Mc Inbur		George Price	
James Kirtland		Jeddediah Mc Inbur		Amos Porter	
Orry King		Bryan Montague		Moses Porter	
Isaac Kellogg		Thomas Marshall		Elijah Porter	
Christopher Kilby		Abel Munroe		David Pratt	
George King	7	Mathem Melony		Peter Phillips	
		Gurdon Munsill		Willm Patterson	
Joseph Lamb		Aaron Merrill		Samuel Phillips	
Thomas Loveland		Adam Mott		Richard Perry	
Levi Latimer		Patrick Mc Donald		Samuel Parker	
Israel Loomis		Saml Meers		Samuel Pufford	
Jeremiah Lord		John McLean		Zera Page	
David Lounsbury		Elisha Mygatt		Daniel Pufford	
Fitch Lamphere		Thomas Morey		William Prior	
William Lewis		Thomas Morgan		John Phillips	
Phillip Lewis		John Mc Ennice	25	Simeon Puffer	
Michael Lana				William Predox	
Lawrence Lewis		Hezekiah Nott		William Powell	
Ebenezer Lee		Samuel Norton		James Pratt	
William Leach		Epaphras Nott		Isaac Payne	
William Laird	14	Thomas Norton		Robert Patterson	24
		Jabez Norton			
Nathan Miller		Norman Newell		Thomas Quigly	1
Stephen Moultor		Francis Nichollson			
Seth Montague		Riverius Newell	8	Asher Russell	
Jonathan Miller				Saml Roberts	
James Millot	5	Timothy Olmsted	1	Amos Raymond	3
	238		**272**		**305**

Moses Ritter	305	Israel Starke	341	Jesse Vibbard	376
Stephen Risley		Joseph Sharpe		Samuel Weaver	
James Ready		Samuel Smith		Daniel Ward	
Joseph Reed		Prentice Stoors		Daniel Williams	
Joseph Robbins		Zacheriah Seymour		William Warner	
Elijah Roberts		David Scribner		Ralph Williams	
Daniel Roberts		Ebenezer Sawyer		William Whiting	
Joseph Rowlandson		John Sweet		David Wood	
Stephen Roberts		Jesse Starr		Jonathan Wood	
Josiah Robbins		Barnabas Stevins		Thomas Welch	
Ozwell Rockwell		Seth Staynard		Alva West	
Noah Roberts		Samuel Sperry		Hugh White	
Boswell Richardson		Thomas Stanly		Isaac Worden	
Amos Rose		Elihu Stowe		Moses Ward	
David Roberts		William Sutton		Thomas Woodward	
Thomas Raymore		William Styles		Prosper Wetmore	
Ephraim Robertson	17	George Smith		James Whayland	
		John Screder	18	Jonathan White	
Daniel Syzer				Gideon Welles	
Daniel Stoddard		Joseph Treat		Ignatius Waterman	
Samuel Spencer		Ezra Tryon		Darius Waterman	
Thomas Scott		John Treat		William Winnons	
Asaph Smith		Phillip Tabor		Amos West	
John Steel		John Turner		Thom⁵ Wattles	
John Swaddle		John Tucker		Joel Welton	
Bela Scovil		John Tucker 2ᵈ		Jesse Wilkinson	
Ely Simons		John Thomas		John Wright	
Joseph Simons		Bates Turner		Ezekel Winchell	
James Spencer		Josiah Treadway		Joshua Welles	
Stephen Scovil		Jacob Teal		Elihu Waterous	
Thomas Stone		William Thrawl		George Warder	
Phineas Shepard		Mathew Thompson		Valentine Wilmot	
Elias Seymour		John Taylor		Bazaleel Washbun	
Aaron Stevens		Thomas Turner	15	Benjamin Weston	
Jehosaphat Starr				Thomas Warner	
Army Sperry		David Vibbard		John White	
Ezra Smith	19	John Vibbard	2	Asa Wright	37
	341		376	Total	414

I do hereby certify that the above named 414 men were enlisted into my Reg.ᵗ in the year 1777, and that they all rec.ᵈ their full bounty excepting from the general sum three hundred fifty four Dollars and a half, which was retained from bounty's of Deserters, which sum was allowed in a settlement with the State of Connecticut and deducted from their State Bounty, as will appear by a Certified copy of their Acc.ᵗ .

SAM.ᴸ B. WEBB Col. 3.ᵈ Connec.ᵗ Reg.ᵗ .

END OF VOL. I.